Worlds Between

Historical Perspectives on Gender and Class

Leonore Davidoff

Polity Press

First published in 1995 by Polity Press
in association with Blackwell Publishers.

Editorial office:
Polity Press
65 Bridge Street
Cambridge CB2 1UR, UK

Marketing and production:
Blackwell Publishers
108 Cowley Road
Oxford OX4 1JF, UK

ISBN 0 7456 0983 X
ISBN 0 7456 0984 8 (pbk)

A CIP catalogue record for this book is available from the British Library.

Typeset in 10 on 12 pt Ehrhardt
by Best-set Typesetter Ltd., Hong Kong
Printed in Great Britain by T.J. Press, Padstow, Cornwall

This book is printed on acid-free paper.

Contents

List of Illustrations

All photographs © Cambridge University Library.

Acknowledgements

Since this collection covers a span of twenty years, it would be impossible to acknowledge all the intellectual stimulation and personal support I have received over that time from colleagues, students and friends, both in Britain and abroad. But there have been those from whose work and advice I have particularly benefited: Carole Adams, Margaret Allen, Meg Arnot, Michèle Barrett, Ava Barron, Judith Bennett, Ida Blom, Gisela Bock, Joan Busfield, Barbara Caine, Anna Clark, Anna Davin, Christine Delphy, Paola DiCori, Delfina Dolza, Suzanne Franzway, Jonas Frykman, John Gillis, Esther Goody, Linda Gordon, Patricia Grimshaw, Catherine Hall, James Hammerton, Karin Hausen, Nancy Hewitt, Olwen Hufton, Angela V. John, Elaine Jordan, Ludmilla Jordanova, Alice Kessler-Harris, Marilyn Lake, Hilary Land, Suzanne Lebsock, Diana Leonard, Jeanne L'Esperance, Jane Lewis, David Lockwood, Ovar Löfgren, Judy Lown, Susan Magarey, Gordon Marshall, Keith McClelland, Judith Newton, Grey Osterud, Alex Owen, Mary Poovey, Jane Rendall, Lyndal Roper, Michael Roper, Ellen Ross, Sonya Rose, Mary Ryan, Raphael Samuel, Alison Scott, Joan Scott, Elaine Showalter, Bonnie Smith, Carroll Smith-Rosenberg, Liz Stanley, Ann Summers, Paul Thompson, John Tosh, Deborah Valenze, Eleni Varikas, Martha Vicinus, Judith Walkowitz, Ulla Wikander, Annie Whitehead and Anna Yeatman.

Thanks also to Sally Alexander for suggesting such a volume, since my essays have previously been scattered among historical and sociological journals and collections.

Brenda Corti and Mary Girling, Department of Sociology at the University of Essex, have been a never-failing source of assistance, encouragement and humour; to them I should like to express my formal thanks here.

The previously unpublished material (chapters 7 and 8) was prepared while on a Fellowship in the Department of History at the University of Melbourne. I am grateful to Professor Patricia Grimshaw who acted as my host at Melbourne and Dr

Jill Matthews, Women's Studies Department, Australian National University, who found me a niche in the Department of History in Canberra. To these departments and their administrative and secretarial staff – Lynne Wrout, Shirley Bradley, Marian Robson and Marree Beer – many thanks for the facilities and kindness offered.

For clerical and computing assistance I should like to thank Jayne Daldry (University of Essex), Susan Janson (University of Melbourne – a wizard with recalcitrant footnotes) and Yvonne Parry (ANU), who so efficiently overcame the British–Australian computing barriers. Miranda Chaytor provided not only impeccable copy-editing but also important substantive advice.

And finally, without the wise and heartening personal sustenance from Leila Berg, Delfina Dolza, Diana Gittins and, in particular, Liz McCormick, I could not have envisioned completing this project.

The following chapters have been previously published and are reprinted here with permission. chapter 1, '*Mastered for Life*: Servant and Wife in Victorian and Edwardian England', first appeared in *Journal of Social History*, vol. 7, no. 4 (1974) and subsequently in Pat Thane and Anthony Sutcliffe, eds, *Essays in Social History*, vol. 2 (Oxford University Press, 1986); chapter 2, '*Landscape with Figures*: Home and Community in English Society', co-authored with Jeanne L'Esperance and Howard Newby, in Juliet Mitchell and Ann Oakley, eds, *The Rights and Wrongs of Women* (Penguin, 1976); chapter 3, 'The Rationalization of Housework', in Diana Leonard Barker and Sheila Allen, eds, *Dependence and Exploitation in Work and Marriage* (Longman, 1976), and subsequently in Diana Leonard and Sheila Allen, eds, *Sexual Divisions Revisited* (Macmillan, 1990); chapter 4, '*Class and Gender in Victorian England*: The Case of Hannah Cullwick and A.J. Munby', in *Feminist Studies*, vol. 5, no. 1 (spring 1979), and subsequently in Judith L. Newton, Mary P. Ryan and Judith R. Walkowitz, eds, *Sex and Class in Women's History* (Routledge & Kegan Paul, 1983); chapter 5, '*The Separation of Home and Work?* Landladies and Lodgers in Nineteenth- and Twentieth-century England', in Sandra Burman, ed., *Fit Work for Women* (Croom Helm, 1979); chapter 6, '*The Role of Gender in the "First Industrial Nation"*: Farming and the Countryside in England, 1780–1850', in Rosemary Crompton and Michael Mann, eds, *Gender and Stratification* (Polity Press, 1986); and parts of chapter 8, '"Adam Spoke First and Named the Orders of the World": Masculine and Feminine Domains in History and Sociology', in Helen Corr and Lynn Jamieson, eds, *The Politics of Everyday Life: Continuity and Change in Work and the Family* (Macmillan, 1990).

Introduction

The essays in this volume come from the margins. In both subject matter and conceptual approach they inhabit a space between those areas which have usually been seen as central concerns of society. They focus in particular on two aspects that traditionally have been taken for granted and/or trivialized. First, they examine activities: domestic preoccupations, the intricacies of housekeeping, the symbolic and material aspects of dirt and disorder. Then they consider people and relationships: domestic servants, landladies and lodgers, farmers' wives and daughters, siblings.

Such topics are often seen as peripheral to historical and sociological interests. Because they are defined as inessential to the real and significant aspects of society, such as class, political, military or cultural affairs and institutions, they have low status. A major reason for this neglect is, arguably, that they mainly involve the lives of women and children, groups already defined as subordinate in the hierarchy of power, resources – and scholarly attention. Trying to draw such issues into the centre has meant swimming against mainstream intellectual and scholarly convention, including much of the radical tradition.

Yet a moment's thought shows that every centre must be defined by its rim – and in social as well as psychic life we are increasingly discovering that the boundaries between centre and periphery are unstable if not permeable. The liminal as well as the repressed will always come back to haunt in some form. A satisfying social analysis must take on the whole circumference.

This holistic approach has meant analysing aspects of society usually swept under the carpet, regarded as too private, too intimately related to the body, too particular. It is the theories (and historical topics) 'that are most divorced from blood, sweat and tears, that have the highest prestige'.[1] But it also may be that these are precisely those areas of life which are often threatening psychologically – and ultimately politically to those with authority to define what is important and worthwhile. Not only autobiographers but also historians have concealed their imaginations and bridled their tongues so that 'the past is . . . often presented as idyllic – totally lacking in smells, urges and bodies'.[2]

Some of the essays explore the position and response of subordinates. Others focus on the way dominant groups created and maintained their centrality – and the material, financial and emotional rewards they reaped by doing so. It has been increasingly recognized that one of the most potent of these advantages is having power to observe, to pronounce, and to gaze on other human beings as subjects. The *flâneur*'s licence to wander, to look, to write from his standpoint and to make that standpoint the template for cultural, architectural and institutional forms is, and has been, one of the greatest forms of mastery that can be conferred.[3]

But, of course, certain groups are subordinate in some situations, while at the same time having power over others. Such was the case of middle-class wives, who were subordinate to their husbands in many ways, while having considerable authority over their servants and children. The truism that power takes many forms and is more a complicated web than a straightforward causal or mechanistic relationship is now widely accepted in late twentieth-century thought.[4] It is also evident that using such simple models in social and historical research is far easier than trying to implement the concept of dispersed or fractured forms of power.[5]

In my own intellectual journey these patterns, and the common threads running through the essays, did not appear all at once. The articles were researched and written over a period of twenty years, starting in the early 1970s, before the advent of the Women's Movement and feminism had raised fundamental questions about how psyches as well as societies have been constrained along gender lines. This was also before 'postmodern' questioning of institutions and categories had appeared on the horizon. The essays are presented in the order in which they were written from chapter 1 which first appeared in 1974 to chapters 7 and 8, published here for the first time. Inevitably some of the concepts and language in the earlier pieces reflect concerns and approaches of the period in which they were written.

My first interest in these subjects began with a post-graduate thesis undertaken in the early 1950s on the employment of married women in England, at that time defined as a 'problem' since marriage was considered most women's primary occupation. To a nascent sociologist, it soon became evident that such a study could not be done without taking into consideration the history of the recent past; Edwardian, even Victorian, culture cast a long shadow over the lives of older women as well as moulding the institutions of post-war England. Thus began an abiding involvement with social history, immeasurably strengthened by the concurrent discovery of 'history from below', the history of ordinary people spearheaded in Britain by the History Workshop movement in the 1970s.

From that study onwards the relationship between kinship/family and the waged economy became one of my central concerns, not least because by far the largest group of married women 'workers' either were, or had been, in domestic service. Nineteenth-century residential domestic service was a twilight world; domestic servants were not really part of the family (as many employers would have liked to believe), but neither were they legally or traditionally seen as unequivocally part of the paid workforce. This anomaly, however, seems to have held little interest either for academic investigators or the public at large. Up through the mid-twentieth century, domestic servants were a taken-for-granted part of the social landscape, of less than passing interest to mainstream and Marxist economists alike. They regarded service as unproductive labour because it added nothing defined as of economic value and was carried on outside a recognized workplace. Even the tiny handful of investigations into women's work tended to neglect servants. Ivy Pinchbeck, for example, in her pioneering study of the late eighteenth and early nineteenth centuries, excluded domestic service on the grounds that servants' work had been unaffected by the industrial revolution.[6]

Furthermore, housekeeping, childcare and the employment of servants were the provenance of women who were themselves often relegated to a biological, and thus non-social, non-historical and naturalistic limbo.[7] My increasing focus on the history of domesticity, housework and domestic servants which emerged from that wider study was seen as quixotic at best, faintly ridiculous at worst.

In any case by the time that study was completed, along with so many women of my generation, I had left the public world of work for a dozen years of housewifery, childrearing and helping to care for an elderly relative. It was that experience – the hours spent sitting by the sand-pit, ironing shirts, mashing baby food, swilling out and trying to dry nappies while coaxing a particularly recalcitrant boiler to stay alight in the depths of winter – which set me to ponder on the division of labour, conceptions of time, space, purpose and rewards which seemed to differ so radically between the world of work and the world of home. Why? What did it mean? How did this division appear in the first place?

The questions were there but the only framework available to answer them lay with the methods, conceptual schemes and theories built around their unacknowledged relevance to a form of intellectual masculinity. The conceptual order on offer was only to be found in a transcendental realm which passed beyond the local and the personal, where my questions seemed to originate, 'the place where body, space, the myriad tasks of the quotidien function'.[8] For example, recognition has come only haltingly that the body is, among other things, 'a theoretical location for debates about power, ideology and economics'.[9]

When at last I returned to social and historical research, these questions resurfaced. What was the source of such a logic of 'rationality' which justified ignoring and thus perpetuating the heavy physical drudgery as well as mental, and often emotional, isolation of so many girls and women within private homes after conditions had ameliorated for many, women as well as men, in public workplaces?[10]

But the meaning of domestic service to the millions of women (and thousands of men) who had worked as servants was especially difficult to fathom. Considering the numbers involved, both autobiography and fiction were strangely silent, while oral historians had barely begun their investigations. Here I had the invaluable advantage of long listening to my mother-in-law's stories of her early days in Yorkshire. Born in the late 1880s, like so many girls raised in the countryside, she was sent away into residential service with no choice in the matter. She went through a series of posts, starting with the first harsh and lonely place as general servant at the age of eleven. Later she moved from parlourmaid in a mill owner's establishment and finally to nursemaid for a doctor's family. Her vivid and detailed recollections of work patterns, emotional reactions and concepts of hierarchy, refracted through a female servant's encounters with the provincial upper-middle-class world while living under the same roof, kindled my determination to give voice to servants as human beings in their own right as well as historical subjects.

As might be expected, higher general standards of living, as well as the revolution in hygiene, had furthered an emphasis on cleanliness. This was undoubtedly one of the reasons for the enlargement of housekeeping rituals and increased employment of servants throughout the nineteenth and well into the twentieth century. But the more I probed into the practice and meaning of housework and the deployment of servants, the more it became obvious that much energy and time were also expended on using these resources to maintain status rituals, to mark boundaries between class strata. The shining brass ornaments and daily whitening of doorsteps, the variety and upkeep of furniture, crockery and dozens of other household items, the servants in neat, clean uniforms to open the front door to visitors, were part of elaborated codes of gentility and respectability.

Furthermore, for decades in the later nineteenth and early twentieth centuries, lower-middle-class and respectable working-class women literally almost killed themselves over the weekly family wash to turn out their sons and husbands in clean white Sunday shirts and their daughters in starched white pinafores. Yet many, if not most, were living on limited, often irregular incomes in households with large numbers of children and a minimum of sanitary facilities such as piped-water supplies. What drove individuals and families at all levels to such lengths for goals which in our relaxed post-sixties, blue-jean-wearing culture seem so unnecessary, even bizarre?

The overwhelming weight given to such signs of social status was also evident among the more affluent, in the etiquette of visiting, dining and calling. Such practices, along with widening access to public-school eduction for boys, enabled English nineteenth-century society, which had been dominated by aristocratic and gentry culture, to absorb a large influx of individuals and families whose wealth was based on commerce, industry and the professions.[11] Far from being trivial, these rituals and patterns of consumption were at the centre of changes in nineteenth-century English society. Economically they provided new demands for a huge variety of products in the home market and stimulated production related to the expansion of Empire. Socially they were key elements in the shift to a broader based politics and culture.

As part of these changes, by the mid-nineteenth century a cluster of forceful and widespread ideas about domesticity, the home and its role in marking boundaries, between classes and class fractions had emerged. Careful demarcations separated the genteel from the vulgar, the respectable from the rough, the civilized from the uncivilized, as well as the English from other nations and races, both on the Continent and in the colonies. In particular, notions about right living in the home, the private sphere as differentiated from the public, had become ever more interwoven with ideas about femininity and masculinity, womanhood and manhood. The dominion of this 'social imaginary' ideal could be found in a multitude of places and forms.[12]

Rapid industrialization, urban growth and the impetus for political inclusion was taking place within a nation of seemingly inviolate island boundaries and a remarkably homogeneous population (with the constant exception of Irish Catholics). Paradoxically, partly due to this lack of external differentiation, nineteenth-century English literate culture appeared to be particularly obsessed with denoting distinctions between sections of that population, especially when confronting a growing waged and urban working class. These distinctions, often based on notions of disorder, pollution and dirt, especially marked out the position of those at the lowest sections of societies.

But these beliefs about 'matter out of place' and disorder were *also* connected to one the most deep-seated classifications entertained: gender. One of Western femininity's most enduring traits has been women's responsibility for coordinating and managing dirt and disintegration, the association of women with polluting aspects of birth and death. While all women partook of this association in some form, it was nuanced as part of class differentiation. In the nineteenth and early twentieth centuries, women who had servants were perceived as more pure, more feminine, more ladylike. The servant (and servant class as a whole) absorbed dirt and lowliness into their own bodies.[13]

Both as symbols and in the work they performed, female servants could represent the whole underside of bourgeois culture. A.J. Munby, for example, one of the most assiduous students of gender and class in this period (and the subject of chapter 4), here describes a young scullery maid of the 1860s washing up in a dirty, evil-smelling cellar:

> She stood at a sink behind a wooden dresser backed with choppers and stained with blood and grease, upon which were piles of coppers and saucepans that she had to scour, piles of dirty dishes that she had to wash. Her frock, her cap, her face and arms were more or less wet, soiled, perspiring and her apron was a filthy piece of sacking, wet and tied round her with a cord. The den where she wrought was low, damp, ill-smelling; windowless, lighted by a flaring gas-jet: and, full in view, she had on one side a larder hung with raw meat, on the other a common urinal.[14]

It was the physical, intellectual, even emotional, work of servants and landladies, as well as wives, sisters, maiden aunts, nieces and daughters, which ensured that others (the employing class and many men) could possess and 'enjoy the benefits of pursuing gainful occupations and intellectual enrichment, the refinement of morals, customs and taste'.[15] Men from higher strata were released from care of their own personal and physical needs by servants and protected by their womenfolk from social and emotional disorder. The fear and distress at the number of 'redundant' women around mid-century focused on potentially independent 'ladies' or impertinent factory girls. Unmarried servants were not a problem, for, in the works of a well-known commentator, they were 'attached to others and connected with other existences which they embellish, facilitate and serve. In a word, they fulfil both essentials of woman's being; *they are supported by, and they administer to, men*' (his italics).[16]

These insights into the symbolic, organizational and material aspects of gender and class were fuelled by my engagement with feminist thinking in the 1970s and 80s. Feminist analysis in several disciplines uncovered layers of gendered metaphor and the hitherto unacknowledged gendered nature of institutions. In particular, there was increasing recognition that the law gives concrete representation to current social opinion as well as moulding constraints or opportunities for living people. Legal classifications in the nineteenth century were built on existing assumptions about gender, the family and work. For example, the idea of a business as a 'personality' rested on the notion of 'person', itself an unnoted masculine concept. Legal debates in this period and changes around marriage, inheritance, the contract of employment and the creation of the business corporation, as well as feminist debates about the gendered definition of 'person', underlie much of the analysis in these essays.

Another key area I was drawn to investigate was the placing of social groups in space – both actual and metaphorical – an approach more often left to historical geographers, architectural historians or anthropologists. Material artefacts, the use of space within buildings as a social marker, the lay-outs of streets, towns and countryside appeared in documents (and sometimes literally on the ground) as a complicated tapestry of gendered meanings. There were the men-only public arenas of office, inn, public house and club, as well as wealthy homes divided between lady's boudoir, children's nursery and school-room, gentleman's smoking-room or study, mixed-sex public drawing-rooms and the back passages or basements inhabited by servants. Lower down the social scale, these divisions were maintained even though they might be reduced to the husband and father's special chair by the fireplace.[17]

Gendered meanings were even mapped out on the grid of the human body itself. Like the prototypical 'other', woman might not only be the tender heart to man's cool, directing head, but sometimes was relegated, along with other social outcasts such as paupers and gypsies, to unsavoury nether regions below the waist. Ideas about beauty and ugliness, morality, sin and desire, all were imbricated in constructions of class and gender, the English and inferior others.

Looking back at this catalogue of hierarchical classification from the perspective of the 1990s, I am filled with wonder at how the dominance of gendered categories could have been overlooked for so long. The very derivation of the word, 'gender', its relation to 'gens' or orders, indicates its centrality to classification systems, particularly those stressing notions of difference. Certainly in Western tradition, gender has operated as a fundamental organizing category at the level of both social relations and the structure of personal identity.[18]

Our world has been constructed along gender lines at all levels. Everyday language, images and expressions carry a tint of oppositional masculinity and femininity, but so too do scholarly models and analysis. How could this basic pattern, now laboriously being uncovered by feminists, have been hidden for so long? A simplified answer to such a complicated question must include the fact that gender categories have been built in terms of power relations, no matter how complicated and involuted these may be.

Women who have opposed accepted notions of feminine inferiority frequently find themselves being questioned simply because they assume a posture or manner of authority and competence which has been central to the construction of masculinity.[19] Part of the effort in these essays, then, is to expose the agency given to those with power. On the whole, it is they who have written the scores within which were produced our supposed harmonies of home and community – and even the occasional recognized discordancy (see chapter 2). Gendered ideas became themselves instruments of control over resources, people and things, and legitimated, in principle, the drawing of boundaries between people. Those in positions of control have had no reason to look behind generalized, given catetories, designations so often based on covert masculine assumptions. They have had no motivation to seek out the supplementary, shadowy presences without which not only their working concepts but their whole cosmology as well as daily life-support systems would melt away.

In an effort to understand the domination of these definitions, British feminist historians in the 1970s and 1980s spoke of a nineteenth-century ideology of domesticity, while Americans emphasized a specifically women's culture from the same period which emerged from the growth of a 'separate sphere' of the home. The latter, it was then argued, had produced a consciousness leading eventually to feminist action. In both these traditions, contrary to the beliefs of some later critics, the investigation of women's constraints within domesticity, and their exercise of power and influence from within its confines, took into account not only prescriptive writing about women (and men), but institutions and the experiences of daily life, including the appropriation of women's physical, intellectual and emotional *work*.[20]

There is still much ambiguity and confusion over how the central features of the sexual division of labour have changed over time. Specialists in every historical period from pre-antiquity onwards have tended to regard their epoch as *the* critical period of transition. All are able to produce evidence of women being defined by identification with childbirth, childrearing, the hearth and the cooking pot. And yet we also know that there have been immense variations in the meaning and deployment of that identification, both over time and among contemporaneous groups. There is as yet – and may never be – no concensus about this issue. But for that matter neither has there been agreement about the related but often-ignored question of what elements are common and what variable in relation to men and masculinity.

Nevertheless, it is fair to ask if there was anything in the emphasis on motherhood and the home in the catalogue of nineteenth-century 'domestic ideology' to distinguish that particular culture from the role of affluent women down through the ages. In a recent critique of the models used in feminist history, Amanda Vickery has claimed that extra resources in a family or household always result in the removal of women from the rigours of income-earning and public life; from the seventeenth century onwards, she argues, there were just more families with the means to free their womenfolk from work in fields, workshops or as traders. 'Domesticity' is inherent in the fact of social mobility in all ages.[21]

A blanket assumption such as this begs all sorts of questions. For example, with an increase in wealth, why not release *all* members of the family, men and women alike, from productive work – as had been normal for the aristocracy and gentry? What was it about late eighteenth- and nineteenth-century English culture which put such emphasis on the elaboration of the home, for men as well as women, and the special derogation of productive work for women at social levels well *below* aristocratic or gentry status? Why not continue to employ adult, married women in the productive enterprise and devolve household chores and childcare to older children, servants, apprentices and the elderly as had been the pattern for centuries past?

In a period increasingly imbued with the 'logic of capitalism', would it not have been more rational to make use of the labour of such adult women in commercial and professional roles, rather than keeping them financially dependent, sometimes at considerable cost to the family and its enterprise, whether farm, shop, factory or professional office? Why was it that forms of business during this period were constructed precisely to maintain a bulwark between productive activity for men and domestic lives for women in such creations as the trust, the annuity, life insurance and, eventually, limited liability, which broke the connection between home and enterprise? Why were the categories employed in the invention of early nineteenth-century statistics framed along gendered lines so evident in instruments of state and social policy such as the censuses of population and occupations?[22] Contrary to such logic, however, in the nineteenth century, gender distinctions were rigidified at all levels from the individual psyche to the national economy while the 'Home' as the natural place for women was reified and naturalized.

While it is important to recognize the actual historical presence of many women in the workforce – their involvement in property and money markets as well as the labour market – upon which such critiques of the models rest, these basic formulations remain as forceful social and historical templates to this day. Of course most women were *not* quiescent angels in the house; they could be as aggressive, as manipulative, as clever, as any man. The qualities necessary to maintain a household with a very small, often irregular, income such as that of the lower-middle-class or respectable working-class housewife, already belie the Victorian stereotype, not to mention the strength of mind, body and spirit of the women which meant survival to the poor.[23]

But even among the wealthy dowagers of Mayfair, as well as their lesser provincial imitators, all of whom acted as social-boundary keepers *par excellence*, the home, as the basis of the more formal nineteenth-century 'Society' functions, could resemble less a haven than the headquarters of a military campaign. Here strategies of acceptance and rejection were planned and launched, rival enemies sighted and routed, a literary or musical lion captured as a drawing card to evening entertainment. The battlegrounds in such campaigns may have been drawing- and dining-rooms, the weapons marshalled may have been troops of servants and dependants, ball gowns, hairdressers, the beauty of a daughter, the net worth of a husband, the planning of an exquisite meal, but the motivation to join in the conflict was clearly present. The view from behind the lace curtain, social regulation via gossip over teacups, over the backyard fence or in the street doorway – the making and breaking of financial as well as marital reputations took place at many social levels.

The essays presented here conclude that there were new elements in this substratum, that domesticity as a concept as well as the home as an actual space were coined and elaborated beyond recognition on a much wider scale and further down the social hierarchy than ever before, in the countryside as well as in towns. By the second quarter of the nineteenth century it became a central part of the new morality propagated by the Evangelical movements within both the Established and Nonconformist churches; it gave a novel twist to the relationship of men to masculinity as well as women to femininity, to desires, to sexuality, to reproduction as well as to work and production. In its various forms it was critical to the bid for political and social inclusion and leadership made by a variety of groups among the middle, and later, the lower strata of English society.

Doctrines of domesticity were a counterpart to what was seen as the growing incursions of the cash nexus and scientific rationality. From the middle decades of the nineteenth century, the decline of patronage, informal contact across class lines and service gave way to the individualistic employer–workman (sic) contract. At the same time, notions of domesticity stressed both duty and a chivalric masculinity encapsulated in men's role as breadwinners. For women, the emotional as well as material attraction in such promises should not be underestimated.

The need for support was emphasized at a time when up to 85–90 per cent of women's lives between their mid-twenties and early forties could be spent in pregnancy and breast-feeding, not to speak of rearing the large numbers of children per family. But the benefits of financial and social maintenance could so easily be undermined by the inability or unwillingness of fathers, brothers or husbands to provide. Women had no real legal or economic sanctions to enforce support for themselves and their children within the secondary status of marriage or adult spinsterhood.[24] Much of the nineteenth-century emphasis on women's 'influence' can be interpreted as just as much a sop to their lack of actual power as it can be seen as a backlash against women's real gains in public opportunities as has been claimed.[25]

It is these issues of independence, dependence, power and subordination that chapters 1 to 7 address. They were prompted by questions which reach into every level of the human condition, from the formation of unconscious desires and fantasies of power and submission laid down in childhood, to the creation and maintenance of economic and political institutions such as markets, forms of housing, workshops, offices and factories, scientific and political societies, universities, lodging houses – the list is endless. To explore such a range even within the relatively narrow time-band of the long nineteenth century (the 1780s to the First World War), has meant making use of every kind of material – from fiction to demographic statistics. It has meant crossing disciplinary boundaries and borrowing methods, not just from history and sociology, but also anthropology, literary studies, historical geography, architecture, psychology, economics and political theory.

Despite the tendency, which I share, for historians to dive for the haven of the detailed archives, it is historians who are, in many ways, uniquely suited to such a generalized and holistic approach. If nothing else, the widespread use of personal testimonies, oral histories, memoirs, diaries and autobiographies has alerted historians to the way lives cross conceptual categories and muddle theoretical models.

It was with this understanding that in the 1980s, together with Catherine Hall, I undertook a detailed study of the provincial middle class, both rural and urban (see chapter 6).[26] It is in detailed historical examples such as this that the links between categories will be discerned in all the richness of individual lives, in local as well as national organizations. The effort to conceive gender – or class or race – as an abstract logical grid without a notion of historical process is doomed for the *categories are only worked out during that process and are emergent in social practices.*[27]

Undoubtedly, there is a difficult balance to be achieved: a context so specific that the findings might not bear on any other case must be countered by linking individual studies to wider conceptual issues.[28] An example would be the apparently similar patterns of violence perpetrated against children, servants and slaves by their elders, masters and owners and which can be seen as similar in many ways to that turned against wives by their husbands (see chapter 1). But such formulations, although of heuristic value in making us think about the constituents of power, are too broad. The extent of the status differential between superiors and inferiors is governed by legal, economic and customary factors which vary. So too do the construction of the superior/inferior categories themselves; for example gender, age, race, class are not of the same order (see chapter 8). And all of these factors are subject to change over time.[29]

It was in trying to bridge the particulars of the historical material with received concepts of hierarchy, knowledge and institutional practice that I became increasingly aware that existing models of social analysis were no longer sufficient. The words and actions of historical actors constantly broke the bonds and slipped through the meshes of all existing prototypes. As my work on domestic service, innkeeping and lodging houses had demonstrated, quasi-familial relationships oozed across unquestioned assumptions about family, home and workplace (see chapter 5). Notions of kinship pervaded the business enterprise. The family home – moral refuge and temple of beauty – also had to be run on strictly business lines. The 'rationality' of science, which by the end of the nineteenth century was replacing a theological world-view, contained a particularly masculine core, exacerbating fears about a displaced moral order so that the *ends* of creating family life and running a home became ever more sacred, while the means remained ambiguously utilitarian (see chapter 3).

Concurrent with that period of my detailed research into the early nineteenth-century English middle class, postmodern and deconstructionist ideas, especially those initiated by feminists, had begun to tug at the edges of even the most basic traditional conceptual boundaries. Their radical contestation of foundations exposed the exclusion of certain voices, arguing that such narrowing was precisely the precondition making possible an agreed political and intellectual agenda accompanying the notion of agency.[30]

The concreteness and separation of each bounded unit such as 'the economic system', or 'the kinship system' was being queried from several directions.[31] Historians and sociologists, for example, found familial models being practised within the business enterprise through the nineteenth and into the late twentieth centuries, not just in small family shops and on farms but also within the heartland of large companies.[32]

In sum, and especially when it comes to issues relating to reproduction of individuals and groups, we have begun to realize that it is *classification systems themselves* which determine what will be understood as 'significant relationships'. This has become evident, for example, in the contemporary social and political controversy over the role and responsibilities of familial relationships in the 1990s. While the discussion has focused almost exclusively on mothers with a nod in the direction of fathers, in historical (and contemporary?) fact, children's lives were moulded by a spectrum of relationships: with siblings, aunts and uncles, servants, lodgers, apprentices, neighbours, teachers, state officials, friends.

This radical questioning of the primary assumptions of social analysis has brought back on to the agenda issues about what is common to the human condition. The peculiarly long infancy of human beings, their physical, emotional and psychic reliance upon caretakers, and the rocky road to a separate identity, seems to

promote special anxieties around issues of autonomy and dependence. Undoubtedly English society, like most Western societies, has for many centuries
placed special emphasis on the value of self-determination. But social life is more
complicated than any free-floating independent individual. It is made up of a
constant reworking and re-experiencing of the paradox of the recognition of others
in which similar yet different beings encounter the agency of the self *and* the
other.[33] Furthermore, recognition implies a first step towards the possibility of
dependence on others. It is in this way that identity, the very stuff of the self is
created, whether the 'other' is a sibling, a neighbour or a distant colonial subject.[34]

This Western emphasis on personal autonomy and a separate notion of self
seems to have buttressed a certain type of masculinity; the ability to control one's
own destiny betokened manhood. Subjugation to the will of another had the
potential to 'emasculate', to make men effeminate. Yet innumerable other societies
also seem to equate manhood with control of the feminine and fear of mastery by
women, whether women's power be expressed through their putatively natural
ability to excite men's desires or their bid for positions customarily seen as men's
preserves. These fears often peak around women's claims for access to the sacred,
whether theological or scientific. A woman in authority may represent (to both men
and women) a relapse into submission to the mother – the terrifying combination
of physical, emotional and spiritual totality echoed by submission to a priestly
office.[35]

Conversely, the essence of Western femininity has been defined as dependence
and service, the obliteration of the self, combined with the enabling of a higher,
dominant, and masculine authority. The equation of effeminacy and submission is
often despised, yet it fascinates too. It has been applied to males of 'inferior'
cultures as well as to women, graphically illustrated once again by the archetype of
the domestic servant, both in Britain and in the vast numbers found serving as
batmen in the armed services, colonial 'native boys', shading into indentured
labourers and concubines in the Empire abroad.

The experiences of the Second World War saw the virtual ending of residential
domestic service. Even affluent women had to assume some of these service
functions. The declining number of children born to each family which had reduced the need for servants was also accompanied by the demise of the older sister,
the helpful aunty, the obliging landlady, as the empirical essays investigate. It is
possible that some of the impetus for the modern Women's Movement was fuelled
by the servantless young middle-class housewife of the late 1960s and early 1970s
confronted with taking on not just the increase in physical tasks of food preparation, washing dishes and clothes and round-the-clock care of small children, but
the additional unrelenting dependence of all family members on her for emotional
attendance, to the detriment of her own interests and identity. Since selflessness
still made up at least part of feminine identity whilst the material, social and psychic
benefits of marriage and motherhood, at least under ideal circumstances, could be

considerable, it has been exceptionally demanding to make manifest the tensions generated by this situation.

These excursions into a range of relationships of hierarchy, dependency and power have raised critical general issues about what is constant and what variable in human societies. In fact, it is becoming evident that we need modes of analysis as well as description which encompass both, for, while time inexorably moves forward and one truly cannot step into the same river twice, timeless principles may still regulate parts – and lead to useful abstractions.[36] In particular, the essential frailty and ultimate mortality of all human beings and the resulting need for societies and social groups to constantly renew themselves demands cooperation. Only an understanding of both commonalities and historical variation can signpost that cooperation.

To come to grips with such complexity as well as with inevitable indeterminacy, the traditional codes and models, based on one-sided perspectives of the powerful (and those who fear the powerless) are no longer sufficient. Chapter 8 seeks to go behind as well as beyond those accepted models – of work and home, abstract and embodied, masculine and feminine, public and private.[37] This essay is a more sustained attempt to confront, at a conceptual level, the issues raised by a long experience of empirical and grounded historical research. In so doing it reaches for a position which would subvert binary modes of thinking 'by seeking the intermediary spaces where boundaries become effaced and Manichean categories collapse into each other'.[38]

Such a re-evaluation, coming from a social and cultural historian and joining with other feminist scholars from a variety of disciplines,[39] is attempted here only as a beginning. But it is a necessary first step in 'not only critically assessing questions of general interest but also commanding a general interest in our own questions', called for by the medievalist Judith Bennett.[40] If nothing else, this foray into the concepts behind interpretations of the recent past confirms that historians as well as all practitioners of the human sciences have hitherto depended on the notion of a gendered (masculine) individual.

Yet far from being marginal or even external to the real business of society, or the focus of historical action, it can be argued that what men are and what men do is at least partially built on conceptions of the female – her body, mind, role and spirit. Women constantly invade men's imagination as muses, fairies, witches, erotic and demonic creatures, while at the same time they are vital human workers and agents in men's lives. Gender always operates in the relationship of one category to the other.

Nineteenth- and early twentieth-century changes built on already deeply held structural and symbolic relationships of men and women. But so also, our own situation, our own time is a palimpsest of past lives and past times. We cannot begin to reveal present problems without a consciousness of those lives and times.

But that consciousness must include everyone's past, humble as well as mighty, colonized as well as colonizer, children as well as adults, women as well as men. The ultimate aim of social analysis surely must be, to paraphrase C. Wright Mills, that all people might become aware of historical structures and of their own place within them.[41] Such a call must be based on a genuine recognition of those whose place up to now has been in the silence and shadows of the non-social, a designation which history has tragically taught may lead all too easily into the darkness of the non-human.[42] But if that recognition is forthcoming, it might possibly lead to sorely needed visions of renewal and reconstruction.

Notes

1 Arthur Stinchcombe, 'The Origins of Sociology as a Discipline', *Acta Sociologica*, vol. 27, no. 1 (1984), p. 52. For a useful discussion of this issue in relation to current feminist work see Michèle Barrett, 'Words and Things: Materialism and Method in Contemporary Feminist Analysis', in Michèle Barrett and Anne Phillips, eds, *Destabilizing Theory: Contemporary Feminist Debates* (Polity Press, Cambridge, 1992).

2 Ovar Löfgren and Jonas Frykman, *Culture Builders: A Historical Anthropology of Middle-Class Life*, trans. Alan Crozier (Rutgers University Press, New Brunswick, NJ, 1983), p. 162.

3 For an illuminating example of this kind of analysis see Judith Walkowitz, *City of Dreadful Delight: Narratives of Sexual Danger in Late-Victorian London* (Virago Press, London, 1992), especially ch. 1, 'Urban Spectatorship'. See also Elizabeth Wilson, 'The Invisible Flâneur', *New Left Review*, no. 191 (1992).

4 Analyses of power, its variety and dispersion, have a long history. See in particular Max Weber, *Economy and Society: An Outline of Interpretative Sociology*, ed. G. Roth and C. Wittich, 2 vols (University of California Press, Berkeley, 1978). The power inherent in knowledge and language has received special attention in the last decade, especially as expounded by Michel Foucault. See, for example, M. Foucault 'Truth and Power', in C. Gordon, ed., *Power and Knowledge* (Harvester, Brighton, 1980). For the gender implications of this approach see Lois McNay, *Foucault and Feminism* (Polity Press, Cambridge, 1992). For problems with Foucault's analysis, particularly his lack of attention to macro-processes, see Nicos Mouzelis, 'Poststructuralism: The Demise of Boundaries', in *Sociological Theory: What Went Wrong?* (Routledge, London, 1995).

5 For an early attempt at conceptualizing these problems see Leonore Davidoff, 'Power as an "Essentially Contested Concept": Can it Be of Use to Feminist Historians?', unpublished paper, Conference on 'Women and Power', University of Maryland, 1977.

6 Ivy Pinchbeck, *Women Workers and the Industrial Revolution* (Frank Cass, London, 1969) p. 4.

7 At that time (and even now not completedly routed) there was a tendency to regard the realm of work and technology as the real (material) basis of society while gender (read women) was part of a symbolic superstructure. This is clear even among non-Marxists such as Talcott Parsons with his division between 'instrumental' and 'expressive' values as institutional as well as personal characteristics. See in particular Talcott Parsons, 'The Family in America', in *Essays in Sociological Theory* (Free Press, New York, 1964). For a critique of this position see David H.J. Morgan, *The Family, Politics and Social Theory* (Routledge, London, 2nd edn, 1985).

8 Dorothy E. Smith, *The Conceptual Practices of Power: A Feminist Sociology of Knowledge* (Northeastern University Press, Boston, 1990), pp. 13 and 17.

9 Bryan Turner, *The Body and Society: Explorations in Social Theory* (Blackwell, Oxford, 1984), p. 59. See also Susan Bordo, *Unbearable Weight: Feminism, Western Culture and the Body* (University of California Press, Berkeley, 1993). Some of the most illuminating historical analysis on this topic has been for the early periods. See Caroline Walker Bynum, *Holy Feast and Holy Fast: The Religious Significance of Food to Medieval Women* (University of California Press, Berkeley, 1987); Peter Brown, *The Body and Society: Men, Women, and Sexual Renunciation in Early Christianity* (Columbia University Press, New York, 1988).

10 In the hierarchy of domestic service it was often the youngest (and overwhelmingly female) servants who did the heaviest work. With the assistance of the Castle Museum, York, I estimated that a full hod of coal weighed around 30 lb as did an average jug of bath water. Before the 1850s, perambulators were unknown and nursemaids or servant-girls had to carry young children in their arms often for hours at a time. The average eighteen-month-old middle-class child of the 1880s weighed 26 lb. See Leonore Davidoff and Ruth Hawthorn, *A Day in the Life of a Victorian Domestic Servant* (Allen & Unwin, London, 1976), p. 78.

11 Leonore Davidoff, *The Best Circles: Society, Etiquette and the Season* (Century Hutchinson, London, 1986).

12 See Cornelius Casteriadis, 'The Imaginary Institution of Society', in John Fekete, ed., *The Structural Allegory – Reconstructive Encounter with the New French Thought* (University of Minnesota Press, Minneapolis, 1984). This term has been used here in preference to 'ideology' which was current at the time many of the essays were written. 'Ideology' has proved to be a confusing concept, used both instrumentally and prescriptively, its double character making it difficult for historians to work with. It is also frequently taken to be a set, or system, of beliefs and institutions/practices which conveys the impression of something that is internally organized, coherent and complete. Mary Poovey, *Uneven Developments: The Ideological Work of Gender in Mid-Victorian England* (University of Chicago Press, Chicago, 1988), p. 3.

13 Jesus Fuenmayor, Kate Haug and Frazer Ward, *Dirt and Domesticity: Constructions of the Feminine* (Whitney Museum of American Art, New York City, 1992), p. 6 – thanks to Nancy Grey Osterud for this reference; see also Phyllis Palmer, *Domesticity and Dirt: Housewives and Domestic Servants in the United States, 1920–1945* (Temple University Press, Philadelphia, 1989).

14 A.J. Munby, Diaries, Trinity College, Cambridge, MSS, 1860, vol. 7, f. 79.

15 Sándor Szalay, *The Question of Urban Servants*, quoted in Gábor Gyáni, *Women as Domestic Servants: The Case of Budapest, 1890–1940* (Institute on East Central Europe, Columbia University, Budapest, 1989).

16 William Greg, 'Why Are Women Redundant?', *National Review*, vol. 15 (1862), p. 451.

17 In the last few years the gendering of space has attracted considerable attention. For an excellent example see Sarah Deutsch 'Women, Space and Power in Boston 1870–1910', *Gender and History*, vol 6, no. 2 (1994).

18 Donna Haraway, '"Gender" for a Marxist Dictionary: The Sexual Politics of a Word', in *Simians, Cyborgs, and Women: The Reinvention of Nature* (Free Association Books, London, 1991).

19 Polly Young Eisendrath, 'The Female Person and How We Talk about Her', in Mary McCanney Gergen, ed., *Feminist Thought and the Structure of Knowledge* (New York University Press, New York, 1988), p. 161.

20 See, for example, Christine Delphy and Diana Leonard, *Familiar Exploitation: A New Analysis of Marriage in Contemporary Western Socities* (Polity Press, Cambridge, 1992).

21 Amanda Vickery, 'Golden Age to Separate Spheres? A Review of the Categories and Chronology of English Women's History', *Historical Journal*, vol. 36, no. 2 (1993).

22 Edward Higgs, personal communication.

23   For a valuable insight into the voices of poor women themselves, see Ellen Ross, *Love and Toil: Motherhood in Outcast London, 1870–1918* (Oxford University Press, Oxford, 1993).

24   See Cecile Dauphin et al., 'Women's Culture and Women's Power: An Attempt at Historiography', *Journal of Women's History*, vol. 1, no. 1 (spring 1989).

25   Vickery, 'Golden Age to Separate Spheres?'

26   This has been published as *Family Fortunes: Men and Women of the English Middle Class, 1780–1850* (Routledge, London, 1994).

27   Robert W. Connell, *Which Way Is Up? Essays on Class, Sex and Culture* (Allen & Unwin, Sydney, 1983), p. 37.

28   Ludmilla Jordanova, 'Gender and the Historiography of Science', *British Journal of the History of Science*, vol. 26 (1993). See also, Nancy Hewitt's analogy with a chemical trace in 'Compounding Differences', *Feminist Studies*, vol. 18, no. 2 (summer, 1992).

29   For historical case studies of these issues see Margaret Hunt, 'Wife-Beating, Domesticity and Women's Independence in Eighteenth-Century London', *Gender and History*, vol. 4, no. 1 (spring, 1992); Cissie Fairchilds, *Domestic Enemies: Servants and their Masters in Old Regime France* (Johns Hopkins University Press, Baltimore, 1981).

30   Judith Butler and Joan Scott, eds, *Feminists Theorize the Political*, introduction (Routledge, London, 1992), p. xiv; see also Judith Butler, 'Contingent Foundations', in the same volume, p. 12.

31   For one of the most perceptive of these efforts see David M. Schneider, *A Critique of the Study of Kinship* (University of Michigan Press, Ann Arbor, 1984), p. 181. Such re-evaluation is taking place in all disciplines, not just the humanities and social sciences. Not only new knowledge but a fundamental paradigm shift has contributed to this liberating but potentially frightening stance. Even the mind itself is no longer seen as a simple system but a diverse, divergent organism which has evolved in 'an almost impossibly complicated way', raising contradictions which come with being human. See Robert Ornstein, *Multimind* (Houghton Mifflin, Boston, 1986), pp. 176 and 179.

32   See, for the nineteenth century, Patrick Joyce, *Work, Society and Politics* (Methuen, London, 1982); and, for the twentieth, Michael Roper, *Masculinity and the British Organization Man since 1945* (Oxford University Press, Oxford, 1994).

33   Laura Lee Downs, 'If "Woman" Is Just an Empty Category, Then Why Am I Afraid to Walk Alone at Night? Identity Politics Meets the Post-Modern Subject', *Comparative Studies in Society and History*, vol. 35, no. 2 (April, 1993), p. 429.

34   There is genuine uncertainty about the origins and strengths of the drive towards separation or autonomy and its implications for human identity. Nevertheless, a transhistorical examination of some basic commonalities is a way of viewing human nature 'without relapsing into reactionary biologisms such as sociobiology, or Freud's theory of instinctual agression'. See Joel Kovel, 'Cryptic Notes on Revolution and the Spirit', in *The Radical Spirit: Essays on Psychoanalysis and Society* (Free Association Books, London, 1988), p. 328.

35   Maggie Kirkman and Norma Grieve, 'Women, Power and Ordination: A Psychological Interpretation of Objections to the Ordination of Women to the Priesthood', *Women's Studies International Forum*, vol. 7, no. 6, p. 492.

36   I have adapted this combination of universal principles with historical time from the discussion of geology in Stephen Jay Gould, *Time's Arrow, Time's Cycle: Myth and Metaphor in the Discovery of Geological Time* (Penguin Books, Harmondsworth, 1987), pp. 58–9.

37   'If it is impossible to think in the Western logo-centred traditions without binary oppositions, then the task of feminist reading [*and I would add writing*], becomes the articulation not of a new set of categories but of the transcendence of categorical discourse altogether. One searches not for a new language but for a discourse at the

margins of language' (Seyla Benhabib, 'On Hegel, Women and Irony', in Mary L. Shanley and Carole Pateman, eds, *Feminist Interpretations and Political Theory* [Polity Press, Cambridge, 1991], p. 130).

38 This strategy has been called *métissage* by Françoise Lionnet in *Autobiographical Voices: Race, Gender, Self-Portraiture* (Cornell University Press, Ithaca, NY, 1989), p. 18. The acceptance of its inherent indeterminacy was clearly set out in the pathbreaking article by Sandra Harding, 'The Instability of the Analytical Categories of Feminist Theory', in *Signs: Journal of Women in Culture and Society*. vol. 11, no. 4 (summer 1986).

39 For a discussion of the disciplinary basis of reconceptualizing categories see J. Gerson and K. Peiss, 'Boundaries, Negotiation, Consciousness: Reconceptualising Gender Relations', and J. Stacy and B. Thorne, 'The Missing Feminist Revolution in Sociology', both in *Social Problems*, vol. 32, no. 4 (April 1985) and in Kate Campbell, ed., *Critical Feminism: Argument in the Disciplines* (Open University Press, Buckingham, 1992).

40 Judith Bennett, 'Feminism and History', *Gender and History*, vol. 1, no. 3 (Autumn 1989), p. 259.

41 Quoted in Phillip Abrams, *Historical Sociology* (Open Books, Shepton Mallet, Somerset, 1982), p. 17. Note that Mill's original and as quoted by Abrams says 'all men' (sic).

42 The use of social in this sense is more abstract and more central than the historically specific creation of an area which came to be designated as 'social' in the late nineteenth century, as distinguished from either the economic or political. This specific development is discussed by Denise Riley, *Am I That Name? Feminism and the Category of 'Women' in History* (Macmillan, London, 1988); and in greater detail in Jane Lewis, *Women and Social Action in Victorian and Edwardian England* (Edward Elgar, Aldershot, 1991).

1
Mastered for Life:
Servant and Wife in Victorian and Edwardian England

During the first half of the nineteenth century, an increasing proportion of the working population was employed as factory labour. Factories and workshops were growing larger. At the same time the nature of farm labour changed as the yearly hiring was gradually replaced by a more casual monthly contract and young, unmarried farm servants no longer lived in their employer's household. Integral to this fundamental change to a more limited contract, was the long and sometimes savage conflict over the abolishing of the Law of Master and Servant and its replacement by the Employer and Workman Act of 1875.[1]

At about the same time, there began a very gradual shift in the conception of the married woman's relationship to society (a process that is by no means complete even now); a move to make marriage a contract, voidable like other contracts involving two legal personalities.[2] This basic change, too, was reflected in some of the legislation that made inroads into the ancient common law concept of couveture: 'the husband and wife are one and the husband is that one', *Blackstone*.

Despite all the political and social ferment these changes generated, the impassioned debates in Parliament and in the press, there were two groups who, almost unnoticed, were hardly touched by the new order. Domestic servants and working-class married women continued, up to the First World War and beyond, in their pre-industrial, almost biblical, subordination to their masters and husbands. Regulation by Factory and Workshops Acts, trades boards or investigations into sweated labour passed them by. Trade union organization proved to be unworkable for servants, unthinkable for wives. Insurance schemes left them aside. Enfranchisement was not for them for they had neither domicile nor property of their own. Their legal definition and, in significant ways, their real situation was closer to the age-old common law doctrine of *potestas*: children, wives and servants are under the protection and wing of the Master.[3] He is the intermediary to the outside world; he embodies the governing principle within the household. It is no accident that such a relationship is called paternalistic, the basic elements of which are given in Max Weber's classical description of what social and political theorists have called patriarchal domination.

> Under patriarchal domination the legitimacy of the master's orders is guaranteed by his personal subjection and only the fact and the limits of his power of control are derived from the 'norms' yet these norms are not enacted but sanctified by tradition. The fact that this concrete master is indeed their ruler is always uppermost in the minds of his subjects. The master wields his power without restraints, at his own discretion and above all, unencumbered by rules insofar as it is not limited by tradition or competing powers.[4]

This term can apply to general expectations for society as a whole, for certain groups within a society or for certain relationships only within a society built on quite other norms, e.g. our attitude towards children in contemporary society. *What* (the franchise, labour relations, etc.) is being studied will determine which one of these is stressed. Here I am concerned primarily with the interpersonal relations between master and servant, husband and wife. *By definition* the subordinate group within each pair had few other links to the wider society.

I

In this essay I should like to examine this relationship in detail, looking at both the conventional expectations embodied in law and expounded by dominant groups as well as the reactions to it by those in subordinate positions. What happened to this doctrine under pressure from an increasingly cash- and market-orientated economy, where home and workplace had become physically separated?[5] What were the forces which led to its decline in service, and its attenuated survival in marriage?

In such a speculative essay, precise documentation is not possible, for necessarily the discussion covers a very long time-span. Much of the argument stems from sociological concern with the nature of authority, stratification, deference and similar abstract concepts. Nevertheless, it is important to make every effort to ground such abstractions in historical time and place. It is at this point that the problems of documenting personal interaction can lead to treacherously simple generalization. Domestic service and working-class marriage are exceptionally elusive areas of study as so much of their activity took place in private homes. Surviving written evidence is overwhelmingly from the superordinates' side and from the more articulate and powerful individuals within even that stratum.[6]

Bearing these problems in mind, the first question that must be asked is how the relationship operated on a day-to-day basis.[7] Second, there is the extensiveness of control through all areas of life for the subordinate. The existence of alternative loci of independence, including the *right* to be independent in any sphere, becomes crucial. For example, the assertion that, because even living-in servants had to sell their labour in the market-place, if only once a year, their relationship to their master was not patriarchal,[8] neglects this dimension. The cash reward may be seen as an extension of bed and board[9] regarded by the servant as a form of enforced savings for young maids and youths before marriage. The existence of cash payment *in itself* does not mean escape from paternalistic control; it only creates possibilities for an alternative way of life. This point is supported by looking at the way the wife's earnings have continued to be seen as part of the family income. The effort to maintain the paternalistic relationship within marriage by denying an *individual* wage to the wife is a thread which runs through debates on family income from the Poor Law of 1834 (which resulted in some unions paying for children to be fostered by strangers rather than pay the mother direct out relief), to the present controversy over the payment of Family Allowance directly to the mother or in the form of tax rebates to the father.[10]

Finally, and perhaps most important of all, is the extent of control over the life-span of the subordinate. Again this can be seen as a matter of degree rather than as a polar opposition, a continuum of control. At one end the father has complete control over the child until one day, no matter what the struggle for independence involves, they both know that the subordinate will break free, if only through the death of the parent.[11] The servant is attached to the master for an unspecified time; often the master wished to believe that the attachment was permanent when in fact many people seem to have served only when they were young and single, causing a high turnover. The wife, on the other hand, knew it was for ever. John Stuart Mill recognized the significance of this point when he said:

> surely if a woman is denied any lot in life but that of being the personal body-servant of a despot, and is dependent for everything upon the chance of finding one who may be disposed to make a favourite of her instead of merely a drudge, it is a very cruel aggravation of her fate that she would be allowed to try this chance only once . . . since her all in life depends upon obtaining a good master she should be allowed to change again and again until she finds one.[12]

By looking at the context in which such relationships took place, asking basic sociological questions about the size and structure of the groups involved,[13] it should be possible to avoid some of the pitfalls of an extreme reductionist psychology.[14] What was the physical setting, how much of the individual's time was spent in this setting through the day, the week, the year? Were there alternative groups for subordinates to identify with and was this identification and interaction 'legitimate' within the system or did it have to be carried out covertly[15] (e.g. was time off given to servants as a right at stated times or did it have to be taken in snatches between tasks)? Could servants see whom they wished when off duty or were their companions overlooked or even banned by the employer (the 'no followers' rule)?

The intense privacy of the English middle-class household in individual dwellings often surrounded by gardens, in isolated settings or suburbs separated from
working-class districts, made English domestic service exceptionally confining.
This was in contrast to continental cities. There the custom was to have all the
maids sleep together on the top floor of blocks of flats. When flats finally began to
be built in London towards the end of the century this feature was deliberately
omitted for fear of losing personal control over the servant.[16]

As the rest of the society changed, the service relationship, always fraught with
potential difficulties, came under increasing pressure. In 1908, Simmel described
this transitional stage as a breakdown in the 'objective idea' which occurs at either
of the extremes of the service relation:

> under the condition of full patriarchal subordination, where the house still has, so to
> speak, an absolute value which is served by the work of the housewife (though in a
> higher position) as well as by that of the servant; and then, under the condition of
> complete differentiation where service and reward are objectively pre-determined,
> and the personal attachment . . . has become extraneous to the relationship. The
> contemporary position of the servant who shares his master's house, particularly in
> the larger cities has lost the first of these two kinds of objectivity without having
> attained the second.[17]

That this is a transitional stage can only be revealed by hindsight. No
unilinear development can be taken for granted. A political and economic regime
pledged to permanent exploitative paternalism can seemingly continue the
relationship indefinitely.[18]

In this context, the most important fact about our period is that the majority of
girls moved from paternal control, in their parents' home, into service and then into
their husband's home – thus experiencing a lifetime of personal subordination in
private homes. This was in growing contrast to boys and to those girls who began
to find other forms of work towards the end of the century.[19]

In the following discussion, I have no wish to strain the analogy between the
situation of domestic servants, *both men and women*, and working-class married
women. In certain respects, most crucially in the presence of dependent children
but also in legitimate expectations for sexual relationships and affection, they
differed. In other, sociologically decisive areas they were similar.

II

The image of a working woman in nineteenth-century England is that of the mill
girl or possibly the milliner or seamstress. Yet it is well known that servants – in the
early part of the century farm and later purely 'domestic' servants – made up by far
the largest occupational group of working women, indeed the largest occupational

group in the whole economy except for agricultural labourers. In 1881, servants of both sexes represented one person in every 22 of the population. In London the proportion was 1 in 15; in Bath 1 in 9, while in Lancashire it was only 1 in 30. However, the great majority of indoor residential servants was made up of girls and women.

Numerically they grew from 751,541 in 1851 to a peak of 1,386,167 in 1891 and never fell below one million until the late 1930s.[20] They were 34 per cent of all women employed in 1891 and still 23 per cent in 1930. A high proportion of female domestic servants was young: those under twenty were 39 per cent of the total in 1860, 42 per cent in 1880 and 31 per cent in 1911. In 1881, 1 in 3.3 girls aged fifteen to twenty was classified as a domestic servant (*Census of Occupations, England and Wales*). A minority remained as servants all their lives, some experienced ten to fifteen years of service and then married; some left after a short time. It is impossible to tell the exact proportions in each category.[21]

Whatever proportion remained as 'career' servants, a great number of working-class women must have gone through some experience of service at sometime in their lives, usually including the formative years of adolescence. At an early age, in the first half of the century as young as nine or ten years old, servants had left their childhood home where they had been entirely subordinated to the authority of their parents. From this household they were transferred to the household of their master, under his direct authority or that of his deputy, the mistress or upper servant. From there, in turn, the servant passed to her husband's home, where, theoretically at least, she remained under his protection and his rule.

Within this large group there was a very wide range of experience. At one extreme was found the better-known form of service in a great house within a graduated hierarchy of servants, which could lead to a measure of autonomy, a high standard of living and a good deal of authority over others. At the other, and numerically more important, extreme was the less visible, less well-known 'slavery' in the lower-middle-class suburban or artisan household or lodging house. Fenimore Cooper, on his arrival in Southampton in the 1830s was shocked at the treatment of the girl where he lodged 'worse off then an Asiatic slave'.[22] The same conditions were still observed in 1897 in a lodging house where the little maid 'believes she belongs body and soul to the missus'.[23]

Despite these vast differences, all service positions shared certain characteristics. The master was expected to provide total support: food, housing and a small cash wage.[24] The servant reciprocated by being entirely at the disposal of the master, to obey his personal authority including directions as to the way in which the work was to be performed. In her demeanour she was to exhibit deference to the higher position of the master and his deputies (mistress, guests; even children). The relationship was residential and located in a private home.[25]

The wages for domestic service did vary very widely from household to household (tables of wage rates in household manuals can give a spurious uniformity) and from area to area.[26] Such variation increased the 'pocket money' character of the cash income because it was a private negotiation between two individuals. In fact, female kin could be and were used as domestic servants without pay. Household service and kinship obligations overlapped to the extent that legally the payment of wages had to be explicitly stated in the contract, otherwise it could be assumed that service was being given voluntarily.[27]

At the beginning of the nineteenth century, ruling groups perpetuated an image of society built on a hierarchy of service. As King is to God, Lord is to King, so servant is to master. All had obligations to serve those above them, to show their loyalty and devotion through service.[28] More prosaically a servant might comfort herself that 'even gentlemen have to bow and scrape to the Royal Family'.[29]

Such an ideal of service to a common and visible goal must be based on a society of small units, limited to a well-defined locality. (Even the great estate households with all their staff, both indoor and outdoor, seldom numbered more than 100 persons.) Such an ideal carries most credibility when the majority of other households in the locality are based on the same principles: therefore it can be as applicable to a farm community as to a castle. In such a setting, an 'external and spiritual community of fate' (Weber), there were no alternatives to challenge the system and 'the elision of "is" in power to "ought" to be in power' is much easier to sustain.[30] Thus employers often favoured servants who had come directly from country districts over those who had had some experience of city life.

It was at about this time, however, that the domination of the older elite, whose wealth had been based on landholding, was being challenged in a fundamental way by groups whose claims to power rested on new wealth garnered from trade and industry as well as by radical forces within the lower class. A consequence of this challenge was the growing concern with stricter controls of admission into the social and political elite, including control over social and personal behaviour. Those with incomes which gave them a substantial surplus were able to take part in the elaborate rituals of 'Society' and sport which had become formalized as part of this control.[31]

At the same time, several other factors had combined to increase both the numbers and scale of servant-employing households. Manufacturers and shop-keepers began moving their households away from mill and counting house to set up separate establishments. The creation of new professions and the expansion of old, meant that more households were established in market towns as well as in the rapidly growing cities, while the wealthier farmers banished work activities, particularly dairy work, from the house and immediately surrounding grounds.

These households were consumption units only. Even those homes where business affairs were carried on under the same roof kept both work activities and accounts separate from household affairs. The goals and activities of such households were dominated by the concern with social placement and social closure necessitating not only a great upsurge in display of material objects but elaborated rituals of etiquette. The surest way of proving social superiority was to surround oneself with 'deference givers', even specialized 'deference occupations'. As J.F.C.

Harrison points out: 'the essence of middle-classness was the experience of relating to other classes or orders of society. With one group, domestic servants, the middle classes stood in a very special and intimate relationship: the one fact played an essential part in defining the identity of the other.'[32]

Domestic servants gave the 'prompt complete respectful and easy obedience' due to their superiors apart from, or even in spite of, the moral or temperamental qualities of the individual master. The superior was thus guaranteed at least a minimum of deference even if he was 'alone' in his own home, i.e. with only his servant or servants.[33] Furthermore, the bestowing of deference can be elaborated to vast proportions through ritual. Such ritual can easily become an end in itself and does not necessarily imply a belief in or even awareness of the symbolic or mystical properties of those involved, either deference givers or receivers. When the elaboration of ritual becomes a whole ceremonial performance, such as the dinner party, the private ball or the house party, it takes on many features of a dramatic performance.[34]

In elaborated upper-class households, upper servants were crucial agents in the performance of these deference ceremonies. In order to be free to receive or give deference, to take part in activities which had symbolic importance or more prosaically to work for the surplus necessary as the basis for these activities, the master (and his family) had to be protected from the mundane pressures of life; the higher the position, the more protection was needed. Not only did servants protect the household from the external world – the kitchen staff dealt with working-class callers at the back door while the butler or parlourmaid dealt with the ritual of calls and card-leaving by social equals at the front door – but within the family, the master and mistress were protected by upper servants from lower servants and children. This protective function reached a point where the most intimate human relationships were mediated through servants in order to give maximum time for preparation and minimum unpleasantness in face-to-face contacts.[35]

Such rituals of deference could only be fully carried out in upper-class households with large specialized staffs. By and large, it is these households which have come to the notice of observers and form the basis of the stereotype of English domestic servants.[36] The typical middle-class family, on the other hand, aimed at having two or three servants,[37] only one of whom was concerned with personal service: answering the door, waiting at table, valeting the master or helping the mistress to dress. In yet less affluent families these functions had to be dispensed with or combined with 'rituals of order' in the material sphere (cleaning, cooking and childcare), tasks which in wealthy households were relegated to lower servants. The underlying rationale of these activities, however, was still the protection of superiors from defiling contact with the sordid, or disordered parts of life. A scanning of household manuals and magazines shows that these cleansing rituals took on heightened significance during this period of rapid social change.[38]

As we know, dirt is essentially disorder. It is matter out of place . . . uncleanness or
dirt is that which must *not* be included if a pattern is to be maintained. In chasing dirt,
cleaning and washing we are positively re-ordering our environment, making it
conform to an idea, separating, tidying and ultimately purifying.[39]

The second factor increasing demand for servants in middle- and upper-class
homes was the survival to maturity of increasing numbers of children.[40] More
children meant potentially more disorder, for children were considered socially
unplaced and therefore had to be kept in segregated parts of the house and fed at
separate times. Young children, especially in large numbers, were also creatures of
disorder in a material sense and therefore required more adults to keep them under
control and to care for them. Generally, greater numbers of servants were needed
to deal with the potentially disruptive and polluting fundamentals of life: birth,
infancy, illness, old age and death, as well as the key sphere of food preparation.
Many millions spent their working lives in this unending struggle: fetching, boil-
ing, steeping their hands in the purifying element of water.[41]

Those who were closest to defiling and arduous activities were, whenever possible, to be kept out of sight. In great houses their very existence was denied. Upper
servants were themselves protected from such defiling activities by having lower
servants to wait upon them. As more men were defined as upper servants, especially
from the 1880s onwards, this meant that the heaviest as well as the dirtiest tasks
could be given either to young girls and boys or charwomen, the two groups
physically least fitted for them.[42] This does not mean that considerate men servants
could not and did not help, for example to carry coal and water, or to clean outside
windows, but they could legitimately ignore this sort of work.

The Victorian preoccupation with rituals of order and cleanliness hardened the
traditional division between labouring and other work. White, shapely hands free
from dirt, burns or callouses were the *sine qua non* of gentility; any woman seen
outside the house without gloves could not be a lady. Again and again attention
is brought to the importance of *hands*. A.J. Munby, in his fascination with both
sex and class differences, continually returns to the contrast between the delicate
hands of the lady, encased in scented kid gloves and the 'brawny, brick red, coarse
grained (work-hardened) hand, with its huge clumsy thumb' that belongs to the
servant-girl.[43]

The need to prove that the advantages of wealth and status were deserved and
the disadvantaged were undeserving, their lowliness in some sense being their own
'fault', meant that this division between dirt and cleanliness, just as the division
between wealth and poverty, was cast in moral terms of good and evil: 'Dirt is the
natural emblem and consequence of vice. Cleanliness in house and dress and person
is the proper type and visible sign of a virtuous mind and of a heart renewed by the
Holy Spirit.'[44]

The symbolic power of cleansing and ordering rituals in warding off the dangers
of social displacement was applied with intensity to those women and girls who had

no family to place them or to those who had been labelled as having fallen outside legitimate society by having (or being suspected of having) sexual relations outside marriage. Whenever possible, they were 'placed' in institutional substitutes for homes: Homes for Orphans, Charity Homes, Homes for Fallen Women – or the Workhouse. Here they were considered to be safe from the dangers of public or street life. Within these institutions, anti-pollution rites combined with problems of discipline led to the use of intensive domestic work as control and as punishment: 'A laundry carefully worked is a capital place for moral training and moulding of the character where sins can be washed away.'[45] Almost without exception, the aim of all these institutions was to prepare the girl or woman for domestic service. For the only legitimate and respected (or respectable) alternative to living with one's own family was living as a servant with another family.

III

In any system of hierarchy expressed in rituals of deference, at a face-to-face level, there will be a continuing tension between identification with the superior (the giver of gifts and rewards) and social distance (protection of independence). How far the subordinate identifies with the goals of the system *and/or the personal superiors*, and by so doing accepts his or her inferior place within it, partly depends on the rewards – both psychic and material – he receives but also partly on how easy it is for him to find compensatory definitions of self-worth. Deliberate, narrow identification with the place of work, 'my kitchen', pride in the job no matter how menial, 'keeping my brass taps always shiny', or pride in the status and possessions of the employing family allowed servants a certain self-respect without total allegiance to or acceptance of the system.

Another device for maintaining dignity and a sense of worthiness was to magnify the dependence of the superior on the subordinate's skill, strength and emotionally supportive activity, a kind of subtle inversion of the relationship. Thus servants often emphasized the 'helplessness' of the gentry. A tweeny in service in the early twentieth century said, 'If it hadn't been for the working class, all the folk in Ryton would have been "hacky dorty", because it took the working class to keep them clean. The majority of people didn't know the right end of a duster.'[46]

These are responses limited to what was possible within the relationship. Strength to resist its encroachments could only come from external sources. Education, especially basic literacy, for servants was important as such a factor. But education, along with the acquisition of skills outside domestic work, posed a dilemma for the master; they made the servant more useful but at the same time potentially more independent. Particularly threatening to the employer was the possibility of the servant earning extra cash, especially from others.[47] Fears of losing control over servants lie behind the master's objections to both the practice of giving vails (gratuities) and board wages (payment in lieu of food) as such payments decreased the servant's dependence: 'by multiplying the hours during which they were free of supervision it increased their opportunities to live a life outside the family'.[48] Servants, on the other hand, deliberately stressed the 'modern' cash side of service partly because other working-class occupations were increasingly seen in this light and partly because by stressing their monetary attachment to the household they had a defence against the persuasive paternalism of service.

Especially when residence and being on call twenty-four hours a day were required, another important device for maintaining self-respect was to accept identification with the employer's household for a time, but then to leave for another situation, apparently without 'reason'. This is the restlessness of servants which was so resented by employers.

Which device was used depended on the particular situation of the servant, including background, age and sex. Accommodation within the relationship might be more characteristic of younger girls under the double discipline of service and femininity. In discussing the vexed question of time off an employer in the 1890s said: 'Men servants can get out for the best of all reasons, that they insist on it. . . . As regards women servants, it is not a disadvantage for them, when they are young, to be under such control as admits of their having only a short time for going out. Restraint is always distasteful to the young and servants share the feelings of the daughter of the house, who would like more freedom in directions which custom deems perilous.'[49] But by the turn of the century, as new leisure-time activities and the possibility of increased mobility by train, omnibus or bicycle increased the expectation of a more independent life for girls, the restraints of residential service became less and less tolerable.[50]

Under the constant pressure for autonomy by their subordinates it is not surprising that the qualities of the good servant extolled by masters were humility, lowliness, meekness and gentleness, fearfulness, respectfulness, loyalty and good temper. Many of these characteristics were equally part of the 'service' ethic whether it was in the armed services, church or public service. In the case of servants, however, they appeared in an exaggerated form, symbolized in behaviour such as walking out of the door backwards, maintaining absolute silence while performing their duties, never sitting down in the presence of their employers and never initiating an action or a speech.

When looked at in a slightly different light, these are also the despised qualities of the menial or lackey (both synonyms for servants as well as being derogatory terms in themselves). Such qualities were considered particularly degrading in men, in an era where 'manliness' was so important, and they often were counteracted by a strained haughtiness and dignity. The relationship I have been describing may, indeed, produce such virtues on the part of the subordinate but also it often results in slyness, evasiveness, a manipulative attitude and an 'uncanny' or 'intuitive' ability to see through the master's weaknesses.[51]

Were these qualities a 'mask' assumed while in the front regions when interacting with the master group, to be sloughed off in private? Or had many servants internalized a belief in their own unworthiness? We do not know. After all, human beings have an infinite capacity for living on many levels at once. As Simmel says in a general discussion of super- and subordination: 'A highly complex interaction is hidden beneath the semblance of the pure superiority of the one element and a purely passive being-led by the other';[52] a dialogue between the superior constantly justifying the legitimacy of his rule, the subordinate constantly restating his self-worth, by seeking 'pockets of resistance'.[53]

Resistance could take other forms than flight or the escape into fantasy of servants' romantic literature. The traditional weapons such as sulking, mishearing, or semi-deliberate spoiling of materials, creating disorder, wasting time, deliberate 'impudence' or 'answering back' were developed to a high art by servants and recognized by both sides. An upper-class employer:

> A housemaid, butler or cook had a unequalled power of taking it out on their master or mistress in subtle ways. Orders could be received with veiled sulks, and insinuations of trouble in the background.[54]

A cook:

> Servants that feel they're being put upon can make it hard in the house in various ways like not rushing to answer bells, sullen dumb insolence and petty irritations to make up for what you're not getting.[55]

The organization of a front- and backstage in larger middle- and upper-class homes gave more scope for such disruptive, individualized reactions including deliberate pollution of a very crude kind.[56]

By the mid-nineteenth century some of the latent hostility of servants focused on the sphere of personal behaviour which symbolized lowly position.[57] The daughter of a coachman recalls,

> I was once told I had to curtsey and my father said, I'll curtsey you if you curtsey. It seemed it was a certain lady my father was coachman to and the gardener's children used to curtsey to them. And my father said, I'll do the curtseying but my child's not going to curtsey. And he said if I find you curtseying I'll give you a good thrashing. So I hadn't to curtsey.[58]

Such hostility reflected the forces which eventually were to undermine the whole fabric of hierarchy and deference. A similar aetiology can be observed in the plantation system of the southern United States in the nineteenth century: the conflict between 'the patriarchialism of the plantation community, and the commercial and capitalistic exploitation demanded by the exigencies of the world market'.[59] In the case of households based on consumption – or the 'production' of social ritual – it was the exigencies of the *labour* market which undermined their rule.

The aversion to domestic service which resulted from the growth of alternative occupations and increasing working-class political awareness first affected men servants. It was they who led the campaign against the most personal and direct effect of subordination, i.e. physical punishment. Some took an ever-increasing manipulative and cynical view of their occupation; some used the contacts they had made while in service as a way out of purely domestic posts, to become shopkeepers or run commercial services. These developments were spread over a long period with beginnings in the eighteenth century. Often there was not a complete break with service because more outdoor non-residential servants were used not only in stable and estate work, but also in the innumerable subsidiary service occupations which were an (as yet uninvestigated) feature of Victorian life. Livery-stable employees, peripatetic clockwinders, couriers, private carriers, etc., all added to the amenities of middle-class life but were no longer under the close personal control of an individual master.

On the whole, employers seem to have accepted the declining use of men servants. It is difficult to find proof, but there are indications that it was not so much the increased cost of keeping men servants but the increased difficulty of controlling them within the house which led to the gradual substitution of girls for men in the 1870s and 1880s.

Girls and women did not make the transition to other occupations so easily. Socialization, the ideology which decreed that the 'natural' place for all women was a private home, and opportunity all conspired to keep them in service positions. Slowly, however, opportunities for alternative work were appearing[60] and, where available, servants were almost always more difficult to recruit.[61] The 400,000 who left service during the First World War were only the most striking case of what was a continuing pattern.

The second force ultimately undermining the master–servant relationship was the concept of citizenship. Once it is admitted that all are equal members of the commonwealth, then the contract must be limited; outside it master and servant meet 'man to man as two British citizens'. Servants were one of the last groups to gain this citizenship either in the form of the franchise or citizen's rights in the form of insurance.[62]

In keeping with my original analogy, however, it is interesting that married women were the very last group of adults to participate fully in civil society; even now vestiges of their status as appendages to their husbands remain and are being debated in questions about pensions, National Insurance and married women's domicile. T.H. Marshall made this point in an aside whose importance even he underestimated: 'The story of civil rights in their formative period is one of the gradual additions of new rights to a status that already existed (i.e., freedman) and was held to appertain to all adult members of the community – or perhaps one should say to all male members, since the status of women or at least of married women, was in some important respects peculiar'.[63]

Middle- and upper-class households defiantly defended themselves against the encroachments of these disruptive forces but the private drives and the gates could not completely keep out the alien influences; for by surrounding themselves with 'deference givers' the stranger was already within their doors.[64] They did everything in their power to deny this was so, stressing the organic nature of the household by devices such as family worship. The danger lurking below the surface, however, was that without the power to enforce loyalty – the vigilant personal enforcement of deferential behaviour – divergence of interest would come to the surface and threaten the whole façade.

In 1826, as a very old and bedridden lady, the famous writer on moral affairs, Hannah Moore, was confined to an upper room alone in her home as her sisters died one by one. The large staff of servants, who had always hitherto been under the rule of the most practical of her sisters, now had such a gay life at her expense that she exceeded her income by £300 in one year and was powerless to stop it; a victim in her own house. At last her friends stepped in and carried her off to lodgings, fired the servants, lamenting that 'the poor old lady had to be made aware that these dishonest and vicious servants were making her appear to tolerate the sins she had testified against through life'.[65]

IV

I have argued elsewhere that the isolation of working-class girls in middle-class homes during the course of their service put them at a disadvantage in the marriage market compared to their less restricted working contemporaries.[66] Under the strict regulations imposed on girls in service, courting had to be done in snatches of time: on their afternoon off, which early in the century could be only once a month, 'at the area steps' or with boys from home whom they might see only once a year.

Once married, whatever the personal qualities and occupations of their husbands, they shared the basic precariousness of all working-class families dependent, at least theoretically, for support solely on the husband's wage, an expectation peculiar to this period of economic development.[67] Married women quickly became absorbed in the arduous battle of housekeeping where purifying rituals had to be carried out by one person in the restricted confines of a working-class home. The content of their work, as in service, was creating order in the house, preparing food and generally dealing with the detritus of personal life. As in service, also, these activities could fill up all the day and some of the night as well – there was no definite time off or time of one's own. Their material equipment was very often makeshift leftovers from middle-class households where 'rational' use of labour was the last consideration; just as working-class homes were often 'rooms' in converted middle- or upper-class houses.

By the latter part of the nineteenth century, the customary division of labour within the household laid most managerial responsibility for household organization as well as the majority of manual tasks upon the wife. Often she had little knowledge of her husband's work or he of hers. Unlike, therefore, an enterprise where the subordinate may defer to the *technical* expertise of the superior, her deference was to his paternalistic status; hers was a subordination of a more pervasive personal kind. Little attention, for example, has been paid to the use (or even more the threat) of physical coercion as a source of the husband's control.[68]

There was undoubtedly great satisfaction to the wife in the knowledge of her power to run the household and control the family's affairs, of her importance as the mainstay of family life. This knowledge, however, increased the pressures on her to protect her husband (and older children who were earning) from knowing how the household was managed to produce meals, clean clothes and rent, much less extras. Such protection from mundane matters paralleled that given by servants to the master or mistress. The husband was freed from 'bother' that he might engage in higher-level affairs (after his often monotonous and arduous work was done), be it the masculine culture of the pub, solitary hobbies like pigeon-racing or, above all, politics. The women themselves summed up their task of constant figuring and planning in such expressive phrases as: 'to contrive and consider', 'to make do and mend'. These decisions had to be made under emotional pressure from the competing demands of husband and children (and possibly elderly parents). Such constraints were compounded by the women's ill-health due to poverty, multiple pregnancies and self-neglect. The price paid was the narrowness of horizons, the closing in of the woman's world.[69]

In both service and marriage, master (mistress) or husband did not see what was happening. This unthinking blindness to what was going on within their own household was not usually the result of deliberate malice or even unkindness; rather it *was built into* the relationship. It was the essence of mastery that the lives of subordinates did not matter, that their concerns were, on the whole, of no interest or importance and were even faintly ridiculous. When the husband gave his wife money over and above the basic housekeeping allowance or other 'treats', or if he helped with heavy washing, or took the children out on a Sunday, it was much in the same tradition as the 'kindly' squire and his lady who gave charitable extras to their retainers and villagers. Very close ties and great mutual affection often existed in such a situation but having either a good husband or 'a real bad 'un' was, in a sense, to be accepted as a stroke of fate in just the same way as the wife accepted the goal of family survival over her individual interests.

If, for any reason, the wife did not receive support and help from her husband, the only alternative recourse for her was to seek help from her family or from her neighbours whose own resources might be limited. But very little is really known about the support available to wives through the network of female neighbours and kin.[70] More attention should be given to the conventions of close-knit communities, such as 'rough music', which were used to control excessive wife abuse or neglect.[71]

The other source of independence I have described for servants, i.e. outside earnings, was vitiated, for the most part, in the case of wives. This was partly because the women's wages were so low and were counter-balanced both by problems of childcare and loss of social status, and partly because all of what was earned almost invariably went into the family budget. If extra money was needed, one of the most frequently used sources was taking in lodgers. Although it solved the childcare problems, it also created more overcrowding and more *work of the same kind* for the housewife while introducing a new, potentially disruptive set of personal relationships into the household.[72] The only possible exception to this pattern was where the wife was highly skilled in a trade which offered work near to where she lived (therefore *not* including many ex-domestic servants) or in textile districts where married women's work was accepted, with consequently higher earnings.[73] But behind the objective problem of low wages lay the basic dilemma of reconciling paternalistic relationships with a market economy nowhere better illustrated than in the legal ruling which required that a married woman who wanted to hire herself out to service must obtain the permission of her husband. An employer who did not gain this permission when hiring her could be sued for 'loss of services', in exactly the same way as an employer could be sued for enticing away a servant. In lay terms, a woman could not serve two masters.

The wife's isolation in a separate household and without colleagues or a work group to enforce expectations of 'fair play' or 'justice' of reward was an extension of the single servant's isolation.[74] Indeed, Marx's well-known metaphor describing the peasants of France is applicable to married women and servants alike.

> The small-holding peasants form a vast mass, the members of which live in similar conditions but without entering into manifold relations with one another . . . in this way the great mass is formed by simple addition of homologous magnitudes such as potatoes in a sack form a sack of potatoes. The identity of their interests begets no community, no national bond, and no political organisation, among them they do not form a class.[75]

Few sources of political education or experience existed for the working-class girl or woman. The slow permeation of individualistic values to their ranks was rather due to increased education, more opportunity for varied work and higher earnings and, above all, to the fall in the birth rate and the accompanying belief that it was possible to control their own fertility.

Given this basic pattern of working-class family life from the second half of the nineteenth century onwards, what were the effects of having been in service? One of the stock defences of domestic service for working-class girls had been the belief that it gave a training for married life, for the girl's natural transition to wife and motherhood. The fact that the key to efficient household management, the budgeting of money and materials, was usually not part of the servant's responsibility was overlooked, nor was it appreciated that the most overwhelming priority for wives was managing on an insufficient or, even more hazardous, a fluctuating income.[76]

The budgeting of time is more problematical. This was less directly taught to the girls than an attitude which they absorbed while in service, for in middle- and upper-class households by the first quarter of the nineteenth century, housework and childcare had been systematically allocated separate units of time. This change from a task-orientated to a time-orientated outlook as applied to personal and home life is one of the most important (and least explored) aspects of Victorian social life. Servants were instrumental to this development. 'As soon as actual hands are employed the shift from task orientation to timed labour is marked',[77] and this applied within the home as well as the workshop. Women who had had some experience of domestic service, particularly in larger households, undoubtedly absorbed at least part of this attitude. However, in their own home, it was the external time constraints of the husband's work, particularly shift-work and, later in the century, the school, which created fixed time points in their day, not social ritual. In the limited framework of their lives, their singlehanded efforts to impose strictly fixed times to family life could be not only inappropriate but even counter-productive.

A few ex-servants were able to save money to use as a dowry or set up with their husbands in trade.[78] A few girls must have married into the master class, or more likely into the lower middle class; some may have been kept as mistresses by upper-class men. For the majority, however, who married into the working class, there must have been very great variations due not only to the diversity of households but to the length of time the girl stayed in service and her experience, if any, of other jobs. If she had accepted some of the preoccupations of order and social ritual already discussed but was not able fully to carry them out because of lack of money, time and space, she had to make do with what meagre external symbols she could, constantly striving to make up deficiencies with her own labour. The whitened doorsteps and net curtains, the struggle to keep children in clean clothes, the whole distinction between 'rough' and 'respectable' can partly be seen in these terms. ('Pollution beliefs can be used in a dialogue of claims and counter claims for status' – Mary Douglas.) Other working-class women with factory or shop experience were also caught up in the struggle against dirt and disorder but it is possible that these distinctions had particular saliency for ex-servants.

Many former servants had very ambivalent attitudes towards their past employers. A few probably maintained personal ties with them, or even more likely with their children with whom they may have had a special relationship. Some found their horizons widened by their experience of service, by having witnessed new ways of living, by having been introduced to new tastes, new forms of beauty in the furnishing, decorations, flowers and gardens of the houses where they worked.[79] Some of these ideas could in turn be passed on to their children along with ambitions for individual advancement.[80] It is even possible that here may be one of the sources of working-class conservatism.[81] It should be remembered, though, that others were deeply ashamed of their servile past: 'How could we have allowed ourselves to be ordered about so, and for that wage?'[82]

Such aspirations tended to be expressed in personal and individual terms for all their experience from early childhood had been of the same personal subordination.[83] 'They are confined within the limits of their imagination of the possible, the relationship is habitual. Insubordination must have not only alternative means of support but an alternative language.'[84] Whereas working-class men were beginning to find a tongue for their wrongs, there were few places where working-class wives could learn to speak of theirs; the Working Man's Club and the public house were often not for them.

In weighing up the relative positions within a paternalistic relationship, the decisive point is what happens when the relationship is broken, given the fact that in theory it should last for life. Only when the servant or wife is abruptly removed from the household and the well-oiled wheels of domestic machinery grind to a halt does the superior realize just how important such services really are.[85] For the master/husband, the first reaction to the loss of the subordinate is outrage at both the inconvenience caused and the disloyalty implied. The depth of this outrage will partly depend on the ease of replacing lost services and this in turn will depend not only on his money resources but also the state of the domestic labour (and marriage) market, both in quantity and quality.

On the other side, the overwhelming fact is that the whole of the life of the servant and wife, from material support to human surroundings, depends on the household of which she happens to be a member: its resources, physical setting, technical equipment and above all the temperament and tastes of the master (mistress)/husband. These resources determine the standard of living, the work-load, the food and other rewards and even help to define the identity of the dependant. When this relationship is broken it is, therefore, bound to be more traumatic and to require greater adjustments for the subordinate.

For in the last analysis, in an industrializing society, particularly a capitalist society at the high tide of liberal economic doctrine, there was no place for those whose social identity was defined primarily in terms of personal relationships, neither servants nor wives. They had no roles to play in the great drama of market forces. In theory they did not exist or at most were residual categories. In reality they had to struggle for survival in what ever way they could, for in such a society 'he who pays the piper calls the tune'.[86]

The majority of such positions have been filled by women, although I have deliberately stressed the fact that *both* men and women servants came into this category in order to demonstrate that this type of relationship is not necessarily linked to sex differences. The fact remains, however, that by and large submission to personal and unlimited authority has been the fate of a majority of women during the stormy history of industrialization.

Recently there have been renewed efforts to find women's place in that history. It is rightly felt that 'a people without a history is a dispossessed people'. Those who wish to seek out heroines, to make us aware that 'female hands ripped coal, dug roads, worked looms . . . that female will and courage helped to push the working class towards whatever decencies of life it has now'[87] are more than justified in doing so. But the heroines must be seen in context. Otherwise there is a danger that they will be frozen for ever in the amber of a new feminist hagiology rather than taking their rightful place in the mainstream of human history.

Notes

1　D. Simon, 'Master and Servant', in J.D. Saville, ed., *Democracy and the Labour Movement: Essays in Honour of Dona Torr* (Lawrence & Wishart, London, 1954).

2　L.T. Hobhouse, *Morals in Evolution: A Study in Comparative Ethics* (Chapman and Hall, London, 1951), p. 231.

3　The point has been made in connection with slavery that it is a mistake to make legal definitions and codes the basis of analysis. David Brion Davis's critique of Tannenbaum and Elkins 'points to the possibility of large gaps between the legal status of the slave and the actual working of the institution' (Ann J. Lane, ed., *The Debate over Slavery: Stanley Elkins and his Critics* [University of Illinois Press, Urbana, Illinois, 1971], p. 8). This is an important warning against sociological naïvety but should not push us to the other extreme of discounting legal conventions, especially court rulings, as historical sources.

4　Max Weber, in *Economy and Society*, vol. 3, ed. Guenther Roth and Claus Wittich (Bedminster Press, New York, 1968), p. 1066.

5　Note that during this period Britain had neither an indigenous nor an imported ethnically or religiously disadvantaged population (with the possible exception of the Irish). Such groups often make up the majority of domestic servants and thus blur the effects of the master–servant relationship. Contrast with the American experience: Lucy Maynard Salmon, *Domestic Service* (Macmillan, New York, 1911).

6　In order to supplement the usual documentary sources in my present research, I have used 200 employer and 75 servant 'autobiographies', both written and oral, including material from Paul and Thea Thompson's 'Family Life and Work Experience before 1918' (Social Science Research Project, University of Essex).

7　Akin to Genovese's basic meaning of 'treatment' in various slave societies. See Eugene D. Genovese, 'The Treatment of Slaves in Different Countries: Problems in the Applications of the Comparative Method', in Laura Foner and Eugene D. Genovese, eds, *Slavery in the New World: A Reader in Comparative History* (Prentice-Hall, New York, 1969).

8　C.B. Macpherson, 'Servants and Labourers in Seventeenth-Century England', in *Democratic Theory: Essays in Retrieval* (Clarendon Press, Oxford, 1973), p. 217.

9　It is also part of the 'pre-industrial' attitude to the use of cash as a work incentive, the belief on the part of employers that servants were looking for only a minimum subsistence income and once given that income any amount of work could be required in return. See Sidney Pollard, 'The Creation of the New Work Discipline', in *The Genesis of Modern Management: A Study of the Industrial Revolution in Great Britain* (Arnold, London, 1965), p. 190.

10　Part of the problem of the decline of family-based domestic and rural employment. See Ivy Pinchbeck, *Women Workers and the Industrial Revolution 1750–1850*, ch. 5 (Cass, London, 1969).

11　For a discussion of the same question at a time when industrialization began to provide alternative means of support for adolescents, boys and girls, see Michael Anderson, 'The Phenomenal Level: Environmental Sanctions, Ideologies and Socialization', in *Family Structure in Nineteenth-Century Lancashire* (Cambridge University Press, Cambridge, 1971).

12　J.S. Mill, *On the Subjection of Women* (Everyman, London, 1965), p. 249. Logically, then, there should be no surprise at the discovery of 'serial marriage' in the 1970s.

13　Georg Simmel, 'Quantitative Aspects of the Group', *The Sociology of Georg Simmel*,

      trans. Kurt H. Wolff (Free Press, Glencoe, IL, 1950).
14   A problem which had bedevilled the Elkins debate. See Ann J. Lane, ed., *The Debate over Slavery: Stanley Elkins and his Critics*, introduction.
15   Hence the importance of servants' quarters and kitchens separate from the house in colonial India and Africa. See Aban B. Mehta, *The Domestic Servant Class* (Bombay, 1960). Large English houses did have a front- and backstage divided by the 'green baize door', but in smaller houses physical separation was much more difficult. See Erving Goffman, *The Presentation of Self in Everyday Life* (Penguin Books, Harmondsworth, 1972).
16   Mrs Loftie, 'Living in Flats', *Social Twitters* (London, 1878).
17   Simmel, 'Quantitative Aspects of the Group', p. 266.
18   M.G. Whisson and William Weil, *Domestic Servants: A Microcosm of 'the Race Problem'* (South African Institute of Race Relations, Johannesburg, 1971).
19   Peter Stearns, 'Working-Class Women in Britain 1890–1914', in Martha Vicinus, ed., *Suffer and Be Still: Women in the Victorian Age* (Indiana University Press, Bloomington, IN, 1972).
20   In 1871 there were 68,369 male indoor residential servants.
21   C. Collett, *Money Wages of Domestic Servants* (Report of Board of Trade, Labour Department), *PP*, XCII, Cmd. 9346 (1899).
22   Walter Allen, *Transatlantic Crossing: American Visitors to Britain and British Visitors to America* (Heinemann, London, 1971).
23   *Toilers in London*, British Weekly Survey (1897).
24   The meaning of this dependency is described in Vilhelm Aubert, 'On the Social Structure of the Ship', in *The Hidden Society* (Bedminster Press, Totowa, NJ, 1965).
25   In weighing up the relative importance of cash versus food, clothes and 'extras', note that domestic servants were specifically excluded from the Truck Acts of 1831 to 1887.
26   Collett, *Money Wages of Domestic Servants*. Wage data from my 275 'memories'.
27   'In England the rule is that the mere fact of service does not of itself ground a claim for remuneration, unless there be either an express bargain as to wages, or circumstances showing an understanding on both sides that there should be payment' (Patrick Fraser, *Treatise on Master and Servant* [London, 3rd edn, 1875]).
28   Harold Perkin, *The Origins of Modern English Society 1780–1880* (Routledge & Kegan Paul, London, 1969), ch. 2.
29   Derek Hudson, *Munby, Man of Two Worlds: The Life and Diaries of Arthur J. Munby, 1828–1910* (J. Murray, London, 1972), p. 310. Booth, in discussing the nature of domestic service in the 1890s, says that it is 'a relationship very similar in some respects to that subsisting between sovereign and subject . . . there is demanded an all-pervading attitude of watchful respect, accompanied by a readiness to respond at once to any gracious advance that may be made without ever presuming or for a moment "forgetting themselves" ' (Charles Booth, *Life and Labour of the People in London* [Macmillan, London, 1903], vol. 4, p. 225).
30   Howard Newby, 'The Deferential Dialectic', unpublished typescript, published (with slightly different wording) in *Comparative Studies in Society and History*, vol. 17 (1975), pp. 139–64; see p. 155.
31   Leonore Davidoff, *The Best Circles: Society, Etiquette and the Season* (Century Hutchinson, London, 1986), ch. 2.
32   J.F.C. Harrison, *The Early Victorians, 1832–1851* (Weidenfeld & Nicolson, London, 1971), p. 110. He notes that Rowntree in his study of York took the keeping of servants (or a servant) as the attribute for inclusion in the middle class.
33   Deference must actively be sought, it cannot be given to oneself (Erving Goffman, 'The Nature of Deference and Demeanor', in *Interaction Ritual: Essays on Face-to-Face Behaviour* [Penguin Books, Harmondsworth, 1967]).

34 John Beattie, 'Ritual and Social Change', *Man*, n.s., no. 1 (1966), pp. 60–74.

35 An emancipated middle-class girl who married into the aristocracy about 1914 was appalled to find that her lady's maid, after helping her into her nightgown, asked permission to go and tell her husband's valet to announce that her ladyship was ready (Ursula Bloom, *A Roof and Four Walls* [Hutchinson, London, 1967]).

36 Alexis de Tocqueville, 'How Democracy Affects the Relations of Master and Servants', *Democracy in America*, vol. 2 (Schocken Books, New York, 1955).

37 J.A. Banks, *Prosperity and Parenthood: A Study of Family Planning among the Victorian Middle Classes* (Routledge & Kegan Paul, London, 1954), ch. 5.

38 This is not to overlook purely physical problems of dirt control, e.g. new conditions produced by factory chimneys and urban living. Nor to deny the importance of the discovery of the germ theory of disease and related public health developments or even the connection of religious beliefs with ideas of purity. All these must be taken into account when discussing the history of the period but they are analytically separate from the above.

39 Mary Douglas, *Purity and Danger: An Analysis of Concepts of Pollution and Taboo* (Pelican Books, Harmondsworth, 1970), p. 12.

40 H.J. Habakkuk, *Population Growth and Economic Development since 1750* (Leicester University Press, Leicester, 1971), ch. 3.

41 Servants, and almost always female servants, dealt with the recurring by-products of daily life: excrement, ashes, grease, garbage, rubbish, blood, vomit. Such tasks are also allocated to wives. 'Protection of the purity of upper strata is an important feature of caste societies' (Louis Dumont, *Homo Hierarchicus: The Caste System and its Implications* [Paladin, London, 1970]).

42 At the Duke of Richmond's castle in Scotland, despite the number of men servants kept, 'on Friday morning an army of charwomen bore down on the place to assist staff with the "rough"' (Muriel Beckwith, *When I Remember* [I. Nicholson & Watson, London, 1936], p. 73).

43 A.J. Munby, Diary (1860), vol. 7, p. 79, Trinity College, Cambridge, MSS. Munby's fixation extended to glorying in seeing his servant (whom he married in 1874) Hannah 'in her dirt', filthy from scrubbing; the dirtier her hands, the more smudged her face, the more he valued her. His fascination with the 'degraded' seems to have included a strong sexual element centred around the themes of mastery and submission. I have deliberately avoided any discussion of servants and sexuality in this paper but this is not to deny its importance as an element in the relationship. See Leonore Davidoff, 'Above and Below Stairs', *New Society*, 26 April 1973.

44 *The Servants' Magazine or Female Domestics Instructor* (1839).

45 Rev. A.J.S. Maddison, *Hints on Rescue Work: A Handbook for Missionaries, Superintendents of Homes, Clergy and Others* (Reformatory and Refuge Union, London, 1898).

46 Barbara Rowlands, 'Memories of a Domestic Servant in the First World War', *North-East Group for the Study of Labour History*, Bulletin no. 5 (October 1971).

47 'I am of the opinion that a man cannot be the servant of several persons at the same time but is rather in the character of an agent' (Rev. V. Goodbody [1838], 8 ct. 665).

48 J. Jean Hecht, *The Domestic Servant Class in Eighteenth-Century England* (Routledge & Kegan Paul, London, 1956), p. 155.

49 Lady Jeune, 'Domestic Servants', in *Lesser Questions* (Remington, London, 1894), p. 265.

50 Some mistresses feared losing control of the servant if they did not constantly find her 'something to do' – that is, show that they owned all of the servant's time. Even on the eve of the Second World War the attitude was: 'with regard to industrial workers the problem is always how many hours they should work; with domestic servants it is how much time they should have off' (Minister of Labour, *Evening Standard*, 14 February

1938); Violet Firth, *The Psychology of the Servant Problem: A Study in Social Relationships* (C.W. Daniel, London, 1925).

51   These have also been both the virtues and vices attributed to wives and slaves. Orlando Patterson, 'An Analysis of Quashee', in *The Sociology of Slavery* (MacGibbon & Kee, London, 1967).

52   Simmel, 'Quantitative Aspects of the Group', p. 186.

53   This ambivalence is even clearer under slavery. See George M. Fredrickson and Christopher Lasch, 'Resistance to Slavery', in Lane, ed., *The Debate over Slavery*; George P. Rawick, *From Sundown to Sunup: The Making of the Black Community*, vol. 1, *The American Slave: A Composite Autobiography* (Greenwood, Westport, CT, 1972), pp. 95–7.

54   Lady Tweedsmuir, *The Lilac and the Rose* (Gerald Duckworth, London, 1952), p. 94.

55   Margaret Powell, *Below Stairs* (Peter Davies, London, 1968), p. 156.

56   In a doctor's family, where the two maids felt that they were overworked and never given sufficient food, the master accused them of stealing the kidney gravy at breakfast. Back in the kitchen, to spite him, one of the maids lifted her skirt and pissed in the gravy pan saying 'she'd see he had plenty o'kidney gravy' (Sybil Marshall, *Fenland Chronicle* [Cambridge University Press, Cambridge, 1967], p. 240).

57   'Lower-class compliance might be more convincingly explained by their pragmatic acceptance of specific roles than by a positive normative commitment to society'. Mann also stresses the role of 'manipulative socialization', in our case through agencies such as Sunday schools. Michael Mann, 'The Social Cohesion of Liberal Democracy', *American Sociological Review*, June 1970, p. 435.

58   P. and T. Thompson, Interview 115.

59   Eugene D. Genovese, *The World the Slaveholders Made: Two Essays in Interpretation* (Allen Lane, London, 1970), p. 98, quoted in C. Bell and H. Newby, 'The Sources of Variation in Agricultural Workers' Images of Society', *Sociological Review*, May 1973.

60   Stearns, 'Working-Class Women in Britain 1890–1914'; L. Papworth and D. Zimmern, *The Occupations of Women* (Women's Industrial Council, London, 1914), p. 23.

61   Doreen Watson, 'The Problem of Domestic Work', University of Leicester, MA thesis, 1944.

62   Kathlyn Oliver, *Domestic Servants and Citizenship* (The People's Suffrage Federation, London, 1911).

63   T.H. Marshall, 'Citizenship and Social Class', in *Sociology at the Crossroads* (Heinemann, London, 1963), p. 79. Paternalistic domination has always been given as a reason for denying the franchise; it was feared that total dependency would influence the vote. As long as slaves, servants and women were regarded as permanent 'grey-haired children' they could never be citizens.

64   Barbara Frankle, 'The Genteel Family: High Victorian Conceptions of Domesticity and Good Behavior', University of Wisconsin, Ph.D. thesis, 1969.

65   Charlotte M. Yonge, *Hannah Moore* (Allen & Co., London, 1888).

66   Leonore Davidoff, 'Domestic Service in the Working-Class Life Cycle', *Society for the Study of Labour History*, 26 (spring 1973).

67   In this section I am speaking in the most general terms. There were variations in husband–wife relationships based on region, types of men's work, opportunity for women's work, degree of urbanization, level of income, as well as over time. There were also working-class families with kinship ties to the lower middle class as well as former members of the lower middle class living on working-class incomes in working-class areas. Ex-servants would be represented in all these groups.

68   It was noted that servants won freedom from physical punishment by about mid-century. Who can *legitimately* beat whom is a social norm, and not based primarily on

physical strength. This aspect of working-class marriage in contemporary America is discussed in Mirra Komarovsky, *Blue Collar Marriage* (Vintage Books, New York, 1967), p. 227.

69 Mrs Pember Reeves, *Round About a Pound A Week* (G. Bell, London, 1913); Alexander Paterson, *Across the Bridges or Life by the South London Riverside* (Edward Arnold, London, 1922); Norman Dennis, Fernando Henriques and Clifford Slaughter, 'The Family', in *Coal is our Life: An Analysis of a Yorkshire Mining Community* (Eyre & Spottiswoode, London, 1956).

70 Colin Rosser and Christopher Harris, *The Family and Social Change: A Study of Family and Kinship in a South Wales Town* (Routledge & Kegan Paul, London, 1965); Michael Young and Peter Wilmott, *Family and Kinship in East London* (Routledge & Kegan Paul, London, 1957); Walter Greenwood, *There Was a Time* (Cape, London, 1967).

71 E.P. Thompson, 'Le Charivari anglais', *Annales: Economies, Sociétés, Civilisations*, March–April 1972.

72 Stearns, 'Working-Class Women in Britain 1890–1914'.

73 C.J. Collett, *Women's Industrial News* (February 1896). For a discussion on this point including family relationships seen as a system of exchange, see Anderson, 'The Phenomenal Level'.

74 This isolation was growing towards the end of the century as improvements in transport and housing led to the growth of working-class suburbs. D.A. Reeder, 'A Theatre of Suburbs: Some Patterns of Development in West London, 1801–1911', in H.J. Dyos, ed., *The Study of Urban History* (Edward Arnold, London, 1968).

75 Karl Marx, 'The Eighteenth Brumaire of Louis Bonaparte', in *Basic Writings on Politics and Philosophy: Karl Marx and Friedrich Engels*, ed. Lewis S. Feuer (Doubleday, New York, 1959), p. 338.

76 'The fluctuation of income makes the problem of housekeeping impossibly difficult for most of the women and the consequent discomfort and privations of the home drive the man to the public house, wear out the health, the spirit and self respect of the women' (Liverpool Joint Research, *How the Casual Labourer Lives* [1909], p. xxvi).

77 E.P. Thompson, 'Time, Work-Discipline and Industrial Capitalism', *Past and Present*, no. 36 (1967), p. 61.

78 Mayhew, quoted in Gareth Stedman Jones, *Outcast London: A Study in the Relationship between Classes in Victorian Society* (Clarendon Press, Oxford, 1971), p. 29.

79 Arthur Barton, *Two Lamps in Our Street* (New Authors, London, 1967); *The Penny World: A Boyhood Recalled* (Hutchinson, London, 1969). Barton's mother had been nursemaid in Lord Tennyson's family. She read poetry to her children and had his portrait on the wall. Richard Hillyer, *Country Boy: An Autobiography* (Hodder & Stoughton, London, 1966).

80 The importance of the *mother's* aspirations in the achievements of children in the educational system is now being recognized. Frank Musgrove, *The Family, Education and Society* (Routledge & Kegan Paul, London, 1966), pp. 76–82. A parlourmaid who had worked in some of the large houses in Kensington during the 1890s described by her niece as 'quite the lady', sent her only son to Eton. Personal interview, Mrs K.

81 Servants as 'culture carriers' is an intriguing idea. It is particularly important in areas of private life, e.g. the adoption of ideal family size. The generation who were young servants in middle- and upper-class households in the late nineteenth century, where completed family size was declining, were the generation of working-class married women whose own family size fell at the beginning of the twentieth century. Of course no direct connection can be drawn between these two sets of facts. J.A. Banks, 'Population Change and the Victorian City', *Victorian Studies*, March 1968, p. 287. For the eighteenth century, see J.J. Hecht, 'The Servant Class as a Cultural Nexus', in *The Domestic Servant Class*.

82 Personal interview, Mrs F.

83 A striking contrast to the 'almost masculine' mateyness of the factory girl. Clementina Black, *Sweated Industry and the Minimum Wage* (Duckworth, London, 1907), pp. 134–5.

84 Sheila Rowbotham, 'Woman's Liberation and the New Politics', in Micheline Wandor, ed., *The Body Politic: Women's Liberation in Britain, 1969–1972* (Stage 1, London, 1972), p. 4. The relations of working-class married women with middle- and upper-class women were almost invariably in terms of patronage or charity. The employment of charwomen was often seen in this light. The contrast in attitudes to relations between men across class lines, who faced each other as employer and workman is brought out in James Littlejohn, *Westrigg: The Sociology of a Cheviot Parish* (Routledge & Kegan Paul, London, 1963), pp. 131–2.

85 When their old cook suddenly died, two grown-up sisters living with their father realized just how helpless they were, both practically and in that 'the "heart" had gone out of the house' (Mrs Josiah Lockwood, *An Ordinary Life 1861–1924* [privately published in London, 1932]).

86 Many Victorians were troubled by the results of the new system. Some of their reactions are discussed in Reinhard Bendix, 'Traditionalism and the Management of Labor', *Work and Authority in Industry: Ideologies of Management in the Course of Industrialization* (John Wiley, New York, 1956). The creation of corporate schemes like Port Sunlight or hierarchical 'paternalistic' institutions like the railway companies whose 'servants' were given security of employment, pensions and bonus schemes was partly an attempt to mitigate the harsh effects of early individualistic capitalism.

87 Jo O'Brien, *Women's Liberation in Labour History: A Case Study from Nottingham*, Spokesman Pamphlet no. 24 (1972), p. 15.

2
Landscape with Figures:
Home and Community in
English Society

Two birds within one nest;
Two hearts within one breast;
Two souls within one fair
Firm league of love and prayer,
Together bound for aye, together blest.

An ear that waits to catch
A hand upon the latch;
A step that hastens its sweet rest to win;
A world of care without
A world of strife shut out,
A world of love shut in.

Dora Greenwell, 'Home', 1863

The house constitutes the realm and, as it were, the body of kinship. Here people live together under one protecting roof. Here they share their possessions and their pleasures; they feed from the same supply, they sit at the same table. The dead are venerated here as invisible spirits, as if they were still powerful and held a protecting hand over their family. Thus, common fear and common honour ensure peaceful living and cooperation with greater certainty.

Ferdinand Tönnies, Community and Society, 1887

In the current renewed discussion of 'woman's place' it is of primary importance to examine how such ideas fit in with other aspects of the society. Little is gained and much is lost in analysing women as a 'problem' separate from what goes on in the economic, political and social structure. In order to make this analysis more explicit we have looked at some of the uses made of sexual differences by our society historically.

We have chosen to do this firstly, because it is marginally easier to stand back and try to see what was going on in a situation a little removed from the present by time, but also because we feel that the period from the end of the eighteenth century was crucial in setting the stage, both in structural and intellectual terms, for the present situation. Girls are still socialized into an on-going role by their female elders, which despite many superficial changes makes the young woman of the

1970s born about 1950 not basically so very different from her grandmother born in 1900 or even her great-grandmother born in 1875.

The ideal setting of women's lives in the home is a constant theme of the whole period. Analogous to it is the theme of the village community as the ideal setting for relationships in the wider society. These ideas had been present in Western thought for a very long time but during the period of which we are speaking they took on a special saliency; they were seen as an important controlling mechanism in the face of unprecedented changes in social relationships. It is our purpose in this essay to make these themes, *home* and *village community* manifest, to draw out the similar ways in which they were used to contain similar kinds of power relationships. Not only were these concepts analogous, however, they were interconnected. The very core of the ideal was home *in* a rural village community. Despite the close parallels between the two themes, however, there were two important differences in the two sets of ideal relationships. The home but not the community included legitimate sexual relations between the superordinate and one of his subordinates, i.e. husband and wife. Second, although the home, like the village, was ideally sheltered and separated from the public life of power – political, economic, educational, scientific – this separation was doubly enforced by the physical walls of the house, by the physical boundaries extending to hedges, fences and walls surrounding its garden setting. The intensity of privacy was, of course, related to the core sexual relationship in marriage. The home, even more than the village, represented an extreme of the privacy in which individualism could flourish. On first sight this individualism might seem the antithesis of the 'community' which our two themes represent. If we look more closely, however, we will see that the individualism refers *only* to the orientation of the master/husband; the privacy was used by him when he cared to invoke it.

To understand the way in which these themes were drawn, the uses to which they were put, the effects which they had on the 'socially invisible' within their orbit, it is first necessary to discuss the ideas themselves and the social structure of which they were a part, in more abstract terms. Only then is it possible, we believe, fully to understand the impact they had on women's lives.

It was Max Weber who most thoroughly explored the structural bases of various forms of social domination. He articulated what many nineteenth-century members of the elite no doubt instinctively felt: namely, that a system based *solely* on coercion, whatever the basis of this domination, was infinitely less stable than one based upon legitimate authority. Weber also recognized that the most stable form of authority was traditional authority – 'the sanctity of the order and the attendant powers of control as they have been handed down from the past'[1] – since authority was granted both to the tradition itself and to the *person* embodying that tradition. This gave those in positions of traditional authority considerable freedom to manœuvre in the face of external circumstances while still maintaining the legitimacy of their rule. The personal nature of the relationship is thus important, for not only is it likely that authority is most effective on the basis of face-to-face contact but it promotes a coherent and consistent set of *ideas* which interpret the exercise of power in a manner that reinforces legitimacy.

What is of central importance in the maintenance of legitimacy is the ability to elide evaluative and factual definitions – not only *does* the individual exercise power but it is believed that he or she *ought* to do so – enabling elite interpretations of the situation to be the only ones. It is not necessary that these ideas make up an 'ideology', as that word is often understood, for they usually become conscious and articulated only in times of crisis and attack. On the other hand, they do constitute an ideology at a much deeper level: a pervasive world-view that structures the taken-for-granted assumptions about social relationships and moulds beliefs and behaviour.

The onset of industrial capitalism increasingly undermined the previous hierarchical economic and social structure as well as the deferential personal relations associated with it. The ideology of home and community persisted as an underpinning to traditional authority in the face of this threat for, as Perkin has pointed out, 'the personal face-to-face relationships of patronage, unlike the impersonal solidarities of class, could only exist in a society distributed in small units, a society of villages and small towns in which everyone knew everyone else'.[2] Because deference to traditional authority is most easily stabilized in relatively small face-to-face social structures, the corollary is an emphasis on the correspondingly small unit of territoriality within which the desired social system could be maintained. It has been overlooked by many historians just how zealous the Regency and Victorian upper and middle classes were in their attempts to re-create wherever possible conditions favourable to a stable deference to traditional authority.

Increased physical as well as social mobility made possible by the railways added to the unease of elite groups, established aristocracy and gentry, as well as the newly wealthy middle class. The necessity for constant redefinition of their 'place' under these conditions made appeals to a nostalgic and seemingly more stable past of rural community even more attractive. Overseas expansion, too, made images of Home amidst the green surroundings of the English village a particularly compelling ideal.

In addition to a reaction to new economic and demographic forces, the desire for stability reflected a fear of the *doctrines* which these forces followed; on the one hand the unrestrained *laissez-faire* market determinism of commercial capitalism (both rural and urban) and, on the other, the appeals to egalitarianism and liberty of the French Revolution.

The growing middle class, who in many ways benefited directly and magnificently from the results of these doctrines were in a dilemma. It was to their distinct advantage, as families, to enter the 'great world' of politics and society as well as business. This entailed a considerable mobility; to foreign countries, to London, to the county seat. But their base of operations was the private home, their ideal location a very local leadership, their identity also a local one. By remaining 'out-of-the-world' they might miss what the world had to offer; by entering it they might become tainted by it. Far better to adhere to an ideal of privacy and local commitment while, in fact, joining the worldly scramble as energetically as possible.[3]

We are concerned in this essay with the home and community as *ideals*. The domestic and rural idyll provided a 'cognitive and moral map of the universe, as a response to the need for imposing order'[4] in an increasingly troublesome, impersonal and alienating real world. As such they contained a number of related dimensions. First, the home and the village community represented two of the small units of territoriality upon which deference to traditional authority depended; each was, so to speak, the spatial framework within which deference operated. However, the home and the village community were not merely geographical expressions, since the physical boundaries were also cognitive boundaries, limiting aspirations and ideas about what was possible and desirable. In this sense 'horizons' were both visually and socially limited.[5] The ideology of the home increased the traditional authority of the household head, emphasizing a solidarity of place while identifying the husband's personal authority over wife, children and servants. Similar ideologies of community were, consciously or unconsciously, put forward to promote integration between the various classes and status groups which made up a particular locality. In each case symbolic – and often substantive – boundaries could be maintained, within which those in the dominant positions could provide compatible definitions of subordinate roles. Within the home and within the community, subordinates 'know their place' because their self-contained situation allows them only limited access to alternative conceptions of their 'place' from outside.

One of the important 'feedback' effects of such a model was that the head of the household, just as the resident gentry in the village, felt that he had the legitimate right to make decisions which affected not only the everyday life but the total future of their subordinates, without consulting them. The resulting ignorance of the outside world was then used as a reason for not giving them responsibility, and their misuse of language and slow responses made them objects of derision. They could be ridiculed as country bumpkins, the 'little woman', or cute children. If they were young and sexually attractive, ridicule took the form of gentle teasing and amusement, or it could become coarse and brutal mockery in the case of, say, agricultural labourers. Such ridicule is particularly devastating within the authoritarian situation we have described above.

The more cut-off, the more 'total' this situation, the greater the likelihood that the definition will remain coherent and thus order and stability maintained; 'outside agitators' were not welcome in either home or village community.

Both settings were also seen as idealized 'organic' communities, hierarchical in structure, with a head, a heart and hands to maintain the life of the organism. For this reason both the home and the village community were incomplete without a full set of characters: 'The family as we understand it, is a small community formed by the union of one man with one woman, by the increase of children born to them and of domestic helpers who are associated with them.'[6] The ideal village also had its resident squire or aristocrat, its prosperous farmers and contented labourers. In each case the individuals fulfilling these roles were seen in stereotyped form; their basic relationship was one of deference and service on the one hand and kindly, protective patronage on the other.

This double-yoked model we have called the Beau Ideal ('that type of beauty or excellence, in which one's idea is realized, the perfect type or model', 1820, *OED*). In the domestic architecture, model villages (in both pasteboard and real bricks or stone), suburban development and new towns of the nineteenth century, the upper and middle classes briskly undertook the task of creating the necessary infrastructure to approximate the Beau Ideal, and, in a circular process, this social image in turn contributed to the physical landscape. Thus was laid the groundplan of retreat from the unwanted and threatening by-products of capitalism (and progress) – destitution, urban squalor, materialism, prostitution, crime and class conflict.

As with any successful legitimating ideology we are aware that there may be some difficulty in perceiving these phenomena *as* ideology rather than as 'reality'. This problem in part stems from its very pervasiveness. It was adopted by a wide spectrum of social groups in all parts of society, and through its physical manifestations as well as through oral and written traditions it remains very much a part of our thinking about the social and physical world.

There are attractive features in the Beau Ideal, but the reality of rural life was something more than a kind of perpetual June with grass forever green, trees in leaf, roses blooming and hot summer sun on waving fields of corn. Of course a warm house, a reasonable degree of domestic order, well-cooked food and an affectionate family are conducive to well-being. But we must be wary of the idea that home and community were 'natural'[7] social arrangements from which everyone benefited. In each case there was an ugly, exploitative underside which it was the purpose of the ideology to overlook and deny. Paternalism easily became either overbearing officiousness or even tyranny; on the other hand it could justify self-centred neglect of subordinates' welfare. Self-sufficiency became isolation, close-knit sociability lapsed into cruel gossip.

What has occurred has been the blurring of the aesthetic, particularly the physical environment, and the social – because it was assumed that the village or the home could be aesthetically pleasing, it was assumed that they contained an equally highly valued social existence. Consequently the model stimulated a particular perspective on the problems of poverty and exploitation. Firstly, where the poverty of the farm labourer (or servant) was acknowledged – and it occasionally was – its importance was overruled by the alleged metaphysical delights of working within such a culturally approved environment. The farm labourer, or the servant, or the wife, or child, was, therefore, not regarded as being exploited, *not* because their subordination was not, at least sometimes, acknowledged but because this subordination did not matter when set beside the domestic and rural idyll.[8]

The emphasis here is either on the aesthetically pleasing surroundings within which the relationships are set or upon the feelings of security consequent on decision-making being taken over by social superiors. To a certain degree the psychological stability that arose from 'knowing one's place' and from having no doubt as to the nature of one's 'place' was real enough, but this is not to say that those at the bottom of the social hierarchy uniformly regarded their existence as a desired one. The 'underworld' of the rural village and below the stairs, much less the darker side of the nursery or even the marriage bed, is evidence enough of this. In each case the system depended upon cheap labour, poverty and a downtrodden, and often socially invisible, working population.

Secondly, the superior's role was not only seen as rightfully his, enveloping him in the merited glow of the contrast between his worthy enjoyment of the fruits of the earth and the menial narrow lives of his subordinates, but this disparity was seen as necessary, a harmonious and indispensable part of the organic whole.

This is not to 'expose' Victorian 'hypocrisy': each age unconsciously recreates its Beau Ideal in its quest for stability and order within a hierarchical and changing society. In this respect the Beau Ideal is an attempt to manage the tensions that arise out of any social hierarchy, tensions that are still with us today.

The Rural Idyll

During the nineteenth century it was taken for granted that real communities could only be found in the English countryside. It was in rural England that the sense of community reigned and where the apparently automatic acceptance of the 'natural order' of things ensured that the norms of deference and paternalism remained at their strongest. One of us has noted elsewhere the easy assumption that community was *par excellence* a rural phenomenon,[9] where the Good Life prevailed amid the placid and the harmonious – 'a beautiful and profitable contrivance, fashioned and kept in smooth working order by that happily undoubting class to whom the way of life it made possible seemed the best the world could offer', as Best has described it.[10] As if to emphasize its rural roots, the term community was often provided with the adjective 'organic'. It was a neat conjunction of the connotations with agriculture and fertility and those with mutual and reciprocal cooperation for the good of all. The organic community was the epitome of the stable social hierarchy which the Victorian upper and middle class wished to preserve, or, where it had been disrupted by the intrusion of industrial and urban growth, re-create. This view of English rural life became such a literary convention that it is now one of our most ingrained cultural characteristics, commonly viewed as man's 'natural' abode, what Ruth Glass has summarized as 'a lengthy, thorough course of indoctrination, to which all of us, everywhere, have at some time or other been subjected'.[11] As it was succinctly summarized in 1806:

Such is the superiority of rural occupations and pleasures, that commerce, large
societies or crowded cities may justly be reckoned as unnatural.[12]

This idiom has been impressed on the mind's eye through the years by vivid visual
images. One such is village and great house joining harmoniously to play cricket on
the village green, bathed of course in the magic golden/green light of an English
summer afternoon. Another is the thatched cottage with heavily scented bowers of
honeysuckle and roses climbing round its porch.

The reality, however, was that the aggrandizement of the landowning class,
which had resulted from enclosure, created a rigid and arbitrarily controlled hierarchy in most rural areas of England. The cohesion of the traditional English
landowning class rendered their power extensive. They were in ultimate control of
all local institutions in many rural villages – economic, political, legal, educational,
domiciliary, religious, etc. – and almost by definition in rural areas they held, either
individually or as a class, a virtual monopoly over employment opportunities. Their
power was, therefore, virtually total, tempered only by their gentlemanly ethic of
obligation to their inferiors – just as the subordination of the agricultural labourer
was equally extensive. By the end of the eighteenth century enclosure had reduced
large numbers of the independent rural population to this position of total subordination, a proletarianization of the rural labour-force which occurred only a short
space of time before industrialism wrought a similar change in relationships in the
towns.

It must be emphasized, then, that the view of the village community as man's
natural habitation, the repository of all that is ancient and immemorial in life, *is* a
convention. The reality of rural experience was *not* laid down on paper by the vast
majority of the rural population – instead, they gave their verdict on the supposedly
idyllic qualities of rural life by voting with their feet and moving to the towns.
Perhaps one brief counter-example will highlight the partiality of the conventional
view. George Crabbe was able to write from centuries of inherited experience of the
Suffolk countryside and, in *The Village*, was not above a little sarcastic humour at
the expense of literary custom:

> I grant indeed that fields and flocks have charms
> For him that grazes or for him that farms;
> But when amid such pleasing scenes I trace
> The poor laborious natives of the place,
> Then shall I dare these real ills to hide
> In tinsel trappings of poetic pride?
> No . . .
> By such examples taught, I paint the Cot,
> As truth will paint it, and as Bards will not . . .
> O'ercome by labour, and bow'd down by time,
> Feel you the barren flattery of the rhyme?
> Can poets sooth you when you pine for bread,
> By winding myrtles round your ruin'd head?

> Can their light tales your weighty griefs o'empower,
> Or glad with any mirth the toilsome hour?

The originality of Crabbe lies in what he includes in his portrait of the rural world –
the oppressive nature of rural society, poverty, *work*. Crabbe's rural way of life
consists not of a 'natural order' but of a very real social hierarchy whose effect on
those at its base was little different from the effect of industrialization on the urban
working class:

> Here joyless roam a wild amphibious race,
> With sullen woe display'd in every face;
> Who far from civil arts and social fly,
> And scowl at strangers with suspicious eye.

Of course, Crabbe stood apart from the mainstream of the English literary tradition
(*The Village*, written in 1783, was in fact Crabbe's counterblast to Goldsmith's *The
Deserted Village*), where the rural idyll and the organic community remained an all-
encompassing theme. From the middle of the eighteenth century it had become
conventional to use the antithetical device of comparing the rural way of life – and
its ecological derivative – with the city. It is a tribute to the endurance of this
convention that even today, to many of us, the adjective 'rural' has pleasant,
reassuring connotations – beauty, order, simplicity, rest, grassroots democracy,
peacefulness, *Gemeinschaft*. 'Urban' spells the opposite – ugliness, disorder, confusion, fatigue, compulsion, strife, *Gesellschaft*.[13] It was summed up by Cowper
writing only two years after Crabbe, in his damning verdict that

> God made the country, and man made the town,
> What wonder then, that health and virtue . . .
> . . . should most abound.
> And least be threatened in the fields and groves?

The characteristics of this literary tradition have been extensively analysed in all
their ramifications by Raymond Williams in his book, *The Country and the City*. As
Williams points out, the idyllic view of rural life, though possessing lengthy ante-
cedents, became dominant during the eighteenth century, when agrarian capitalism
triumphed: '. . . you might almost believe – you are often enough told – that the
eighteenth-century landlord, through the agency of his hired landscapers, and with
poets and painters in support, invented natural beauty'.[14] The idealization of the
rural world and its associated social order was taken up by the nature poets in their
use of nature as a retreat, as a principle of order and control. Life in the countryside
was viewed as one of harmony and virtue, as static and settled. It consisted in
Gray's words of 'peace, rusticity and happy poverty'. It was this idealized version
of rural continuity and virtue that was increasingly used as a yardstick by which to
measure the degradation of urban society.

In the early reaction to urbanization, however, another image overlay this: the view of the organic community as the life of the past – John Clare's 'far-fled pasture, long vanish'd scene'. The organic community, in other words, was always slipping away. This was partly due to the problem that many rural writers had of incorporating the manifest changes of rural life into an overriding image of it which eliminated any dimension of change. Change could thus only be considered by placing it against an unchanging institution instilled with tradition and antiquity. Hence the rural community was particularly susceptible to the 'Golden Age' syndrome, the nostalgia for a half-remembered past, especially as migration was occurring *from* the countryside *to* the towns. The largest share of the responsibility for idealizing and popularizing a mythical merrie England in the countryside belongs to Cobbett. A host of nineteenth-century writers repeated Cobbett's vision of an ideal rural society, a society which consisted, in the words of his biographer, of 'a beneficent landowner, a sturdy peasantry, a village community, self-support-ing and static'.[15] They were also to repeat his idealization of the Middle Ages which was to become so prevalent in nineteenth-century social criticism, and which Chandler has summarized as 'a dream of order'.[16] Cobbett in an argument with a contemporary wrote: 'You are reducing the community to two classes: *Masters* and *Slaves* . . . when *master* and *man* were the terms, everyone was in his place and all were free.'[17] Cobbett's arcadian vision of a happy peasantry and a sturdy beef-eating yeomanry was a picture repeated by Coleridge – 'a healthful, callous-handed, but high and warm-hearted tenantry'[18] – by Carlyle, Kingsley, Engels, Ruskin and many others. Indeed, to trace in detail the scope and pervasiveness of this deeply rooted cultural trait would be to construct an inventory of virtually all nineteenth-century British social thinkers as well as myriads of poets, writers, artists, intellec-tuals, etc. This view of countryside and village society as natural – 'the proper place for the proper Englishman to dwell in'[19] – continues in often subtle and uncon-scious ways to affect English literature and art, aesthetic ideas, politics, physical planning – and indeed its social science.[20]

It was, then, to the village community that the Victorian middle class looked as a haven from the industrial world. This was not simply a matter of the aesthetic qualities of green fields as opposed to city streets, but of the kind of society into which the individual fitted. The whole concept of community was invested with an emotional power which made it much more than merely locality; it had a greater sense of integration and meaningfulness, a sense of being more attuned to the realities of living, simply of 'belonging'. As one nineteenth-century American visitor pointed out, a country house meant much more than a house in the country:

> They have *houses* in London, in which they stay while Parliament sits, and occasion-ally at other seasons; but their *homes* are in the country. Their turretted mansions are there, pictures, tombs. . . . The permanent interests and affections of the most opu-lent classes centre almost universally in the country.[21]

Ensconced in this pastoral world the 'opulent classes' could indulge their rec-
reational tastes – hunting, shooting, picnics, parties, balls – secure in the knowledge
that the rural working class would remain quiescent and obliging – except in the
hidden – and, therefore, publicly unacknowledged – class warfare of poaching. For
as long as the village community remained a largely isolated and remote social
world, the influences and judgements of the traditional elite members remained
paramount within it. There was no opportunity to question the justice of *which*
rights were being exchanged for *which* obligations. As Lord Percy was later to point
out, any landowner, great or small, 'could manage men with whom he could talk'.[22]
By their ideological alchemy they were able to convert the exercise of their power
into 'service' to those over whom they ruled and a rigid and arbitrarily controlled
hierarchy became the 'organic community' of mutual dependency. It was not,
therefore, surprising that their leadership should be widely regarded as natural.

The Domestic Idyll

As the nineteenth century progressed and England became more urbanized, the
real countryside became less accessible to the urban middle class. The custom of
holidays in the country which had begun in the 1840s meant that most children
grew up knowing only the superficial sun-filled pleasures of the country in summer;
the thatched-cottage ideal of family life was thus annually reinforced. This ideal
was, of course, deeply interwoven with the same quest for harmony. The home was
to a house what community was to a locality.[23]

Although from the seventeenth century onwards there had been an emphasis
within the middle class on the home as a moral force, these arguments became more
widespread, closely allied to the reform in temperance and the religious revival of
the late eighteenth and early nineteenth centuries. They were part, too, of the great
moral transformation of that time. The intensity of concern can be traced through
the spate of literature from the early part of the century – advice manuals, tracts,
poems, etc.[24] In a direct comparison with events in France, a writer in 1841 said:
'Household authority is the natural source of much national peace: its decline is one
of the causes of the reckless turbulence of the people.'[25]

Cobbett illustrates the fusion of the two ideals. Again acting as the radical with
a nostalgia for a golden past, he sighed for the self-sufficient household, in an heroic
effort to stem the intrusion of wage work into family economy. He idolized cottage
life where each is busy with his allotted task, the women never so attractive as when
busy in the dairy making their own butter, kneading their own bread. Nostalgia was
here too for a past when servants knew their place, children obediently followed
parental directions and wives were untouched by siren calls from the great world
and misguided prattlings about independence.

The underlying theme of 'Home' was also the quest for an organic community;
small, self-sufficient and sharply differentiated from the outside world. Like the

village community it was seen as a living entity, inevitably compared to the functional organs of a body, harmoniously related parts of a mutually beneficial division of labour. The male head of this natural hierarchy like the country squire, took care of and protected his dependants.

> The Master: the Husband, the Father, the Head of the House, the Bread-Winner is the responsible individual whose name and power upholds the household. . . . He holds the place of highest honour; he is the supporter and sustainer of the establishment. He is also legally and politically responsible for all the other members of the family . . . such are the duties of a master, a husband and a father.[26]

It was he, therefore, and he alone who could be joined to the wider society as an individual and a citizen. His dependants, in turn, responded to him with love, obedience, service and loyalty. Ideally no taint of market forces should corrupt the love–service relationships within the domestic citadel.

In keeping with the functional analogy, members of the household were to be sharply differentiated by task, sex and age. Legitimate relationships were seen as vertical only. Subordinates' whole lives were to be spent within the community thus ensuring total loyalty, privacy and trust. Wives, servants and children, the major subordinate constituents of the household, were never to leave the precincts of the 'domestic domain' except under the closest scrutiny and control.

In the construction of this 'country of the mind', the idea of domesticity as a general good was intimately tied to the powerful symbol of the home as a physical place. The house became both setting and symbol of the domestic community. In the upper-income ranges, the house's carefully guarded entrances with drives, gates and hedges, its attended portals and elaborate rituals of entrance created a sense of security as well as preserving its inmates' rank from pollution by inferiors. Throughout the middle class and in respectable working-class homes, the front privet or iron fence, whitened doorsteps, clean curtains and shining brass door furniture presented the household to 'the World'.[27] The 'temple of the hearth' became a powerfully evocative image, not only in literature but in house design, and in spending resources of servants, labour and income in the lavish use of open coal fires in a deliberately wasteful manner.

> Then as the dusk of evening sets in, and you see in the squares and crescents the crimson flickering of the flames from the cosy sea-coal fires in the parlours, lighting up the windows like flashes of sheet lightning, the cold cheerless aspect of the streets without sets you thinking of the exquisite comfort of our English homes.[28]

Servants were separated behind soundproofed baize doors in the back regions of the house and children were confined to the nurseries (even if this was no more than one small upstairs room). There was also a strong tendency to segregate the sexes physically within the house. In larger houses this took the form of male study or smoking-rooms for the men, a ladies' boudoir, separate staircases and water closets – and even separate bedrooms for the master and mistress.[29]

Although the idea of home had such a universal appeal, what was not usually explicitly stated was the point of view of the speaker or writer. Even when the writer was a woman, the underlying imagery is the unacknowledged master of the household looking *in*, so to speak, at the household he has 'created'. The 'domestic interior' awaits his coming, his return.[30] Little explicit information is given about where he has gone or what he does when away from home. Ideally, he remains, as a country gentleman, part of the extended rural idyll. As squire his house has a study or business-room full of masculine features, where he sees his tenants, does his accounts, acts as magistrate and lawgiver to his dependants and retainers. This room is entered by the master from the house but has its external entrance from the backyard only. Ideally there should be no need for him to leave his estate and village to enter the sordid world of commerce or manufacture. Military exploits and service overseas might be necessary as a 'higher duty' to king and country; but his heart was always turned to home, 'the place of Peace, the shelter from all fury' (Ruskin); it was for the master's benefit that the shelter existed.[31]

In fact, of course, the mythology of home primarily appealed to the professional and bourgeois groups who did face the 'cold winds' of the market-place. To the doctor coming home late in the evening:

For home opened its wide door to him he thought and seemed to say 'come in'; here you have a right to enter, a right to be loved; whatever befalls you without, come in; forget your suspense, put away your fears for tonight. Welcome, Welcome![32]

The house mistress, ideally the wife, was the linchpin of the static community.[33] It was she who waited at home for the return of the active, seeking man. Her special task was the creation of *order* in her household, the regular round of daily activity set in motion and kept smoothly ticking over by continued watchfulness; doing everything at the 'right' times, keeping everything and everybody in the 'right' place. The function is made explicit in one of the best-known sources of this concept, Ruskin's lecture 'The Queen's Garden'.

The woman's power is not for rule, not for battle – and her intellect is not for invention or creation, but for *sweet ordering, management and decision*. She sees the qualities of things, *their class, their places*. (our italics)[34]

In literature, from highbrow to popular, the wife–mother–house-mistress image often merged with the physical symbol of the house so that it became difficult to visualize the woman as having a separate identity from the house; in a sense she *became* the house. This symbolic elision is clear in literature. As Richard Gill has said of Mrs Ramsay in *To the Lighthouse*, 'it is this quiet but intuitive woman who creates community within the house'. Of Mrs Swithin in *Between the Acts* and Mrs Wilcox in *Howard's End* he writes, 'they are healers, the unifiers and within their communities they are symbolized in every case by the houses they inhabit'.[35]

If the husband (grown-up sons or brothers) looked for action, adventure, amusement away from home, then it was a fault of the domestic atmosphere, and wives (daughters, sisters) must strive to win them back by making home more attractive, warmer, better organized, more comfortable, more sprightly to counteract the weaknesses of male human nature. For the domestic organic community was the upholder of moral order in a chaotic external world. Women created this order by 'being good' themselves. There was, in fact, very little they could do actively to change their men; it was rather their general example and passive influence which ultimately alone could save men from their baser selves, through their redeeming power 'to love, to serve, to save'.

In the early part of the nineteenth century, this moral redemption was stated in religious terms, the 'sanctity' of home was described in a religious idiom. Family worship symbolized this fusion. The basic concepts of domestic peace and salvation, however, remained deeply part of a secular morality well into the twentieth century.

The essence of domesticity in the daily round, the weekly and seasonal rituals within the home, emphasized the cyclical and hence timeless quality of family life in opposition to the sharp disjunctive growth and collapse of commerce and industry. The stability and timelessness was often enhanced by nostalgic memories of one's own childhood home and the attempt to re-create it for one's children. These qualities were seen as part of the naturalness of domestic life; the family was felt to be part of nature (ideally, of course, located in its rural, natural setting) in opposition to the unnaturalness of factory or counting house.

However, as we have seen within the rural idyll, it was 'natural' in selected aspects only. Mothering and nurturing in a general way were important elements in domestic symbolism. The mother–wife was the protector, guide and example of morality. Women's sexuality, on the other hand, was denied, as well as the sexuality of children and servants. This was one of the reasons for the 'no followers' rule and for trying to oversee servants' and children's activities day and night. Since it was obviously an impossible task, indications of sexual activity by household subordinates had to be denied or ignored whenever possible.

Sexual passion was cast out of the domestic ideal partly because it could be used to found the basis of an alliance among subordinates which would run counter to the legitimate bonds of authority and deference within the hierarchy. In any case what was called natural was a carefully selected, trimmed, even distorted view as only a very limited form of sexual behaviour could be formally admitted. The problem was to contain sexuality for procreation only within married love. The elevation of the home to mystical levels of sanctification, the sacredness of 'the walled garden', demanded an intensification of the double standard despite marriage on the basis of personal choice and love, not on that of parental arrangements.[36] The carefully cosseted married woman (and her forerunner the even more carefully guarded pure, innocent, unmarried daughter) living at home, never going into public places except under escort and then only on the way to another private home, surrounded by orderly rooms, orderly gardens, orderly rituals of etiquette and social precedent was in stark contrast to the woman of the streets, the outcast, the one who had 'fallen' out of the respectable society which could only be based on a community of homes, to the *ultima Thule* of prostitution.

As the patriarchical family had been held up as the ideal base unit of both state and church since the rise of Protestantism, those people who had no place within it constituted a threat to social order. Despite the strong drive to envelop everyone within the domestic framework, Victorians, even more than their predecessors, had to come to terms with the existence of unattached adults. (Single women, of course, were particularly threatening, especially as the sex ratio became more unbalanced in marriageable age groups through the emigration of young men and a rise in the age of marriage.)

The cult of domesticity rested firmly upon the double standard of sexual conduct. One rule for men and another for women demanded that the latter, of course, be divided into two groups: the 'pure' and the 'fallen'. The two groups must never encounter each other, and the pure must pretend not to know of the existence of the others. The home was the habitat of the pure; the city streets the haunt of the fallen. The separation of women into two classes was well established by 1750 and was based on a combination of economic and ideological changes. In the late seventeenth century, the word 'spinster' was used in an opprobrious sense for the first time[37] and that of 'old maid' was invented. Daniel Defoe spoke of the 'set of despicable creatures, called Old Maids' and there are innumerable literary caricatures of the type in eighteenth-century literature.

Part of the problem was of course due to the growing emphasis on the degrading effects of work on women with any pretentions to gentility:

> There are many methods for young men . . . to acquire a genteel maintenance; but for a girl I know not one way of support that does not by the esteem of the world, throw her beneath the rank of a gentlewoman.[38]

The publication of Richardson's *Pamela* in 1740 finally crystallized a new stereotype of femininity. The model heroine is very young, very inexperienced and so delicate that she faints at any sexual advance; essentially passive, she is devoid of any feelings towards her admirer until the marriage knot is tied. This view of women's sexual nature, of course, ran counter to the commonly accepted idea in previous centuries that women's desires were much stronger than men's and that married men should beware of unduly arousing their wives lest they become insatiable.[39]

If purity was the prime female virtue it was particularly endangered by the promiscuous life of the city. The multifarious pleasures of eighteenth-century London could only represent the road to damnation for the virtuous woman; it is significant that Richardson's Clarissa finally 'falls' because of her unfamiliarity with wicked city ways. The life of the streets, of inns and public gardens once commonly enjoyed by men and women of all classes, became more and more restricted to poor women, or to the appropriately named 'women of the town' who could no longer have any pretence to respectability or decency.[40] By about 1820 prostitution had become '*the* sin of the great cities' and the opposition of pure country girls and abandoned town women was well established. The city streets were the downfall of many virtuous men who 'would have escaped the sin altogether, had they not been exposed to the incessant temptations thrown in their way by the women who infest the streets'.[41]

To the nineteenth-century thinker man's sexual needs were so overwhelming there could be little hope of changing masculine behaviour; control of the women was the way to ensure that young men escaped the supposedly debilitating effects of fornication. Medical opinion especially campaigned vigorously from the 1840s for police control and medical inspection of the 'women of the town', ostensibly in the interest of public health, but revealing in their language, a close approximation in the minds of the writers between the refuse of the streets and the women.[42] 'We object *in toto* to Ladies' Committees,' wrote the *Quarterly Review* in 1848 in an article on Penitentiaries. 'We cannot think a board of ladies well suited to deal with this class of objects . . . we may express a doubt whether it is advisable for pure-minded women to put themselves in the way of such a knowledge of evil as must be learnt in dealing with the fallen members of their sex.' But during the next twenty years women themselves protested against their isolation from their sisters and contested with the many middle-class men, who, like Charles Dickens, had become passionately involved in rescue work, their suitability for this task. 'It's a woman's mission,' wrote Mrs Sheppard who ran a home for the fallen in Frome, 'a woman's hand in its gentle tenderness can alone reach those whom *men* have taught to distrust them'.[43]

Rescue work became an acceptable part of the multiplicity of philanthropic activities in which middle-class women now involved themselves and for which their essentially domestic nature was supposed especially to suit them. Within the village, charity and cottage-visiting were part of the duty of the mistress of the house; given her special moral qualities she forged the link in the hierarchical chain; made palatable the subordination through her gracious loving kindness. 'For it is this human friendship, trust and affection, which is the very thing you have to employ towards the poor (of the country parish) and so call up in them. . . . Visit whom, when and where you will; but let your visits be those of woman to woman.'[44] All married women had, at least, tasted the fruits of knowledge. Single women in their purity, on the other hand, were particularly suitable (and conveniently available) for such good works.

But within the city there were no such bonds:

The rich, the refined, the educated and the religious are leaving the centre of London (the poorer parts of London) and going, through the medium of railways and steamers, to the beautiful suburbs, to live in the midst of green fields and under the shade of charming trees, there they can breathe the perfume of flowers, where there is no profligacy, drunkenness or crime. They are leaving the poor, and the working class to fester together in filth, ignorance, misery and crime.[45]

The organized charity of the latter part of the nineteenth century was an attempt somehow to reproduce the organic community (and its controls) within the impersonal city to bridge the terrible gap and reaffirm the bonds of deference.[46] For this alone women might leave their homes, their place.

The Beau Ideal

We have seen that the rural and domestic idylls had many features in common. Territorially, these two areas merged together in the symbolism of the garden where nature could be enjoyed but was also tamed and controlled. About 1800 there was a move to unite the great house with its surroundings. Terraces were reintroduced, often balustraded with urns and other 'garden-furniture' which helped link the house with the garden which became another bounded space for social interaction.[47]

Throughout the nineteenth century the art of landscape gardening expanded rapidly. In 1851, these were 4,540 domestic gardeners; by 1911 they had increased to 118,739. While women were urged to take their share in this interest, there was still a basic division between indoor and outdoor activity being appropriate to females and males respectively. As an instrument of education, however, the garden was considered ideal for both sexes, and, indeed, the metaphorical equation of gardens, growth, fruition through tender care was a strong one in literature about children of this period: childhood as part of the organic community.

It was in the 1820s, 1830s and 1840s too, that the Scottish émigré landscape gardener John Claudius Loudon edited his very successful *Gardener's Magazine and Register of Rural and Domestic Improvements*. His primary audience was the newly wealthy middle class who were investing in large suburban villas with gardens rather than grand parks as his own model semi-detached house and garden in Bayswater indicated. This emulation went down the social scale:

> that this was a matter of class is very clear from one rather curious phenomenon: the man who, although he lived in the country, say upon the outskirts of a county town, but felt himself to be, in income and social habits, a member of the urban small burgers class, had not a cottage garden but a garden which in style and plant material was a suburban garden.[48]

Loudon's goals for the middle-class house and garden were suffused with the longing to approximate the orderliness and functions of the great country house. Robert Kerr, another very influential ex-Scotsman and architect, succinctly summarized this aspiration in his well-known book *The Gentleman's House* (1864) in which he set out the fundamentals of England's 'peculiar model of domestic plan, the *Country-Seat*'. 'Let it be again remarked that the character of a gentleman-like Residence is not a matter of magnitude or of costliness, but of design – and chiefly of plan; and that, a very modest establishment may possess this character without a fault.'[49]

In 1883, Loudon published what was, in effect, a utopian fantasy which the anonymous author – an architect – admitted was no longer really feasible in times when great disparity of wealth was no longer so acceptable (sic) yet he calls it 'The Beau Ideal' of an English villa, a picture of a modern English villa as it ought to be, and follows this with a thirty-page description of an imaginary country house, its gardens, its farm, its village.[50] This was to be in fact 'the true home epitomizing social, historical and cosmic community'.[51] Twenty-five years later, in the heyday of country-house building, architects were no longer so reticent.

> Providence has ordained the different orders and gradations into which the human family is divided, and it is right and necessary that it should be maintained. . . . The position of a landed proprietor, be he squire or nobleman, is one of dignity. Wealth must always bring its responsibilities, but a landed proprietor is especially in a responsible position. He is the natural head of his parish or district – in which he should be looked up to as the bond of union between the classes. To him the poor man should look up for protection; those in doubt or difficulty for advice; the ill disposed for reproof or punishment; the deserving, of all classes, for consideration and hospitality; and *all* for a dignified, honourable and Christian example. He has been blessed with wealth, and he need not shirk from using it in its proper degree. He has been placed by Providence in a position of authority and dignity, and no false modesty should deter him from expressing this, quietly and gravely, in the character of his house.[52]

The English country house, seen in this way, was 'the great good place' and embodied in its social relationships to its attendant village, its setting in gracious gardens, the 'unity of past, present and future; unity with nature . . .' In an era of travellers, wanderers and seekers the country house remains a 'still point' in an ever-turning world, 'the sense of home, of place'.[53]

The large-scale English country house of the Beau Ideal could, in fact, only be achieved by a small minority. A true estate employed everyone in the area as labourers and ideally recruited all servants, both indoor and outdoor, from the children of estate workers. But even in the early part of the nineteenth century middle-class bankers, professional men and merchants, divorcing their source of income from their personal living started developing suburbs in imitation of this ideal.

This is born out in the detailed study of the development of Hampstead.

> The prime object of this exercise was to create a series of residential estates, each house set in its few acres of park-like grounds and surrounded by its own paddock and meadows to give a perfect impression of a country estate in miniature; a rural-illusion

which was yet, in the early nineteenth century, more than a half-truth, and one which
was within reach of the successful business or professional man whose affairs did not
demand an excessively punctilious attendance at the office.[54]

As time went on, the scale of these suburban villas decreased as land near city
centres became scarce and the meadows and paddocks disappeared, but the illusion
of rural community remained as the basis of all suburban development.

In fact, this development has always been a commercial venture based on the
market value of land and houses, but the shape and lay-out of the houses and
gardens, the favoured gabled or mock-tudor style, reflects the yearning for the rural
community. When the widened gulf between the classes was becoming painfully
clear in London in the 1880s one proposed solution, the 'true answer to the bitter
cry of outcast London' was to revitalize the declining village with the transfer, and
thus the regeneration, of the urban population; the creation of industrial villages.
Although this idea never became a serious commercial venture, it did have an effect
on the Garden City movement.

Suburban life is the ultimate experience in the *separation* of classes. From the
time of its origins in the eighteenth century the very rich and the very poor were
excluded, and the middle-class pattern could develop unmolested, safe both from
the glittering immorality of the fashionable world and from the equally affronting
misery and shiftlessness of the poor.

The growth of professional landscape gardening and the increasing popularity
of suburban homes were the enduring physical expressions of the Beau Ideal. The
harmonious community of village and home, however, appeared in every guise. It
was the unmistakable message of sermons, hymns, poems, popular songs, wall
texts, household manuals, annuals, tracts, magazines and novels. The written word,
an important new medium for a mass audience, was supplemented by illustrations
in periodicals, advertisements and calendars. (This has continued to the present
day in colour photographs and posters such as the 'Come to Britain' campaign of
the British Tourist Board.) And the whole genre of nineteenth-century children's
literature is full of paeans to family and village life.[55]

The Beau Ideal in Action

As with the rural idyll, discussions of conflict or constraint were avoided in descriptions of domestic community. In fact, of course, the household could be not only an
'earthly paradise' but its opposite, a 'hell on earth', a prison.

The fact that no other external relationships were sanctioned for its inmates, at
least below the rank of master, could make men tyrants over their wives, mothers
over their daughters and both over their younger children and servants. The home
could be not only a walled garden but also a stifling menagerie of evil forces
unchecked by interference from any higher authority.[56] Even if such depths were

not reached, middle-class homes not 'in' the fascinating social game of upper-middle or upper-class Society, could be the incarnation of routinized boredom. Men and boys had alternative living places in, first, boarding schools, then college halls, barracks, clubs and chambers where they could be 'serviced' and find companionship. They might, indeed, feel guilty about such escapes but nevertheless they could legitimately flee to them. Without nunneries and with the suspicions cast on sisterhoods of any kind and the lack of openings overseas, girls and women had *no* alternative unless it be the homes of other relatives or friends.

Because one of the goals of family life was in keeping up a front, if not to rise in the ranks of society, at least to keep up respectability, the impetus always was to aim at the highest standard of living possible. This meant a constant urge to live beyond the means of the household and to make up the difference by exploiting the labour of the most subordinate members, i.e. young servants, children, unmarried daughters and, in lesser households, wives. The cash worth of such labour was played down, the ideal was the old family retainer, whose love and loyalty to the family was reward enough, no matter how hard the work. The spiritualized dwelling-place often bore little resemblance to the realities of half-cooked mutton, egg-stained table-cloths, recalcitrant boilers and wailing, puking babies of real life. But the fact that the ideal, if it was even attempted, depended on hard, unremitting drudgery performed by often lonely, tired out, young maidservants secreted away in underground basements, sleeping in freezing attics, carrying hods of coal and heavy toddlers from early morning to late at night was not allowed to intrude on the dream; no one ever asked subordinates how they viewed the household. Joyce Cary described his childhood home in London in typical imagery:

> It was hierarchic ... everyone had his place in it. ... There were enormous pressures, as in every human society, but in Cromwell House at that time they were in balance. And the result was a society highly satisfactory to everyone's [sic] needs of body and soul – imagination, affection humour and pride – a house unforgettable to those who knew it.[57]

The power relationships which included controlling the definition of the situation permitted overtly sexual exploitation within the household without admitting it as such. It is clearly very difficult to find direct evidence on this subject, to sort out what was a voluntary response by girls and what was part of their confined and powerless position within the household. Virginia Woolf's much older stepbrother's visits to her bedroom when she and her sister were in their early teens seems to have been such a case. The shame and secrecy surrounding sexual matters was a useful screen which the superior could usually count on to protect him from the consequences. A young servant-girl dare not tell her own family of the master's advances for fear *she* would be punished.[58]

Family life was even more deeply wracked, however, by the contradiction in the whole basis of the domestic idyll, for the standard of living of the household depended ultimately on income. The reality of middle-class life was not centred on a country gentleman's estate but on the product of mainly urban livelihoods from investments, commerce, the professions and manufacture. Especially in the early years of the nineteenth century, this income was insecure, liable to sudden shifts and drops. Home as stability and a haven unsullied by change was in reality exceptionally vulnerable to bailiff's men and forced removal to living in lodgings, which represented the symbolic breaking up of home because it was particularly degrading to share a house with others on a commercial basis.

The harmonious ideal of home not only obstructed a more realistic view of its economic base but also had far-reaching secondary effects on all members of the household; effects particularly momentous for the female and the young. Inculcation into appropriate attitudes and behaviour started in early childhood. The middle-class girl was seen as responsible for setting an example to younger brothers and sisters when she was hardly out of infancy herself, for keeping them quiet and orderly by demonstrating ladylike behaviour.

> The little girl in the nursery is quite ready to set herself up as guide and monitress to brothers two or three years older than herself; girls became mentors at a very early age and how many husbands are kept in good order by the love of training that is in the nature of their wives![59]

Little boys, on the other hand, were to be manly, to observe the etiquette of doffing caps, opening doors, offering chairs to ladies, to protect their sisters from insult and physical harm. In fact, of course, there was bullying and teasing, hero worship and snubbing cutting across sex lines. The framework of expectations, nevertheless, did put severe restraints on girls, from the physical immobility because of their clothes to the imaginative restrictions resulting from the strictures of genteel etiquette. It was girls, after all, who grew up with a special and personal obligation of filial obedience and deference.

Although the conventional picture was of man, wife and children, the tensions of sexuality in such households meant that many of the idealized households in fiction were of brother and sister, father and daughter, uncle and niece, where obedience, moral purity and gentle influence could be brought to perfection, without the disturbance of physical sex.

In any case, girls and women actually spent a good deal of their time only with other women. They were very often educated at home, or if at school only with other girls, and afternoon calls were almost entirely female affairs in the middle class. House parties, balls and dinners where the sexes mixed were highly ritualized. Just as many of men's closest and most meaningful relationships were with boys and men at school, in college, in the army or in the all-male office or club, so much of women's emotional life was centred on other women: kin, friends or even servants.

In terms of economic support, however, the effect of the domestic idyll on the livelihood of middle-class girls and single women was pernicious indeed. The vast reorganization of work patterns which took place from the 1750s onwards meant that more single young women came to the city in search of work than ever before. Daughters and single women in pre-industrial society had worked on farms, in domestic industry and in the shops of craftsmen alongside other family members. But the cult of gentility meant that by the third quarter of the eighteenth century the increasing pressure for girls to give up any economic activity and become accomplished young ladies living at home had had an effect. This development long *antedates* Victoria's reign and is a concomitant of the acceptance and the ideal of female purity. By the 1840s the plight of the unsupported middle-class single woman forced into underpaid governessing, became one of the best-documented problems of mid-Victorian society. Governessing, or being a 'companion', was the only respectable occupation for middle-class women because it was located in a private home and could be regarded as a pseudo-familiar position with either very little or even no cash reward to degrade her femininity.

Such a solution, however, was always seen as second best. Within the ideal a woman should always remain in the home of a male relative yet the single, dependent woman was in a particularly deprived state within that home. Although her help could be used within the home to aid the wife and mother in her multifarious responsibilities, her presence there always held a threat. The controversy over the Deceased Wife's Sister's Bill shows the fears which could prey upon the family over the sexual and authority position of the wife and single woman.

With the growth of industrial towns, however, many working-class girls became factory workers or came to residential towns as servants. These hordes of unattached women were seen as a more threatening problem than young men, for one fallen woman could ruin so many men.[60] The battle to bring girls within the domestic sphere lies behind a great deal of the charitable efforts throughout the nineteenth century; for example, Dr Barnardo on factory employment:

> The East End of London is a hive of factory life and *factory* means that which is inimical to *home* . . . they [the factory girls] are easily thrown upon the world to 'fight for their own hand'; there is bred in them a spirit of precocious independence which weakens family ties and is highly unfavourable to the growth of domestic virtues.[61]

In the late 1850s many organizations were founded to provide a home for milliners, seamstresses, shop assistants and flower sellers who were felt to be at risk in the city.

> In every district of London, and of every other large town or populous neighbourhood indeed, wherever there are young females who are neither employed in domestic service, nor under the tender guardianship of a mother or other relatives – provision should be made to supply them with home society, love and care.[62]

Such arrangements were considered makeshift substitutes for the home. On the other hand, it was recognized that working-class girls in reality had to be self-supporting, and thus domestic service within a private home where the servant could be enfolded once again within the bonds of community was felt to be the ideal occupation, for

> they [domestic servants] do not follow an obligatorily independent, and therefore, for their sex an unnatural career: – on the contrary, they are attached to others and are connected with other existences which they embellish, facilitate, and serve. In a word, they fulfil both essentials of woman's being: *they are supported by and they administer to men.* (author's italics)[63]

Yet servants out of place were also without a home. Although charitable efforts were made to provide a place for them to go, such as the Female Servants Home Society, the impetus was a fear of unattached young women. Thus it is no accident that the secretary of the FSHS was David Cooper, also secretary of one of the leading organizations for the reclamation of fallen women, The Rescue Society. Domestic servants were in fact one of the major sources of prostitution but this was due to economic and social forces at least partially produced *by* the domestic ideal. In towns such as Dundee which was a major centre of women's employment in the jute industry, prostitution was almost unknown.

From the founding of the first penitentiaries domestic service had been seen as the future of the repentant fallen. The Rescue Society even offered training in housework and laundering as part of its programme of reclamation and most of its 'graduates' did indeed go into service, yet of 450 girls in their Homes in 1870–1, 412 *had been* domestic servants. That the loneliness and privations of the life of a woman in a small household might make even prostitution look attractive was never considered. Even the organizations specifically created for the social and organizational needs of working-class girls were both structurally and ideologically based on family imagery often reinforced by constant references to the Royal Family.

The structure of such a society emphasized personal relations between the working-class girl 'member' and upper-class 'associate' operating as a family relationship (although significantly, as Harrison points out, a family without fathers or brothers). Thus any potential political activity for working-class girls and women was snuffed out at its source under the pervasive familistic model.[64]

It is still very unclear how far working-class men or women accepted the domestic idyll for married women, even in a watered-down version, as part of their own life-style. Clearly it varied widely from place to place and within occupations and over time. It does seem to be, at least in its negative form – i.e. the wife not working and 'keeping house' full time – a strand in the definition of the desired working-class respectability.[65]

For example, Martha Vicinus has noted how even working-class writers who had personally experienced the process of urbanization, even in the latter half of the century, were unable to come to terms with it except by reinvoking a half-remembered idyllic rural past, a garden metaphor, and translating this by 'taking nature into the home, behind the red bricks, so that a metaphoric refuge has been created'.[66]

Ben Brierley's solution to the 'Bedlam' of Victorian Manchester was as follows:

Bedlam, however, was not a social desert without its oasis. Stiffy's home glimmered out in the cloudy void like a green spot upon which a streak of refreshing sunlight had settled. It was a home that you would think ought to have had more genial companionship than could be found among squalid dens, where vice and unkindly feelings gendered and grew in festering loathsomeness. It was a home that ought to have had such associations as green meadows, blossoming hedgerows, gardens, the song of the wild bird, and the breath of the sweet moorland breeze. But had it been placed among the wigwams of some savage tribe it would have been just the same, for 'woman' had made it what it was; and she has the power to make such a place a Paradise or Pandemonium, whichever she wills.[67]

Middle-class commentators, however, were more explicit; by insisting that wives both could and should be supported at home, they defined this problem out of existence. As a result, working-class married women formed the army of casual workers: chars, washerwomen, harvesters and fruit-pickers, outworkers, the most exploited section of the whole economy.

Work for girls and single women became one of the rallying points of the nineteenth-century feminists, yet it was seldom clearly seen as related to the question of work for married women – and widows. Two overwhelmingly important results of the application of domestic ideology were often admitted as regrettable but inevitable. Firstly the overcrowding of girls and women into a narrow sector of wage work and secondly low wages:

Women's earnings are, rightly or wrongly regarded for the most part by both employers and employed as merely supplementary to those of the head of the family and the rate of wages is fixed on this assumption.[68]

Into the Twentieth Century

The direct continuity between the nineteenth-century Beau Ideal of the rural organic community and the twentieth-century approach to town and country planning has been traced in detail by Peterson, Thorns and many others.[69] The desire for an ordered social world which prompted the construction of model villages and towns like New Lanark, Saltaire, Port Sunlight and Bournville also stimulated Ebenezer Howard's Garden City movement in the first decade of the twentieth century. The Garden Cities – a wonderfully felicitous Edwardian phrase which captured exactly the desired balance of rusticity and propinquity – were planned experiments in utopian living outside London, at Letchworth and Welwyn. They were the precursors of the British New Towns, which were to be similarly inspired by a utopian zeal. The Garden Cities conveyed a uniformly suburban appearance which has since spread to estate design both in Britain and the United States.

Suburbia became the last refuge of the Beau Ideal for architects and planners. Here they attempted to create the conditions for an arcadian existence – 'city homes in country lanes' – what one critic has summarized as lying 'somewhere on the urban fringe, easily accessible and mildly wild, the goal of a "nature movement" led by teachers and preachers, bird-watchers, socialites, scout-leaders, city-planners and inarticulate commuters'.[70] To many dwellers (but not so often their isolated wives) suburbia meant the sylvan, the natural, the romantic, the lofty and the serene, the distant but not withdrawn, neither in nor of the city, nor the country-side, but at its border. 'Living in the country' as one commuter announced to *Harper's Weekly* in 1911, meant 'allowing the charms of nature to gratify and illumine, but not to disturb one's cosmopolitan sense'.[71] Here one was offered 'the cream of the country and the cream of the city, leaving the skim-milk for those who like that sort of thing'.[72] The Garden City movement became a focus for such sentiments in Edwardian England. Here, in Howard's own words:

> The town is the symbol of society – of mutual help and friendly cooperation, of . . . wide relations between man and man. . . . The country is the symbol of God's love and care for man. All that we are and all that we have comes from it. . . . It is the source of all health, all wealth, all knowledge. But its fulness of joy and wisdom has not revealed itself to man. Nor can it ever, so long as this unholy, unnatural separation of society and nature endures. Town and country *must be married*, and out of this joyous union will spring a new hope, a new life, a new civilisation . . .[73]

After the First World War, the basis of middle-class housing shifted to ownership rather than rental in the new outer-suburban developments. For the first time, too, there was a chance for the expanding white-collar sector and even upper-working-class families to own the by now ubiquitous semi-detached house with the poss-ibility of having a 'tradesman's' entrance at the back, the illusion of privacy, gardens to give an air of rural surroundings.

> Many of the Londoners dreaming of a new house in the suburbs were seeking to renew contact with the rural environment . . . they looked for at least a suggestion of the country cottage in their new suburban home . . . assiduously, often clumsily they strove to evoke at least a suggestion of that rural-romantic make-believe which was the very spirit of suburbia.[74]

They were seeking very much the same qualities that their grandfathers had sought, 'the subtly mixed aromas of Pears soap, Mansion Polish and toast . . . the ambience of peace and stability'.[75]

At the heart of the suburban dream was the housewife. The immediate post-war unease, the signs of many women wanting to pursue a new social consciousness and a reluctance to return to the old domestic confines were stifled and forgotten. In terms of one of the most powerful cultural reflections of women's position, 'the new periodicals [for women] dedicated themselves almost without exception to uphold-ing the traditional sphere of feminine interests and were united in recommending a purely domestic role for women'.[76] The celebration of domesticity had obvious connections with the need to sell consumer durables, connections made evident in the model mock-ups of homes in the annual *Daily Mail* Ideal Home Exhibitions which began in the 1920s. Ironically, one of the greatest pressures to renew the domestic idyll at this time was the increased work-load on middle-class wives because of the exodus of domestic servants from middle as well as lower-middle-class homes after the First World War. Servants had few illusions about the domestic idyll as we have seen and few hesitated to leave when alternative work was available.

The Depression atmosphere of the 1930s also favoured the saving and protecting aspects of home life. The rhetoric of home continued to be a powerful rallying point throughout the Second World War, despite the mobility of all family members and especially the wider opportunities war offered to women.

> I believe the value of a comfortably run home and family to be of immense moral and civic importance . . . that Woman not only has, but should confidently wield a special influence over Man. The feminine spiritual vision sees, or rather senses, further than man's.[77]

This was written in nineteen, not eighteen, forty-five.

In the course of the twentieth century, however, middle-class girls, as opposed to older women, were increasingly able to shun some of the demands of home discipline and obligation. They gained a degree of economic independence through the growth of the clerical sector for jobs and even social independence in bedsitters and flats. As the 'daughter-at-home' expectation waned, the married woman and mother became more than ever the identifiable constituent of the home. Increased educational opportunities for girls widened this generation gap.

The more that the wider society grows in centralized corporate and state power, in size of institutions and in alienating work environment, the more that the home becomes fantasized as a countering haven.[78] Home-baked bread, French farmhouse cookery, wine-making, organic gardening – the whole gamut of 'creative homemaking' have become the suburban substitutes for the fully fledged return to the self-sufficient smallholding, only made real by a tiny minority.

When the rosy spectacles are laid aside, however, it is clear that what to the husband and children can be a refreshing hobby – after all they are more often than not the consumers, not the producers, of the home-made jam – to the wife can be another variant of the natural-mother image and in everyday terms can mean longer than ever hours at the chopping-board. Moral and nutritional reactions to packaged foods in the 1970s are as inextricably confused as the same reactions to tinned foods three generations ago.

The point has been made that the Beau Ideal was a model, a way of composing reality that helped to create that reality in a very concrete way, often embalmed in the bricks and mortar of houses, the lay-out of roads and services with which we are still living. Both the village and home sectors of this ideal represented a defence against various attacks on the social structure which made, particularly members of the middle class, fearful of disorder in every sphere of social life. The model was seen to stress consensus and affective ties. It thus shifted attention away from exploitation of groups and emphasized individual relationships.[79] It denied the reality of, and thus made less viable, the existence of households with other structures – namely, without male heads, with working wives and mothers.

Ideal communities are supposed to be both self-sufficient and self-regulating, therefore there is no need to protect the weaker members because protection is inherent in the relationship. The concern with harmony and control meant that there was a tendency to see the social/spatial world as a theatre, the unfolding of carefully selected roles. This theatre was complete with a front- and backstage so that disrupting elements could be kept out of sight and, it was hoped, out of mind.

But the ultimate end of perfect order is sterility, even death. Despite the organic imagery, the leafy bowers and garden setting, this strain towards absolute harmony was full of tension. The anonymous creator of the 'Beau Ideal of the English Villa' sensed this dilemma. He recognized that the gentleman's residence should be within sight of, but well screened from, the village; that living creatures – i.e. cattle and labourers – must be present as a generative force, although carefully regulated and kept in the background.

> As the most beautiful landscape is incomplete without figures, so the general effect of a park is always lonely, unless it have a footpath frequented by the picturesque figures of the labouring classes and giving life and interest to the scene.[80]

Similarly within the house, after giving an extremely detailed catalogue of furniture and decoration, he notes that in the drawing-room, 'most of the tables must also have something upon them, to make them appear of use'.[81]

A stage-set, after all, is only a pretence of life, it produces nothing. It has no base of transforming energy, either human or mechanical, Yet the effects of uncontrolled energy were the very elements that were feared; the novel and mighty energy of steam which could multiply goods a hundredfold, on the basis of which wealth could be created overnight, which left havoc and waste on the physical landscape and bitter rebellious poverty among the working class of wage labourers. Within the home, it was social and sexual energy, the thrust of the *parvenus* (at all social levels) and their offspring, which was so threatening to established ideas of hierarchy, to the 'debased pastoral' of the middle classes.[82]

Such tension between order and change has always been one of the main themes of political and social debate in English society. In the nineteenth century the struggles for greater participation in the responsibilities and rewards of society took place on many fronts. In the public debate, the desire for order was experienced in increasingly controlling legislation in the interests of public health, in the classification of prisons and workhouses and of all those who were deemed not to belong in the mainstream of national life. The Beau Ideal, however, separated women and family from public concerns and gave them their own sphere of social influence in the home.

We have lived for so many generations with this separation, which *in itself* has become such a forceful method of control, that it comes as a surprise 'that such personal and elemental feelings as those about love and women would have been so strongly influenced by the hard competitive world of business or by the pressure of intellection and doubt'.[83] The realization that this division is not a given of the universe, not a timeless and natural phenomenon, lies behind the discovery of what has been called 'sexual politics' as well as contributing to the recent interest in family history.

Much of the idiom of the model we have been discussing has been at a subliminal level, in the form of visual images and a social map where sex and class divisions are confined to certain specified physical areas. This means that it takes a special effort to see the model from the outside. It also has made the rebellion against the barren segregating categories of the hierarchy, against the ritualized narrow and stereotyped behaviour demanded by the model, a particularly disturbing one aimed primarily at an equally idealized search for life-giving self-fulfilment through unfettered sexuality.[84]

At the same time, women, especially married women, have been still left with the task of defending the remnants of the Beau Ideal, at least in its bare essentials of socializing young children into civilized behaviour and in nurturing and watching over their men.[85] In their suburban homes, wives are still expected to create a miniature version of the domestic idyll, set in subtopian pseudo-rural estate surroundings while their male counterparts swarm into central city offices and factories. Wives remain protectors of the true community, the 'still point'; a basic moral force to which the workers, travellers and seekers can return. In the archetypal portrayal of everyday life they still wait, albeit with less resignation as well as less hope, for the hand upon the latch.

Notes

1 Max Weber, *The Theory of Social and Economic Organization* (Free Press, Glencoe, IL, 1947), pp. 341–2. For an elaboration of the theoretical arguments covered in this paragraph, see Howard Newby, 'The Deferential Dialectic', *Comparative Studies in Society and History*, vol. 17, no. 2 (1975), pp. 139–64.

2 Harold Perkin, *The Origins of Modern English Society 1780–1880* (Routledge & Kegan Paul, London, 1969), p. 51.

3 The way part of this tension was handled by a sexual division of labour is discussed in Leonore Davidoff, *The Best Circles: Society, Etiquette and the Season* (Century Hutchinson, London, 1986), chs 1 and 2; John Foster, *Class Struggle and the Industrial Revolution: Early Industrial Capitalism in Three English Towns* (Weidenfeld & Nicolson, London, 1974), ch. 6; see also Robert K. Merton, 'The Idea of Locals and Cosmopolitans', in *Social Theory and Social Structure* (Free Press, Glencoe, IL, 1957).

4   'Ideology', in *International Encyclopedia of the Social Sciences*, vol. 7 (Macmillan, New York, 1968), p. 69.

5   For the way such 'maps' can be built up from childhood, see Peter Gould and Rodney White, *Mental Maps* (Pelican, Harmondsworth, 1974).

6   *Cassell's Book of the Household: A Work of Reference on Domestic Economy* (London, 1890), vol. 1, p. 27.

7   'It is important to stress how difficult it is for anyone in any social or moral context to say what they mean by "natural" and why it recommends itself as good. Two distinct steps are involved here: defining what is meant by "natural" and arguing that what is natural is good' (Christine Pierce, 'Natural Law, Language and Women', in Vivian Gornick and Barbara K. Moran, eds, *Woman in Sexist Society: Studies in Power and Powerlessness* [Basic Books, New York, 1971], p. 243).

8   There is an underlying tone in much that has been written on this theme concerning rural society: workers are viewed as contented cows – happiness is abetted by a bovine intelligence. See some of the contributions to E.W. Martin, ed., *Country Life in England* (Macdonald, London, 1966). Elsewhere the position of women has been directly compared with that of horses. 'I believe we must have the sort of power over you that we're said to have over our horses. They see us as three times bigger than we are or they'd never obey us' (Virginia Woolf, *The Voyage Out* [Penguin, Harmondsworth, 1970], p. 210). Of course the word 'pet' has similar connotations when used as a term of endearment towards wives and children.

9   See the introduction to the first section of Colin Bell and Howard Newby, eds, *The Sociology of Community* (Cass, London, 1974); also Howard Newby, 'The Dangers of Reminiscence', *Local Historian*, vol. 2, no. 3 (1973), pp. 334–9.

10 Geoffrey Best, *Mid-Victorian Britain, 1851–75* (Panther, St Albans, 1973), p. 85.

11 Ruth Glass, 'Conflict in Cities', in CIBA Foundation Symposium, *Conflict in Society*, ed. Anthony de Reuck and Julie Knight (Churchill, London, 1966), p. 142.

12 J.C. Loudon, *A Treatise on Forming, Improving and Managing Country Residences* (London, 1806), p. 5.

13 Glass, 'Conflict in Cities', p. 142.

14 Raymond Williams, *The Country and the City* (Chatto & Windus, London, 1973), p. 120.

15 W. Baring Pemberton, *William Cobbett* (Penguin, London, 1949), p. 139.

16 Alice Chandler, *A Dream of Order: The Medieval Ideal in Nineteenth-Century English Literature* (Routledge & Kegan Paul, London, 1971).

17 *Political Register*, 14 April, 1821.

18 Cited by Raymond Williams, *Culture and Society, 1780–1850* (Penguin, London, 1961), p. 34.

19 Peter Laslett, *The World We Have Lost* (Methuen, London, 1965), p. 25.

20 The chief importer into the sociological tradition is Ferdinand Tönnies. This has been well exemplified by Charles P. Loomis and John C. McKinney in their introduction to *Gemeinschaft und Gesellschaft* (Harper & Row, New York, 1963), pp. 12–29. See also Glass, 'Conflict in Cities'; R.E. Pahl, 'The Rural–Urban Continuum', in R.E. Pahl, ed., *Readings in Urban Sociology* (Pergamon Press, Oxford, 1969); R.J. Green, *Country Planning: The Future of the Rural Regions* (Manchester University Press, Manchester, 1971).

21 Cited by Richard Gill, *Happy Rural Seat: The English Country House and the Literary Imagination* (Yale University Press, New Haven, 1972), p. 4.

22 E. Percy, *Some Memories* (Eyre & Spottiswoode, London, 1958), cited by D. Spring, 'Some Reflections on Social History in the Nineteenth Century', *Victorian Studies*, vol. 4 (1960–1), p. 58. Also Newby, 'The Deferential Dialectic'.

23 Winifred Peck, *Home for the Holidays* (Faber, London, 1955). Many middle-class memoirs speak of the custom of renting vicarages or even school houses in the country for family holidays.

24 Mrs Sarah Stickney Ellis is one of the best known writers of these advice books. For a fuller list, see J.A. and O. Banks, 'The Perfect Wife', in *Feminism and Family Planning in Victorian England* (Liverpool University Press, Liverpool, 1964), pp. 58–70.

25 A mother and mistress of a family, *Home Discipline; or, Thoughts on the Origin and Exercise of Domestic Authority* (London, 1841), p. 106.

26 *Cassell's Book of the Household*, p. 31.

27 'The front fence . . . gives no real visual or acoustic privacy but symbolizes a frontier and a barrier' (Amos Rapoport, *House Form and Culture* [Prentice-Hall, Englewood Cliffs, NJ, 1969], p. 133).

28 Augustus Mayhew, *Paved with Gold* (1858), p. 8, quoted in Myron Brightfield, *Victorian England in its Novels 1840–1870*, vol. 4 (University of California Library, Los Angeles, 1968), p. 349.

29 'One curious feature of Victorian houses is the increasingly large and sacrosanct male domain . . .' (Mark Girouard, *The Victorian Country House* [Clarendon Press, Oxford, 1971]). On the social meaning of physical separation, see Edward T. Hall, *The Hidden Dimension: Man's Use of Space in Public and Private* (Doubleday, New York, 1966).

30 A new category of paintings, 'Domestic Pictures', was created by the Royal Academy in 1852. 'The return of the man from work, from war, from the sea or from a journey was a very popular theme' (Helene E. Roberts, 'Marriage, Redundancy or Sin? The Painter's View of Women in the First Twenty-Five Years of Victoria's Reign', in Martha Vicinus, ed., *Suffer and Be Still: Women in the Victorian Age* [Indiana University Press, Bloomington, IN, 1972], p. 51).

31 Economists, sociologists and historians have continued to use the concept of *the household* assuming identity of interests up to the present day – an identity which greatly benefits the superordinate. See J.K. Galbraith's critique in *Economics and the Public Purpose* (André Deutsch, London, 1974).

32 Anon., 'Out of the World', *Cornhill Magazine*, VIII (September 1863), p. 374.

33 'In our traditional and largely subconscious opinion, what the marriage ceremony does is to consecrate a woman and a house-mistress' (Lord Raglan, *The Temple and the House* [Routledge & Kegan Paul, London, 1964], p. 34).

34 John Ruskin, *Sesame and Lilies* (London, 1868), p. 145.

35 Gill, *Happy Rural Seat*, p. 201.

36 Keith Thomas, 'The Double Standard', *Journal of the History of Ideas*, April 1959.

37 Richard Steele in *The Spinster* (1719) recalls that the word was not originally opprobrious but referred to the laudable 'industry of female manufacturers'.

38 Jane Collier in her *Essay on the Art of Ingeniously Tormenting* (London, 1753).

39 Jean L'Esperance, 'Woman in Puritan Thought', McGill University, MA thesis. 1955.

40 Robert Palfrey Utter and Gwendlyn Bridges Needham, *Pamela's Daughters* (Russell & Russell, New York, 1972).

41 *Meliora*, vol. 7 (1858), p. 75. Patrick Colquhoun in his *Treatise on the Police of the Metropolis* (London, 1979) refers to prostitutes as brazen lower-class hussies who should be kept from the sight of respectable women by the police. The classification of 'good' and 'bad' women is, of course, made by men in the masculine interest.

42 'The details of a control over prostitution need not form the subject of a separate bill,' argued the *British and Foreign Medical Chirurgical Review* in January 1854, 'any more than the Commissioners of sewers require a new clause for each clearage. The object would be completely accomplished by its being enacted that prostitution, meaning the demanding or receiving of money for sexual intercourse, is a criminal act; and that as a

punishment, the individual shall be placed under the control and surveillance of a commission, and that the commission be authorized to make such arrangements as may be considered necessary for the public safety.'

43   *The Magdalen's Friend, and Female Homes' Intelligencer*, June 1860, p. 93.

44   Charles Kingsley, 'Woman's Work in a Country Parish', *Sanitary and Social Lectures and Essays* (Macmillan, London, 1880), p.13.

45   'Lights and Shadows of London Life', *Meliora: A Quarterly Review of Social Science* (1867), p. 270.

46   For a discussion of the attempt – and its failure – see Gareth Stedman Jones, 'The Deformation of the Gift: The Problem of the 1860s', in *Outcast London: A Study in the Relationship between Classes in Victorian Society* (Clarendon Press, Oxford, 1971).

47   Elizabeth Burton, 'Gardens', in *The Early Victorians at Home, 1837–1861* (Longman, London, 1972).

48   Edward Hyams, *The English Garden* (Thames & Hudson, London, 1966), p. 273.

49   Robert Kerr, *The Gentleman's House; or, How to Plan English Residences from the Parsonage to the Palace* (London, 3rd edn, 1871), p. 66. The most influential builder of country houses of the period was also a Scotsman, William Burn. The influence of Scotsmen in architecture and landscape gardening was part of the growth of these pursuits, a separation of the expert and the consumer (Girouard, *The Victorian Country House*).

50   J.C. Loudon, *An Encyclopaedia of Cottage, Farm and Villa Architecture and Furniture, Containing Numerous Designs for Dwellings From the Cottage to the Villa* (1883), ch. 2, pp. 780–2.

51   Gill, *Happy Rural Seat*, p. 112.

52   Sir Gilbert Scott, *Secular and Domestic Architecture* (1857), quoted in Girouard, *The Victorian Country House*, p. 2.

53   Gill, *Happy Rural Seat*, p. 15.

54   F.M.L. Thompson, *Hampstead, Building a Borough, 1650–1964* (Routledge & Kegan Paul, London, 1974), pp. 91–2.

55   One of the most famous and enduring was Mrs Sherwood's *The Fairchild Family* which was first published in 1818, ran to fourteen editions before 1847, and was still in print in 1913. The book begins: 'Mr and Mrs Fairchild lived very far from any town; their house stood in the midst of a garden . . .' The Fairchild rural paradise is inhabited by the family of parents and children, the devoted servants and assorted loyal villagers.

56   A few well-known examples from the nineteenth century are: Samuel Butler, *The Way of All Flesh* (Penguin, London, 1947); Florence Nightingale, 'Cassandra', in Ray Strachey, *The Cause: A Short History of the Women's Movement in Great Britain* (G. Bell, London, 1928); Betty Askwith, *Two Victorian Families* (Chatto & Windus, London, 1971); Ruth Borchard, *John Stuart Mill* (Watts, London, 1957). Cynthia White cites the year-long correspondence in the *Englishwoman's Domestic Magazine* in the 1850s on the subject of corporal punishment of children, 'in the course of which the corrective measures employed were fully described, throwing a new and sadistic light on the concept of the "pious" Victorian mother' (*Women's Magazines, 1693–1968* [Michael Joseph, London, 1970], p. 46).

57   Joyce Cary, *To be a Pilgrim* (Michael Joseph, London, 1942), quoted in Gill, *Happy Rural Seat*, p. 204.

58   Quentin Bell, *Virginia Woolf: A Biography*, vol. I, *Virginia Stephen, 1882–1912* (Hogarth Press, London, 1972); P. and T. Thompson, 'Family and Work Experience before 1918', Social Science Research Council Project, interviews.

59   'At Home and at School', *All the Year Round*, 8 October, 1859, p. 572.

60   Hence the banning of women from underground work in the mines and fieldwork in agriculture, and the attempt to ban them from work in factories can be seen as part of

this attempt at control (as well as in the humanitarian progress usually emphasized by historians). Angela John, 'Pit Brow Lasses – a Test Case for Female Labour', unpublished paper, 1974.

61 T.J. Barnardo, 'Something Attempted, Something Done' (published by the offices of the Barnardo Institution, London, 1889), p. 30.

62 *The Magdalen's Friend*, no. 4 (July 1860), p. 113.

63 W.R. Greg, 'Why Are Women Redundant?', *National Review*, Vol. 15 (1862), p. 451.

64 Brian Harrison, 'For Church, Queen and Family: The Girls' Friendly Society, 1874–1920', *Past and Present*, November 1973.

65 Not to speak of the variations produced by the continued existence of domestic manufacture and craft. For the difficulty of evaluating this response, see E.P. Thompson, *The Making of the English Working Class* (Gollancz, London, 1963), pp. 414–7; R.Q. Gray, 'Styles of Life, the "Labour Aristocracy" and Class Relations in Later Nineteenth-Century Edinburgh', *International Review of Social History*, vol. 18 (1973).

66 His solution is not political or economic reform but, like Mrs Gaskell, greater love between the classes. Martha Vicinus, 'Literary Voices of an Industrial Town: Manchester, 1810–70', in H.J. Dyos and Michael Wolff, eds, *The Victorian City: Images and Realities* (Routledge & Kegan Paul, London, 1973), vol. 2, p. 756.

67 Ben Brierly, 'Out of Work', *Lancashire Stories*, VI, 1884, pp. 77–8.

68 Mr Steel-Maitland, *Royal Commission on the Poor Laws*, vol. 43 (1909), p. 182.

69 W. Peterson, 'The Ideological Origins of British New Towns', *American Institute of Planners Journal*, vol. 34 (1968). David C. Thorns, *Suburbia*, (MacGibbon & Kee, London, 1972) and 'Planned and Unplanned Communities', *University of Auckland Papers in Comparative Sociology*, no. 1 (1973).

70 Peter J. Schmitt, *Back to Nature: The Arcadian Myth in Urban America* (Oxford University Press, New York, 1969), p. xvii; and see John Betjeman's poem on Letchworth.

71 Eugene A. Clancy, 'The Car and the Country Home', *Harper's Weekly*, 4 (6 May 1911), p. 30, cited by Schmitt, *Back to Nature*, p. 17.

72 William Smythe, *City Homes on Country Lanes* (Arno Press, New York, 1974), p. 60.

73 E. Howard, *Garden Cities of Tomorrow*, quoted in B.I. Coleman, ed., *The Idea of the City in Nineteenth-Century Britain* (Routledge & Kegan Paul, London, 1973), pp. 197–8.

74 Alan A. Jackson, *Semi-Detached London: Suburban Development, Life and Transport, 1900–1939* (Allen & Unwin, London, 1973), p. 136.

75 Ibid., p. 143; Lawrence Hanson, *Shining Morning Face: The Childhood of Lance* (Allen & Unwin, London, 1949).

76 White, *Womens's Magazines, 1963–1968*, pp. 99–100.

77 Dorothy Paterson, *The Family Woman and the Feminist: A Challenge* (Heinemann, London, 1945), p. 37.

78 Peter Berger and Hansfried Kellner, 'Marriage and the Construction of Reality', in Hans Peter Dreitzel, ed., *Recent Sociology* (Patterns of Communicative Behaviour, no. 2) (Collier-Macmillan, London and New York, 1970).

79 Domestic servants, agricultural labourers and married women were the last categories (bar children) to gain citizenship rights in the twentieth century. Married women are not quite full citizens to this day, see Leonore Davidoff, 'Mastered for Life: Servant and Wife in Victorian England', this volume, ch. 7.

80 J.C. Loudon, *An Encyclopaedia of Cottage, Farm and Villa Architecture and Furniture, Containing Numerous Designs for Dwellings From the Cottage to the Villa*.

81 Ibid.

82 Kirk Jeffries, 'The Family as Utopian Retreat from the City: The Nineteenth-Century Contribution', *Sounding: An Interdisciplinary Journal*, spring 1972.

83 W.E. Houghton, *The Victorian Frame of Mind, 1830–1870* (Yale University Press, New Haven, 1957), p. 393.

84 In a writer like Dylan Thomas, for example, middle-class and middle-aged women are seen as life *deniers*; men are perpetual boys, escaping their moral strictures, glorying in sexual and alcoholic adventures. See *Under Milk Wood*. This is simply a variation of the 'woman as saviour' theme; whichever is emphasized, women embody in themselves the moral order.

85 'It should be noted that the particular and peculiar pairing of "passivity" and "responsibility" may account for many aspects of the behaviour of adult women' (Harriet Holter, *Sex Roles and Social Structure* [University of Oslo Press, Oslo, 1970], p. 60).

3
The Rationalization of Housework

Do everything at the proper time
Keep everything in its proper place
Use everything for its proper purpose.

This chapter is an attempt to put forward some very preliminary ideas about a subject which, until a few years ago, was not only neglected but, on all levels, treated with contempt. The idea of asking serious questions about housework seemed unthinkable. Until about 1970, only the amusing and provocative American piece by Pat Mainardi, *The Politics of Housework*, circulated within the Women's Movement, even raised the issue.[1] She ends with her husband saying: 'Housework? Oh my God, how trivial can you get. A paper on housework!'

Housework, like housewife, is a catch phrase covering a multitude of activities and attitudes. In contemporary society both tend to be residual categories used to fall back on when an activity or person cannot be classified in any other way. Yet neither of these terms, nor their meaning to us, is universal or 'natural', rather they are culturally and historically specific. Housework can, for example, be looked at as *work*, including physical, psychological and social components, although for reasons, some of which are considered here, it is systematically left out of both popular and sociological discussions of work.[2] Housework can also be analysed as part of an overall economic system.[3] And as in this chapter, it can be considered as part of the culture of the society. It is hoped that this general discussion can be illuminated by looking at a specific historical case – late eighteenth- and nine-teenth-century England.

The focus of the following discussion will be on middle- and upper-class (i.e. servant-keeping) households. This is justified, first, because I believe that the sexual division of labour which developed throughout the nineteenth and twentieth centuries had elements which cut across all class lines, and that this similarity has increased in recent times. (Whether this was a result of deliberate ideological manipulation by dominant groups or because of economic and social developments in the total society is an open question.)[4] Thus what I have to say has relevance for all sections of society today. Second, the majority of recent economic analyses of housework have in the main been related to working-class households only.[5]

In studying the development of households in the nineteenth century, the most striking facts are the separation of the household from public concerns into an intensely private sphere and the elaboration of domestic life. In the twentieth century, both these patterns, but particularly the latter, have been reversed. Domestic life has become less rigid and formal. Specialized activities in the home have been merged. Even architecturally we have moved to the 'open-plan' house where functions like cooking have been reincorporated into general family life. The problem is to account for this change as it developed at this particular historical time.

A clue to understanding the pattern of nineteenth-century domestic life may be found in the fact that the same period was also the time of an intense emphasis on the purity of women and the idea of a double standard in moral affairs.[6] The evolution of these ideas was a slow process and can be traced back to the end of the seventeenth century. This was also the period when English society was faced with the disruptive effects of nascent capitalism, in agriculture as well as in commerce and manufacturing. The establishment of a free market and the attendant concept of individualism were making inroads into received notions of hierarchy. It was in the middle class that these developments were most marked and it was given to middle-class women to become the moral protectors of society. Women began to be seen as more moral, more pure (and more clean) than men. They had to be kept so, segregated in private homes free from the taint of market forces which would have weakened paternalistic authority.[7] Eventually, the fear of market activity as an agent in undermining the purity of women extended to any work which included manual labour even within the home. Obviously, by this definition truly genteel and pure women could only be a relatively small proportion of the total female population. Those who must work, therefore, were ideally only to be engaged in work which protected the purity of others, i.e. as domestic servants, washerwomen, charwomen – or prostitutes. Women became the purest, most ethereal, most unworldly of all creatures, but they also, as protectors of the moral order, had constantly to wrestle with the impure.

Three questions must then be asked about the historical case under discussion. Why were women singled out for this special task? What part did the elaboration of housekeeping play in this pattern? Finally, how did these two factors interact – how did the household become more 'rationalized' in order to serve as the moral centre of society, while at the same time this goal raised fundamental contradictions to the process of rationalization itself?

For an attempt to answer such questions we must first turn to a more abstract level of analysis.

Culture, Domestic Work and the Sexual Division of Labour

Because the components of housework have existed since biblical times (and before), it is often assumed that housework itself is a constant feature of all societies.

But even though the activities may be timeless, the context and meaning are not. Who does it, where, when and for what reasons – both acknowledged and latent – are the important questions to be asked. Take, for example, sweeping a floor, an activity which has changed technologically very little over the years. Sweeping can be a form of ritual; making patterns in dirt, sand or gravel with magical and/or aesthetic meaning, periodic ritual cleansing as in spring cleaning, or even a kind of exorcism. But sweeping a floor can also symbolize a humble position, a special kind of relationship to the social order. As the well-known stanza runs:

> A servant with this clause
> Makes drudgery divine
> Who sweeps a room as for thy laws
> Makes that and th'action fine.

Such subordination can merge into sweeping, or scrubbing floors as a humiliation and punishment, as in the army, prisons, orphanages and mental hospitals, where the most menial domestic work is also used as discipline to keep order. On the other hand, it can be seen as part of 'scientific' dirt control to combat diseases by removing places for them to breed. Or, most often, it can be all of these combined.

Significantly, too, such activities have not always and everywhere been carried out by women, particularly adult women; it is only our stereotypical thinking that equates domestic work completely as part of the adult feminine role. Indeed the concept 'domestic work' itself is culturally dictated.[8] Very often such tasks as fuel-gathering, simple cookery, child-minding and water-carrying have been turned over to young children, and old or handicapped people of either sex, i.e. those too physically weak or socially marginal to be involved in productive tasks.[9] In colonial societies, it was very often native men who were used for domestic work for the foreign dominant group.[10]

Note also the use of batmen in the armed services and the arrangement of domestic work in all-male situations, such as on board ship or in mining camps.

In the most basic sense, housework is concerned with creating and maintaining order in the immediate environment, making meaningful patterns of activities, people and materials. The most important part in the creation of such an order is the separating out of the basic constituents and making clear the boundaries between them. For example, cooking food is the transformation of raw ingredients into a new substance. This process makes the ingredients into an element which can then be used in family or social ritual. In this sense the raw food has now 'participated in the family – by cooking, food is made to pass from the natural to the human world'.[11] More than this, however, when the cooked food is eaten, it penetrates the boundaries of the body, truly binding together those who 'break bread' around a common table.

A meal itself is made up of ritually prescribed patterns of cold and hot, sweet and savoury food. Unless it is patterned in this way it is felt that it is not proper food.

Yet changes in the rigid daily meal pattern can signify changes in the season or a holiday release provided by the deliberate inversion of this formality.[12] Who partakes of the meal, when and where, helps to create the boundaries of the household, of friendship patterns, of kinship gradations. Only the family eat hot Sunday dinner together, lesser acquaintances are invited for drinks, not a full meal, etc.[13] These eating patterns vary between and help to define the boundaries of classes, ethnic, religious, age and sexual groups.[14]

Cleaning (clearing, tidying and washing) is another operation of the same kind, which is very widespread although perhaps not as ubiquitous as cooking. In separating wanted from unwanted matter, defining what is to be saved and what is rubbish, we are imposing a pattern, defining boundaries. As Mary Douglas has said, 'dirt is essentially disorder . . . eliminating it is not a negative movement, but a positive effort to organize the environment . . . making it conform to an idea'.[15] But the idea must precede the efforts to maintain the boundaries and, therefore, the disorder must first be perceived. The perception of disorder is a cultural artefact which changes through time and place:

> Cleanliness or tidiness is a relative idea. Shoes are not dirty in themselves, but it is dirty to place them on the dining table; food is not dirty in itself, but it is dirty to leave cooking utensils in the bedroom or food bespattered on clothing; similarly bathroom equipment in the drawing room; clothing lying on chairs; out-door things in-doors; upstairs things downstairs; under-clothing appearing where overclothing should be; and so on. In short, our pollution behaviour is the reaction which condemns any object or idea likely to confuse or contradict cherished classifications.[16]

Freedom from the responsibility of maintaining these particular boundaries or of even perceiving them is one of the rewards of power positions. The enforcement of basic order can be ignored because it can be delegated to others. Although I have indicated many exceptions, by and large, everywhere and at all times, women have been more concerned with these 'core' boundary-maintaining functions than men. Why?[17]

If we look more closely at the core activities of cooking and cleaning, we see that they are attempts to impose cultural patterns upon the natural world. Pollution and purity rituals often seem to be part of this relationship between nature and culture. They are an attempt 'to generate and sustain systems of meaningful forms (symbols, artefacts, etc.) by means of which humanity transcends the givens of natural existence, bends them to its purposes, controls them in its interests'.[18] Since women are for a longer period of time more involved with physiological processes (menstruation, childbirth and lactation) they are seen as closer to nature than men. They also bring forth new unplaced individuals for the society to absorb. Because they are usually assigned to care for small children, they spend more of their lifetime with those who are unsocialized and thus 'uncivilized' forces. Men are seen as people, but women are ambiguous simply by the fact of being also conscious beings who are not men but who do take some part in the culture of the society. Yet women are active beings in their performance as a 'mediating agency' between nature and culture: the raw and the cooked.[19]

Thus women are a moral force of the utmost importance, the first line of defence against fundamental symbolic as well as physical disorder. Because of their marginality and ambiguity, however, they are in danger of being unclean or threatening themselves. 'Those nearer to the "non-structure", i.e. those who are more marginal, can unleash more dangerous powers, are more polluting.'[20] As a result, even when they are engaged in maintaining the purity of others and of the environment, they are often segregated spatially into limited areas of action. This physical segregation becomes an integral part of the system, a feature long recognized by anthropologists but until recently ignored by many mainstream sociologists whose conceptions of social systems often seem to exist in free-floating space. Physical invisibility is also social invisibility and this is one of the reasons why much of women's activity has been systematically left out of sociological and other analysis.

Housekeeping activities are not only concerned with segregating and maintaining categories, they are, as I have indicated, related to the ways in which these categories are ordered in terms of power.[21] Hierarchical boundaries are always some of the most salient in any society. This has two important implications for our discussion. First, those who deal with potentially polluting activities, such as transforming the raw into the cooked, and dealing with the detritus of personal life, are very often those at the bottom of the hierarchy, indeed sometimes even outside it, i.e. 'outcasts'.[22] For example, body substances in many societies are regarded as *boundary overflows* and therefore particularly dangerous.[23] Hence those who deal with such defiling material must be defilers themselves.[24]

Second, societies which are exceptionally concerned with hierarchical ranks will be also usually concerned with maintaining distances between them and fearful of the confusion caused by the blurring of their boundaries. In every case, of course, these boundaries are ultimately enforced by power. But there is also a whole symbolic system used by the agencies of power to legitimate their rule. When the power base is shifting, the symbolic system becomes doubly important. A preoccupation with the *listing* of hierarchy and the forbidden contacts between groups seems to be a feature of such a situation when, *at the same time*, a great deal of actual mixing is going on.[25]

Domestic Work and Hierarchy in the English Historical Context

In eighteenth- and nineteenth-century English society, hierarchical boundaries were under attack. There were no legal restrictions on entry into various social strata, and new sources of wealth were being used to build up what was potentially a new definition of legitimate rule outside landowning groups. The order based on the mixture of domestic industry and agriculture was increasingly challenged by manufacturing interests.[26] In this situation a rigid classification of hierarchical ranks was officially proclaimed.

> The rich man in his castle
> The poor man at the gate
> God made them high or lowly
> And ordered their estate.

was sung in Sunday schools across the country, but social boundaries were, in fact, permeable. Although mobility was not easy to accomplish it was quite possible if limited in degree. The response to this situation seems to have been, indeed, a preoccupation with classifying and segregating various strata of the society (by *sex*, *age* and '*usefulness*' or moral worth, in addition to class), as well as great pressure to build up the moral force of the society to take part in the task of keeping disorder at bay. The rise of Methodism, the Evangelical movement within the church and the beginnings of the temperance movement (whose rhetoric with its emphasis on purity, e.g. 'My Drink is Water Bright' is interesting in this context) can all be seen as part of this process.

Another separating and ranking device emerging at this period and given into the keeping of women was the idea of 'Society' – the category of being *in* as opposed to *out* of 'the World'.[27] Within this concept of a clearly demarcated Society, the older ideals of gentility, based on honour, were recast in the new and more flexible definition of *lady* and *gentleman* as understood in the nineteenth century.[28] According-ing to the aristocratic code of honour, work itself, any work, implied a drop in status whether it was in trade, manufacture or in the professions. The manual, physical side of work was beneath contempt while, at the same time, manual *skills*, in sport, in swordsmanship and other arts of war or in intricate embroidery or music-making had high esteem. In middle-class culture, on the other hand, work activity was highly valued for itself and it was only the actual physical or literally manual work which came to be particularly despised as ungenteel. Following on from this, it is not accidental that *hands*, their whiteness, smoothness, smallness, their encasing in gloves, or conversely largeness, filthiness, roughness, redness, bareness, should become a preoccupation of this period.[29]

The symbolism of hands was only a part of the division between dirt and cleanliness which increased as the nineteenth century progressed. The striving for order and control by keeping dirt away, by washing and brushing, polishing and sweeping, had been associated with various groups in earlier periods (e.g. many Protestant sects and even medieval burgher households), but these tended to be small minorities easily ridiculed for their finicky ways. On the whole, up to the middle of the eighteenth century, the distinct life-styles of the rich and the poor had depended on the amount and type of food, of gold or silver ornaments and plate and sumptuousness of clothing. Most people in all classes had lice and diseases associated with dirt.[30] The concern with personal and domestic cleanliness, with the stricter ordering of things and people in the house came later. And it emerged as an important way of marking the middle classes off from those below them, well before the germ theory of disease was discovered, much less understood by the general public. It is true that by the second quarter of the nineteenth century there was a growing feeling that somehow a connection between dirt and disease existed. For example it was acknowledged that drinking water, so polluted that it was brown and stank, had something to do with the scourge of cholera. But the connections were dimly appreciated and often based on explanations such as 'myasmic contagion'; a vagueness that caused many problems for real control through bacterial destruction.[31] Historical explanations of sanitary improvements solely in terms of what William James has dubbed 'medical materialism'[32] have too glibly overlooked this question of the timing of the reforms.

Part of the preoccupation with cleanliness was due to the obtrusiveness of new kinds of dirt, e.g. the increased use of coal in large cities and manufacturing areas which produced unusable by-products of cinders, smuts and dust. Also in large cities garbage and sewage which would have been useful as fertiliser in the country became sheer waste as it festered on the curbs and in muck-heaps by the doorsteps. (Housewives still often refer to garden soil as 'clean dirt'.) New definitions of what was and was not waste were part of a new definition of the relationship of human beings to nature which was taking place at the same time in, for example, the Romantic movement in the arts.

The point to be stressed, however, is that nineteenth-century cleanliness really had more to do with tidying and polishing – sparkling glasses, gleaming silver, brass, copper and polished wood – than our notions of dirt control. Tidiness was seen to be as much a moral as a physical attribute (A Place for Everything and Everything in its Place). Indeed, furnishing, equipment and clothing were all so elaborated, embossed, carved and trimmed that they inevitably harboured and even created dirt.

Women's place in this control system was clearly stated in the tracts, manuals, advice books and fiction of the period. Women were purer than men, they were by nature more moral and should be cleaner. 'There can be no love of long duration, sincere and ardent love in any man towards a *filthy* mate', wrote Cobbett in 1829 and he went on to urge the prospective suitor to look between his intended bride's fingers and behind her ears for traces of grime.[33]

> Lords of Creation are neither in practice nor is it their province to be as domestically clean and orderly as ladies. . . . Even those men who have some degree of satisfaction in seeing that things *are* clean, are apt to be unreasonable and impatient if obliged to witness the operations that must make them so; whilst the implements of domestic purification are their confessed abhorrence.[34]

It was assumed then, and is to an extent to this day, that boys are by nature dirtier than girls. It was women and girls who spent so much of their lives carrying, heating, and steeping their hands while washing things, clothes and people in *water* – that fluid element which dissolves matter and is so often used in rituals of purification: 'water symbolizes the primal substance from which all forms come and to which they will return'.[35] The middle- and upper-class house, within its walls and continuing down its front steps and path (ideally maids were supposed to wash both back and front paths as well as steps every day) was the clean tidy haven in the midst of public squalor and disorder.[36] It was the housemistress's responsibility to make it so.

Even more important than the equation of femininity with cleanliness was, of course, the equation of cleanliness with class position, part of the parcel of behaviour and attitudes bundled together in that imprecise but vital concept *respectability*. Whatever the other strands in respectability – church-going or temperance – cleanliness was supposed to be its hallmark. In the nineteenth century the labouring classes, the poor, the proletariat were, in middle-class minds, 'The Great Unwashed'; they *smelled* uncontrolled and disordered.[37] This view persisted well into the twentieth century, and George Orwell is one of the very few writers to discuss openly the implications of this fact. He was in no doubt as to its effect on efforts at social equality. 'That was what we were taught – *the lower classes smell*. And here obviously you are at an impassable barrier' (his italics)[38] – a barrier created in childhood and so doubly difficult to break down.

Smell and sound as well as sight of dirt and disorder were more obtrusive in crowded cities than in the countryside, and the idealization of Nature as pure compared to towns as impure may be connected to this fact. 'The great unwashed were socially unclean, too, the typical attitudes first expressed to this emergent group by those above them were [also] stereotyped – a blend of contempt, fear, hate and physical revulsion.'[39] Himmelfarb notes a disturbing habit of Victorian observers of using the same word to describe both the sanitary condition (Chadwick) and the human condition (Mayhew) of the poor; i.e., 'residuum' was the offal, excrement or other waste that constituted the sanitary problem; and was also the name applied to the lowest layer of society.[40]

Conversely, manual work and hence dirt, or the absence of cleanliness became associated with ideas of masculinity.[41] Personal habits associated with dirt and mess, e.g. spitting, chewing tobacco and smoking, became strictly masculine from the end of the eighteenth century onwards. Similar attitudes were part of an aggressively proletarian identification, and held by the type of radical who was 'goaded to fury by the sight of a clean shirt'.[42]

A second element used in the separation of classes was fresh air. Again, the recognition of the value of fresh air undoubtedly had much to do with new forms of physical pollution – smog was already a feature of London life in the eighteenth century. But the metaphorical use of the term 'fresh air' to blow away and cleanse social problems was also a constant theme. Newman in his *Apologia* wrote: 'Virtue is the child of knowledge, vice of Ignorance. Therefore education, periodical literature, railroad travel and ventilation seem to make a population moral and happy.'[43] 'Morality was intimately connected with the free circulation of air – exposure to public gaze.'[44] Middle-class children were told that servants' bedrooms were inevitably fuggy and stale-smelling because they did not understand the benefits of fresh air. Charity workers and others brought the message home to their working-class (largely female) audience with tracts such as those put out by the Ladies' Sanitary Association, 'A Word About Fresh Air', 'The Black Hole in our own Bedrooms', etc. (c.1850). And until very recently, the 'airing' of rooms, bedding and clothing was seen as one of the English housewife's indispensable daily tasks.[45]

I have indicated that one of the rewards of a superior position within a hierarchical structure is the protection of the superordinate from potentially polluting activities. The ultimate nineteenth-century ideal became the creation of a perfectly orderly setting of punctually served and elaborate meals, clean and tidy warmed rooms, clean, pressed and aired clothes and bedlinen. Children were to be kept in nurseries with nursemaids; animals and gardens cared for by outdoor servants; callers and strangers dealt with by indoor servants. In other words there was to be a complete absence of all disturbing or threatening interruptions to orderly existence which could be caused either by the intractability, and ultimate disintegration, of things or by the emotional disturbance of people.[46] In the nineteenth century this ideal of perfect order could only be approximated by the small group of wealthy and powerful individuals who could command the attendance of numerous domestic servants. Below this small group, *men* – that is, all middle-class men and to a certain extent the best paid, most regularly employed of the working class – were provided with an intensely personal form of ego-protection and enhancement by their wives (or daughters, nieces and unmarried sisters), aided by female general servants.

This process must be recognized as a relational aspect of social stratification. It should not be substituted for an analysis of the distributive aspects of inequality. Drawing attention to the part such interaction plays in the maintenance of stratification, however, emphasizes the way the system was divided along *both* class and sex lines.

The attitudes and behaviour relevant to nineteenth-century middle-class house-keeping – cleanliness, order, the segregation of activities in time and place, careful overall planning, diligence and hard work – had all existed and been commended for a very long time. Not only do they appear in Puritan and other Nonconformist precepts, but they go back as far as the moralists of Roman husbandry. They are echoed in fourteenth- and fifteenth-century Florence by such writers as Alberti and continued in various places where trade and commerce flourished as far apart as sixteenth-century Holland, Defoe's London and eighteenth-century Pennsylvania. There the rubric reached its fullest expression in the writings of Benjamin Franklin, 'the perfect bourgeois', particularly in his *Autobiography* and *The Way to Wealth*.[47] The purpose of all these guides to conduct was, in every sphere, to make life more calculable, to balance expenditure with income in an effort to save. Thrift in regard to both time and money was the cardinal virtue. The goals of saving might vary (a dowry for a daughter, an extra piece of land), but the primary drive, for continued saving, for saving as a way of life, was to create capital for commercial expansion. And it was the growth of capitalist commercial enterprise which was responsible for the critical organizational change: the separation of the business 'house' and the domestic household. Even more important than physical separation was the budgetary division of these units.[48] Strangers began to be admitted as partners into what had been an organization of kinsmen, brotherhoods or guilds. This process reached a critical point in the adoption of detailed accounting and eventually the introduction of double-entry book-keeping into business practice (an invention of seventeenth-century Holland).[49] With this development, business and commercial activity were finally cut loose from other goals of family life, allowing the systematic accumulation of capital. Such expansion of the enterprise is not possible without the use of rational accounting, which in turn must use an all-purpose medium of exchange – money. Only then can any true calculation of input and output, of profit or loss be made.

It is also true that the rational ordering of life is quite possible whatever the chosen ends, even if they are 'unworldly' ones. This is a point worth remembering in the context of the present discussion. For example, European monasticism was just such a system of living, for the glory of God, with its minutely calibrated daily activities rigidly prescribed by the constant ringing of bells. Yet even under monasticism, such attitudes seem to mesh most easily with the rationalization of economic life, for the monasteries were also very often large farming and productive enterprises. As Weber noted, 'the Reformation took rational Christian asceticism and its methodical habits out of the monasteries and placed them in the service of active life in the world.'[50] In this way, the stage was set for economic expansion, in enterprises which had 'no boundaries to this process of addition',[51] and it is this type of enterprise and its descendants which has been the concern of social commentators from the seventeenth century onwards.

Few have asked, however, about what happens to the household which has been thus disengaged from production. Before trying to answer that question it should be remembered that this separation was a very slow process, starting with a few mercantile and tradesmen's households which were exceptions to the general case of more or less self-sufficient units which drew their sustenance directly from the land; which ranged in scale from great landowners to cottagers. A high proportion of the income of such households remained in kind, not cash. The large numbers of rural households which were partially dependent on outwork (e.g. textiles, straw-plaiting, lace-making) further complicates the total picture. Nevertheless, the trend was for more and more household relationships to involve a cash nexus, whether in the form of proletarian wage earner, salaried or professional occupation, tradesman, rentier, capitalist or a mixture of these. This shift was associated with a higher proportion of families living in towns, and, although this was an important aspect of the change, it is not possible to discuss it here. The final and complete break, however, was not reached in England until full extension of limited liability with the passing of the Company Acts of 1856–62, which once and for all freed business activity from any restraints imposed by kinship obligations.

The very slow pace of the separation of household and enterprise and the persistence of home production of a great many commodities did not prevent attempts to rationalize activity in bourgeois homes as well as commercial enterprises. In particular there seems to have been a transfer of the values of business into the home. But these attempts were, and are to this day, unsuccessful for two fundamental and interrelated reasons. The first, and probably the most obvious, concerns the limited size of the household. Neither vertical nor horizontal extension is really possible and this means that economies of scale and the benefits of specialization are not practicable for a household. While the goal of economic rationality is always the expansion of the enterprise, there are inherent and quite narrow limits to household expansion.

Of course it is possible to point to examples of really large establishments, but these are very exceptional. While one of the biggest in the nineteenth century, Woburn Abbey, had fifty to sixty indoor servants and could house several dozen guests, the mean household size in Social Class I in York in 1851 was 6.02.[52] As far as growth through devices such as mergers or takeovers is concerned, there was a certain amount of transfer of income and/or services between households across generations or between siblings, but the whole tendency has been for each family unit to act independently.[53] In addition, because of other effects of nineteenth- and twentieth-century capitalist developments, households have tended to grow smaller as measured by house size and numbers of inhabitants.[54]

The second point concerns the goals of family and household (it should be noted that although the two terms are now almost synonymous this has not always been the case). The problem here is not that non-pecuniary ends cannot be reached by rational means, but that the goals themselves – the maintenance of hierarchical boundaries and ego-servicing of superiors – *deny* the use of rational calculation.

The struggle to keep unlimited calculation – 'the need to see the world in terms of figures'[55] – from creeping into every sphere of life was a long-drawn-out and even bloody one.[56] Nowhere was it more visibly demonstrated than in the segregation of women and of the home from market forces. The use of money means that there are no longer 'mysterious incalculable forces that can come into play, but rather that in principle all things can be mastered by calculation'. Money is the most rational and formal means of orientation because it makes possible calculation *within* a unit and *between* units. It is the demystifying instrument *par excellence*. The resistance to the application of rational calculation to the family, and hence women, is of utmost importance; and because it reflects a primordial concern for order, for protection from pollution, it has a deeper basis in collective life than social theorists have so far acknowledged. In this sense, housework has remained not a residuum left over from a previous mode of production, but it is seen as a positive purposive activity in capitalist and non-capitalist societies alike.

The analysis of housework by contemporary Marxist economists is quite correct in showing that the real productive labour-power of women in domestic tasks is obscured; and that this particular obscuration is superimposed on the general obfuscation (and thus legitimation) of extraction of surplus-value within the capitalist mode of production. The labour of the housewife in preparing and sustaining the husband for his labour, as well as in producing new workers in the form of children, is mediated through the labour (and thus the wage) of the husband. It is true that for this kind of analysis 'it matters not at all that the concrete conditions of domestic labour are privatized';[57] but sociologically, and for the women themselves, this is crucial.[58]

Simply exposing this double obscurity, and the double oppression it implies, does not show why the oppression takes the *form* which it does. Indeed, if we look at the early period of industrial capitalism in England, the overwhelming need for workers, together with a reluctance to use adult male labour, led to a factory system based mainly on female and child labour, which was more tractable, and cheaper, than the former. But this practice was met with storms of protest from all sections of the society and it is just at this period that the ideology of women's domestic place was being most intensely propagated. Capitalists, as public men, were supporting the cult of domesticity, while at the same time, as rational entrepreneurs, they were recruiting women workers into their mills and mines through the back door. However, the whole history of this period has yet to be systematically studied.[59]

The Movement towards the Rationalization of Housework in Eighteenth- and Nineteenth-Century England

I turn now to look in more detail at the move towards rationalization of housework in a more specific historical setting. A useful way of proceeding is to consider the physical artefacts left by those groups who were most subject to the appeal of rational calculation. The whole development of middle-class housing and furnishings from the sixteenth century onwards is one of increased separation and specialization of function. The hall or large living place gradually gave way to separate smaller rooms for cooking, eating and, eventually, solely for sleeping. The massive central chimney provided flues for 'kitchen and parlour' instead of 'hall and service'. As time went on, beds were no longer found downstairs in sitting-rooms or doubling as seats for receiving visitors. This evolution eventually affected all social classes, although obviously resources varied enormously and up until very recently working-class families were still cooking in the 'house-place' or living-room rather than in a separate kitchen. On the other hand, this arrangement was very often made in order to free another room, the parlour, for ceremonial or frontstage purposes analogous to the middle-class drawing-room where ceremonies of integration and exclusion could take place at ritually defined times, e.g. Sunday, Christmas, weddings and funerals. This is a prime example of rational segregation for non-worldly ends.

It is known that in the nineteenth century the level of consumption of food, furniture, china and decorations rose rapidly with increasing middle-class prosperity, but if we look closely at the way these resources were deployed – for example, separate cutlery and crockery not only for nursery, kitchen and dining-room but for every day and holidays – the divisions represented by the allocation of these resources indicate which categories were most important to the participants in the rituals. In the period from about 1800 to 1840 meals changed in character.[60] Dinner began to be eaten later in the evening. Instead of having one or two large courses, including a selection of as many as twenty-five different dishes, set on the table at once in a mixture of roasts, 'made-up' dishes, sweets, tarts and jellies, the meal began to be served sequentially, starting with soup and moving through a variety of tastes and textures to a sweet, a savoury and finally dessert. This order was accompanied by the proliferation of specialized utensils and dishes to prepare and present the extended meal and much more labour was needed to serve it. At the same time there was, at least for family meals, a move to make food predictable. Increased resources were not used to allow choice to run riot. Rather the sentiment was that 'it was an excellent plan to have certain things on certain days' (1827), and this laid the basis for the Victorian rigidity of joint on Sunday, cold on Monday, hash on Tuesday, etc., which dominated English cuisine for generations afterwards.

The spate of housekeeping books of the late eighteenth century and early nineteenth century shows that this was a period of experimentation with various forms of rationalizing household affairs. It was during this period, for example, that the keeping of strict and detailed household accounts was continually advocated, and these accounts dealt with both income and expenditure within various time-spans:[61]

> Those articles extracted from the Cook's and Footman's books, or paid for in ready money, are to be entered in the first column and transferred to the cash-book as weekly sundries. Those bills which are paid monthly or quarterly, to be in the second column as a register to the consumption, that the weeks be compared with each other: and the mention of the number of persons in the family and what guests dine either accidentally or by regular invitation, will be found useful, as a standing explanation of any excess in the weekly bills.
>
> Make an exact estimate of your *Net* Income; reserve two-fifths of net income for emergency. To ensure this compare your *Weekly* Expenses with a computation which you may easily make of how much your *Annual* income will afford every *Week*.[62]

From the above quotations it can be sensed that there was coming into use a new time structure which was made up of shorter, controllable units and which was freed from intimate dependence on the agricultural calendar of sowing and harvest. In prosperous households, instead of the quarterly orgies of washing of huge stocks of dirty linen, the span between launderings dropped first to every six weeks, then to three weeks, until by the mid-nineteenth century the weekly wash was the norm.[63]

Housework schedules began to be drawn up with regular daily, weekly, monthly and annual tasks to be followed; and the remnants of these survive in our rituals of spring cleaning. Early rising was the constant exhortion to mistress and maid alike. Artificial light was improved to even out the day and night throughout the year, and thereby to increase the time so carefully hoarded. An often-quoted maxim from early in the century warns:

> Lost, yesterday, somewhere between sunrise and sunset;
> Two golden hours, each set with sixty diamond minutes.
> No reward is offered for they are gone forever.

Gongs and house bells were now used to mark times for rising, for prayers, for meals, for dressing for meals. The generally increased use of clocks and watches for timing household operations as well as accurate weights and measures in cooking are all indices of the same tendency.

> In a well regulated family all the clocks and watches should agree . . . the Dining room should be furnished with a good going clock; the space over the kitchen fire place with another, vibrating in unison with the former so placed that the cook may keep one eye on the clock and the other on the spit

stated Kitchiner in one of the most influential early nineteenth-century cookery books.[64]

In the critical sphere of social relations, middle- and upper-class housemistresses kept visitors' books, or calling books, into which they transferred the information from visiting cards left and received.[65] A commonplace book of the 1830s belonging to a merchant's wife had dated double-headed columns for each month of each year to record visits received and visits paid, gifts received and gifts given, evenings spent at home and evenings spent out – a kind of commercial balance sheet of home and social life.[66]

The most fundamental index of rationalization, however, was the vastly increased employment of specialized domestic servants and the concomitant withdrawal of the housemistress from actual household tasks to a supervisory position, even within quite small establishments. The early nineteenth century was the period when the concept of the 'domestic' as opposed to the farm servant became established in both popular and legal terminology. Of course nineteenth-century servants were paid in cash as well as board and room, but the ideology of the home stressed the familial and service side of their attachment. Within the household a symbolic head/hands hierarchy was established, either by the mistress herself directing one to three servants, or, where larger staffs were employed, by their separation into upper and lower staff.

Running the house was broken down into minutely specified spheres of action: cook cleans back passage and steps, housemaid cleans front steps, hall and landing only, parlour maid is responsible for dining-room and drawing-room. The records covering three generations of an upwardly mobile banking family show that in the 1830s two maids did every sort of job including gardening. In the 1870s the daughter-in-law had three maids, subdivided as cook, housemaid and nursemaid, and the third generation added a gardener and under-housemaid in 1900. While it is true that the increase in numbers of servants in this family was related to its increasing wealth, the form of specialization, for instance as between indoor and outdoor, between kitchen and house side, is significant.[67]

In studying the housekeeping books of the nineteenth century culminating in that often-cited monumental volume, Mrs Beeton's *Book of Household Management* (first published in book form in 1861), I have come to suspect that what they provide is more a legalistic model, a 'grammar of conduct . . . concerned more with what ought *not* to be done rather than what should be done',[68] as opposed to an account of what *was* actually going on in many households. Interview material and careful reading between the lines of memoirs indicates that there was, in fact, a good deal of transfer of personnel as well as blurring of the job demarcations and that the mistress of the house did more manual work herself than was admitted publicly (even if it was with blinds drawn as in Mrs Gaskell's *Cranford*!).

Nevertheless, there is still no question that the final aim was a rigid division of front- and backstage and a relegation of household work to special times and places. In England particularly there was an unusually strong effort to remove the house-mistress, even in quite modest households, from her core function of cooking. By 1845 Mrs Loudon (an extremely practical and working gardener herself) could recommend that a charcoal stove be set up in the housekeeper's room so that the housemistress might be able 'to make any dishes in French cookery, or any cakes or preserves that you may take a fancy to do yourself, with the assistance of your maid, apart from the observation of the other servants'.[69] The segregation of activities became so important that it included an intense dislike and fear of cooking smells in front rooms or even the sounds of any domestic activity, such as clinking dishes or thumping of irons. An examination of house guides and architectural books shows that architects of the period clearly saw provision for the separation of facilities for domestic work as a major part of their brief.

Here is clearly a case of specialization for ritual ends. Fears about female purity had reached such a pitch that an introduction to a mid-century cookery book says:

> In the higher ranks an idea is entertained that any consideration connected with eating is injurious to the delicacy of the feminine character; this notion being strengthened as it descends, by an indisposition to undertake the toils which attention to the table must necessarily involve. Eating is an unpoetical thing: Lord Byron disliked to see women eat . . .[70]

This attitude was bemoaned by writers, preachers and housemistresses them-selves, but by and large it was accepted and represented a very real shift in norms from the eighteenth century where a young woman's diary could record: 'read a little Greek, then made custard and tarts – which was very notable, then set the codlin' bar in order, produced myself in the parlour and were mighty agreeable.'[71]

Most of these attempts at rationalization were eventually abandoned; those that remained produced contradictions that are still with us, for middle-class, much less working-class, households neither are nor were rational economic organizations. On the contrary, as I have tried to show, their aims are principally concerned with boundary maintenance at various levels. As Dorothy Smith has written, 'in a capitalist society, the house constitutes a dead end. The surplus above subsistence which enters it does not pass beyond it into a productive activity with others' – rather it performs a display function which is used to mark off the household's position, and 'thus the household order enters a semiotic structure . . . money stops at the family, there is nowhere else for it to go'.[72]

Consequences of the Contradiction Between Rationalization and the Purposes of the Household

The attempts at rationalization within a context of incommensurable ends had, and to a certain extent still have, several consequences for household management. When pre-industrial traditions of labour distribution within the home broke down, there was, theoretically, no rational check on labour input. Any deficiency was made up by more intensive labour on the part of the housewife and servants; it was not only 'in the abodes of the poor [that] every defect of spending power has to be made good by the toil of the woman's muscles'.[73] In principle, only the physical exhaustion of the wife (and/or children), or in the case of servants the availability of alternative opportunities (other jobs or marriage) which enabled them to quit, put a check on the length of the working day or the expenditure of energy in housework. Although the individual husband (or master) might have tried to ease his wife's burden by *giving* her help either in the form of better equipment or hired help when he could afford it,[74] housework had to remain labour intensive because there was no way of genuinely calculating alternatives to the woman's labour in the form of capital investment of labour from the external market.[75] Conversely, middle- and upper-class women could be carried as completely unproductive members of the households because ideology refused to allow the 'costing' of womanly love and service. (The fact that such women were in actuality constantly reminded of the cost of their support was a bitter portion of their dependence.) The other possible ways of limiting the work-load and of estimating the efficiency of housework – i.e. by governmental investigations or trade union pressure – were of course completely absent. How many women were maimed or even killed, and how many became ill through exhaustion and the close nature of their work we will never know. Drinking among cooks was considered a joke, not an occupational disease.

Second, because it can never be really accepted that women's efforts in house-work and household management should be measured in monetary terms, the worth of all women's work is affected. The census classification itself over the nineteenth century reflects this ambivalence, making something of a mockery of refined attempts to analyse the female labour market in purely statistical terms. The Registrar General warned in 1901 that the apparent 'remarkable decrease' of occupied women from 34.4 per cent in 1891 to 31.6 per cent was due to struggles with classification rather than empirical fact, because

> In 1881 and earlier, daughters and other female relatives of the Head of a Family, who were described as assisting in household duties, were classified as unoccupied. In 1891, however, it was considered that, the nature of daily occupations of such persons being thus evident, they would be properly reckoned in Domestic Service. . . . In deciding on the rules of guidance of the clerks at the recent census (1901) however, we came to the conclusion that, on the whole, it would be better to revert to the method of 1881.[76]

Domestic service as a position between paid work and family attachment is, therefore, the crucial example of this equivocal orientation and from about 1850 to 1950 it was *the single most important form of employment of women and girls* (over a million and a quarter in the last part of the nineteenth century and never less than a million until the mid-1930s).

What is wage work in the life of Mary H. (born 1876)? At thirteen she went by the day as companion-guardian to a mentally ill neighbour after helping her mother at home morning and evening (as she had done before leaving school). From fourteen to sixteen she was a paid living-in nursemaid to a publican, then spent almost a year living with her married sister to help with a new baby, receiving board and room only. This was followed by another nursemaid's job at 3s 6d a week, then six months living at home helping in the house and another nine months with an aunt to help with the housework and young baby. Back to London as a house/parlour maid at 4s a week, promoted at age twenty-two to head housemaid at 7s 6d a week, she then married a tram conductor and, as his wife, kept house for him, receiving set 'housekeeping' and thus no longer officially 'working'.[77]

Secombe may be correct in saying that the spurious attempt to calculate the 'wage' value of housewives' work is 'an exercise in bourgeoise reasoning, i.e. wages as a measure of the value of work done rather than a monetary package paid to en-sure the family subsistence'.[78] Nevertheless we now live in a fully wage-orientated society where only cash can buy support. If women are, in this sense, as individuals, not fully and legitimately within the labour market – which in the nineteenth century they certainly were *not* – then they must find support in the only other way they can, through the marriage market and its corollary, prostitution.

For with the falling away of economically 'mixed' households depending on smallholding, craft-type workshops and even the taking in of washing and/or lodgers, more and more households exist solely as consumption units.[79] A consumption unit cannot by itself either create or increase income; it can only save by cutting expenditure. Some saving can, of course, benefit the family in the form of house purchase, for example, but the amount of saving that is possible on most salaries let alone wages makes this a remote aim. The point is that household support really depends on cash currently coming into the household. If no 'housekeeping' is brought into the home by the husband for *whatever* reason, from personal spite to unemployment, there is no money for the housewife to live on or for the support of the dependent children. Because of this a goodly proportion of poverty, however measured, was, and to a certain extent is, female and child poverty. In 1910, the Webbs wrote:

> The amount of destitution in the country, generally, caused by the death, absence or desertion, of the male head of the family . . . we should estimate to be 35% of the whole.[80]

An example, among dozens, of the confusion caused by the failure to grasp this point is from Littlejohn's *Westrigg*, where he tries to show how the wife in the working-class family can maintain the status of the household

> and can be responsible for its downfall into the non-respectable 'slum class' . . . the difference between 'rough' and 'respectable', bare boards versus cloth, china versus enamel, cooked meals, clean clothes, lack of debt to salesmen are all part of the household and therefore female economy.[81]

Granted that there are variations in the ways in which money can be spent and in the energy and skill which women put into household management, yet no miracle of 'make do and mend' can create china or lino, or the fuel to cook meals, or the soap to wash clothes.

It is almost impossible to tell what proportion of their husbands' income wives in various social classes received or how these levels were arrived at, or whether the housekeeping rose during inflation. It is notoriously difficult to gain this information now – women tend to be woefully ignorant about family finances in general and their own families in particular – so that trying to reconstruct the distribution of income within the family historically will be a daunting task.[82] However, it is clear that our ignorance of these matters is not fortuitous and is due not so much to the husband's meanness about disclosing his total income but rather to the fact that it is thought to be *inappropriate* to apply cash reckoning to family life.

Another crucial area of calculation which can only be briefly mentioned here is the supplying of the household through buying in goods; that is to say 'shopping', which is a peculiarly modern urban phenomenon in that no supplies are grown by the family or traded for at a local market. One of the acknowledged and lamented, but never questioned, penalties for the nineteenth-century urban working class was the necessity to buy in minute quantities every day, or even several times a day, from the corner shop:[83] 'screws' of tea, ounces of sugar and dabs of jam. And even if the poorest sections of the population could have bought in larger quantities they had nowhere to store the provisions.

However, given some margin of expenditure, what would be the most 'rational' way to buy in various kinds of provisions, both perishable and non-perishable? When a household no longer lives off its own produce, is it 'economy' to buy in bulk and store goods or is it a 'good general rule never to purchase anything until you absolutely need it'?[84] Both of these incompatible courses were (and still are) urged on housekeepers. The fear of wasting time and materials, became a leitmotiv of nineteenth-century writers on domestic life. But what is waste in this context when there is no standard to measure expenditure by? In the household there is a constant tension between the aims of hospitality, generosity, lavish display (or 'wilful waste') on the one hand and the aims of economy, rational planning and careful fore-thought (or meanness) on the other; in nineteenth-century idiom, the tightrope between 'Profligacy' and 'Parsimony'. These two orientations can be seen as the contrasting characteristics of upper-class and middle-class life-styles, an antago-nism of outlook which goes back at least 300 years.[85] The major problems of many nineteenth-century households were due to the fact that they tried to combine both.

Finally, the lack of calculability in the housewife's work has meant that the 'striving for perfection, the ingenious refinement of the conduct of life and attain-ment of increasing mastery over the external world', which is the *modus operandi* of rationalization,[86] is constantly being brought up short, being thwarted. Thus 'the physical disorder of the house is marked by the housewife's own psychological disorder'[87] and housework is seen as a battle, with the housewife waging war on dirt and chaos, and the dirt and chaos constantly attacking her. This is basically a defensive operation, under ordinary circumstances, a struggle to stay out of debt while maintaining certain standards of living. It is brought out most clearly in times of war or economic crisis when the housewife is exhorted to save and to 'contrive and consider' every action. It is a mentality of going from shop to shop looking for lower prices, turning cuffs and collars, saving string, making casseroles out of leftovers and unravelling old pullovers to knit into gloves.

The attitudes bred by this situation were fatalistic and passive. Only those with aims and resources to enter Society through elaborate entertainment could begin to direct their activity to a more positive goal, and even that had traditional limits. In contrast, the capitalist entrepreneur's mentality was a product of the internal pressure to expand. He must 'conquer, organise, deal, speculate and calculate' into a 'boundless infinity'.[88]

The housewife's position, reinforced by isolation and subordination to her husband's authority, produced the feeling that it was right for her to adjust to the lack of calculability, indeed that this adjustment could be a moral virtue. Far from seeking efficiency, it was 'better' to prepare food by hand, to use a hair sieve rather than a moule, and the use of tinned foods carried a moral stigma which lingers on to our day (a separate issue from both taste and nutrition but often confused in discussions of this point). Such attitudes of resignation and passivity are the antithesis of an entrepreneurial ethic; indeed they were positively viewed by both men and women as a *protection* of society from the full effects of that ethic.

Nowhere is this attitude more evident than in the lack of pressure to rationalize the physical plant of the house and in the reluctance to invest in basic equipment such as hot running water.[89] This fatalism is prominent in literature for housewives. A typical statement is by Fay Inchfawn ('the Poet Laureate of the Home'):

Within My House
First, there's the entrance, narrow and so small,
The hat-stand seems to fill the tiny hall;
That staircase too, has such an awkward bend,
The carpet rucks, and rises up on end!
Then, all the rooms are cramped and close together;
And there's a musty smell in rainy weather.
Yes, and it makes the daily work go hard
To have the only tap across the yard.
These creaking doors, these draughts, this battered paint,
Would try, I think the temper of a saint.

However, while washing the breakfast dishes she stops grumbling and starts to pray:

'Lord' (thus I prayed), 'it matters not at all
That my poor home is ill-arranged and small;
I, not the house, am straightened Lord, 'tis I!
Enlarge my foolish heart, that by-and-by
I may look up with such a radiant face
Thou shalt have glory even in this place;
And when I slip, or stumble unaware
In carrying water up this awkward stair
Then keep me sweet, and teach me day by day
To treat with patience Thy appointed way.
As for the house . . . Lord, let it be my part
To walk within it with a perfect heart.'[90]

The Application of Science and Technology

The ethos which I have been discussing was not only linked to rational calculation in every sphere of life, but it also promoted a utilitarian approach to most problems, an 'insistence on empiricism and experimentation, the expenditure of physical energy, the equation of contemplation with idleness, the handling of material objects with industry';[91] in short, a set of characteristics congruent with both a scientific outlook and good housewifery. The application of science to production whether directly in textile manufacture or, for example, in the improvements in coach construction and road surfacing at the end of the eighteenth century, were characteristic of many spheres of life. But household management, even though it was partially based on many empirically provided dicta, never progressed very far beyond the 'cook book' (sic) stage of scientific development. To this day housework remains an art, making use of a mixture of traditional maxims, empirically proved rules of thumb as well as more fully 'scientific' procedures;[92] e.g. 'to take fruit stains out of table linen, boil 3 pints of water with 4 tablespoons of lemon juice, steep for four hours, rinse and dry in the open air' could equally well have come from an eighteenth-century manual, a nineteenth-century cook book or a twentieth-century woman's magazine.

Not only was the fundamental contradiction discussed in the last section an important element in the limited application of science and technology, but the predominant forms of household authority relationships also blocked any such development. Within the private household, housework was done in accordance with the wishes and beliefs of the superior. In the case of servants, part of the definition of service was the legal requirement to do the work in the way that the superior prescribed.[93] Hierarchy had to be maintained as well as order in a material sense. For example, it must have been known by experience that soaking very dirty pans in water overnight made it both much easier and much quicker to clean them, but it was the rule that every single pan had to be scoured and polished and put away before the servants were allowed to finish work, no matter how late the hour, and young scullery maids could be hauled out of bed to scrub the pans if they had neglected this duty.[94]

A scientifically based criterion of cleanliness (in the sense of destroying all bacteria as in a hospital) was not the standard of the family wash. What, then, is cleanliness in, for example, clothing: how is it to be defined: how clean is clean? In the nineteenth century the internal organization of a household on traditional lines came into conflict with the demands of the external economy and no objective scientific level of cleanliness was, or could be, invoked to settle the issue. Considerable strains were put on water supplies and tempers because:

They that wash on Monday
Have all the week to dry
They that wash on Tuesday
Are not so much awry
They that wash on Wednesday
Are not so much to blame
They that wash on Thursday
Wash for very shame
They that wash on Friday
Wash in sorry need
They that wash on Saturday
Are lazy sluts indeed.[95]

Contrast this ubiquitous rhyme with an excerpt from an investigation into laundries:

The washing does not arrive at the laundry, as a rule till Monday afternoon, and must be returned on Friday. Hence the necessity of working young girls till 10, 11, or even 12 at night. This argument exalts a domestic custom to the dignity of a law of nature. There is nothing in the constitution of the universe which demands that dirty linen should be collected on Monday, washed on Tuesday, dried on Wednesday, ironed on Thursday and sent home clean on Friday. There is no reason in the nature of things why families with a normal supply of linen should not have their 'washing' called for on a certain day of the week and returned on the same day in the following week.[96]

Again, is it scientific disease control that is the rationale for an affluent linen cupboard (*c*.1890s) to be marked 'guests, adults, children, servants and sides-to-middle' (for illness)? Or is this another instance of status and ceremonial segregation and the creation of categories which required a large investment in money and labour? The resistance to the installation of more efficient stoves and heating apparatus has been the despair of engineers from Count Rumford in the 1790s onwards, but until very recently the open coal fire remained one of the most potent symbols of the boundary between the private domain and the world, the focus of hearth and home.[97]

Really fundamental changes in food preparation came from outside the private home, from, for example, people like Alexis Soyer, who significantly was a chef first in a club and then in the army of the Crimea, where his innovations in army cooking were as important as Nightingale's in medicine. What must be kept in mind is that technical improvements in equipment, such as those exemplified by the use of the small electric motor, are not of the same order as a fundamental change in the organization or aims of housework. A washing-machine may be used, for example, to produce more efficiently a clean, white linen tablecloth for every meal. Yet the use of the cloth is still for ceremony and display, a purpose whose effectiveness can, in turn, by its nature never be subject to scientific tests of efficiency.[98]

How women were introduced to scientific ideas and how the latter were absorbed into the women's conception of her role in the nineteenth century have all to be explored. An organization such as the Ladies' Sanitary Association has left records showing how closely ideas of physical cleanliness were related to ideas about social and moral purity. The assimilation of scientific ideas also involved reconciling the need to teach domestic skills to girls who, according to the ideology of the time, were domestic creatures by nature. The whole domestic economy movement which started as early as the 1870s was an attempt to deal with a situation produced by the primacy of social goals among the middle class and lack of domestic experience of working-class girls employed in factories. It was couched in terms of a return to the traditional skills, a girl's birthright, which had been somehow taken away from her by the over-civilizing effects of modern life. In fact, girls in neither class were necessarily 'by nature' fitted to carry out domestic tasks and needed to be equipped to cope with *new* demands created by higher standards of living on every level of society. (If you don't sleep on beds, you don't have to know how to make beds.)

In its attempts to become more and more 'scientific', the growing unreality of the domestic economy movement culminated in the idea of the kitchen as a workshop, in the 1920s. The 'time and motion' study approach of Frederick Taylor was imported from the United States in an effort to maintain the standards of middle-class households faced with a drastic shortage of labour.[99]

The Twentieth Century: The Importance of Childcare

In middle- and even upper-class households some of these contradictions between rationalization and non-calculable ends began to be exposed in the decades just before and increasingly after the First World War, when domestic servants were harder to recruit and more difficult to control. Family and social life had to be simplified, tasks had to be combined, and ceremonial polish neglected. The mistress of the household now faced more directly the problems of food preparation, dirt and refuse control, as well as childcare. Alternative investment in technical improvements or domestic service began to be more closely appraised, but the outcome remained uncertain until lack of servants forced a change of goals. In 1932, the upper-class journal Queen solemnly ran an article to query whether it was worth the investment in gadgetry to continue entertaining on Sunday evening which the maid had acquired the right to take off:

> You can't entertain without a maid and look after your guests as you would like if you have not reduced catering to a fine art. The equipment needed includes a dumb waiter, dinner wagon, electric coffee percolator, electric toaster, table cooker and refrigerator.[100]

Because of these threats, earlier generations had made more serious moves in several directions to change radically the pattern of middle-class life. One was the growth of service flats and residential hotels. (Some upper-middle-class men had always been able to live, at least part of the time, in colleges, chambers, clubs and barracks, while middle- and some working-class men could live as lodgers and thus be 'serviced' without the complications of marriage.) On the fringe, there were people such as Edward Carpenter who tried to pare and simplify domestic life to a bare minimum by a Thoreauian retreat from the world.[101] John Brett, a minor artist and architect, designed and built his own flat-roofed, centrally heated, completely 'labour-saving' house in Putney in the 1870s.[102] Many schemes for various forms of cooperative living and shared services were proposed in this period, although few were actually tried. Clementina Black, in 1919, urged municipal cleaning services which she called, even then, 'home help'.[103] Yet none of these proved viable on a larger scale, and through the twentieth century middle-class housewives carried on trying at first to maintain considerable ceremony, particularly in crucial boundary areas like answering the front door and mealtime ritual. Working-class wives were also caught up in the pattern: the hearth-stoning and black-leading may have faded in significance but other cleansing activities have taken their place: the shining sinks, polished floors and sparkling windows of the media image.

It is now commonplace that childcare has moved into the forefront of house-keeping as fewer children are born but more of them are expected to reach adult-hood. Previously in all sections of society childcare was, in a sense, subordinate to other household aims and activities. When the standard of living was high enough not to have to make use of child labour, children tended to be cordoned off into areas, times and activities which were separated from the main concerns of the household, and the whole philosophy of childcare was one of containment. Middle-class child-training in the nineteenth century, in keeping with the other patterns I have discussed, placed great reliance on rigidity of routine, and segregation by time and place. Obviously this was only completely possible with specialized servants to give their whole attention to the children but it was the principle that applied to all childcare. A nursemaid recalled in the 1950s that changes in discipline are the most striking of all:

> not that we were strict with the children, but they led such quiet lives, and had so little time to themselves. You see, with the two walks (morning and afternoon), meals regular as clockwork and the hour downstairs from which they were back in the nursery by six o'clock sharp . . . in a well-run nursery with everything to time out-breaks of naughtiness were rare and soon suppressed.[104]

In the 1920s and 1930s it took a scientifically-based psychology and the insti-tution of progressive schools to rediscover and reintroduce the idea that children's joy in unbound limbs – bare feet, ungloved hands and bared heads – was important for their health and development. A central part of this educational reform was play with dirt and water in the carefully provided sand-pit and paddle-pool.

The change in views of early childhood care, and the accompanying concern with imagination and language formation, have brought out conflicts *within* the basic constituents of housework, i.e. boundary maintenance through dirt control and tidiness, the latter often incompatible with the socializing of young children when given a new tolerance of their 'disruptive' behaviour.[105] On the surface, changes in children's clothes, particularly for girls – from starched white pinafores to blue jeans – illustrates this development. A closer look, however, shows that the more casual clothes still have to be kept 'Persil' clean, and while all housewives are torn between these aims there seem to be important class and educational differ-ences in the tasks which housewives favour.[106]

Conclusion

Despite some public shifts in attitudes, it is still women who are seen today as basically responsible for servicing members of the family, protecting them from the pollution of dirt, waste products and untidiness, for transforming the raw into the cooked; and for transforming 'little savages' into civilized adults. In the vast majority of cases it is women (particularly mothers, but also the women responsible for the elderly and chronically sick) who peel the potatoes, wash, sort and put away the socks, mop up the vomit, change the nappies and the sheets. These activities are still performed for love (and support). Mary Stott asked in a *Guardian* article ('Are You a Slave or a Slut?'):

> When you buy a new piece of equipment – washing machine, dishwasher, etc. . . . is it because it will save money, save time or because you rather fancy it? Do you cost your time in relation to the purchase – or for instance in relation to whether you take the washing to the launderette?

At the end of the article she gives no answer, because, I believe, there is no answer.[107]

How much longer will this continue? Are our concerns with pollution and boundary maintenance so fundamental that women will always remain within the cluster, housewife? I do not know, but it is significant that J.K. Galbraith gives a central place to women and their role in what he coyly calls 'the administration of consumption', i.e. housework.[108] Such recognition is only the first step. A great deal more needs to be learnt about how such patterns evolved in the past in order to help understand how they operate now. One thing is certain, however. Historians, economists and, above all, sociologists can no longer go on turning their attention to everything *but* the kitchen sink.

Notes

1 Cf., however, Suzanne Gail, 'The Housewife', in Ronald Fraser, ed., *Work: Twenty Personal Accounts* (Penguin, Harmondsworth, 1968), pp. 140–55; and the work of Helena Znaniecki Lopata, *Occupation: Housewife* (Oxford University Press, New York, 1971); Catherine Hall, 'The History of the Housewife', *Spare Rib*, no. 26 (1974); and Ann Oakley, *Housewife* (Allen Lane, London, 1974) and her *The Sociology of Housework* (Robertson, London, 1974).

2 For an example of the usual assumption that work can only be located in a 'workplace', see Dorothy Wedderburn and Christine Craig, 'Relative Deprivation in Work', in Dorothy Wedderburn, ed., *Poverty, Inequality and Class Structure* (Cambridge University Press, Cambridge, 1974), pp. 141–64.

3 Jean Gardiner, 'Political Economy of Domestic Labour in Capitalist Society', in Diana Leonard Barker and Sheila Allen, eds, *Dependence and Exploitation in Work and Marriage* (Longman, London, 1976), pp. 109–20; Wally Seccombe, 'The Housewife and her Labour under Capitalism', *New Left Review*, no. 83 (1974), pp. 3–24.

4 Leonore Davidoff, Jean L'Esperance and Howard Newby, 'Landscape with Figures: Home and Community in English Society', this volume, ch. 2.

5 Seccombe, 'The Housewife and her Labour under Capitalism'.

6 These ideas on purity and its relation to women's work have developed in discussion with Jean L'Esperance.

7 Leonore Davidoff, 'Mastered for Life: Servant and Wife in Victorian and Edwardian England', this volume, ch. 1.

8   Margaret Mead, *Male and Female: A Study of the Sexes in a Changing World* (Penguin, Harmondsworth, 1970).
9   Alice Clark, *Working Life of Women in the Seventeenth Century* (Frank Cass, London, 1968). In fourteenth- and fifteenth-century England upper-class boys began their apprenticeship by serving in aristocratic households, service which included laying out body linen, fetching water and emptying slops; F.S. Furnivall, 'For to Serve a Lord', in *Boke of Nurture*, ed. John Russell (London, 1888).
10 Aban Mehta, *The Domestic Servant Class* (Bombay, 1960).
11 Louis Dumont, *Homo Hierarchicus: The Caste System and its Implications* (Paladin, London, 1972), p. 183.
12 The Pic Nic Society dates from 1802 – the more formal middle- and upper-class dining etiquette became, the more attractive eating *au naturel* seemed (G. Battiscombe, *English Picnics* [Harvill Press, London, 1949]).
13 Mary Douglas, 'Deciphering a Meal', *Daedalus*, no. 101 (1972).
14 One of the sharpest breaks between the 'respectable' and 'rough' elements in the nineteenth-century English working class was mealtime behaviour; P. Thompson and T. Thompson, 'Work and Life before 1918' (SSRC Project, University of Essex).
15 Mary Douglas, *Purity and Danger: An Analysis of Concepts of Pollution and Taboo* (Penguin, Harmondsworth, 1970), p. 12.
16 Ibid., p. 48.
17 The emphasis in this essay on women's role in boundary maintenance should not blind us to the sheer power of men over women, power partly derived from physical strength but mostly from the vulnerability of women with very young children – which is, in part at least, the cause of their powerlessness. In this way they are locked into their subordinate position (J. Brown, 'A Note on the Division of Labour by Sex', *American Anthropologist* [1970], p. 1073).
18 Sherry Ortner, 'Is Female to Male as Nature Is to Culture?', in Michelle Zimbalist Rosaldo and Louise Lamphere, eds, *Woman, Culture and Society* (Stanford University Press, Stanford, 1974).
19 Ortner, 'Is Female to Male as Nature Is to Culture?'
20 Douglas, *Purity and Danger*, p. 118.
21 'Both Durkheim and Marx have shown us that the structure of society's classifications and frames reveals both the distribution of power and the principles of social control' (B. Bernstein, 'On the Classification and Framing of Educational Knowledge', in Richard Brown, ed., *Knowledge, Education and Cultural Change: Papers in the Sociology of Education* [British Sociological Association and Tavistock, London, 1973]).
22 Dumont, *Homo Hierarchicus*.
23 S.J. Tambiah, 'From Varna to Caste through Mixed Unions', in Jack Goody, ed., *The Character of Kinship* (Cambridge University Press, Cambridge, 1973).
24 M.N. Srinivas, *Religion and Society among the Coorgs of South India* (Asia Publishing House, New York, 1965).
25 Tambiah, 'From Varna to Caste through Mixed Unions'.
26 Harold Perkin, *The Origins of Modern English Society 1780–1880* (Routledge & Kegan Paul, London, 1969); E.P. Thompson, *The Making of the English Working Class* (Gollancz, London, 1964).
27 Leonore Davidoff, *The Best Circles: Society, Etiquette and the Season* (Century Hutchinson, London, 1986).
28 Howard Newby, 'The Deferential Dialectic', *Comparative Studies in Society and History*, vol. 17 (1975), pp. 139–64.
29 The first chapter in a little handbook (*c.*1860) on *How to Behave – A Pocket Manual of Etiquette* is completely taken up with care of the hands and 'a lady can always be known by her hands'. Hence the whole panoply of the Victorian 'language of gloves', e.g. a

pair of white gloves for a maiden's funeral wreath, keeping one glove of a lover, etc. A.J. Munby is a case of this cultural preoccupation becoming a private obsession; see Derek Hudson, *Munby, Man of Two Worlds: The Life and Diaries of Arthur J. Munby, 1828–1910* (John Murray, London, 1972).

30 A late eighteenth-century country gentry family living in County Durham had lice, fleas and ringworm. Yet they spent part of every year in London, for the season, where the father was in Parliament (Ethel Colburn-Mayne, *The Life and Letters of Anne Isabella, Lady Noel Byron* [Constable, London, 1929]).

31 George Rosen, 'Disease, Debility and Death', in H.J. Dyos and Michael Wolff eds, *The Victorian City: Images and Realities*, vol. 2. (Routledge & Kegan Paul, London, 1973).

32 Douglas, *Purity and Danger*, p. 44.

33 William Cobbett, 'Advice to Young Men', in *Cobbett's England: A Selection from the Writings of William Cobbett*, ed. John Derry (Folio Society, London, 1968), p. 170.

34 Anon., *Home Truths for Home Peace, or 'Muddle' Defeated* (Edinburgh, 1852).

35 Mircea Eliade, 'Water and Water Symbolism', in *Patterns in Comparative Religion* (Sheed & Ward, New York, 1958), p. 188.

36 Davidoff, L'Esperance and Newby, 'Landscape with Figures'.

37 Richard L. Schoenwald, 'Training Urban Man: A Hypothesis about the Sanitary Movement', in Dyos and Wolff, eds, *The Victorian City*, vol. 2.

38 George Orwell, *The Road to Wigan Pier* (Secker & Warburg, London, 1959), p. 129.

39 Dyos and Wolff, eds, *The Victorian City*.

40 G. Himmelfarb, 'Mayhew's Poor: A Problem of Identity', *Victorian Studies*, March 1971.

41 David Lockwood, *The Blackcoated Worker: A Study in Class Consciousness*, (Allen & Unwin, London, 1958), pp. 122–5.

42 Stan Shipley, *Club Life and Socialism in Mid-Victorian London* (Ruskin History Workshop Pamphlet, no. 5, London, c.1972).

43 G.M Young, *Victorian England: Portrait of an Age* (Oxford University Press, Oxford, 1966), p. 7.

44 Gareth Stedman Jones, *Outcast London: A Study in the Relationship between Classes in Victorian Society* (Clarendon Press, Oxford, 1971).

45 Over the years 'airing' has come to mean both letting air circulate and warming or drying. For example one puts ironed clothes back outside on the line for a final 'airing' or 'airs' them around the fire.

46 Davidoff, *The Best Circles*.

47 Werner Sombart, 'Middle-Class Virtues', in *The Quintessence of Capitalism: A Study of the History and Psychology of the Modern Business Man*, trans. M. Epstein (Howard Fertig, New York, 1967).

48 Max Weber, *Economy and Society: An Outline of Interpretive Sociology*, vol. I, ed. Guenther Roth and Claus Wittich (Bedminster Press, New York, 1968).

49 Under the system of double-entry book-keeping *everything* that is encompassed by business activity is accounted in monetary terms: 'The essence of the double-entry system is that the value recorded in the accounts shall always reflect the balance sheet equation. Hence for every debit entry there must always be a corresponding credit entry of equal magnitude, and for every credit an equal debit' (*Chambers Encyclopedia*, vol. I, p. 38).

50 Max Weber, *The Protestant Ethic and the Spirit of Capitalism* (Allen & Unwin, London, 1971).

51 Werner Sombart, 'Medieval and Modern Commercial Enterprise', in F.C. Lane, ed., *Enterprise and Secular Change: readings in Economic History* (Allen & Unwin, London, 1953).

52   John Robert Russell, Thirteenth Duke of Bedford, *A Silver-Plated Spoon* (Cassell, London, 1959); Alan Armstrong, *Stability and Change in an English County Town: A Social Study of York, 1801–51* (Cambridge University Press, Cambridge, 1974), p. 189.

53   It might be argued that the aim of the household is to expand over time through generations, or at best to endure. However, except in very specific cases as in the aristocracy, this does not seem to follow empirically, or, according to economists, theoretically (M. Bruce Johnson, *Household Behaviour: Consumption, Income and Wealth* [Penguin, Harmondsworth, 1971]).

54   Government Statistical Office, *Social Trends*, no. 4 (HMSO, London, 1973), pp. 12–13.

55   The resistance to rational calculation as part of woman's mission may be one of the reasons why girls are 'naturally' less able to do mathematics and technical subjects in *all* modern societies.

56   Thompson, *The Making of the English Working Class.*

57   Seccombe, 'The Housewife and her Labour under Capitalism', p. 9.

58   Other economists use the idea of 'non-pecuniary income' but, I believe, the same objections could be raised to its application. Under systems of barter – of services as well as goods – counting and recording do take place and must make use of some sort of unit of accounting, but surely the point is that this type of unit is not transferable from its very local associations.

59   Angela John, 'Pit Brow Lasses – A Test Case for Female Labour' (unpublished paper, 1973).

60   W.A. Henderson, *The Housekeeper's Instructor; or, Universal Family Cook* (Stratford, London, 1975); Hannah Glasse, *The Art of Cookery Made Plain and Easy* (London, 1748).

61   A Lady, *The Home Book; or, Young Housekeeper's Assistant* (London, 1829), p. 15a.

62   William Kitchiner, *The Housekeeper's Oracle: A Plain and Easy Plan of Keeping Accurate Accounts of the Expenses of Housekeeping* (Whittaker, London, 1825), p. 7.

63   Christina Hole, *The English Housewife in the Seventeenth Century* (Chatto & Windus, London, 1953); Rosamund Bayne-Powell, *Housekeeping in the Eighteenth Century* (John Murray, London, 1956).

64   William Kitchiner, *The Cook's Oracle: Containing Receipts for Plain Cookery on the most Economical Plan for Private Families, the Quantity of each Article is Accurately stated by Weight and Measure: being the Actual Experiments Investigated in the Kitchen of Wm. Kitchiner* (M.D. Whittaker, London, 1823), p. 30.

65   Davidoff, *The Best Circles.*

66   M. Young, Common Place Book, 1828–1840, 300.01; 48. 85/3 (London Museum Library).

67   Anne Vernon, *Three Generations: The Fortunes of a Yorkshire Family* (Jarrolds, London, 1966).

68   Tambiah, 'From Varna to Caste through Mixed Unions', p. 15.

69   Jane Loudon, *The Lady's Country Companion; or, How to Enjoy a Country Life Rationally* (London, 1845).

70   Mrs Rundell (A Lady), *A New System of Domestic Cookery* (London, 1845), p. xi.

71   *The Receipt Book of Elizabeth Raper, and a Portion of her Cipher Journal 1756–1770*, ed. Bantle Grant (Nonesuch Press, London, 1924).

72   Dorothy E. Smith, 'Women, the Family and Corporate Capitalism', in Marylee Stephenson, ed., *Women in Canada* (New Press, Toronto, 1973), pp. 21–2.

73   Clementina Black, *Married Women's Work* (Women's Industrial Council, London, 1915). This goes some way to explaining why, despite the introduction of labour-saving devices, time spent on housework has not decreased substantially in recent

years. None of the housewives in Ann Oakley's study was working less than 40 hours a week, many were working 70 to 80 hours, four were working over 90 while the longest working week was 105 hours (Oakley, *The Sociology of Housework*).

74 Davidoff, 'Mastered for Life'.

75 Hence the meaninglessness of recent attempts to 'cost' a wife. In the US, for example, the average housewife works a 99.6 hour week doing twelve different jobs worth $8,285 per annum, or collectively $250 billion a year; 35 per cent of the GNP (Chase Manhattan Bank, 'What Is a Wife Worth?').

76 *Census of Population and Occupations*, General Report, *c.*2174, vol. CVIII (1904), p. 76.

77 Anonymous MS, courtesy of Anna Davin.

78 Seccombe, 'The Housewife and her Labour under Capitalism', p. 13.

79 The existence of credit systems – from being carried on the tradesmen's books in the middle class to the pawnshop in the working class – complicates this picture but does not fundamentally alter the point.

80 Sidney Webb and Beatrice Webb, *English Poor Law Policy* (Longman Green, London, 1910), p. 103.

81 James Littlejohn, *Westrigg: The Sociology of a Cheviot Parish* (Routledge & Kegan Paul, London, 1963), p. 123.

82 L. Oren, 'The Welfare of Women in Laboring Families in England 1860–1950', *Feminist Studies*, 1 (winter–spring 1973).

83 This emphasizes the importance of the consumer cooperative movement, although this only affected the regularly employed, mainly in the north.

84 Anon., *The Home Book of Household Economy* (London, 1854).

85 Lawrence Stone, *The Crisis of the Aristocracy, 1558–1641* (Oxford University Press, Oxford, 1967).

86 Julien Freund, *The Sociology of Max Weber*, (Allen Lane, London, 1968).

87 Oakley, *The Sociology of Housework*.

88 Sombart, 'Middle-Class Virtues'.

89 In 1945, 20 per cent of those in the lowest income groups (below £160 per annum) had to heat water for washing clothes in pans and kettles on a fire, stove or range. I am not underestimating the effects of tenancy patterns here, but I believe that landlords' interests were the immediate not the ultimate cause of this neglect – a point which can be strengthened by looking at the amenities provided in council houses (Political and Economic Planning, *The Market for Household Appliances* [Wartime social survey, Heating of Dwellings Inquiry] [Oxford University Press, Oxford, 1945]).

90 Fay Inchfawn, *The Verse-book of a Homely Woman* (Girls' Own Paper, London, 1920).

91 Robert K. Merton, *Science, Technology and Society in Seventeenth-Century England* (Howard Fertig, New York, 1970), p. 93.

92 A. Ravetz, 'Modern Technology and an Ancient Occupation: Housework in Present-Day Society', *Technology and Culture*, vol. 6 (Society for the History of Technology, University of Chicago Press, 1965).

93 Personal control is crucial to the definition of who is a servant; 'a person is under the control of another if he is bound to obey the orders of that other, not only as to which work he shall execute but also as to the details of the work and the manner of its execution' (A.S. Diamond, *The Law of Master and Servant* [Stevens & Son, London, 1946], p. 1).

94 Jean Rennie, *Every Other Sunday: The Autobiography of a Kitchen-maid* (Arthur Barker, London, 1955).

95 Nursery rhymes are an important source for the traditional sexual division of labour. 'It can be safely stated that the overwhelming majority of nursery rhymes were not in the first place composed for children' (Iona Opie and Peter Opie, *The Oxford Dictionary of Nursery Rhymes* [Clarendon Press, Oxford, 1951]).

96   Fabian Society, *Life in the Laundry*, Fabian Tract, no. 112 (July 1902).
97   A. Ravetz, 'The Victorian Coal Kitchen and its Reformers', *Victorian Studies*, June 1968; T.P. Teale, *Economy of Coal in House Fires* (Churchill, London, 1883).
98   'For purposes of the theoretical definition of technical rationality, it is wholly indifferent whether the product of a technical process is in any sense useful'; and Weber cites the example of a supremely efficient machine for producing oxygen; M. Weber, *Economy and Society*, vol. 1.
99   Christine Frederick, *Scientific Management in the Home* (Routledge, London, 1920).
100 'Sunday Night Supper', *Queen* (October 26, 1932).
101 Edward Carpenter, *My Days and Dreams: Being Autobiographical Notes* (Allen & Unwin, London, 1916).
102 'John Brett (1831–1902)', *Dictionary of National Biography*, Twentieth-Century Supplement (1911).
103 'Le Ménage', *Queen* (March 29, 1919).
104 Noel Streatfeild, ed., *The Day before Yesterday: First-hand Stories of Fifty Years Ago* (Collins, London, 1956).
105 John Newson and Elizabeth Newson, *Infant Care in an Urban Community* (Allen & Unwin, London, 1963).
106 Oakley, *Housewife*.
107 In 1973 a French manufacturer began a sales campaign to push paper nappies in the English market – his efforts were unrewarding and the results of a market survey showed that resistance was not only on the basis of cost but also on the belief that disposable nappies were not 'really clean'. Significantly, while a commercial nappy service has been attempted in large cities, a municipal nappy service has never even been proposed.
108 John Kenneth Galbraith, *Economics and the Public Purpose* (Houghton Mifflin, Boston, 1973).

4

Class and Gender in Victorian England: The Case of Hannah Cullwick and A.J. Munby

> Her strong, bare, sinewy arms and rugged hands
> Blacken'd with labour; and her peasant dress
> Rude, coarse in texture, yet most picturesque,
> And suited to her station and her ways;
> All these, transfigured by that sentiment
> Of lowly contrast to the man she served,
> Grew dignified with beauty and herself
> A noble working woman, not ashamed
> Of what her work had made her
>
> A grace, a glow of quick intelligence
> And ardour, such as only Nature gives
> And only gives through Man . . .

A.J. Munby, *Ann Morgan's Love: A Pedestrian Poem*, 1896

Symbolism and Reality: The Creation of a World-View

In investigating the connections between class, gender and sexuality a detailed study of one case can be a useful check on either prescriptive literature or listings of household and family structure.[1] This essay attempts to show how the themes of fantasy and the manipulation of symbols in one such study can throw light on the dynamics of a whole society. But first it is necessary to look at the meaning of class and gender divisions at a more general level and at the mechanisms by which they were created.[2]

The nineteenth century was the time when traditional social boundaries were being eclipsed by the rapid development of a market economy and the creation of a 'class' society. All social relationships including gender divisions were affected by these changes. During this period, class designations came to carry gender overtones. The status characteristics associated with *gentility*, for example, differed for men and women; and the concepts *manhood* and *womanhood* which are peculiar to the nineteenth century have very different resonances. (It was on the basis of claims to *manhood* that the independent respectable working man petitioned for both a living wage and the right of entry to full citizenship through the franchise.)

What makes the analysis of the interaction of class and gender so difficult, however, is that the same forces which produced a world-view dividing the society between masculine and feminine, working class and middle (upper) class, urban and rural also separated physicality, e.g. bodily functions in general and sexuality in particular, from the public gaze. This is an example of the privatization we have come to associate with the development of industrial capitalism and was part of a changing view of men's and women's positions in the cosmos and of their relation to Nature.

The world-view of Victorian society which has been handed down to us was mostly the creation of those persons in positions of power who had the resources as well as the need to propagate their central position. Within this world-view, those categories of people who are furthest away from the centres of decision-making are ranked accordingly; and they are also visualized in images that emphasize their powerlessness and degradation as well as their potentially threatening and polluting effects on those persons closer to the centre who exploit their labour and their persons. Middle-class Victorians, as middle-class persons in many other societies, expressed this powerlessness by associating peripheral groups with physiological origins.[3] This association was then used in a circular fashion to lock such people into menial positions for life.

> The unskilled, uncreative occupations whose incumbents order very little, handle brute matter as brute matter, express little that is vital and do not penetrate intellectually into the nature of anything, rank very low. The occupations whose incumbents handle only the detritus of man's existence and do so only by manipulating it directly come lowest.[4]

It should be remembered, however, that it is not the tasks themselves that degrade; it is the power of the dominant groups which defines what tasks are to be considered degrading and then forces the incumbents of socially constructed categories to perform these tasks.[5]

The degradation of peripheral groups was also expressed in body images, for Victorian social commentators, including early sociologists like Herbert Spencer, often used a body metaphor in an effort to stress the organic nature of their society. This image was set in explicit contrast to both the mechanistic visions of the eighteenth century and the conflict models put forward by early Victorian radicals. According to the organic view, society was able to operate as system because of its hierarchically ordered but interdependent parts. The adult middle-class (or aristocratic) man, representing the governing or ruling group, was seen as the Head of the social system as well as the Head of his household which was in turn a society in miniature. The Hands were the unthinking, unfeeling 'doers', without characteristics of sex, age or other identity. (The implication of the word 'Hands' for workers is mercilessly castigated by Dickens in his novel *Hard Times*.) Because work was central to Victorian society, the implication was that middle-class men did brain work while the hands did menial work. Middle-class women represented the emotions, the Heart, or sometimes the Soul, seat of morality and tenderness. Women performed these functions as keepers of the Hearth in the Home, and here we find a body/house connection which figured widely in the Victorian world-view.

The final section of this mental map was not as often or as openly expressed, for middle-class Victorians shrank from naming their own bodily functions. Still, Victorians visualized the 'Nether Regions' of society which, by their definition, were inhabited by the criminal classes, paupers, beggars and the work-shy as 'stagnant pools of moral filth' comprising the 'effluvia of our wretched cities'. Historians, in fact, have recently drawn attention to the disturbing equations made by commentators, such as Mayhew, between the sanitary and the human condition, to 'the cloacal imagery of the social investigators [who] pursued the social "offal" and "moral refuse"'.[6] Prostitutes, who were seen as the potential source of both physical and moral contagion for middle-class men, were also cast into this region. Defenders of prostitution saw it as a necessary institution which acted as a giant sewer, drawing away the distasteful but inevitable waste products of male lustfulness, leaving the middle-class household and middle-class ladies pure and unsullied. None of the inhabitants of this twilight zone could ever aspire to be included in the 'body politic' but had to be hidden and controlled whenever possible. Indeed, by the third quarter of the nineteenth century, there were drives to segregate certain groups by sexual designations as well as by class labels. The separating out of a criminal class was followed by the creation of a homosexual subculture and a hardening of the lines between professional and casual prostitution.[7]

In keeping with this body imagery, certain groups were seen to be closer to nature than the rational adult middle-class man who dominated educated opinion. These groups included not only women, children, servants and many other elements in the working class, but also natives in the colonies and by extension all non-whites. Their supposed affinity with nature also helps to explain the animal analogies which were often applied to them in literary writing as well as popular sayings. The position of animals, of course, had changed during the growth of industrial capitalism. From being the central source of energy and production, the 'first circle of mediation between man and nature', the relationship between man and animal became much more metaphoric; and in this latter stage two themes were always stressed: what animals and man had in common and what differentiated them.[8] ('Man' is here put forward as a generic term but quite clearly the implication is that it really referred to adult men, preferably middle-class educated men.) The belief in an organic hierarchy, finally, provided the basis for scientific theories about biological divisions which were refurbished within a Darwinian evolutionary framework.[9]

Within this framework, sexuality – particularly male sexuality – became the focus of a more generalized fear of disorder and of a continuing battle to tame natural forces.[10] The social as well as psychic importance of this focus is clear in Max Weber's analysis, which considers sexuality as a non-social, even anti-social force:

> ... the drive that most firmly binds man to the animal level. ... Rational ascetic, alertness, self-control and methodical planning of life are threatened the most by the peculiar irrationality of the sexual act which is ultimately and uniquely unsusceptible to rational organization ... the more rationalized the rest of society becomes, the more eroticized sexuality becomes.[11]

The effort of adult middle-class men to maintain their positions of power within the society as a whole and the 'little kingdoms' of their own households, as well as in regard to their own sexuality, seems to have created a kind of 'psychological backlash' within their own personalities. They combined excessive fears of pollution, disloyalty and disorder from subordinates with a desperate search for a moral order which would help to control all three, as well as the immoral forces of the market. Indeed, with the help of religion, the restraint of male sexuality came to be seen as a great feat of self-control, one of the hallmarks of middle-class gentility. But this was a gentility reserved for middle-class men. The working class and native blacks supposedly allowed their sexuality to spill out over their total lives, diverting them from the goal of achievement through work, wasting their energies and draining their vital forces. In Victorian language they displayed a lack of self-control resulting in incontinence.[12]

One well-documented solution to the problem of controlling middle-class male sexuality had been to see middle-class women (ladies), particularly within marriage (the golden chain that binds society together), as agents of salvation,[13] and with the crisis in religious faith, the image of a desexualized Madonna took on increasing saliency.[14] Madonnas, however, imply Magadalenes; and Victorian culture and social institutions provided both. A dual vision of women was already available, of course, as a legacy from classical culture, a culture inculcated through the curriculum of the grammar and public school, which emphasized hierarchical and misogynist interpretations of society.[15] The dualistic view of women was also a keystone of Christian theology, which justified the subordination of female to male on the grounds of woman's potential 'carnality'. Since femaleness was equated with the body, so the female must be subordinated to the male 'as the flesh must be subject to spirit in the right ordering of nature'.[16] Victorian women, therefore, were not only divided between working class and middle class, they were divided between 'ladies' and 'women', categories which signified as much gender as economic and social meaning. In viewing Victorian women it is as if we are looking at a picture through a double exposure.

Indeed, the dual vision of women, as woman and lady, becomes mixed with other polarities such as those between white and black, familiar and foreign, home and Empire. In a perceptive discussion of these polarities, as expressed in literature, Cleo McNelly cites the following:

> . . . [in] the binary opposition between here and there, home and abroad . . . home represents civilization, but also order, constraint, sterility, pain and *ennui*, while native culture, the far pole of the myth, represents nature, chaos, fecundity, power and joy. The home culture is, moreover, associated always with the ability to understand by seeing, abstractly, while the other culture is associated with black, with the sense of touch, the ability to know by feeling, from within. The far pole of the tropical journey is indeed the *heart* of darkness.
>
> At either end of this journey stand two figures, each of which has a profound mythological past: the white woman at home and her polar opposite, the black woman abroad. These figures come from a long and well-entrenched tradition in the West. The first of them, the white woman, is not only Beatrice, she is Rowena and even Mrs Ramsay as well. At her best she is 'a star to every wand'ring bark,' gentle, courteous and endowed with the immortality of the gods. At her worst she is Virginia Woolf's 'angel in the house,' the angel of death and sterility. In either case she tends to be sexless and *familiar* in every sense of the word. She is mother, sister or wife rather than mistress or friend.
>
> The second figure, the black woman, is her mirror image. She is the ever-present exogamous mate, the dark lady of the sonnets, savage, sexual and eternally other. At her best she is a 'natural woman,' sensuous, dignified and fruitful. At her worst she is a witch, representing loss of self, loss of consciousness and loss of meaning. In either case she is most emphatically *not* familiar. She is an unknown quantity, and in her strangeness lies, both her value as an object and her ability to fascinate the white man.[17]

These are stereotypes which are deliberately cast in terms of opposites. There cannot be one without the other, and politically one of the key functions of this particular set of oppositions is to separate white women from black women and, by extension, middle-class ladies from working women to insure that they relate only through men.[18] The opposition also ensures that real women are given an identity and destiny which they can only approximate and never fulfil. Above all, it is an identity cast upon them by the dominant group, for no matter what the locus of the dual image of women – art, literature, advertising, costume, song, pornography, even architecture and landscape – it is man (middle-class educated man) who is the active observer and doer. Not only women but the whole world, extending to the farthest reaches of the Empire, becomes his object. And though in fact active manipulation of such objects was often severely constrained, in fantasy, as well as in the range of activities from anthropology to photography, middle-class men appear to be engaging in a kind of voyeurism which comes out of their privileged position as actors and doers. This voyeurism, for example, is particularly evident in the preoccupation with child pornography and child prostitution, not to mention father–daughter incest,[19] which is such a strong, if underground, theme in Victorian middle-class culture.

It is striking, moreover, that middle-class men's interests in rescue work, in the plight of working women, as well as pornographic imagery, focused on girls and *young* women, that it was they who carried the burden of purity and pollution, and indeed of projected male sexuality. For this obsessive concern with keeping young girls in innocence, preserving the 'bloom of ignorance' is built on an obvious paradox. If girls were 'by nature' innocent why were they so easily aroused, why all the need for protection and suppression of sexual knowledge? As Gorham has shown, the attempt to combine the two views, of the girl child as totally pure but also as naturally wicked and corrupted gave rise to two powerful but opposed images, the child as redeemer (little Nell) and the child as evil incarnate,[20] a parallel to the dual vision of women in general.

This preoccupation with young women, of course, is directly related to the power structures of gender and class;[21] and it was reinforced by the legal system and such customary practices as the large discrepancies in age between middle-class husbands and wives, both in reality[22] and in fantasy.[23] It was not unknown, for example, for an upper-middle-class man to raise a ward or poor relation with the intention of making her his wife when she reached her middle or late teens.[24] The cult of domesticity, moreover, removed married women, particularly mothers, from the sexual arena. Thus we have many images of older middle-class men in relation to young girls (sometimes middle class, sometimes illicitly working class) but almost no images of the older middle-class woman in relation to working-class men or younger men at all, except in the all-powerful, deliberately desexualized mother–son image.

It seems clear from the preceding argument that many of the preoccupations of the Victorian middle class and many of the dichotomous themes which pervaded their world-view were laid down in childhood, even infancy, and that, even though the mechanisms are not yet completely understood, class as well as gender divisions were, partially at least, created in the nursery.[25] The dual vision of women, for example, has much to do with new divisions of labour in the middle-class home. From the end of the eighteenth century, a middle-class life-style had evolved which emphasized the importance of a well-ordered, and increasingly, a materially well-stocked home. While the responsibility for the management of the home and the emotional demands of husband and children were the domain of the wife and mother, there was a continued effort to shift the manual work, or at least the heavier, dirtier tasks on to domestic servants.[26] Of course this division of labour depended very much on the financial resources of the family as well as on the number of children. Nevertheless, there was increasing pressure to employ domestic servants in larger numbers and, as the century progressed, for more specialized functions.

Although in the eighteenth century, female and male servants had been equally employed, by the mid-nineteenth century the proportion of male servants had dropped substantially; and by the 1870s even the upper middle class was substituting women, partly because of expense (for other occupations such as schoolteaching attracted men), but also because working-class definitions of masculinity and independence made domestic service less and less palatable to young men.[27]

By the 1850s there were already 750,000 women employed as residential domestic servants, and by the 1890s this figure had reached 1,300,000. The majority of these women were young and unmarried. The evidence from servants' as well as from employers' memoirs suggests that in households where there were young children, even where only one servant was employed, she would spend a good portion of her time helping to care for them. Upper-middle-class ladies in households with two or three servants were unlikely to have taken any active part in the physical care of infants or toddlers.[28] It was the nurse or maid who fed, nappied, washed, dressed, potted, put to bed and directly disciplined the infant and small child. Within the nursery domain she had total power over her charges; yet middle-class children learned very quickly that she was their inferior and that they were both, children and servants alike, subject to a higher authority. It was very often these girls and women who first awakened sexual as well as other feelings in the child.

This was the case with Freud himself, although psychoanalysts have been remarkably uninterested in the role of nursemaids. Recently, however, the importance of the social background of the maid and her position of dependency in the household, combined as it was with 'derived' power over the child, has been recognized in a discussion of Freud's self-analysis and confirms many of the findings in upper-middle-class memoirs and autobiographies.[29] Freud's nurse was actually a maid who had worked in the family before he was born and who had other duties in addition to looking after him. This was a much more common experience than the specialized nanny we expect from nostalgic fiction. Freud's nurse was of Czech working-class and Catholic origin so that her employment by a bourgeois, German-Jewish family implied cultural, social, economic and ethnic inferiority, 'a potent combination to be carrying into a relationship with an infant boy'.[30]

In many households, the maid in charge of the children would be very young, scarcely more than a child herself; so it is not surprising that both bribes and threats were used to keep order and to control her charges, and it is likely that sexual stimulation was one of the ways nursemaids amused and quieted infants. In his analysis of Freud's case, Swann notes the parallel with the American South where white infants were nursed by black mammies and grew up into a culture that idealized white women. 'The same splitting is present, in society and psyche alike, to make the idealisation possible':[31] 'White women are lovely but not carnally lovable; they are more like the Virgin Mary. But there is the maid or mammy, the black mother figure, at once the real thing and a substitute.'[32]

The extent of the splitting would obviously depend on the resources of the family, e.g. space available, number of children, number of servants. It became extreme in the wealthiest households and was a particular ideal of the English upper class whose trained nannies were famous the world over. In her memories of this division of labour an upper-middle-class woman of the 1890s said: 'To me she was the perfect mother. I would not have liked her to dose me, bathe me, comfort me or hold my head when I was sick. These intimate functions were performed by Nanny or by Annie our nurserymaid. . . . I did not like mother even to see me in the bath.'[33] Ideally the mother in this type of household would direct the intellectual and particularly the religious and moral upbringing of her children. She would see them only either in the nursery when it was set in order for her visit or when they were taken to see her, specially washed and dressed at the appointed 'children's hour'. Whether the nurse was loved, hated or simply endured, this split remained.

R.L. Stevenson wrote of his beloved nanny: 'My second Mother, my first wife / The Angel of my Infant life'.[34] Yet servants also dealt with the underside of household life, and their work was seen to be dirty and menial. They were thus more intimate and earthy than middle-class adults who were debarred from many activities because of taboos, manners and etiquette. Children soon learned that servants talked differently, walked differently, even smelled differently. Memories, for example, are evoked of a maid's hands which smelled of dishwater when dressing a child, or of the fusty smell of servants' bedrooms. A lady in her sixties still remembered the maids' stories about their courting escapades, stories whispered in an atmosphere redolent of the exciting mingled smell of 'hair oil, pantchouili and body odour'.[35]

Victorians of the middle class, in contrast, were affected by a drive for personal cleanliness and sanitary reform which began early in the nineteenth century. Some middle-class Victorians even suffered from a type of obsession such as that suggested in the recent account of the life of Charles Kingsley, an active sanitary reformer who was constantly preoccupied with personal cleanliness and cold baths and who could not bear to wear clothes that were dirty.[36]

Despite this drive (or possibly even in reaction to it), the naturalness, even 'rankness' of working-class people, and servants in particular, could have a subtle attraction. (In the context of class domination, of course, this attraction was as falsely romantic as the opposite fears of depravity and bestiality.) A country clergyman's son remembers the illiterate charwoman who lived in a cottage at the foot of his house, a woman he regarded as his 'second mother': 'She was a woman always poor, always comfortable, always free, rich and racy in her mind and in her speech, pagan and fearing neither God nor devil.'[37] Middle-class children liked to slip down into the kitchen and laugh and play with the servants, cadge scraps of forbidden adult food, and listen to less inhibited conversation than they usually heard; and the direct accessibility of servants, who were not governed by the etiquette rituals of middle-class front-door conventions, continued to have a particular appeal to many middle-class adults who remembered with pleasure visits to the homes of servants when they were children: 'A cottage with an open door, not closed till day is done.'[38] Indeed, the fascination with the alien, often forbidden but exciting, world of the servants is a common theme in middle-class memoirs:

In the maid's room I read romances . . . bound volumes which lay concealed beneath Karoline's underclothes in the bottom drawer. Without the exchange of a word, we both knew that I would not have been allowed to read them if I had asked my mother. And indeed, I read them with something of a bad conscience but it was more than that . . . there was something in these romances which made one think of tainted water that has been forgotten in a carafe; of all the foul and unwholesome smells whereby the town became familiar to my senses.[39]

This fascination with the forbidden world of the working class had obvious sexual overtones. Herman Hesse, for example, described in his novel *Demian* (1913, written immediately after his psychoanalysis), how, at least for boys, attraction to working-class life took on an explicitly sexual character. Hesse is speaking of his hero as a pubescent boy, who sees the world in terms of dark and light forces: the light being the bourgeois world of parents, sisters, law and order; while the dark world, the world of his awakening sexual desires, inextricably draws him to the maidservant. The equation of working class, sexuality, disorder and guilt has been well-established. In fact, not only symbolically but physically and often with covert social sanctions the young servant was available to the middle-class male adolescent. The first sexual experience in the long and notorious career of the protagonist of *My Secret Life* takes the form of just such an encounter (although this incident, as he recounts it, can be described more as a rape than as a seduction). And there are enough reminiscences by domestic servants to confirm the characteristic nature of these relationships.

For middle-class children, these social divisions and their erotic overtones were also reflected in a spatial view of their world – a view which started with their own bodies, extended to the houses where they lived and eventually to their village, town or city. Just as society was often symbolized by a body metaphor, so house and body images were conflated. Within the house the child was safe and warm in the cosy nursery or sitting-room with the glowing hearth at its centre, an image very often associated with the mother. The servants, on the other hand, lived and worked in the dark underground parts of the house or slept in the inaccessible, often spooky attics. Their territory was the 'back passages' (nursery euphemism for anus) where the working parts of the household machine were visible and where waste and rubbish were removed. Such images carried over into adulthood and help to explain the often irrationally divided and inefficient design of middle-class housing.

Thus spatial segregation was associated both with control over servants (and by extension over other members of the working class) and control over polluting aspects of the body. Control over one's own body became, in turn, associated with both the ability and the right to control and dominate others. The natural extension of this bodily domination was, of course, legitimate physical punishment; the right to beat or strike a servant was only removed in the 1860s[40] while the legitimacy of wife-beating, not to mention physical punishment of children, remained unchallenged long into the twentieth century.

Middle-class children not only learned that certain social spaces belonged to certain social groups, they also learned to use their bodies to express class and gender boundaries. Little ladies and gentlemen did not sit on steps; they stood absolutely straight; they did not whistle, scuff or slouch. By imitating middle-class adults they learned habits of command through silent body language, through the way they looked at people, through tone of voice as well as accent.

Servants in return, showed deference in the way they used their bodies, a point also observed by the children of the house. Servants stood when spoken to and kept their eyes cast down, they moved out of a room backwards, curtsied to their betters and were generally expected to efface themselves; doing their work and moving about the house so as not to be visible or audible to their employers. In an extreme case they were made to turn their faces to the wall when the employer passed by.[41] One instruction book for young servants devotes a whole section to *Standing and Moving* and shows the extra burden which the need to express deference placed on the already heavily worked servingmaid class:

> I was once in the nursery bedroom when Anna came in panting with a can of water. As I spoke to her she sank down on a chair saying 'Excuse me, ma'am, I am so tired,' but I could not excuse her. She acted very rudely. It would have been but a small effort to stand for a few moments, however tired she might be and girls who are not capable of such an effort are not fit for service.[42]

In the street, servants, male or female, walked a few paces behind their master or mistress. They walked on the outside of the pavement if escorting a lady in a rough or dirty street, just as a middle-class man would have, to act as her protector.

Servants also contributed to the growing child's mental map of their social geography outside the home: 'The servants of the house made windows for us into the outside world.'[43] After all, one of the primary tasks of servants in even lower-middle-class homes was to take the children out for walks and the small child's first view of the neighbourhood may have been very much through servants' eyes. Many of these children were first- or second-generation suburban dwellers as the middle class started to move away from the city centres where factories poured out both wealth and filth. Servants passed back and forth between the 'good', clean, orderly but dull suburbs and the 'bad', dirty, disorganized but exciting centre. A school-master's daughter living in a south London suburb expressed this feeling in her attitude towards Deptford, the dockland home of the general servant girl who had charge of her: 'This name meant for me unimaginable squalor. I was never taken there; somehow I was brought up to think of it as dark, dirty, common, low. Yet I hugged a secret fascination with the very idea of it.'[44]

Without claiming some sort of implicit functionalism it is still possible to observe that the housing, the life-style, and the childrearing practices of the middle class helped to create and maintain a structure of authority and a personality suited to the group which was instrumental in running the business, of governing, and reaping, the rewards of Victorian society. This is not to deny that the structures so created did not produce major contradictions both at the individual and group level, especially in the realm of sexuality.[45]

Freud, for example, believed that it was almost impossible for the 'love of civilized man' to avoid the split between affection and sexuality because of the need to avoid direct erotic attractions to the mother (incest). For him the whole sphere of love remained divided into sacred and profane (animal) love: 'Where they love they do not desire and where they desire they cannot love.' For him it is this which underlies the double standard, including the tendency of men in the highest classes to choose a woman of a lower class as a permanent mistress or even a wife, in the need for a debased object, since the 'sexual act is seen as something degrading which defiles and pollutes not only the body'.[46] This theory takes for granted the existence of women of the lower class and, therefore, does not need to explain the stage at which they enter the individual drama or any active role that they might play. Ultimately, as with most nineteenth-century thought, it rests on a conception of society in which hierarchical divisions of both class and gender are natural. The relationship of master to servant, of men to women, that is, was seen as natural and organic in contrast to the newer and much more threatening relation of employer and workman.

Natural in this context has two related meanings: the relationship was taken for granted; it was a given. It was also part of nature as opposed to the civilized, the man-made, which was unnatural. Some sensitive men struggled against a world-view which posed such polar opposites and especially which split the world into masculine and feminine, or into lady and woman. Edward Carpenter, E.M. Forster and William Morris, for example, in their lives and in their writing, have given us a glimpse of the anguished efforts needed to break through the constraints, conscious and unconscious, which it produced. The minor poet and man of letters who is the subject of this study, A.J. Munby, also senses this dilemma posed by the dual vision of women as the following passage from his diary, written in his characteristically sententious style, illustrates. He is visiting with friends in an old house in Kent.

It became necessary for me to retire for a space; but the men-servants had gone to bed, and amongst the intricate passages [sic] of the old house I could nowhere find the spot I wanted. So, encountering in the hall the waiting maid, a ruddy domestic damousel, I had no recourse but to ask her the way. An unpleasant process! With much hesitation and awkwardness I strove by delicate circulocations to hint to her my needs: but the girl's rude mind could not comprehend them – she looked at me with respectful wonder, and at last I was obliged to say bluntly 'could you tell me, where is the water closet?' She would blush, I half thought and stammer, and I should regret having said it. Not at all! it was only the reflex of one's own training that made one think so. [The maid takes him to the door of the water closet.]

Significant of several things. Not certainly of vulgarity or any culpable coarseness, rather of a rude simplicity and innocence of shame. We are brought up to ignore these ultimate necessities of nature, and to be animals only by stealth: but your housemaid has had quite a different schooling in knowing that such things exist, sees no harm in speaking of what she knows.[47]

Arthur J. Munby and Hannah Cullwick: A Double Portrait

It is one thing to identify a world view and its possible sources, but another to analyse the way in which it was incorporated into everyday life: 'People are living in the middle of their cosmology, down in amongst it; they are energetically manipulating it, evading its implications in their own lives if they can, but using it for hitting each other and forcing one another to conform to something they have in mind.'[48]

While one should be fully aware of the power of symbols and images, it would be a mistake to see these phenomena purely in symbolic terms. Fear of pollution and obsession with dirt and degradation had a very real basis. Victorian cities were filthy with soot, smoke, mud and appalling muck-heaps lying in the streets; and cholera was a very real threat to life. Indeed, the effort to enforce sanitary reform had to start with the middle class before moving on to controlling the habits of the working class.[49] Similarly, the images of women as domestic beings produced feedback which restricted their lives to the extent that many of them *were* insipid, under-exercised, narrow-minded and neurasthenic.

In the record left by two obscure Victorians,[50] however, it is possible to catch glimpses of the world-view I have outlined and of the way these divisions operated in practice since one of the pair was male and upper middle class and the other was female, not only of a working-class but also of a rural background and a domestic servant. She was one of the great army of working-class women who did, in fact, spend a good deal of their lives in direct face-to-face contact with the middle class. (Both in reality and fantasy it was young female servants who bore the direct personal brunt of class interaction. Independent working men could protect their manhood by remaining within social contexts of their own kind and it was they who were the first to confront employers as members of a *class*.) A detailed examination of such a relationship can show that the private lives, even obsessions of two individuals, far from being simply psychological quirks or even aberrations, flowed directly from the social situation of these two typical individuals.

The main source for understanding that relationship is the private diary, letters, drawings and photographs of a minor poet and writer, A.J. Munby, and the companion diary of his disciple, servant, and eventually his wife, Hannah Cullwick. By Munby's instructions the diaries were locked up until 1950 by which time, as he had foreseen, the shock and degradation of such a story would have died away. Munby's diary, which he kept regularly from 1859 to 1898 with scattered entries after that date, runs to millions of words. In addition, there are about 800 letters as well as dozens of drawings and photographs. (Because of his special interest in working women, the collection has already become known as a valuable source for historians.) It is interesting to note that although the content of the diary is so unusual, the form is conventional for its period.[51]

A.J. Munby's avocation (and private obsession) in making encounters with, observing and collecting information on, working girls and women was not as unusual as it may appear at first sight. The passion for collecting information on and statistics about the working class, particularly working-class women, has a streak of voyeurism which can be sensed behind the work of a journalist such as Mayhew, as well as in the detailed accounting of moral depravity in the pages of staid publications such as the *Journal of the Royal Statistical Society*. This voyeurism also appears in both the lives and writings of men like George Gissing and Somerset Maugham. 'Rescue' work among fallen women or simply the compulsion to nocturnal wanderings in search of conversation with 'women of the streets', which figure in the lives of men like Gladstone, have some close affinity to the sexual scoring and collecting described at length in the notorious diary, *My Secret Life*.[52] ('Walter', the anonymous author, came from much the same background as Munby, was also born in the mid-1820s, and also had an obscure job in the civil service which allowed him the same time and freedom of action for his pursuits.) While 'Walter' was concerned with strictly sexual encounters, Munby was collecting examples of women at work; but the pattern of wandering from place to place in search of encounters, the emotional urgency and the sense of culmination with each 'find' lies below the surface of both diaries whose form is similar.

Unlike Mayhew or Booth, Munby's observations were not commissioned by any official body, nor were they intended to answer public questions or even written for publication. Rather, as with sexual diaries such as *My Secret Life* or the diary of the homosexual, A.J. Symonds, Munby seems to have been using the diary to construct a meaningful identity by using themes from his culture – both those that were explicitly admired and those that were forbidden – and reinterpreting them to fit his own psychic structure. It is only in his poetry that he expressed some of his views to the public, if in a somewhat muted form (see appendix).

Arthur Joseph Munby was born in 1828, the eldest child of a York solicitor and the daughter of a wealthy clergyman. He had been brought up from infancy by a nurse called Hannah Carter who remained the faithful servant of the family for twenty-eight years. Six younger siblings were born in the span of ten years and his mother, not surprisingly, was delicate to the point of spending much of her time lying on a sofa, weak in health and with a tendency to become hysterical. Munby always viewed her with exceptional awe and love. He described her as charmingly 'old fashioned', with a 'fair delicate face and golden-auburn hair and dainty figure'. He remembered her best for her pious, gentle way, as one who 'believed as devoutly in my father as he believed in God and Christ'. Her whole being was in the affections, 'her husband first and her children next . . . her love was so tremulous and tender, and her health so delicate always, that each of us felt it might kill her, if he went into the army or navy, for instance, or went away very far or very long'.[53] With such a mother, no disturbing or distasteful subjects could ever have been broached. Sexuality, much less any bodily functions, would have been completely taboo.

The family had an assured social position and Munby, although having a provincial and country childhood, received a traditional middle-class boy's education first at a local private school supplemented by private tutoring from a local clergyman and then at Cambridge. Unfortunately we know little more than this about his early life. He became a barrister despite his distaste for the law, probably in deference to his father and his position as eldest son. However, he did not practise law but moved to London where he lived 'in chambers', i.e. in a set of rooms within one of the Inns of Court. Here he remained for the rest of his life, partly supported financially by his father. At the age of thirty-one, he found a position with the Ecclesiastical Commission, work he disliked for the most part but felt obliged to take in order to have some financial independence. Despite his middle-class Victorian belief in work, therefore, in his own life, work was always a burden and a distraction.

In his lifetime, A.J. Munby was known only in a small circle. He passed his life as an undistinguished but respectable civil servant, teacher, amateur poet and artist, who was on the fringes of both the Pre-Raphaelite and Christian Social-ist circles, particularly through his teaching for the Working Men's College. His real interest lay in his self-created avocation, the observation and collection of the lives of working women. Although he was in no way a radical, he did occasionally protest at moves to keep women out of manual work even to the extent of heading a delegation to Parliament on behalf of the collier girls of Wigan.[54]

For the most part, however, he enjoyed the modest comforts of a professional bachelor, strolling through London to look on at the building of the Embankment; to dinner at his club; or to play-writing games at the Pen and Pencil Society; to a late supper in a friend's rooms in London's Inn where politics, art, and writing were discussed; meandering home at four a.m. amid Covent Garden porters: watching, talking to anyone in the street, walking anywhere with perfect ease. His diary thus emphasizes the freedom of action enjoyed by a middle-class man, even on a small but assured income, in contrast to the lack of freedom imposed on middle-class women.

His first love was for what he persisted in calling 'peasant' or 'country wenches'. He idealized the rural and the out-of-doors, which may be a partial explanation for his fascination with a ruddy countenance and suntanned skin. This rural nostalgia, of course, was widespread among the recently urbanized Victorian middle class.[55] In his country wanderings Munby sought out farm girls; the 'flither girls' of the north-east coastal region who made their living by being lowered over the edges of cliffs to collect sea-bird's eggs and limpets; and, above all, the 'pit brow lasses' who worked in the coalfields sifting cinders and hauling carts at the pit surface. They not only worked outside in a primarily man's world but they were covered in coal dust and, at least in Wigan, wore trousers.

In the city he favoured women in outdoor occupations: flower sellers, milkmaids and prostitutes. He was particularly interested in circus women and acrobats and made a large collection of photographs of these performers.[56] Although he sought out entertainment places used by female clerks and shop assistants, these girls were approaching too near to the lady to really attract him: 'Commend me to the honest roughness of a solid maid of all work rather than to the hybrid fine ladyism of Miss Swann and Edgar'[57] (a large clothing store in the West End). It was not work or even financial independence *per se* which he found so fascinating in women, but menial work. In common with many other upper-middle-class Victorians, not absolutely sure of their own position, he disliked those who tried to rise above themselves. In a typical passage describing one of his country rambles he contrasts his 'ruddy farm servants and true peasant women' with the upper servants he saw at North Repps Hall, 'lean, pale-faced insolent looking hussies in would-be lady's clothes'.[58]

Munby's attitude illustrates the appeal of working-class openness which we have observed as a theme laid down in childhood:

> Nothing is more striking than the contrast of behaviour which even courteous gentlemen exhibit in dealing with a lady or a quasi-lady and in dealing with a servant or other labouring woman. To the lady, you are all deference and smiles: you smooth your phrases and put away all allusions to things coarse or common, you do things for her, you would not hear of her doing things for you. To the servant, you are civil, indeed, but you speak plainly and frankly to her about things which may not be mentioned to a lady; you call her by her Christian name though you never saw her before and expect her to call you Sir in return; you order her about and expect or allow her to fetch and carry for you as indeed it is her calling to do so.[59]

> Deep down in the great shifting mass of the people, their own histories and names have for them nothing private or sacred. . . . They are accustomed to be close questioned about themselves by mistresses and to be called 'Anne' or 'May' by anyone who chooses to address them. To be asked bluntly 'What is your name?' or 'How old are you' by a stranger, does not seem to them at all offensive or impertinent.[60]

Munby does not acknowledge that this quality he so much admires was at least partly a result of his position as a dominating middle-class man, who for sixpence could feel a girl's palm and for a shilling could take her to a photographer to have her picture taken in whatever pose he chose to put her. It was economic necessity combined with the service role which made his 'wenches' so available. It is noticeable that Munby seldom tried to approach a Lancashire mill girl or even a London factory worker.

Because of this position of economic and social power we know a considerable amount about the middle-class, particularly male, world-view. We know very little about the way working-class children, particularly domestic servants, were moulded by the social structure into which they were born. This makes Hannah Cullwick's diary, with its detailed record of childhood memories, conditions of work and work performed, wages, hours, recreations, relationships among fellow servants, and many other details, a unique and precious document. However, it must be remembered that she was writing it for Munby's eyes alone, a further way in which he could dominate and even 'create' her life. Thus, the diary has to be interpreted with caution. Still, through a reconstruction of her relationship to Munby, as interpreted by both of them, it may be possible to gain some insight into

Plates 1 and 2: Symbolism and Reality: Watercolour sketch by A.J. Munby of himself and a colliery girl; photograph of the same (photographer unknown).

the construction and acceptance of deferential interaction based on both class and gender, an interaction which female servants must have carried back into the working class when they married and had children.

Hannah Cullwick was born in 1833 and raised in Shropshire, but through her work as a servant she came to London when she was in her late teens. Except for her relationship to Munby her life was typical of literally millions of women of the period. Hannah started in service when she was eight years old, which was not atypical for the 1830s. Her rural background is important as an element in her acceptance of the status quo because there were no alternatives to some form of personal service for her or her family. Her father had been both a farm servant and worked in a gentlemen's stables. Her maternal grandmother had been in service before marriage and returned to residential service after she was widowed. Her mother had been a lady's maid and companion to the Lady at the Hall near their village of Shifnal. This lady became Hannah's godmother and had wished Hannah, as the eldest child, to be named after her, Anna Maria Dorothea, but Hannah's mother thought that this was too pretentious for one of her station. Hannah's first memory is of a visit to their cottage by the butler from the Hall when she was five years old. He came with gifts of a bible for Hannah and a print dress for her mother, and he summoned them to come up to the Hall: 'I remember it because it seemed so grand to me and i polished my shoes as well as ever i could and i trotted up by Mother as fast as possible o' purpose to see my godmother who was a *lady*'.[61] The little Hannah curtsied as her mother had taught her and the lady kissed her, gave her cake and wine and a toy. Later, this all-powerful and beneficent lady sent her special clothes and paid her fees for the charity school which Hannah attended from the age of five to eight, the only formal schooling she ever had.

Her first employer was a farmer who was a friend of her mother's. Here her position was much like that of an extra daughter, but one who had certain special duties to perform. The family was kind to her; she was taught to cook and sew; the farmer took her fishing and opened a savings account for her. This kind of gradual introduction to the authority system of service in which discipline was enforced first through the mother and then often through female teachers, relations or friends is one of the factors which made it possible to maintain the institution of domestic service for so long and make it seem so 'natural' even to those who were subordinated and who gained very little in real terms from their positions.[62]

By the time she was fourteen, Hannah had left the farmer's family which could no longer afford her higher wages. After a short spell as a 'pot' girl at the local Red Lion pub (a position of which neither her mother nor the farmer and his family approved), she was sent to the vicarage at Ryton to be nurserymaid under a nanny to eight children. This position meant a heavy load of cleaning, fires to be made, bath water to be carried up and down, as well as children to look after. She had only been there a month when fever struck her home village. Her mother wrote to her of her father's death but no one told her of her mother's death a fortnight later until a neighbour happened to call by the vicarage. Although it was only three miles away from her home, Hannah was not allowed to go, even to see what had happened to her younger brothers and sisters (a ban possibly laid down because of the fear of infection but also to maintain discipline). Whatever the cause of the prohibition, Hannah was devastated. Her goal of earning money to send to her mother which had made her situation bearable was suddenly gone: 'i *thought it was* no use tho i ax'ed to go and all my strength seemed gone.' She was ordered to go back to the school-room to start work immediately.[63]

The total power of the employing class over her existence was again brought home to Hannah, then about fifteen, in her next place of third under-housemaid in an aristocratic household. She had been very proud to be taken on in this position and enjoyed working in the beautiful surroundings, learning how to make a bed and 'do out' the long gallery and great rooms. One sunny day, she and the second under-housemaid were outside cleaning the sixteen copper kettles used daily by the household: 'Maria and me was cleaning our kettles in the yard and *playing* over it, for we was young things; and My Lady, see'd us out o' the nursery window and sent the housekeeper to give us warning.'[64] Hannah's pleas were useless and she was sacked on the spot. She then had to take a job as scullery maid in another large household near by: 'i couldn't help crying when i come to clean the stew pan and great spits and dripping pan and live only in a rough out-house next the kitchen', a shed with no window which she could only reach through the coal hole.[65]

Hannah learned at a very early age that her world was made up of powerful middle-class and upper-class people and that only her strength to labour gave her a footing in that world. She was particularly vulnerable having been orphaned early but this was by no means an unusual state at this period. In any case, servant memoirs emphasize that their own families, almost always under pressure for income and house room, could do little for them. There was also the question of sexual power. In the course of her service in country houses, visiting gentlemen as well as menservants, tried to 'make a pass' at Hannah. In one instance when she has been offered a ride home in a carriage with one of these gentlemen, she was set down with him 'in a lonely spot' to walk the rest of the way home. He tried to kiss her and she threatened him: 'if you offer to touch me again I'll do something you won't like, so you go your way and i'll go mine.'[66] Like many working-class girls, she learned early in life that strength of body and personality were her chief resources for both work and self-protection.[67]

Like so many girls, particularly of rural origin, Hannah accepted her position (not for nothing did employers prefer girls fresh from the countryside, 'uncorrupted' by urban life). She tried to gain a sense of dignity and worth both in the work she did and through the love she craved. With Munby she achieved that sense of work and love, although it was on his terms and ultimately at a very high price. Running throughout her diary, however, there is a sense that the system as it stood had cheated her, that the pious platitudes about the dignity of service were not believed in even by middle-class employers. Over the years, the tone of her diary subtly changes as her life experience and education through Munby widened her horizons. In one of the very last entries she made, after she had been married for about nine months, and thirty-five years after her first experience of residential domestic service, Hannah wrote:

> I went out to service too soon – before I really understood the meaning of it – and at the Charity School i was taught to curtsey to the ladies and gentlemen and it seem'd to come natural to me to think them *entirely* over the lower class and if it was our place to bow and be at their bidding and I've never got out o' that feeling somehow.[68]

Images, Games and Transformations

In 1854, When A.J. Munby was twenty-five he met Hannah Cullwick, aged twenty-one, on a London street. In his usual manner he struck up a conversation with her. She combined all the qualities he prized most highly: she was from a country background; strong and robust but good-looking; a maid-of-all-work, but exceptually intelligent and lively. From then on she was the centre of his emotional life as he was of hers. For nineteen years until their marriage they were involved with each other, although during all that time he remained a nominal bachelor living at 6 Fig Tree Court, the Temple, and she living in various residential servant situations. It is not clear from the sources we have whether theirs was, in conventional terms, a sexual relationship and there are some indications that Munby may have been impotent. In any case, there were no children nor indications that Hannah ever thought she was pregnant, a situation which might have totally altered their relationship.[69] Munby and Hannah finally married in 1873 when he was forty-four and she was thirty-nine. She lived with him for just over four years as his servant, not openly as his wife. After a period of increasing tension in their relationship, she returned to her people in Shropshire and lived for the rest of her life in a cottage provided for her by Munby where he visited her regularly. Her relatives and friends accepted him; while his middle-class circle, with the exception of two of his closest friends, never knew of her existence.

Soon after their relationship began, they started a series of games and play-acting in which they used the differences between them to emphasize their love and devotion. They were intensely aware of the impression that they made on other people. In public, Hannah would act the perfect servant, demurely walking behind Munby, carrying his heavy luggage, calling him Sir and meekly obeying his orders. He would act especially 'masterful', give her ostentatious tips, and send her off to do his bidding. Later they would meet in his rooms and giggle like children over the incident revelling in the 'if they only knew' aspect of their situation. This is, of course, not an unknown phenomenon:

> On occasions, individuals will come together and find that they share each other's bizarre fantasies. The fantasy ceases to be a personal mental resource to be drawn upon intermittently during the course of everyday life; now it can be elaborated with

Plate 3: Hannah carrying slop-pails. Photograph by A.J. Munby.

the help of another and may shift into the centre of our lives. The classical description of this phenomenon is *folie à deux*: a situation in which two individuals actively cultivate their extreme fantasy to the point at which scripts may be assembled.[70]

The point about Hannah and Munby's 'scripts' is that they were written around the theme of class and gender differences played out through games of mastery and submission.

In following these themes through the diaries, it becomes clear that Munby's inversion of the usual Victorian stereotypes suggests the possibility of transformations, of passing back and forth from one 'side' to another at will. Black becomes white, degradation becomes love, masculine becomes feminine, working class becomes genteel. All this happens at the will of the middle-class male protagonist who creates the situation and engineers the transformation. Through the use of his position as an upper-middle-class man, Munby was able to find a partner and carry through into reality at least some of these fantasies. Hannah, although much more clear-sighted about the reality of her own situation, was driven by her economic and emotional needs to act willingly as this partner. She was, indeed, very jealous of his interest in one or two of his charity cases, particularly the 'girl without the nose', but seems to have been quite accepting of his friendship with women of his own class.

Most of the themes which preoccupied Munby and, to a lesser extent, Hannah, clustered around the question of dominance and subordination, strength and weakness, autonomy and dependence. The dichotomies and contrasts allied to these subjects are characteristic of much Victorian culture: respectable/not respectable, lady/woman, pure/impure, clean/dirty (and by extension white/black), indoor/outdoor, fairness/suntanned or ruddy (blushing was thought to be a sign of sexual arousal in middle-class women), clothed/uncovered skin and, above all, of course, feminine/masculine. Many of these themes are related either directly or indirectly to the major Victorian preoccupation with *work*: what was it, who did it? where did they do it? This produced another set of contrasts: work/leisure, work/home, manual work/brain work.

Connected to both sets of contrasts and in keeping with the body imagery we have already mentioned, *hands* take on a special significance and play a central role in both class and gender imagery, e.g. 'the language of gloves'. They also carry an explicitly sexual connotation for Munby and, one would guess, for many other Victorians as well.[71] White, dainty hands indicated gentility as well as femininity. They were symbolic of inner breeding but also of life-style. George Augustus Sala, who was a contemporary and friend of Munby's, a man-about-town and commentator on the social scene (as well as a connoisseur and collector of erotica), wrote a novel in which the middle-class hero rescues a 'fallen woman' who turns out to be a lady by birth. He literally pulls her out of a horse trough and takes her to a café where he listens to her story: 'As she spoke she laid her right hand on the filthy table-cloth. The woman's hand was, considering her stature, small, but the fingers were long and tapering, the nails, although grimy, filbert-shaped. Otherwise it was a handsome hand, and very very white'.[72]

When Munby tried to persuade Hannah to dress as a gentlewoman he wanted her to wear gloves, but she resisted saying 'they baffle my hands so'. He quotes this statement approvingly, however, for contrary to what had usually been considered attractive, Munby is fascinated by, even addicted to looking at, touching (at times cutting the skin from) large, rough, red, work-hardened hands of working girls. With monotonous repetition Munby's diary entries and poems dwell on the motif of hands, their colour, shape and texture:

> For she is still a working wench
> and sits with hands still bare[73]

Hannah deliberately rubbed the bars of grates and cleaned knives with her bare hands, despite the unpleasant feeling, in order to harden them in a paean of love for Munby, expressed through work.

A similar, although slightly less compelling, preoccupation of Munby's was with women who either had large masculine-looking feet or who wore heavy boots; in fact Hannah often wore his old boots. He writes approvingly of a colliery girl: 'Her

Plate 4:   Hands. Photograph by A.J. Munby.

ponderous boots with iron on the sole, shod like a horse's hoofs'. Here Munby connects this image with one of his favourite animal analogies. Small, dainty feet and hands, of course, were the pride of middle-class Victorian women and figure widely in descriptions of feminine attractiveness, a physical characteristic evoked in characters from Dora, the wife in *David Copperfield*, to Meg in *Little Women*, or Rosamund in *Middlemarch*. This concern extended to doubts about working women who did not conform to the expected distinction. In 1862, a private factory welfare officer for a silk firm wrote: 'I immediately remarked the small delicately formed hands of the weavers, and I have seen the smallness to be, in a domestic point of view, a great disadvantage to women in that condition of life . . .'[74]

The animal/human analogy which Munby used for his colliery girl pervades his diary. It indicates lowliness and degradation, but also a brute strength and dumb loyalty expressed through love and service. In his poetry, girls and women are compared to cows, horses, dogs, and in the case of the 'ebony slave girl' (who eats on all fours out of a bowl on the ground), even an elephant. Note that all these are examples of domesticated animals who have been 'trained' and 'broken in' by man. This analogy is, as we have seen, by no means unique to Munby. The comparison of the 'handling' of women to horses has a long history in literature about the relations between the sexes.[75] In some writers, middle-class women may appear as 'spirited fillies', but for Munby the domesticated animal evocation is more often expressed in a fondness for watching women standing and working in lowly positions. He was a firm believer in the importance of curtsying, for example, and he finds the young milkwoman he saw stooping to take up her new yoke looking 'proud as a young cart horse'. He imposes the same image on a servant washing the kitchen floor in a country inn: 'I spoke to her first, she did not understand me: but leaning on her hands which were spread upon the wet brick pavement like forefeet . . . she scrubbed away busily under tables and dresser, folks stepping over her whenever they came in her way.'[76] Fascination with love expressed through drudgery, dirt, defilement and even disfigurement reaches its height (or depth) in a poem which no publisher would accept. It combines all these themes with one of Munby's favourite locations, a coal-mining area. In this poem his heroine works underground and is eventually hideously disfigured in a mine explosion. (Coal miners had a general fascination for Victorians. They were the troglodytes who produced the power on which the whole edifice of comfortable middle-class life rested but they were hidden away under the ground.) Munby's imaginary pit lass:

> . . . thinks it sweet to walk all day upon her hands and feet.
> With a full wain behind! To rejoice in being a quadruped?
> To give her voice for such degradation?
> Let her go, disgusting creature!
> Ah! You little know the ways of women and the rights of love.[77]

The special importance of dirt or blackness for servants should be obvious. They spent a great deal of their lives maintaining cleanliness in middle-class homes.

Plate 5:   Hannah scrubbing steps. Photograph by A.J. Munby.

Their most important job was to remove dirt and waste: to dust; empty slop-pails and chamber-pots; peel fruit and vegetables; pluck fowl; sweep and scrub floors, walls and windows; remove ash and cinders; black lead grates; wash clothes and linen.[78]

The equation of servants with dirt and pollution, however, and the equation of dirt with blackness had particular overtones in mid-Victorian England, as some of the literary symbolism cited has already indicated. In Western culture blackness has always carried strong symbolic meaning: 'being the antagonist of white which is God, it becomes the symbol of personified evil'.[79] From the sixteenth century onwards, this symbolism was enlarged by its associations with the Dark Continent and the slavery of black peoples.[80] As Jordan points out, embedded in the concept of blackness was its direct opposite – whiteness: 'Every white will have its black.' White and black connotated purity and filthiness, virginity and sin, virtue and baseness, beauty and ugliness. From the Elizabethans onwards, whiteness had been the colour of perfect human beauty, especially female beauty, implying the desirability of a fair rose and white complexion.[81] It should not come as a shock, therefore, that Hannah's pet name for Munby was Massa, that is, what they took to be the Negro slave's word for Master. Three years after they met she began to wear a leather strap around her wrist and a chained collar with lock around her neck to which Munby held the key. He particularly enjoyed seeing her face and arms blackened – in his phrase 'in her dirt'.

Again, these associations were commonplace in the Victorian era. In the classic children's book, *The Water Babies*, written by Munby's friend and contemporary, Charles Kingsley, the climactic scene shows Tom, chimney-sweep boy, leaping out from the chimney covered in soot, 'looking like a little black gorilla', into the spotless white bedroom of Ellie, the golden-haired middle-class child. Tom has to be purified by dying and becoming a water baby, that is, washed clean and returned to a non-sexual infant innocence before he can join Ellie in heaven.[82]

Natives, particularly African slaves, were also associated with nakedness and by implication were heavily sexualized in contrast to buttoned-up, controlled Englishmen. Showing oneself uncovered and dirty in public was thus considered especially degrading. In their memoirs, several servants emphasized the humiliation they felt at having to kneel (thus showing legs and petticoats) to scrub the front doorsteps and paths every morning, open to the stares of passers-by, the whistles and importunings of men and boys. The symbolic meaning of cleaning in public helps to explain the use of 'step girls' by those who could not afford any other domestic services. Hannah reported that the mistress she served in summer when there were lodgers and visitors in the house 'told me she would try to do with no servants in winter – only for the errands and for cleaning the front door steps – she says "i *cannot* do them" – and i felt sorry for her – i can do them and always do everywhere i like, but she seem'd to think it degrading and of course it would be to her.' She added, 'it wants nerve to stand or kneel in the street before everybody – feeling that you're despised and degraded before them all.'[83]

Plate 6:   Hannah as a slave. Photograph by A.J. Munby.

It is only by understanding these symbolic meanings that the fantasy games which Hannah and Munby played can be appreciated:

> I got up early, for Massa was coming at $^1/_2$ past eight to see me clean the steps and do the *sign* of my 'lowness' like i did awhile ago . . . and i wanted to be black from doing' the grate as well . . . i did the dining room fire – got my arms blacked and wiped my mouth and nose across with my black hand . . . I washed the doorsteps and flags and when I saw Massa coming I got the door mat out and shook it well in the road and then i laid it on the causeway [pavement] & knelt on all fours and swept it well o' both sides wi the hand brush & last of all i knelt an wiped my face on the dirty mat in front of all the folks what pass'd by and Massa was looking on from a few doors up . . . & then i rubbed my face on it & put my lips again it & i thought now i was one o' the lowest drudges as could be – but Massa loved me & i love my work, both for its and also Massa's sake & i felt so happy.[84]

The power to create or transform another human being and in so doing to reaffirm upper-middle-class masculine identity provided, as we have seen, the compelling attraction of rescue work as well as the rationale for the phenomenon of the child bride. In 'Susan: A Poem of Degrees', 1893, it is Munby, thinly disguised as the hero, who speaks of creating 'the new Pygmalion':

> He look'd at her: a Juno covered in coal,
> With lustrous eyes and firm devoted soul;
> Goddess within, beneficent and brave,
> Yet outwardly a negress and a slave

She flings herself at his feet. He raises her up (a favourite phrase in 'rescue work') and 'kisses her foul lips' until they 'again grew ruddy from their black eclipse'. There are, indeed, several photographs in the Munby collection of collier girls in their filthy, masculine pit clothes with the same girl neatly dressed in her Sunday best, looking like any other respectable working-class woman in crinoline, bonnet and shawl. Hannah was also photographed as slave, drudge, neat serving-maid, middle-class lady and 'angel'. After their marriage she would work in the basement kitchen in Fig Tree Court all day but sit with him, 'dainty in black silk', in the evening. 'Is she not a servant during the day, and a lady in the evening? and fulfils either part so well, that for the time being she seems incapable of the other.'[85]

For Munby, as we have seen, one of the most important transformations was the crossing of sex lines. The more sharply that gender was differentiated in dress, looks, voice, walk, colouring and size, the more intriguing and exciting passing through or reversing these boundaries could be. Victorian writing, costume and visual imagery constantly emphasizes the largeness, hardness, and muscularity of men as opposed to the smallness, fragility and roundness of middle-class women. The Victorians took every opportunity to emphasize and create differences between the sexes just as they did between the working-class woman and

Plate 7: Hannah as a neat serving-
maid

Plate 8: Hannah as a middle-class
lady

Plate 9: Hannah as an 'angel'

Plate 10: Hannah dressed as a man
Photographs by A.J. Munby.

middle-class lady. Or in Munby's phrase the shoulders of the girl farm servant, who he compares to a young guardsman, are three foot broad and 'square, massive, muscular, made for work, just as those sloping white ones of a drawing room were made for show'.

Munby was fascinated by working girls and actresses who dressed in men's clothes. He often had pictures of himself taken with the pit girls in their working dress and in the diary compares himself, his stature, his hands, and feet with theirs.[86] In several places, Munby compares his size with that of Hannah. We know that she was five feet, seven and a half inches tall and weighed nearly as much as he did, eleven and a half stones (161 lb). At various times he measured her biceps and the size is given variously as thirteen, fourteen and once even eighteen inches round. Hannah in her diary too glories in her strength and size relative to 'Massa'. Her hands are too big to wear his gloves. 'i can heave my Master easy and carry him as if he was a child, nearly'.[87] She was even photographed by Munby with hair cut short and dressed in men's clothes. (She also recorded in her diary in various places that she wrestled a calling tradesman and floored a young, male fellow servant, neither of whom were amused.) The sex-reversal theme, then, just as the class-transformation theme, figures in their fantasy games. In one of his dialect poems Munby wrote:

> Look at mah Master, then an' look at me
> Wi' his fine fingers an' his dainty ways
> He's like a lady – an Ah often thinks
> He *is* a laady, when Ah waits on him –
> An me a common mon[88]

Again, women dressing as men, especially as 'gentlemen', was a favourite music-hall turn and a common frolic below stairs reported in servants and children's memoirs.[89]

The other major theme in these reversal games was the city/country division. Munby liked to see Hannah not only with bare arms and rough hands, but also wearing old-fashioned short frocks and peasant bonnets or picturesque white caps. He loved her 'countrified' speech and kept lists of dialect words she used; he delighted in her rural simplicity juxtaposed to the sophistication of the drawing-rooms where he met middle-class women. As we know, many of his contemporaries were also trying to rediscover country customs, dialect, and song in the beginnings of the 'folk culture' movement popularized by people such as Cecil Sharpe. Pre-Raphaelite painters, too, took as a motif the warm red and brown skin tones of rural figures, often dressed in folk costume.

Although Hannah was a country woman by origin, the long years in London had cut her off from a genuinely rural culture. Although she could switch to her Shropshire dialect at will, she also had learned some French from Munby and German from a fellow servant. Her diaries, especially the later ones, are vividly written if not perfect in spelling and grammar. Munby himself introduced her to many classical authors and liked to discuss them with her. She enjoyed suprising

Plate 11:   Hannah as a rural maiden. Photograph by A.J. Munby.

him with her ability to do household accounts and add up columns of figures. She copied manuscripts for him, wrote letters, and even checked references. Yet, to please him, she made a French peasant's bonnet from a picture he had shown her and continued to wear it despite ridicule from fellow servants.

Some of their games and activities had a strong mother (nurse/child) theme. Sometimes *he* sat on *her* lap: 'Massa sits on me, feet and all on my knees – at first he thought i couldn't bear him, but i said "oh i can", so ever since then i expect to nurse him after dinner.' She would then usually fetch a basin of water and kneel down to wash his feet.[90] One of their favourite activities in the Shropshire cottage was to bathe each other. Hannah, of course, had fetched and heated the water and prepared everything beforehand. She would rub his back and wash him, an office which he says only a mother or wife (or nurse) could perform. After his bath, she would get into the tub using the same water and he would wash her back. Indeed at one point he specifically says of Hannah: 'Let me be refreshed by a mother's love *and* by that of one so different.'

Not all their games were so benign. Over the years Munby had taught Hannah to value her lowliness. He cut out of his diary those passages which explicitly explain what this 'training' in love through degradation was, but it most certainly included kissing his feet and licking the mud off his boots. (In *My Secret Life* when the hero is still in his teens, he was inflamed with lust when the maidservant had to kneel to take off his boots, a standard part of a maidservant's duties.)

As in the ritual 'sign' of lowliness previously described, with Munby and Hannah, both bodily and spatial symbolism were exaggerated. We have already noted his use of animal analogies and fascination with women in a kneeling position. Hannah would lurk in the basement of Fig Tree Court, she would revel in going into the backs of coal holes and water-closets to clean them out, she would climb up the chimney to clean it (twice in the nude) and would curl up inside it, 'like a dog' and covered with soot. She deliberately would allow lodgers to walk over her while she scrubbed on hands and knees. While she was kneeling to hammer down a new carpet, a lady kicked her and she was glad for she could put it in her diary to show Munby.[91]

Nine years after they had first met and their relationship was firmly established, Hannah had a dream which she recorded in her diary. She dreams she is at 'Massa's'. She is on the floor and he is showing her a book; a gentleman walked in and looked astonished. She asks Munby what to do. He says lie still but she creeps around the table 'and lay curl'd up like a dog under the window' and 'Massa talking to the gentleman and he didn't seem to notice me nor hardly to know i was a girl [note she was thirty years old] laying there and i was glad of that.'[92]

In the two-room cottage in Shropshire where Hannah went to live, the parlour was kept solely for Munby. In this room his desk and writing equipment, the symbols of his work and attachment to the wider world, took pride of place. This scene is laid in one of Munby's barely disguised verses describing their relationship:

His parlour an' mah kitchen is as near
To one another, an' an mooch unlike
As him an' me is . . .

The kitchen's *my* home, Sir, an always was
An always will be.[93]

Their compromise situation of master/husband and servant/wife was literally
reproduced in space.

Contradictions

It seems evident that Hannah tried and, to an extent, succeeded in accepting and
believing in Munby's equation of dirt, lowliness, even degradation with love and
inner worth. On the other hand, she admits that most servants, herself included
before her 'training', would have wanted to rise above scullery work or a maid-of-
all-work position if they could. She too had internalized conceptions of respectability, order and cleanliness. It was, after all, partly her task to create that order.
After the incident where she rubbed her face in the dirt and kissed the mat on the
pavement in front of Munby, she records her feelings: 'i was glad i'd done it, but i
felt so overcome somehow with the feeling of love and degradation – been in the
street like that – so low and so dirty – yet liking the work so and especially for
Massa's sake that it was some time afore i could feel calm.'[94]

Her training in degradation was a lesson with contradictory repercussions. At
one time she took a place as a 'skivvy' in a lodging house in the Strand to be nearer
Fig Tree Court. This kind of service was the lowest in status and the most onerous
in heavy, dirty work required; it was often done by girls who had been brought up
in the workhouse. It was winter and the frost had cracked Hannah's hands into
open chilblains which had become ingrained with soot (a very common and painful
complaint of both domestic servants and working-class housewives whose hands
were constantly in water). One day she slipped out to visit Munby hoping to please
him to be seen thus 'in her dirt' but even Munby was appalled. In another place she
was left to 'clean down' a large house that had not only its full complement of
London grime and soot aided by three coal fires in the house, but also a railroad
running at the bottom of the garden. The family had gone away on holiday while
the cleaning was being done (the usual practice) and Hannah invited Munby to
come and visit her: 'i wanted him to see what a big gloomy dirty house this i have
to live in, and what a deal o' work was left for me to do all by myself, and i felt *so*
dirty and miserable too, for after all too much dirt & too much work is sickening,
& i was not surprised to see Massa look disgusted.'[95]

As early as 1860, Munby himself began to realize the ramifications of his
scheme. When he was on a visit to Hannah, then a maid-of-all-work in a dreary
suburb, he noticed how five years of 'scrubbing & cleaning, of sun & wind out of
doors and kitchen fires within' have coarsened Hannah's looks:

And she was pleased with the change – *pleased* that she is now so much rougher and coarser – because it pleases me, she thinks. Truly, every smear and stain of coarseness on her poor neglected face comes of love. And now, it is high time that all this discipline should cease, but I have no means of ending it! To be a smart parlour maid, or even lady's maid are distinctions far above her reach: she would smile incredulous if I proposed them. Che sera, sera.[96]

In 1864 when Hannah was working as a maid-of-all-work in a prosperous trademan's household, she was told to remove the wrist-strap she wore as a badge of servitude to Munby. She refused and was sacked on the grounds that it made her too dirty to wait at table. The constant need to wash and change from work clothes to a clean apron at any minute to be summoned upstairs or answer the door was a complaint of both Hannah and many other domestic servants. The effort to maintain a clean frontstage and working backstage was an extra burden on servants when there was only one employed. After she had lost her job, Hannah wrote bitterly: 'i felt a bit hurt to be told i was too dirty, when my dirt was all got with making things clean for them.' This is her satisfaction, the work that her strength and skill can accomplish:

> How shamed ladies'd be to have hands and arms like mine and how weak they'd be to do my work and how shocked to touch the dirty things even what i black my whole hands with every day – yet such things must be done and the lady's'd be the first to cry out if they was to find nobody to do it for 'em – so the lowest work i think is honourable in itself and the poor drudge is honourable too providing her mind isn't coarse and low as her work, both cause its useful and for be'en content with the station she is placed in.[97]

Once Hannah even made the dangerous connection between this strength and the constraints of her deference and dependency. In a tiff with an employer, occasioned by her visits to Munby, she noted: 'i told Massa how it was to feel a great big wench & strong as i am, as could crush a weak thing like Miss Margaret is with one hand (though of course i *wouldn't* & she must know that) – for her to *trifle* with me about going out when i'd got leave to – & *play* with me as if i was a child' (Hannah was thirty-eight years old at this time). Hannah was resentful at Munby's taking the lady's part and not helping her. She claims she wasn't rude, only 'spoke up plain' but 'humble as i *ought* to be to them above me'. It was not a pleasant evening she spent with Munby after this incident 'but i could see he didn't exactly *dislike* me for showing *spirit*'.[98]

Here was one of the paradoxes of their relationship. Hannah was in many ways a more independent agent than Munby as she had supported herself from the age of eight while he was financially and in many ways still emotionally and socially dependent on his parents. Yet for all her strength and independence, Hannah's position forced her into a childish dependency on Munby. Both referred to her moods and outbursts as 'being naughty'. When she is put in an intolerable situation by her employer, Munby gives her a double message; backing up the authority of the employer yet obviously enjoying her show of spirit especially as he knew that he had ultimate loyalty over her life through love:

> Obeying other folks' commands
> Although she was my own[99]

Munby especially delighted to subtly attack middle-class women through Hannah: his love was stronger than their legitimate authority. In 'Queen Kara' he says:

> From Nature's sanctum: whose degree is sure
> And even a slave obeying finds reward
> That Woman still should mould herself to Man
> And not to Woman. Masculine regard
> Is hers by right for blessing or for ban.[100]

He believes that Hannah, like all young servants while outwardly respectful, regards 'the ladies as her natural enemies' but the gentlemen as her allies. This is very like the childhood alliance of children and servants against the moral authority of the mother. Munby was incapable of realizing that while Hannah was subservient and hard-worked by all middle-class employers, the women varied just as much as the men. The ex-governess for whom Hannah worked in Margate was particularly kind and uncondescending, talking to her at length, teaching her about astronomy and loaning her books.

The same psychological shallowness is evident in Munby's reaction to any illness or even fatigue on Hannah's part. On these occasions, in contrast to his attitude to his mother's perpetual illnesses, he both panics and becomes angry with her like a child depending on an all-powerful, never-exhausted mother figure if she shows any sign of weakness:

> And again my Massa, why shd you be put out cause I had the Lumbago & them sweats & languid feelings – I shall not like telling you if anything's the matter if it puts you out o'sorts, as you say – I know you'll say it's love & all that, but i know how *soon* you *wince*, & are really put out if all doesn't go to your liking, & if you was a married man with a family & delicate wife & kep a lot a servants you'd often ha' things to vex I can tell you . . .[101]

In the year before they were married, Hannah was working for an eccentric maiden lady who lived alone. She often made Hannah get up in the middle of the night and search the house from coal cellar to dust hole in the yard for 'wicked men'. Munby scolded Hannah for exposing herself to yet more colds and rheumatic pains for she had been ill on and off for some months:

> I told Massa how i'd got a cold from it, he was angry with me for running the risk but i said 'if my missis orders me to do a thing i must *do* it' & i said 'if it costs one's life we ought to do it, else what's a servant good for?' Massa said 'Yes you *shd* obey your

missis of course but shouldn't you obey *me* first?' So i said 'Yes Massa & if you'd bin there & told me *not* to go in the coal hole i wouldn't.'[102]

In the face of such potential degradation and dependence, Hannah sought sources of self-respect and meaning in what was a rather lonely life. Brought up from early childhood in the charity school, imbued with the tracts and hymns which were the staples of Victorian reading matter, religious observance had become one such source which added beauty, music and a spiritual dimension to her sordid daily life. Although Hannah had no illusions about the role of the church as mainly the preserve of the better-off and thought, for example, that her sister's compulsive church-going was rather too much, nevertheless, religion was of consequence to her and she resented the limited time she could give to public worship. Over the years, partly through her association with Munby but also on her own, she managed to become something of a connoisseur of the liturgy, sermons and music of the services.

Most important of all, religious belief and mutual church-going provided the couple with a joint experience. Particularly for Hannah, in the eyes of God, she and her Massa were equals. She specifically mentions the solace of silent prayer together; kneeling at the altar with Munby provided a silent communion and reconciliation between them.[103]

In addition to these psychological contradictions, there was an economic problem. With her skill, experience and intelligence, Hannah could have earned upwards of twenty pounds a year as an upper servant. She did try a place as cook with a kitchen maid under her at twenty-two pounds but she soon gave it up and didn't try again:

indeed it was only nonsense for me after being used to the lowest only and Massa teaching me to love rough dirty work . . . i dislike the thought of being over anybody and ordering things not only cause i'd rather do the work myself but for fear anyone should think me set up and proud . . . for freedom and true lowliness there's nothing like being a maid of all work.[104]

Hannah, by her own admission, was very glad to turn her financial affairs totally over to Munby whom she trusted implicitly. It is probable that part of this financial dependency was the product of her blocked ambition and her acceptance of her lowliness. In February 1871, on Munby's advice, she withdrew £100 of her savings (a very substantial amount by working-class standards of the period – Munby himself only started his job at £160 a year). She was given the money in sovereigns and notes but she records in her diary that she didn't even count it: 'it seem'd such a lot & confused me, for though i like saving and being careful, i hate going to the bank or having anything to do with money affairs, so i feel glad to get rid of it as long as its safe, & glad that Massa doesn't mind managing it for me, for i certainly would do nothing with it myself.'[105]

Nevertheless, Hannah's relationship to Munby in his persona as *gentleman* was extremely important to her. She claimed several times that she had 'seen his face in the tea-cups' before she met him; in other words that she was psychologically attuned to finding someone of higher status as proof of her own self-worth. She muses in her diary at various points about whether she could have ever fallen in love with a man of her own rank and comes to the conclusion that it is doubtful. Yet, as with women of any class, without marriage, the final mark of her dependent status was the lack of a home of her own. Unmarried female servants no matter what their age, were always considered 'girls'. The mythology of the middle class maintained that these women would be taken care of as Munby took care of his old nurse, Hannah Carter, by giving her a pension in her old age. (Munby himself published a collection of *Epitaphs and Obituaries of Faithful Servants* in 1891, material culled mostly from tombstones found in his wanderings.) The Royal Commission on the Poor Law inquiry at the turn of the century confirmed that, for those domestic servants who were single and had never had a home of their own, a much more common fate was for them to seek indoor relief in the workhouse when they could no longer work.[106] Hannah felt this gap in her life increasingly as her relationship with Munby drew her further away from her childhood roots in Shropshire. Some of the entries in her diary show her often desperately 'homesick'. The cottage she finally had in Shropshire partly made up for this and made her resigned to living apart from Munby.

Munby too was torn by the contradictions implicit in his relationship with Hannah. He resented what he felt to be her underestimation of what he had sacrificed in remaining loyal to her. Most importantly, he didn't see, as most employers of servants didn't see, the physical and mental burden of the work-load a servant such as Hannah was expected to carry. Despite the vivid, detailed description of her daily work that Hannah provided in her diary, and his own observations of working women, Munby, who had never worked with anything heavier than a pen in his life, romanticized manual work. He delighted in the fact that Hannah spent her Sunday afternoons off with him, doing his housework, getting his tea, washing his feet. She also took his laundry, mending and sewing away to do in her spare time.

After they were married, Hannah not only did all the housework, shopping and cooking for Munby; but because she was nominally the housekeeper for the whole building at Fig Tree Court, she worked for the other tenants as well. Writing of this period, Munby exults half-jokingly in his diary: 'She emptied slops, she drew water, and brought up the full can and pail, she dug coals and carried up the full scuttle; which things she does daily without any help from her Brutal Husband.'[107]

Although he taught working women Latin at the Working Women's College, Munby believed that the working girl should remain simple. In his poetry he sneers at the 'listless pale imitations' of gentility into which such girls develop who strive to become educated. Rather, their education should consist of 'Nature, Labour and Life'. While thoroughly appreciating Hannah's inborn refinement and obvious intelligence, he lists her best characteristics as 'Devout purity, homely household skill, love of nature, strength, humility and artless simplicity'. A careful reading of Hannah's diaries, however, conveys the impression of an extremely efficient administrator as well as hard worker with a wide knowledge of the social nuances of her several worlds and a shrewd skill at manipulating her employers within the limits of her service relationship.

Munby's 'not seeing' Hannah's distress and physical exhaustion was part of the natural relationship of the servant/wife. After they were married he did, indeed, consider that he owned all her loyalties and legally, of course, he gained control of her income and savings. After their marriage Hannah at last took off the wrist-strap, collar and chain which she had secretly worn all the years of their courtship.

He was fond of quoting Ruskin's words to her: 'that the best of all service is unpaid because it is done for love'. In a poem written after her death in 1909 in which Munby openly acknowledged their relationship, he calls Hannah 'my faithful servant wife' and he equates love and labour as one and the same thing:

> Happy in her humble calling
> Happy on her hands and knees
> Nothing checks her – nothing daunts her.
> Til her daily work is done;
>
> And she does it not for merit but to prove
> That no labour is too low to be
> The language of her love[108]

In *Ann Morgan's Love* he repeats his favourite theme that a woman's true love will be expressed through loyalty and labour:

> Of sacrifice, of self-abandonment
> Of pure devoted, unregarded toil
> For him to whom she gives herself: for *me*

In many ways Hannah was, in fact, a creature of his fantasy. He could not face the fact that she was a real human being with wishes and needs of her own. After they were married for a short time, Munby persuaded Hannah to dress and live as a lady and openly become his wife. It worked very briefly while they were on their wedding trip in France and for the odd week or two in hired rooms in the country. But after their return to Fig Tree Court, Hannah refused to continue and Munby, with secret relief, allowed her to remain as his housekeeper. His fascination with the pretending and transformation game made this enjoyable at first and they could now at least live in the same house.

Munby was obviously afraid of his father's wrath and the effect on his frail, unworldly mother if he revealed the truth about his marriage. And yet after his parents' death, he seemed to become even more ambivalent about the relationship. The games were beginning to lose their charm as Hannah gained more understanding of middle-class life at close quarters, and the 'strange trials' and nineteen years of waiting had left their mark on both of them. Hannah clung more than ever to her servant identity as her one claim to independence, but to Munby it seemed rather that she had learned the lesson of lowliness only too well.

In middle-class Victorian terms, A.J. Munby failed to become a full social adult, for he never set up and supported a household complete with wife, children and servants. His relations with women of his own class were mostly formal; his secret despising of their weakness was compensated by extreme chivalry and courtesy in his dealings with them in person.[109] His diary reveals that he felt much more at ease in the company of his male companions. He was especially hostile to any claims made by what he considered to be feminist women. He considered that they had neither the attractions of his 'rustic maidens' nor the acknowledged, fragile femininity of their own class; rather they were unsexed beings who were viciously determined to take away real men's vocations and he remained opposed to women's suffrage all his life.[110]

Clearly, Munby was no radical in the sphere of sexual politics. Once at a party in Campden Hill he made a special effort to speak at length to a young lady with whom a close friend and contemporary was deeply in love. (He and Munby were in their early forties at the time.) 'A lively good natured very pretty girl of nineteen: voila tout! Yet there is something noble in that worship of beauty and girlish weakness which makes a brave high-minded man fall down before such an object in despite of his own judgement.'[111]

Munby himself had twice become involved with young middle-class women and even thought of proposing marriage, but before long he withdrew. The impression from the diary is that he was never seriously emotionally drawn to any of those from his own class. In any case, marriage to a middle-class woman would have meant his obtaining a level of income and life-style which Munby could not and would not do.

It may have been, as in the case of many other middle-class men who turned to working-class girls (or men) for their emotional life, that the split image was too great for him to maintain in a traditional marriage.[112] Nevertheless, this inability also sharpened his awareness of the contradictions in his society. He was attracted to Hannah and the women like her, degraded and dirty for his sake, but also for the independent spirit of her life in refusing to be a 'lady' and thus losing that independence. Munby said of service that 'it may blunt the home affections' but it gave a 'sturdy independence, self-reliance and shrewdness' to the character. He quotes approvingly from one of his servant informers, 'I know if I don't take care of myself, nobody else'll take care of me.'[113]

Despite his, to us, repellent fascinations with certain symbolic themes: the equation of dirt and degradation with female strength and love; the comparison of women to brute beasts, of both to black slaves; and the identification of all these inferior breeds as agents of a threatening but compelling Nature, Munby did recognize, if only dimly, a fundamental contradiction of Victorian society. The sheltered lives that middle-class ladies were ideally supposed to lead depended directly on the labour of working-class girls and women, who through their services created the material conditions necessary to maintain a middle-class life-style for men and women alike.[114]

He went further than expressing his concern about this contradiction in more normal activities like the moral reform of individual women or the 'rescue' of symbolically important, but marginal, groups such as child prostitutes. He wanted to see working women remain independent and in charge of their own destiny through economic and social control of their own lives. The tragedy was, of course, that his championship of this cause remained at the individual level, and stopped short at the significant barrier of manual work.

Conclusions

A detailed study of such a source as the Munby collection brings alive the connection between social structure and personality. The pervasiveness of both class and gender categories, which it illustrates, stems from the effect of often unconscious, highly-charged, emotional expectations laid down in childhood, which in many cases appear in the form of subliminal images. The mutual preoccupations of Munby and Hannah with boundaries and their experience of crossing these boundaries in both fantasy and reality can tell us a great deal about the way the fabric of Victorian society was created and maintained.

Hannah's experience of both sides of the class barrier, in particular, while emphasizing the monotony and sheer drudgery of domestic work, it provides insights into the constraints as well as privileges of middle-class women. Hannah obviously valued the social, physical and spatial freedom of movement open to a servant but denied to any woman who had pretensions to gentility. In her experiments with ladies' clothing and life-style she demonstrates in a very human way the constraints which such apparently trivial factors meant in daily life. On her wedding journey to France, she had changed her short servant's skirt and jacket to dress as a lady, complete with felt hat with a feather and veil, 'a grey frock with frill round my neck, and white cuffs and grey kid gloves, and carrying my striped sun shade – all different to anything i had got used to, that one day in the train i got almost ill tempered at being so muffled up, and i felt i'd much liefer feel my hands free as they used to be.'[115]

When set against background knowledge of the period, the omissions in the diaries can be as revealing as what is recorded. Munby, for example, scarcely ever mentions working-class men in detail, even those he taught at the Working Men's College. If he does, they are noted without emotion, as figures in the landscape or occasionally as part of Hannah's circle: her brother, uncle or fellow servants. He seems to have concentrated almost exclusively on women, though heavily 'masculinized' women. Yet it is known at this period that cross-class homosexual relations exercised both intense attraction as well as fear for many men of Munby's background and education.[116] Working-class youths, as well as girls, could represent the natural and uncorrupted domain. Edward Carpenter expressing his love for the poor and uneducated 'thick-thighed, hot, coarse-fleshed young brick layer, with the strip around his waist' uses language very reminiscent of Munby's.[117] The lure of the unknown appears especially strong in the image of the dusky native boy so easily available to colonial soldiers, administrators and adventurers.

This view at times comes close to a vision of the working class as representing 'true' masculinity, the power of manual work. Such a force would revitalize the effete, over-urbanized, even feminized, middle class; but at the same time, it is equated with fear of the threatening working-class mob. Munby, as well as reformers of many varieties and even radicals, tried to use personal (sexual) relationships to bring the classes closer together, to bridge the artificial gap between human beings – consider E.M. Forster's cry of 'only connect'. Yet cross-class relationships always displayed a certain ambivalence for they were ultimately based on power and exploitation; first and foremost the power of money, but also of education and life-style, while within heterosexual relations these powers were augmented by the rights traditionally due to the man.

A.J. Munby had a dim sense of this ambivalence, for he had spent his whole life in trying to come to terms with the dilemma of class and gender while at the same time making full use of the prerogatives of his status as an upper-middle-class man. He expressed his unease in a passage from his diary where he focuses, as so often, on the metaphor of *hands*.

In 1860 he was dining with some of his men friends at a country inn. One of his favourite types of 'country wench' with big, red hands and bare arms waited at table and Munby mused:

> Are the relations of the sexes really inverted when three men sit at table, with hands delicate and jewelled, and a woman stands behind and waits, offering the dishes with so large coarse a hand that makes her master's look almost lady-like: And is it the proper thing, that the *women* should sit as at a ball supper, drawing the gloves from their dainty fingers, and waited on by *men* whose hands that seemed so ladylike by comparison with Molly's, look sinewy and labourious by the side of Blanche's tender tips? If *this* is right for one class is that for the other? In short, what, in the Equation of Life, is the respective value of the terms *sex* and *station*.[118]

In the course of studying this one relationship in depth it has become evident that the separation of spheres for women and men, which had begun as an attempt to solve the contradictions created by the pursuit of economic power and rationality through the market, had itself created intense contradictions for the individual men who reaped its benefits. At the same time, it also becomes clear that the interconnection of these hierarchical divisions could blight innumerable lives of those who were made most vulnerable by that system, particularly young working-class women.

Appendix

From A.J. Munby, *Benois: Poems*, 1852

The Sexes

O, you are fair – you have soft turtle-eyes,
　　Not flush'd with vulgar passion, clouded not
With stains of folly, – whose transparent lymph
　　No shadows dull, no fretful eddies blot:

Your souls are precious oratories, closed
　　And curtain'd in from all things not divine;
Where smoothest sounds enrich the loving air,
　　And moons alone and silver cressets shine.

You dwell in peace among your pleasant hours –
　　You hear no echoes from the far-off strife;
You lift your shining eyes, and all the place
　　Feels happier – feels the magic of your life.

But we – for us in the thick thronging days
　　No shrine, no bower, no oasis appears;
No path is left whereby we might have climb'd
　　Back for a moment to the better years:

We have forgotten all – we hear not now
　　Our mothers' teachings, – see not in the land
Its ancient beauties. – look on you as dreams
　　Too fair to love, too high to understand:

We are uncover'd – the rank, stagnant air
　　Infects our breath – our curdled souls endure
A press of crawling horrors – and vile sounds
　　Hiss in our dull ears: how can we be pure?

Two Hands

I

This is her hand, her cool and fragrant hand:
　　Long lissome fingers, soft as the south wind;
　　A roseleaf palm, which Love's own kiss would find
Sweet as the rose; and many a thin blue strand
Vein'd in the white, our homage to command.
　　All grace of form and colour has combined
　　To give us this fair index of a mind
Pure as her hands, and not less nobly plann'd.

Ah, tender toys, so slight, so flexible!
    Can they too share the strenuous work of life,
And help their owner to do long and well
    The duties of a woman and a wife;
Or, may they brook no labour more severe
Than just to charm the eye and soothe the ear?

II

This is her hand, her large and rugged hand:
    Strong nervous fingers, stiff with homely toil,
    Yet capable; for labour cannot spoil
Their native vigour, nor their swift command
Of household tools, indoors or on the land.
    What if rough work must harden and must soil
    Her massive palms? They are but as a foil
To that sweet face which all can understand.

Yes, all enjoy the beauty of her face;
    But few perceive the pathos and the power
Of those broad hands, or feel that inner grace
    Of which they are the symbol and the flower:
The grace of lowly help; of duty done
Unselfishly, for all – for anyone.

Notes

I should like to thank Pat Bradford, Angela John, Ann Kallenberg, Jean L'Esperance, Helen Hirsch, Steff Pixner, Jeff Weeks and members of the University of Essex Research Seminar for help and suggestions in preparing this essay.

1   Throughout this essay I shall be using gender to refer to the socially constructed categories, masculinity and femininity, while sex refers to the biological categories, male and female. See Ann Oakley, *Sex, Gender and Society* (Temple Smith, London, 1972).

2   Anthropologists have made use of this approach far more often than historians have. For example, 'Gender is very much made use of in Hagen to talk about things other than men and women, and the fact that it is so used has a feed-back effect on how the sexes are perceived. . . . The logic inherent in the way such notions are set up must be understood in relation to general values in the society' (Marilyn Strathern, 'The Achievement of Sex: Paradoxes in Hagen Gender-Thinking', in Erik Schwimmer, ed., *Yearbook of Symbolic Anthropology*, I (McGill-Queen's University Press, Montreal, 1978), p. 171.

3   Mary Douglas, *Natural Symbols: Explorations in Cosmology* (Pelican Books, Harmondsworth, 1973).

4   Edward Shils, 'Charisma, Order and Status', in *Center and Periphery: Essays in Macrosociology* (University of Chicago Press, Chicago, 1975), p. 269.

5   Christine Delphy, 'Proto-Feminism and Anti-Feminism', in *The Main Enemy: A Materialist Analysis of Women's Oppression* (Women's Research and Resources Centre, London, 1977).

6 Geoffrey Pearson, *The Deviant Imagination: Psychiatry, Social Work, and Social Change* (Macmillan, London, 1975), p. 162; Michael Steig, 'Dickens's Excremental Vision', *Victorian Studies*, 13 (March 1970), pp. 339–54; Gertrude Himmelfarb, 'Mayhew's Poor: A Problem of Identity', *Victorian Studies*, vol. 14 (March 1971), pp. 307–20. See also H. Hallam, 'Report of the Council of the Statistical Society of London from a Committee of its Fellows appointed to make an investigation into the state of the poorer classes', *Journal of the Statistical Society of London* (August 1848), p. 193: '. . . since the population [St Georges in the East] is, to some extent, the drainage from the grades next above it, we should rather hope to find a cure by cutting off the supply of degradation than by attempting to reform and elevate it in the lowest depths to which it can sink.'

7 Jeffrey Weeks, *Coming Out: Homosexual Politics in Britain from the Nineteenth Century to the Present* (Quartet Books, London, 1977); Judith Walkowitz, 'The Making of an Outcast Group: Prostitutes and Working Women in Nineteenth-Century Plymouth and Southampton', in Martha Vicinus, ed., *The Widening Sphere: Changing Roles of Victorian Women* (University of Indiana Press, Bloomington, IN, 1977).

8 John Berger, 'Animals as Metaphor', *New Society*, 10 March, 1977, pp. 504–5. The idea that women are both part of but outside 'society' is a point of view still expressed in discussions of sexual divisions. It has recently been the centre of a debate: nature/culture = female/male. See Edwin Ardener, 'Belief and the Problem of Women', in Shirley Ardener, ed., *Perceiving Women* (Dent, London, 1977); and a critique, Nicole-Claude Mathieu, 'Man–Culture and Woman–Nature?', *Women's Studies International Quarterly*, no. 1 (spring 1978), pp. 55–65.

9 Examination of physical features such as skull capacity and other 'evidence amassed from the very beginning tended to relegate the female, with the Negro, to a sub-ordinate position' (John S. Haller and Robin M. Haller, *The Physician and Sexuality in Victorian America* [University of Illinois Press, Urbana, IL, 1974], p. 48).

10 Yet we as observers should know that the way sexuality and particularly rituals surrounding sex are used can tell us something not so much about sex *per se* as about the society. See Mary Douglas, *Implicit Meanings: Essays in Anthropology* (Routledge & Kegan Paul, London, 1975).

11 Max Weber, 'Religious Ethics and the World: Sexuality and Art', in *Economy and Society*, trans. and ed. Guenther Roth and Claus Wittich (Free Press, Glencoe, IL, 1968), vol. 3, p. 603.

12 G.J. Barker-Benfield, *The Horrors of the Half-Known Life: Male Attitudes Toward Woman and Sexuality in Nineteenth-Century America* (Harper & Row, New York, 1976); Peter Cominos, 'Late Victorian Sexual Respectability and the Social System', *International Review of Social History*, vol. 3 (1963).

13 Carroll Smith-Rosenberg, 'Sex as Symbol in Victorian Purity: An Ethnohistorical Analysis of Jacksonian America', in John Demos and Sarane Spence Boocock, eds, *Turning Points: Historical and Sociological Essays on the Family American Journal of Sociology*, vol. 84, supplement (University of Chicago Press, Chicago, 1978).

14 Eric Trudgill, *Madonnas and Magdalens: The Origins and Development of Victorian Sexual Attitudes* (Heinemann, London, 1976).

15 Sarah B. Pomeroy, *Goddesses, Whores, Wives, and Slaves: Women in Classical Antiquity* (Schocken Books, New York, 1976).

16 Rosemary Radford Ruether, 'Misogynism and Virginal Feminism in the Fathers of the Church', in Rosemary Radford Ruether, ed., *Religion and Sexism: Images of Women in the Jewish and Christian Tradition* (Simon & Schuster, New York, 1974).

17 Cleo McNelly, 'Nature, Women and Claude Lévi-Strauss: A Reading of *Tristes Tropiques* as Myth', *Massachusetts Review*, vol. 16 (winter 1975), pp. 10–11.

18 Ibid.

19 Anthony S. Wohl, 'Sex and the Single Room: Incest among the Victorian Working Class', in Anthony S. Wohl, ed., *The Victorian Family: Structures and Stresses* (Croom Helm, London, 1978).

20 Deborah Gorham, 'The "Maiden Tribute of Modern Babylon" Re-examined: Child Prostitution and the Idea of Childhood in Late Victorian England', *Victorian Studies* (spring 1978); Trudgill, *Madonnas and Magdalens*.

21 Steven Marcus, *The Other Victorians: A Study of Sexuality and Pornography in Mid-Nineteenth-Century England* (Bantam Books, New York, 1971).

22 Charles Ansell, *On the Rate of Mortality at Early Periods of Life, the Age of Marriage and Other Statistics of Families in the Upper and Professional Classes* (C. and E. Layton, London, 1874).

23 C. Carey, *Wee Wifie* (F.M. Lupton, London and New York, 1869).

24 Betty Askwith, *Two Victorian Families* (Chatto & Windus, London, 1971).

25 Theresa McBride, ' "As the Twig is Bent": The Victorian Nanny', in Anthony S. Wohl, ed., *The Victorian Family: Structures and Stresses* (Croom Helm, London, 1978); James Bossard, 'Domestic Servants and Child Development', in *The Sociology of Child Development* (Harper & Row, New York, 1954).

26 Leonore Davidoff, 'The Rationalization of Housework', this volume, ch. 3.

27 Leonore Davidoff, 'Mastered for Life: Servant and Wife in Victorian England', this volume, ch. 7.

28 Jonathan Gathorne-Hardy, *The Rise and Fall of the Victorian Nanny* (Hodder & Stoughton, London, 1972).

29 McBride, ' "As the Twig is Bent" '; and Leonore Davidoff, 'Forbidden Territories: Children, Servants and the Victorian House', unpublished lecture delivered to the Victorian Society, spring 1978.

30 J. Swann, '*Mater* and Nannie: Freud's Two Mothers and the Discovery of the Oedipus Complex', *American Imago: A Psychoanalytic Journal for Culture, Science and the Arts*, spring 1974; and Kenneth A. Grigg, 'All Roads Lead to Rome: The Role of the Nursemaid in Freud's Dreams', *Journal of the American Psychoanalytic Association*, vol. 21 (1973), pp. 108–26.

31 Eugene D. Genovese, *Roll, Jordan, Roll: The World the Slaves Made* (Pantheon Books, New York, 1974), pp. 354, 361.

32 Calvin C. Hernton, *Sex and Racism* (André Deutsch, London, 1973). In his section on 'The Sexual Gain', John Dollard discussed the illicit but acknowledged sexual exploitation of black women by white men in the American South. In a period when black and white cultures varied it is possible that diet etc. produced body odours which differed, but it is also possible that the difference was perceived as greater than it really was. In any case it has obvious similarity to the case I am discussing. 'It may be that just those odours which are revolting when one is in a conventional mood may be exciting in a sexual mood' (John Dollard, 'The Sexual Gain', in *Caste and Class in a Southern Town* [Doubleday Anchor Books, New York, 1949], p. 144).

33 Mary Lutyens, *To Be Young: Some Chapters of Autobiography* (Rupert Hart-Davis, London, 1959), p. 15.

34 Robert Louis Stevenson, *Collected Poems*, ed. Janet Adam Smith (Rupert Hart-Davis, London, 1950), p. 361.

35 Ursula Bloom, *'Mrs Bunthorpe's Respects': A Chronicle of Cooks* (Hutchinson, London, 1963), p. 42.

36 Susan Chitty, *The Beast and the Monk: A Life of Charles Kingsley* (Hodder & Stoughton, London, 1974).

37 Geoffrey Grigson, *The Crest on the Silver: An Autobiography* (The Cresset Press, London, 1950), p. 51.

38 Arthur J. Munby, 'Dichter und Baverin', *Relicta* (Bertram Dobell, London, 1909);

Leonore Davidoff, *The Best Circles: Society, Etiquette and the Season* (Century Hutchinson, London, 1986).

39 Alrik Gustafson, *Six Scandinavian Novelists* (University of Minnesota Press, Minneapolis, 1966), p. 292.

40 Legal protection for servants from being physically punished was only provided as part of the Offenses Against the Person Act of 1861 and complaints had to be made to two JPs. See J.D. Caswell, *The Law of Domestic Service* (Grant Richards London, 1913).

41 Ronald Blythe, *Akenfield: Portrait of an English Village* (Delta Books, London, 1971).

42 Mrs Motherly, *The Servants' Behaviour Book: Hints on Manners and Dress for Maid Servants* (Bell & Daldy, London, 1859), p. 49. 'Humility is expressed in all postures which involve bowing, crouching or lowering the body' (Michael Argyle, *Bodily Communication* [Methuen, London, 1976], p. 284).

43 Stephen Tallents, *Man and Boy* (Faber & Faber, London, 1943), p. 10; Sigrid Undset, *The Longest Years*, trans. A.G. Charter (Cassell, London, 1935).

44 Jennifer Wayne, *Brown Bread and Butter in the Basement: A Twenties Childhood* (Gollancz, London, 1975), p. 43.

45 Cominos, 'Late Victorian Sexual Respectability and the Social System'.

46 Sigmund Freud, 'On the Universal Tendency to Debasement in the Sphere of Love', *On Sexuality* (Pelican Freud Library, Harmondsworth, 1977), pp. 251–4.

47 Trinity College, Cambridge, MSS, Munby Diary, September 1860.

48 Douglas, *Implicit Meanings*, p. 61.

49 Richard L. Schoenwald, 'Training Urban Man: A Hypothesis about the Sanitary Movement', in H.J. Dyos and Michael Wolff, eds, *The Victorian City: Images and Realities* (Routledge & Kegan Paul, London, 1973) vol. 2, pp. 669–92.

50 Munby's story has been told and excerpts from his diary sensitively edited in Derek Hudson, *Munby, Man of Two Worlds: The Life and Diaries of Arthur J. Munby, 1828–1910* (Abacus, London, 1974); and Arthur J. Munby, Diaries 1859–1898. I am very indebted to Hudson's work and interpretation. All quotations from the diaries are by permission of the Master and Fellows of Trinity College, Cambridge. I have retained spelling, punctuation and underlining (represented by italic) exactly as they appear in the original. I have also followed the general convention of referring to Arthur Munby by his last name only while Hannah Cullwick is invariably called simply 'Hannah'. Nevertheless the status and power implications of this naming convention should not be overlooked. The adult middle-class man is given the impersonal dignity of his surname while the female servant retains the personalized, childlike use of her first name only. See also Arthur J. Munby, *Benois: Poems* (John Oliver, London, 1852); Arthur J. Munby, *Verses: New and Old* (Bell & Daldy, London, 1865); Arthur J. Munby, *Dorothy: A Country Story* (Kegan Paul & Co., London, 1880); Arthur J. Munby, *Vulgar Verses (by 'Jones Brown')* (Reeves & Turner, London, 1891); Arthur J. Munby, *Susan, A Poem of Degrees* (Reeves & Turner, London, 1893); Arthur J. Munby, *Ann Morgan's Love: A Pedestrian Poem* (Reeves & Turner, London, 1896); Arthur J. Munby, *Poems, Chiefly Lyric and Elegiac* (Kegan Paul & Co., London, 1901); and Arthur J. Munby, *Relicta* (Bertram Dobell, London, 1909).

51 Robert A. Fothergill, *Private Chronicles: A Study of English Diaries* (Oxford University Press, London, 1974).

52 Anon., *My Secret Life* (Grove Press, New York, 1966).

53 Letter from Munby, quoted in Hudson, *Munby: Man of Two Worlds*, p. 39.

54 Angela V. John, *By the Sweat of their Brow: Women Workers at Victorian Coal Mines* (Croom Helm, London, 1980).

55 Leonore Davidoff, Jean L'Esperance, and Howard Newby, 'Landscape with Figures: Home and Community in English Society', this volume, ch. 2; and John Henry

Raleigh, 'The Novel and the City', *Victorian Studies*, vol. 11 (March 1968), pp. 291–329.

56 Actors, especially circus performers and travelling players, like gypsies, held a special place in the pantheon of Victorian fantasy. Their independence from the duties and constraints of work, the element of play in their lives, held a special attraction as well as moral opprobium. See, for example, the place of the circus people in Charles Dickens's *Hard Times*.

57 Munby, Diary, June 1859, quoted in Hudson, *Munby: Man of Two Worlds*, p. 35.

58 Munby, Diary, 1860.

59 A.J. Munby, Hannah's Volumes 2, 1877.

60 Munby, Diary, 1860.

61 A.J. Munby, Hannah's Places, 1841–1872.

62 This point has been made by Pam Taylor, Centre for Cultural Studies, Birmingham, in her study of domestic service in the interwar period.

63 Interestingly, it was the governess who comforted her in her sorrow. Governesses, especially retired or 'broken down', were often noted by Hannah throughout her diaries. The two maiden ladies whom she worked for in Margate and who were very kind to her were ex-governesses who were trying to run a boarding house. Hannah was always slightly pitying of such women, not real ladies, yet trying to live a genteel life without the resources to do so and unable to do a thing for themselves, not even sew their own clothes. Hannah's diary confirms the social and metaphorical, not to be confused with statistical, importance of the governess in the Victorian view of gender and class. See also Leonore Davidoff, 'The English Victorian Governess: A Study in Social Isolation', unpublished paper, 1971; M. Jeanne Peterson, 'The Victorian Governess: Status Incongruence in Family and Society', in Martha Vicinus, ed., *Suffer and Be Still: Women in the Victorian Age* (University of Indiana Press, Bloomington, IN, 1973).

64 A.J. Munby, Hannah's Volumes, 1875.

65 A.J. Munby, Hannah's Places, 1841–1872.

66 A.J. Munby, Hannah's Places, 1841–1872.

67 Cissie Fairchild makes the point that it was the physical, social and economic vulnerability of lower-class women which made them susceptible to seduction by their masters (masters' sons, relatives or friends) or to promises of marriage from their swains. See Cissie Fairchild, 'Female Sexual Attitudes and the Rise of Illegitimacy: A Case Study', *Journal of Interdisciplinary History*, vol. 9 (spring 1978), pp. 627–67.

68 Hannah Munby's Diary of Her Life As A Servant in the Temple, September 1873.

69 D. Hudson, *Munby: Man of Two Worlds*. Personal communication, Pat Bradford, Archivist, Trinity College, Cambridge, who catalogued the Munby collection.

70 Stanley Cohen and Laurie Taylor, *Escape Attempts: The Theory and Practice of Resistance to Everyday Life* (Allen Lane, London, 1976), p. 92. For the recent discovery of another case of double playacting which expresses themes of mastery and submission in a sexual context, see the case of Charles and Mary Kingsley (Chitty, *The Beast and the Monk*).

71 At the level of the individual psyche, hands were also regarded as the agents of the 'dirty' work involved in masturbation, an obsessive concern of the middle class at this time. See Trudgill, *Madonnas and Magdalens*. 'It is just as plausible to examine sexual behaviour for its capacity to express and serve non-sexual motives as the reverse' (John H. Gagnon and William Simon, *Sexual Conduct: The Social Sources of Human Sexuality* [Aldine, Chicago, 1973], p. 17). Feet and hands as fetishes often screen actual relations from oneself and others. See Gertrud Lenzer, 'On Masochism: A Contribution to the History of Phantasy and its Theory', *Signs: Journal of Women in Culture and Society*, vol. 1 (winter, 1975).

72 G.A. Sala, *Margaret Forster: A Dream Within a Dream* (T. Fisher Unwin, London, 1897), p. 15.

73 A.J. Munby, *Vulgar Verses (by 'Jones Brown')* (Reeves & Turner, London, 1891).

74 Mary Merryweather, *Experience of Factory Life: Being a Record of Fourteen Years' Work at Mr. Courtauld's Silk Mill at Halstead in Essex* (B.R. Parkes, London, 1862), p. 9. A late Victorian health visitor noted that this perception by the rich that the poor have large hands and feet resulted in the giving of cast-off clothing, particularly boots, which never fitted properly: see M.E. Loane, *The Next Street but One* (Edward Arnold, London, 1907). In fact, given differential feeding, standards of living and the effects of grinding physical work, we know that the poor would have been of smaller physique than the middle class or even regularly employed working class.

75 See the following seventeenth-century description of the perfect wife: 'When shee submits herselfe with quietness, cheerefully, even as a well-broken horse turns at the least check of the riders bride, readily going and standing as he wishes that sits upon his back', in William Whately, *A Bride-Bush or a Wedding Sermon*, quoted in Kathleen Davies, '"The Sacred Condition of Equality" – How Original were Puritan Doctrines of Marriage?' *Social History*, vol. 5 (May 1977), p. 572. Davies goes on to say that 'the metaphor of horse breaking was a favorite one'.

76 A.J. Munby, Diary, 1863.

77 A.J. Munby, 'Leonard and Elisabeth: A Subterranean Story', unpublished poem, 1896, kindness of the late Dr A.N.L. Munby and Dr A. John.

78 Davidoff, 'The Rationalization of Housework'.

79 Arrah B. Evarts, 'Color Symbolism', *The Psychoanalytic Review*, 6 (April 1919), pp. 124–57.

80 James Walvin, *Black and White: The Negro and English Society 1555–1945* (Allen Lane, London, 1973). According to the *OED* definition from that period black implied 'deeply stained with dirt, soiled, dirty, foul . . . having dark or deadly purposes, malignant, pertaining to or involving death, baneful, disasterous, sinister – an emotionally partisan colour, the handmaid and symbol of baseness and evil'.

81 Winthrop D. Jordan, *White over Black: American Attitudes Toward the Negro, 1550–1812* (University of North Carolina Press, Chapel Hill, 1968).

82 Chitty, *The Beast and the Monk*.

83 Hannah's Diary, February 1872. Munby and Hannah have constructed these 'signs of lowness' on the base of 'socially valid and institutionally recommended standards of "preference"' given by the position of Victorian domestic service. See H. Garfinkel, 'Conditions of Successful Degradation Ceremonies', in Earl Rubington and Martin Weinberg, eds, *Deviance: The Interactionist Perspective* (Collier-Macmillan, London, 1973), p. 89.

84 Hannah's Diary, April 1870.

85 A.J. Munby, Diary, May 1873, quoted in Hudson, *Munby: Man of Two Worlds*.

86 This is a kind of selective perception which still influences our behaviour. 'If pairing were random, the woman would actually be taller than the man in 1 out of 6 couples' (Judith Stiehm, 'Invidious Intimacy', *Social Policy*, 6 [March/April 1976], p. 12).

87 A.J. Munby, Diary, 1859.

88 A.J. Munby, *Ann Morgan's Love: A Pedestrian Poem*.

89 Edith Olivier, *Without Knowing Mr. Walkley: Personal Memories* (Faber & Faber, London, 1938).

90 Hannah's Diary, February 1870. To 'nurse' implies cuddling a baby or child on one's lap rather than the American usage which specifically means breast-feeding.

91 Hannah's Diary, July 1864.

92 Hannah's Diary, February 1863.

93 A.J. Munby, *Ann Morgan's Love*.

94   Hannah's Diary, April 1870.
95   Hannah's Diary, July 1871.
96   A.J. Munby, Diary, February 1860, quoted in Hudson, *Munby: Man of Two Worlds*, p. 52.
97   Hannah Cullwick, A Maid of All Work's Diary, 1864.
98   Hannah's Diary, May 1871.
99   A.J. Munby, 'Dichter und Baverin'.
100 A.J. Munby, *Vulgar Verses (by 'Jones Brown')*.
101 Letter from Hannah to Munby, 1886 December 5, quoted in Hudson, *Munby: Man of Two Worlds*, p. 411.
102 Hannah's Diary, April 1872.
103 Hannah's Diary, 29 October 1871 and booklet, 'Hannah', 1871.
104 A.J. Munby, Hannah Cullwick's Account of Her Own Life, 1873.
105 Hannah's Diary, February 1871.
106 *Royal Commission on the Poor Law* (Statistical Appendix, 1910, vol. 53).
107 A.J. Munby, Hannah's Volumes, 1875.
108 A.J. Munby, *Relicta* (1909).
109 Hudson, *Munby: Man of Two Worlds*.
110 The contradiction between the beliefs and practices of upper-middle-class men who accepted the idea of middle-class women as pure gentle creatures in need of protection from the rough and tumble of the public world has been discussed in Albie Sachs and Joan Hoff Wilson, *Sexism and the Law: A Study of Male Beliefs and Legal Bias in Britain and the United States* (Martin Robertson, Oxford, 1978). See also Brian Harrison, *Separate Spheres: The Opposition to Women's Suffrage in Britain* (Croom Helm, London, 1978).
111 A.J. Munby, Diary, 1863.
112 'The man almost always feels his respect for the woman acting as a restriction on his sexual activity, and only develops full potency when he is with a debased sexual object, and this in its turn is partly caused by the entrance of perverse components in his sexual aims, which he does not venture to satisfy with a woman he respects' (Sigmund Freud, 'On the Universal Tendency to Debasement in the Sphere of Love', *On Sexuality*, p. 254).
113 A.J. Munby, Diary, 1860.
114 Gorham, 'The "Maiden Tribute Of Modern Babylon"', p. 378.
115 Hannah Munby's Diary of Her Life As a Servant in the Temple, August 1873.
116 Weeks, *Coming Out*, and 'Inverts, Perverts and Mary Annes: Aspects of Male Prostitution in the 19th and early 20th Centuries', *Journal of Homosexuality*, vol. 6, nos. 1 and 2 (fall/winter 1980–1).
117 Weeks, *Coming Out*, p. 41.
118 A.J. Munby, Diary, 1860.

5

The Separation of Home and Work? Landladies and Lodgers in Nineteenth- and Twentieth-Century England

There is a long-standing belief that urbanization and industrialization necessitated the 'separation of home and work'. It can be argued, however, that this division as we now know it was not simply the inevitable result of technological developments or even a side-effect of the emergence of first a bourgeoisie and then the working class. On the contrary, particularly in the period 1780 to 1850, the definition of masculinity and femininity, together with their social location in work and home, became an arena of conflict.[1] The process of redefinition was taking place through-out society, although it was interpreted in different ways by different class groups.

It was undoubtedly the urban middle class who were the most zealous in promoting the separation of spheres, proseletyzing their message to both the upper and developing working classes. The central belief that emerged during this period was that of a male breadwinner gaining a livelihood through work and maintaining his female (and child) dependants within the home, as well as representing them in political activities appropriate to his station. In this view, husband and wife were the archetype, but father and child, brother and sister, uncle and niece, master and servant reproduced the relationships of clientage and dependency. These expecta-tions were not only themes in contemporary commentaries; they were embodied in important new legal codes such as the Poor Law of 1834.

Historians have tended to accept the prescriptive literature on the separation of spheres and the domestic ideal as a description of reality, partly because the sources for historical analysis are cast in these terms.[2] But it is equally necessary to ask what people were actually doing, how and where they were living, and whom they were living with.[3]

Whatever the expectations within the domestic ideal, in an increasingly urban as well as cash-dominated society, women had to find ways to earn income in lieu of or in addition to support from father, husband or other male relatives. Family ties precluded residential domestic service except for the young and single. Factory work was often problematic, both practically and morally, and in many areas simply not available. One alternative was outwork – from squalid, miserably paid fur-pulling, matchbox-making, etc., to respectable work such as tinting Christmas cards. The other major sources of income were activities like casual cleaning, child-minding, washing in other people's homes, taking in washing into their own homes or providing houseroom and domestic services to lodgers and boarders. In the middle class, similar strategies included becoming companion to an older woman or resident teacher of young children. For all classes of women, these surrogate family activities could contain maternal or sexual elements, evident in roles as diverse as housekeeper or prostitute. It could be argued that these marginal activities were part of an inevitable 'transitional' stage of the economy, on the way to a more clearly demarcated and rationalized labour system. But such sweeping and deterministic assertions often obscure many times and places where the outcome was by no means certain. By looking at one of these activities – the provision of lodging and boarding[4] – it should be possible to throw some light on the formation of both gender and class divisions.

Landladies, Lodgers and Social Observers

Historians, as well as other social commentators, have tended to regard lodging as an insignificant phenomenon in recent history. When they have noticed it at all, it has been treated primarily as a housing category. Urban sociologists, following social investigators of the late nineteenth and early twentieth century, have equated the existence of boarding and lodging with urban decay, a practice often located in a 'twilight zone' within the city.[5] Family sociologists have confirmed this picture. 'The demonology of boarding is characteristic of the entire theory of family break-down under the impact of industrialisation and urbanisation.'[6]

Recently this view has been challenged by both urban and family historians who have seen lodging as a housing arrangement particularly suited to migrants[7] and as a phase in the family life-cycle.[8] According to the most detailed study of boarding and lodging to date, this type of living arrangement contributes to the conclusion that under the impact of industrialization, 'the family was not fragile, but malleable'.[9]

While this perspective has added greatly to the understanding of family patterns and urban development, it still suffers from the disadvantage of seeing the family as a unit interacting functionally with the economy in a process of 'moderniza-tion'.[10] Although divisions within the family are recognized, there is a prior as-sumption of equality between all family (and household) members. This assumption, in turn, underlies the rational–choice models which are used in these studies.[11] It is significant that, within this framework, the Hareven and Modell study of boarding and lodging reproduces the division between home and work by explicitly excluding boarding and lodging *houses* from their discussion and in this they follow other historians.[12] This exclusion limits the historical analysis even before it begins.

Recent Marxist theory, too, emphasizes the boundary between domestic and socialized labour (wage work). Indeed, the whole notion of 'domestic labour' is premised on the existence of a fully developed system of capitalist enterprise with a proletariat (who is included in that term is immaterial for this argument) living in nuclear-family homes run by housewives. In this way, the 'domestic labour debate'[13] as a whole seems to be not only ahistorical but couched at a level of abstraction which must overlook the intermediate forms of enterprise where women were so often located.[14]

Similarly, it is becoming evident that an analysis based on individual occupations, as in the concept of 'occupational segregation', also takes the division between home and work, the private and the public, as given.[15] 'The emphasis . . . is on the structure of the labour market and the question of men and women's place in the family in this paper is relegated to the status of an explanatory factor.'[16]

In both schemes, all activities carried out within the home are assumed to be for consumption by the family. The women who do this work are not directly related to 'the economy', since the economy by this definition is located *outside* the home. The conceptual limitations of this division between the labour market and the home are clear when trying to analyse a situation such as residential domestic service: the largest single occupation for women, numbering over 1,000,000 well into the 1930s. This activity was viewed by employers as familial (and therefore particularly suitable for young women). Servants, on the other hand, despite the fact that they were performing domestic tasks in a domestic setting, stressed that they were selling their labour as in any other occupation, and where possible they rejected the paternalistic features of the situation. This divergence should prompt us to inquire what kind of an organization this entity called a household was, and what were its goals?

Such an approach is akin to the analysis of the form and size of the enterprise in the analysis of the Third World today.[17] As in these countries now, in nineteenth-century England it was not at all clear whether subsidiary household tasks were for producing a profit. Nor, in fact, was it clear that members of the household regarded themselves as engaged in profit-making activities. Rather, an activity such as the housing and feeding of lodgers can be understood as a kind of subsistence employment, one of a variety of forms of labour existing side by side or even carried on by the same people: a way of life, as much as making a living.

The creators of the census in the nineteenth century were aware of the contradictions in dealing with domestic activities. Some discussion of this problem can be found in the introduction to every decennial census. In the development of the census over the century, statistical categories were successively changed in the direction of a stricter demarcation between domestic and market activities. New instructions in 1911 tried once and for all to eliminate the ambiguity with regard to the occupations of women:

> The occupations of women engaged in any business or profession including women regularly engaged in assisting relatives in trade or business must be fully stated. No entry should be made in the case of wives, daughters or other female relatives wholly engaged in domestic duties at home.[18]

The ambiguities in the position of those people performing these domestic duties, however, presented even greater difficulties. For several decades Class II was the Domestic Class of the occupational census, subdivided into Orders 4 and 5:

> The persons in this class are all employed, if they are employed at all, in houses. Some supply simply service, others with it supply board and lodging. They are paid wages (servants) or they are paid for the board and lodging and attendance they supply (inn-keepers, etc). Wives perform at home for the bulk of the population the same kind of duties as persons in Order 5 perform, but they are not paid directly in money for their services as they form a part of the natural family, and consequently they are dis-tinguished in a separate Order 4. . . . The Fourth Order consists entirely of women; it embraces the majority of the women engaged in the most useful of all occupations, that of wife, mother and mistress of a family . . . and includes daughters of 15 and upwards at home.[19]

The implication of this statement is that within the family these activities are carried out only by women.[20] In turn, one of the results of such a definition was the construction of a concept: 'the natural family'.[21]

Lodging, Boarding and the Domestic Ideal

There have always been strangers or 'sojourners' living with the basic nuclear family, although the definition of who belongs to this category has varied. In the seventeenth century an elderly yeoman explained that 'his wife being dead and his children grown up, he now lived as a soujourner with one of his sonnes'.[22] In eighteenth-century London, rented furnished rooms probably formed the main type of housing; an arrangement which shaded off into the 1 d per night common lodging house, lowest in the finely graded social scale of housing. This 'custom was by no means confined to the poorer sort; there were furnished lodgings for all classes and the letting of lodgings was a great industry, besides being, as Adam Smith pointed out, a by-industry of London shop keepers'.[23] The importance of this living arrangement increased as the custom of having living-in farm servants and apprentices slowly died out. This involved not just a change in housing, but an important shift in authority patterns. 'With the breakdown of the paternalistic practice of apprentices living in their master's houses in the late 18th century, the number of lodgers living in a household but not under the control of its head must have increased considerably.'[24] This shift was part of the substitution of cash payments for labour, instead of paying by providing training and payment in kind. While it appealed to the theorists of political economy, in practice many middle-class householders feared the consequences.

From that period on, lodging and boarding began to carry moral opprobrium. On the part of both lodger and householder it came to be considered a necessary evil and a sign of the loss of genteel status. In memoirs, novels and official reports alike there are ambiguous, mostly negative reactions to the practice. George Gissing, the lower-middle-class novelist, was particularly attuned to the social meaning of living arrangements. In his novel *In the Year of the Jubilee* Mary Woodruff is the ex-servant of the main character, Mrs Nancy Tarrant. Mary has been left a small income by a former master and rents an unfurnished house in Harrow-on-the-Hill. She lets the two front rooms furnished to Nancy Tarrant, who is living with her child, apart from her husband. While Nancy writes her novel, Mary takes care of the child and much of the housework is done by a very young residential servant kept by Mary. Nancy Tarrant was considered a lodger, in Gissing's words 'seeing that she paid a specified weekly sum for her shelter and maintenance; in no other respect could the wretched title apply to her. To occupy furnished lodgings is to live in a house owned and ruled by servants; the least tolerable status known to civilisation.'[25]

Taking in lodgers acted as a social indicator throughout the nineteenth and early twentieth century. The daughter of an ex-nursemaid married to the manager of a grocery shop remembers how her mother's experience in genteel service meant that her own childhood was dominated by ideas of respectability which kept her family very isolated. She and her siblings were not allowed to play with the children of a neighbouring family that took in lodgers, even though the family was materially better off than her own.[26]

In reality, the ability to take in lodgers on a regular basis and provide even basic services for them could only be managed at a certain level of income and organization. This was at least tacitly recognized within the working class, where the condemnation of lodging was by no means widespread. In fact, the decline of an area in Camberwell from 1871 to 1881 is characterized by the fall in the proportion of households with lodgers, from 15 per cent to 4 per cent. 'Few indexes of poverty and overcrowding could conceivably be more significant than the inability to sub-let even sleeping room.'[27]

Middle-class failure to recognize this fact, and disapproval of lodgers who were less firmly under the control of the head of the household than apprentices had been, do not, however, explain why there was such a change in middle-class acceptance of the practice in the early nineteenth century. Nor was it simply a recognition of the sanitary and medical effects of overcrowding. Admittedly, in the eighteenth century in the middle class 'it was a matter of custom that the family lived in two rooms and rented out any excess space as furnished lodgings. The cramped way of life of the comfortably-off classes is illustrated by the popularity of beds concealed in various articles of furniture. . . . All classes' lived so much at coffee-houses, ale-houses or clubs that houseroom was a secondary consideration. The necessary "good address" was provided by the coffee-house or tavern.'[28] But at the end of the eighteenth century a new consciousness of privacy began to be stressed – a privacy which would keep the family inviolate behind the walls of the home.[29] As the Registrar General said in the introduction to the census of 1851: 'The possession of an entire house is strongly desired by every Englishman; for it throws a sharp well-defined circle round his family and hearth – the shrine of his sorrows, joys and meditations.'[30]

Living in lodgings, then, with its sharing of part of someone else's house, was a sign that the family could no longer be kept private and implied a loss of caste. In a mid-century tract, when loss of income forces two spinster sisters to live in lodgings, the elder admonishes her sister to resignation: 'Look at all the comforts we have in these respectable lodgings where we can be all by ourselves' and the sisters have stipulated (improbably) that the couple with whom they lodge shall not take any other lodgers with whom they would have to mix.[31] Mrs Craik, the author of the bestseller, *John Halifax, Gentleman*, summed up this repugnance when one of her characters says:

> . . . not temporarily, but permanently sitting down to make one's only 'home' in Mrs Jones's parlour or Mrs Smith's first-floor, of which not a stick or a stone that one looks at is one's own. . . . To people with family feeling living in lodgings is about the saddest life under the sun.[32]

Privacy was necessary for genteel status because it kept 'the family' free from the taint of the market-place. If family relationships became commercialized, there would be no way of maintaining the careful façade of strict sexual divisions and, by extension, no way of enforcing sex and age hierarchies. For both men and women, the fear was that all the vaunted domestic felicities might not in reality stand up to the temptations of being able to live in situations where cash could buy most, if not all, of the 'comforts of home' without assuming the long-term obligations and emotional entanglements of marriage and domesticity.

Since men had both greater freedom of action and greater financial resources, the pull of independence which such an arrangement promised was more threatening for them. The definition of masculinity which stressed the responsibilities of the male breadwinner also had an escape clause which maintained that the 'natural inclinations' of the male could, at least occasionally, allow him to slough off these responsibilities with impunity. The way this masculine prerogative operated across classes is brought out in Booth's discussion of common lodging houses in London:

> The provision to be found in the Metropolis for those who are 'homeless' – or perhaps it would be more accurate to say, those who enjoy no family life – has a wide range. From the luxury of the West End residential club to the 'fourpenny doss' of Bangor Street is but a matter of degree. The club loafer of Piccadilly or Hyde Park Corner,

and the unkempt and ill-clad vagabond sleeping away the summer day on the grass of
St James Park, are often influenced by much the same desire – to attain the advantages
of the associated life without the cares of housekeeping – and the election which the
one has to undergo to pass a 'clubable' man finds its counterpart in the unwritten law
which makes certain common lodging houses accessible only to the 'game 'uns'.[33]

The idea that lodging was an evil, although possibly a necessary one, acted as a
powerful force in middle-class attitudes towards working-class housing and living
arrangements. The necessities of working-class life, as well as its cultural traditions,
resulted in a great deal of mobility and flexibility in living arrangements of a kind
incomprehensible, if not downright immoral, in middle-class eyes. The extent to
which people lived 'on the road', even slept out in the open despite the English
climate, is hard for us from a twentieth-century vantage point to understand; it was
a practice hounded by the authorities throughout the period.[34] This mobility
implied a casualness of relationships, the mixing of age, sex and social groups which
was also viewed with revulsion by Victorian middle-class observers who were
hypersensitive to social boundaries. The drive to eliminate all forms of living
arrangements except the nuclear family (with servants) was, then, in part a con-
tinual effort to strengthen current definitions of masculinity and femininity, to
separate sexual as well as class groups. Given this context, it is not really surprising
that one of the first and most punitory interventionist pieces of Victorian legislation
was the Common Lodging Houses Act of the early 1850s (subsequently modified
by later legislation). The immediate aim of these acts was to control both the
sanitary and moral living conditions of this mobile population, particularly in the
large cities, the 'working of an Act of Parliament reaching to the homes and health
of the people benevolently intruding on their habits . . .'[35]

One of the main reasons put forward for the introduction of this legislation was
to control the problem of overcrowding that undoubtedly existed in the fast-
growing cities of the early Victorian period. However, as in much subsequent
nineteenth-century housing legislation, overcrowding was often understood as
synonymous with taking in lodgers. In evidence taken from Birmingham, for
example, a witness reported that 'there has never been any serious overcrowding
within the limits of the borough. The habits of the people are to have separate
houses; they do not to any very considerable extent take in lodgers.'[36] This view is
similar to the opinion held in America, where social observers 'explain the dangers
of overcrowding just as though biologically related persons required less space than
unrelated individuals. Social, not physical, space was the question.'[37] In reality,
crowded living conditions were directly related to low wages and the condition of
the labour market.[38]

The common lodging house legislation gave specially appointed agents of the
Metropolitan Police (and soon afterwards their provincial counterparts) the right of
entry and search at any time of the day or night to check on the numbers of people
sleeping in a house, the sanitary state of the building and the mixing of the sexes in
sleeping arrangements. Lodging houses were seen as 'the great source of contagious

and loathsome diseases, the hot-beds of crime and moral depravity' in the words of
Captain Hay, one of the most assiduous of the commissioners, who used two a.m.
raids to catch his elusive quarry.[39] Ironically, the overcrowding which was believed
to be caused by lodging was really feared because it, in turn, was believed to lead to
incest, a preoccupation of middle-class Victorians, although one which was seldom
openly acknowledged.[40] In an inspection by the special police it was reported that
'in many cases the law is no doubt evaded; lodgers and landlord falsely asserting
relationship of parties occupying the same room. . . . Where such relationships
really exist and many adults are herded together night and day, in the narrowest
limits, all decency must be lost and frightful evil is the consequence.'[41]

Since the private home was sacrosanct by both law and custom, this type of
draconian measure could only be taken against what were presumed to be the larger
lodging houses. But no definition of a common lodging house was ever laid down,
so that people taking in lodgers might find themselves open to inspection and
regulation. It was quite clear, however, as with much other interventionist legislation, that the authorities had specific groups in mind:

> The opinion of the law officers of the Crown with regard to lodging houses does not
> give any definite idea as to what constitutes a common lodging house and we have very
> great difficulty in discriminating. All they said was that private hotels and houses to
> let to the upper and middle classes do not come within the provisions of the Act.[42]

It was where paternalistic schemes existed, often with additional controls through
tied housing, that the prohibition against lodgers could be most effectively enforced. On the Duke of Cleveland's estate, where 500 cottages were let to lead
miners, lodgers were not permitted and the bailiff informed the agent if anyone
went into lodgings. The Duke of Bedford owned 1,830 cottages on his estates,
which were inspected annually. Where there was room to spare, and with permission, a lodger could be taken.[43]

Lodging, in fact, is an excellent illustration of a familiar Victorian dilemma
where moral commitments and the wish to control the lives of the working class ran
counter to the free play of market forces. At the start of the large-scale municipal
housing programmes after the First World War, this contradiction was brought out
into the open:

> House room is a commercial commodity and in the absence of express restrictions its
> conversion at the will of the possessor into money or money's worth can hardly
> occasion comment. But the free exercise of any such right is presumably contrary to
> the intention of municipal housing estates . . .[44]

The prohibition, or at least regulation, of lodging was regarded as only a partial
solution. As with many other Victorian social problems, proscription was to be
softened by charity. Model lodging houses were to be built on land donated by the
municipality, the best known of these schemes being the Lord Rowton Houses for

homeless men in London. Permissive legislation passed in 1851 – the Labouring Classes Lodging Houses Act – conferred on local authorities the power to borrow money on the rates and apply it to the erection of lodging houses; in effect the earliest form of municipal housing in Britain.[45] While some authorities did take up this option, most did not, and many of those who did ended up providing single family units.[46] The truth was that private enterprise could not provide sufficient housing for the population, and lodging was a sensible, flexible arrangement, no matter how much it outraged middle-class sensibilities.[47]

Both municipal and charity schemes were deliberately aimed at the 'casualities' – those considered to be outside the ideal family structure. They were never intended to be an alternative living arrangement, and many of them had punitive regulations which made them all too reminiscent of that ultimate lodging place – the workhouse. Their character is also reflected in the fact that many more places were provided for men than for women and children.

Indeed, by now it should come as no surprise to discover that women and girls in lodgings were considered even more reprehensible than men. There was an expectation that girls should be living at home under the control of their parents, or in domestic service under control of their employers.[48] Part of the distaste for factory work for girls was that it often meant they had to go into lodgings to be near their work and thus, in Dr Barnardo's words, developed that 'precocious independence' so inimical to home life.

In Nottingham in the 1880s, when lace work began to offer increased employment for girls, there were schemes to lay on special trams to take them to lodgings in the suburbs. There was such a public outcry against this in the town that employers and philanthropists joined in building about ten barrack-like Homes for Working Girls in the city centre.[49] Even where it was recognized that such housing must be provided, attempts were made to domesticate the inmates. The Duchess of Marlborough, addressing the National Conference on Lodging House Accommodation for Women, stressed the need for providing moral and hygienic lodgings for women and girls, with someone on the premises to teach the duties of home life and motherhood in such surroundings.[50] Some felt, however, that such girls should be urged to 'start earning their own living by domestic service rather than in the precarious employment of the mill and factory', for 'any arrangement which, by supplying cheap accommodation encourages young women to leave the shelter, however poor, of their own home and offers them an opportunity of living without any restrictions or oversight . . . exercises a decidedly harmful influence'.[51]

The Problem of Definition

Before going on to discuss the practice of lodging in detail, three points about Victorian and Edwardian living arrangements must be understood. First, pre-industrial patterns of production and service included the bringing of raw materials to the craftsman by the customer, to be made up or finished. So also in lodgings, many people provided their own food, even fuel, either to cook for themselves or have others cook it. Fires were lighted in any hearth in the house, not just for heat but to make tea, toast or even meals. Artefacts such as toasting-forks, wash-stands to which water had to be carried, chamber-pots which had to be emptied, show that the division of function and space within the house was not yet entirely fixed. This was true for all levels of society. The poor would cook wherever they could get access to a fire; hence the large communal kitchens in common lodging houses. (This also goes part of the way to explain the intense dislike of the workhouse practice of ladling out the 'skilly' [gruel] individually to the inmates, giving them no choice or control of their diet.) The wealthy too could have cooking and serving done for them in their own 'rooms' when in lodgings or in inns (the forerunner to room service). They could provide their own linen, plate, etc., as well as bringing their own servants to wait on them, providing they could afford to pay for their keep. On census night in 1871, the Clifton Ville Hotel in Margate had thirty-two adult and four child guests. They were waited on by forty-two servants, eleven of whom had been brought as private servants by the guests.[52] Further, middle-class families and individuals expected – and could pay for – an extraordinarily wide range of services from working-class people, particularly women and children, much in the manner of Third World countries today. This was the day-to-day face of class interaction, in the street as well as in the home. These were not just regular domestic services, but casual errand-running, lifting and carrying everything from luggage to messages. Working-class people's *time* as well as labour was at their disposal.

In a similar manner, so too were the facilities of working-class homes. Many middle-class people felt that they had the right to inquire into the lives and enter the homes of the working class in the name of charity; how much more they assumed service and attention on working-class premises if payment were offered. For example, a French mid-century tourist explained how, on leaving London by train for an excursion to the country, he got out impulsively in a small village. He stopped on the edge of the common and knocked on a door at random. He was shown by the woman of the house into a 'modest room but very well furnished. "If monsieur needs a little apartment this parlour and one or two rooms are free." Climbing the stairs she showed me a bedroom as fresh and comely as the parlour. "How much do you want for them and will you be able to feed me?" "Yes," she said "22 shillings per week for board and room and I promise you that you will be satisfied."' He decided to stay several weeks 'in this solitude'.[53]

Note that some of the great social investigators of the late nineteenth and early twentieth centuries made full use of this prerogative. Charles Booth made a regular practice of living in working-class lodgings in the East End, proclaiming that he preferred their diet and timetable to the upper-middle-class routine of his own nine-servant establishment.[54] George Orwell, Stephen Reynolds and others used lodgings for shorter or longer periods to give flavour, favourable or otherwise, to their commentaries on working-class life. Intellectuals like E.M. Forster, among many others, could dip into working-class culture in this way, believing that they understood it from the inside. Note, too, that almost all these examples are single males who could use the freedom and flexibility of lodging to its greatest advantage.

Finally, the division of the sexes and the creation of a special domestic sphere with higher standards of cooking, cleaning, laundry and mending had promoted male expectations of being 'serviced' by women; not only by mothers and wives, but also daughters, sisters, nieces, aunts, cousins, female servants and even neighbours. Hence the colloquial phrase that has now almost completely disappeared: 'to *do*' for someone.[55] Unless a man was living at home with his mother, or married, or employing paid servants, inquiry would be made about his living arrangements: 'Who does for him?'. In extreme conditions, for example, as a widower, a man could 'do' for himself and even his children, but this was felt to be an unnatural arrangement. When Hannah Munby's aunt died, a cousin of hers who had been a lady's maid in London had to give up her place and go back to Shropshire to 'do' for her uncle, as he could not look after himself.[56] This element of personal female service is crucial in understanding the special relationship of landladies (and their servants) to boarders and lodgers. For lodging was in some ways only semi-commercialized. Note for example, the connotations of the word *landlord* (one who owns property and collects rent) as compared to *landlady* (one who, usually living on the premises, provides house room and services for cash). Such a relationship, just as in domestic service, could include covert sexual services. There was, after all, a deeply rooted expectation that any man living with a woman would provide support, as a husband did, in return for services; the position of housekeeper very easily ran into common law wife.[57] Some Poor Law Unions, in fact, imposed a rule under which no woman receiving outdoor relief could take in a *male* lodger without permission from the relief committee.[58]

It is not surprising, therefore, that not only the Special Commissioners of the Metropolitan Police found difficulty in defining the categories *lodger* and *boarder*. Historians, too, have been known to give up the attempt and list them as 'residuals', together with visitors, etc., in their analysis of household structure.[59] 'There are two problems here. One is to overcome the varying practice of the [census] enumerators in discriminating between lodgers and either tenants or independent households at the same address. . . . The second problem in classifying lodgers is more fundamental. When is a lodger not a lodger?'[60]

Nevertheless, ambiguities, which might appear to be a methodological disaster, especially when using statistical sources such as the census, may point to important historical insights. For example, the confusion in the census between *visitor* and *lodger* is revealing. When Hannah Munby, general servant, was not employed, she would move in with friends for a few days or weeks and help to pay for food in cash and/or do extra cleaning, wash curtains or whitewash a scullery, in return for her keep. But when she was in a town where she had no friends, she lived for a while on exactly the same basis with a woman whose house she had found simply by knocking on the door.[61]

The problem of definition in the nineteenth century was partly a creation of the Registrar General's Office itself. The basic unit in the census was taken to be the family, whatever actual living arrangements may have been, for example, kin who paid cash for services, house sharing by kin, unrelated people or even fictive kin.[62] From the beginning of the census, the convention was adopted that boarders were part of the family of the occupier but lodgers were to be counted as single families having their own separate census schedule:

> The family in its complete form consists of a householder with his wife and his children; and in the higher classes with his servants. Other relatives and visitors sometimes form a part of the family; and so do lodgers at a common table who pay for their subsistence and lodging [e.g. boarders].[63]

Enumerators would persist, however, in confusing the two, as well as being inconsistent among themselves. Reviewing the situation in 1851, the Registrar General observed gloomily:

> Mr Rickman [the first Registrar General] adverts to the difficulty of defining in an Act of Parliament, the degree of connection between the head of a family and lodgers who reside under the same roof. For in the Census of 1831 it had been stated that: 'those who use the same kitchen and board together are to be deemed members of the same family. But he [Rickman] proceeds to say, 'even then remains the question whether a single person inhabiting a house solely, or lodging, but not boarding, in another man's house is to be deemed a family. This admits only of an unsatisfactory reply 'that it cannot be otherwise' and by this negative paralogism is decided in the affirmative'. A lodger, then, who did not board in the house in which he lived, was by this decision 'a family'. Whether a family can be constituted by a person who lives alone in a house or a lodger who either boards in a family or only occupies the chamber in which he sleeps and, as in Paris or London, lives in the daytime at coffee houses, clubs or other places, may be disputed.[64]

This period, when the shape of the private household was thus being officially defined, was also the time when large institutional units were being created for all those who did not come under the domestic rubric: workhouses, hospitals, orphanages and purpose-built barracks for soldiers. It is significant that, in his task of creating categories, the Registrar General specifically saw the *lodging and boarding house* as an 'intermediate form between the institution and the private family'.[65]

The difficulty in defining lodging goes back to the status of the tenancy of the occupier, in both custom and law. Most houses were occupied by tenants; that is, a relationship created simply by the acknowledgement that one party was the tenant of the other, who was the owner of the property. A lodger, on the other hand, was one who resided with the landlord (landlady) on the premises. Of course this landlord may have been – indeed probably was – himself or herself also a tenant.

The question of who actually was the lodger and who the tenant was important, but could be problematic. According to law, the occupier had to 'retain his quality of master, reserving to himself the general control and dominion over the whole house. If he does, the inmate is a mere lodger'. The position of master, then, ultimately depended on who had control over the outer door.[66] In this context it should be remembered that the franchise had always been based on property qualifications. But in 1867 it was extended to every man who occupied the same lodgings for twelve months if the yearly value of the premises, unfurnished, was over £10. Nevertheless, this recognition of lodging as a normal part of working-class life was in name only, as it was generally acknowledged that the 'lodger's franchise' remained a dead letter because of complicated registration procedures.[67]

The Demand for Lodging

Some of the concern over lodging may be due to the belief confirmed by historical research that lodgers tended to be the 'semi-autonomous young persons'[68] who have always made authorities anxious. Their abundant energy with potential for both work and violence, their budding sexuality with its potential for 'unregulated' reproduction, have made problems of control over this group seem particularly acute. In rural and pre-industrial society, living-in farm service, apprenticeship, as well as peer-group sanctions, had provided much of this control.[69] But by the nineteenth century, the masses of young people flocking into cities, combined with a relatively high age of marriage, created a new situation. Residential domestic service for girls was seen as one solution, while young men went into lodgings. A witness to a government inquiry in the 1880s said 'I suppose it would lie between a young unmarried man of 20 living at home with his family or becoming a lodger with some family or getting married.'[70] In fact, male lodgers usually outnumbered female by between two or three to one.[71] According to this view, domestic service may be seen as an alternative to lodging, with apprenticeship as a situation halfway between the two.[72]

The demand for certain types of labour greatly increased the numbers of people, particularly young people, constantly on the move. For example, railway employees needed lodgings at the end of the line if they could not return home after a journey. At first the companies rented room and board in private households, but eventually built their own lodging houses.[73] One of the greatest areas of employment through-out the century was in building, from private housing to the huge public buildings which transformed Victorian cities. Building needed labour for irregular periods of work; both labourers and craftsmen moved from site to site and were affected by the seasons. 'At Kinson, Dorset in 1865 . . . many of the men were employed in building work at Bournemouth. Some came home only weekly, living in lodgings while away.'[74] Others would stay on until the work was finished. When a journey-man stonemason came to London to seek work, he found lodgings under the same roof as his foreman. He describes the foreman's 'good lady' as a stout, burly woman:

> . . . pretty clean in herself and her household, a pretty good cook and of an exceed-
> ingly mild and willing disposition never seeing it a trouble to cook or do anything for
> us even if it happened out of the common way so that we were quite at home here,
> although there were eight men lodging in the house, six of the number working
> together with me.[75]

As in this case, occupational links between landlord and lodger could be as important as place of origin (see figure 5.1).

Moving about the country was a well-established part of many trades or even a
way of life. 'Tramping was not the prerogative of the social outcast, as it is today;
it was a normal phase in the life of entirely respectable classes of workingmen; it
was a frequent resort of the out-of-work; it was a very principle of existence
for those who followed itinerant callings and trades.'[76] Lodgings were the fixed
points in these circuits, and certain streets in every town were known for their
lodging houses for travellers. One of the greatest benefits that the card-holding
'tramping artisan' gained by his membership in a trade organization was the contact that provided respectable, comfortable lodgings in a strange town, either at
the pub where the local chapter met or with the families of local fellow artisans,
where the wife (or daughter) provided service. This institutionalized arrangement
was not available to women or girls, as they were usually ineligible for union
membership and, in any case, not often found in the type of occupation that
provided such benefits. The few young women who had seasonal occupations –
such as the herring girls from Scotland who followed the catch to East Anglia –
made full use of the freedom from parental and community surveillance while in
their lodgings.[77]

In the first half of the century, pubs and inns were important way-stations for
all classes of lodgers, including billeted soldiers. 'Drink-sellers provided lodgings
for homeless or itinerant working men, and sheltered lodgers whose landladies
allowed them on the premises only to sleep.'[78] Pubs also provided lodgings for
sailors and seamen, occupations which created a steady demand for temporary
accommodation, a demand undoubtedly associated with prostitution. Prostitution,
in turn, included 'private lodgings where they [prostitutes] were more likely self-

Figure 5.1   Household 1: 146 High Street, Margate, 1871

John Hyland	Head	Married	Age 33	Bricklayer
Clara Hyland	Wife	Married	Age 22	Coffee-house keeper
May Hyland	Daughter		Age 1	
Charles Hyland	Son		Age 9	
Mary Higgs	Visitor	Single	Age 18	Domestic servant
Frederick Jones	Boarder	Single	Age 23	Bricklayer

employed and less physically segregated from a general working–class neighbour-hood. . . . Prostitutes tended to reside in dwellings with two or three other women, often run by an older woman but in a capacity as landlady, not "madam".' This accommodation was scarcely distinguishable from low–class lodging houses or, often, even 'externally respectable establishments', and seems to have been an example of a strong female network resulting in good fellowship and sociability among the prostitutes, physically located in these female lodging houses.[79] Signifi-cantly, the use of such temporary lodgings might very well not show up in the census figures, for they were often the result of seasonal or migratory patterns, while the census was always taken on one night at the end of March or beginning of April.[80]

There were, however, less peripatetic groups, such as clerks and shop assistants who came to the cities, particularly London, and filled the respectable lodging houses or lived as lodgers in private households in districts such as Kennington or Camberwell. In those areas where little housing was available, the provision of lodgings helped to attract young, single workers. In rural Essex a scheme was established by the silk–manufacturing firm of Courtauld whereby their purpose-built housing was let to their workers on a sliding scale, provided the tenant also lodged the single girls who often returned to their families in the villages on Saturday and walked back to Halstead on Monday morning. It was even possible for the tenants to be paid a small sum or at least live rent free, as in the case of Miss Greer who housed ten lodgers.[81]

All the activities associated with travel greatly expanded as a result of the railways, better road surfaces and river and coastal steam traffic. With this in-creased travel came demand for overnight or longer–stay lodgings. There were also special occasions when middle–class people were on the move: parents visiting sons at college or boarding school, staying near relatives for festivities or in times of illness when they could not stay with kin. There were the groups of kindred spirits who booked rooms for a few weeks at a time to pursue common interests, such as the reading parties of the famous Cambridge 'Apostles'. Lytton Strachey, on one such occasion, wrote from Penmenner House in Cornwall: 'We are quite close to the sea. The house seems very comfortable. We have two sitting rooms. There is another party of young gents from Oxford in the house.'[82] Race meetings, royal occasions, or any other public event would bring a rush of people to the area.

Above all, there was the increase in holidays, first in spa and seaside towns, later in the country, for which medical ideas about rest, recuperation and good air provided part of the justification. The period of growth of middle–class resorts was from the mid–eighteenth century to 1820 and 'once the reputation of a resort was established, people were willing to build lodging houses, shops and other amenities to cater for the visitors'.[83] Later in the century the better paid, more regularly employed, of the working class joined in, at first only for day excursions by rail, but later for weekends and even whole weeks. At the heart of a city created to cater for holiday–makers (Blackpool, for instance) was the seaside boarding house.

What Was Provided

The basic services provided in lodgings seem to have been 'attendance, light and firing'. 'Attendance' included services such as cleaning, carrying water and coal, emptying slops such as waste water and chamber-pots, making fires, running errands (with the kiss on the stairs if the lodger could snatch it).[84] In furnished lodgings, the lodger could supply some of his own effects, or alternatively, the arrangement could be 'all found', virtually as in a hotel.

Anderson found that most of the working-class lodgers in Preston had room, candles and coals provided, paying extra to the landlady for washing or for washing materials.[85] A report from London confirms that 'in furnished rooms the "keeper" provides the bedding as a rule, but it is generally understood that the lodger is responsible for washing bed linen'. Either coppers were provided for the tenants or 'women made use of the public wash-houses'.[86] This indicates that male lodgers might receive (and pay for) more services than female lodgers; Anderson cites a report that 'single women ordinarily pay a sum per week for cooking their own food'.[87] Most often lodgers ate at the same table with the family, whether or not they had provided their own food, with the exception of lodgers who themselves formed a family unit, where they would probably have had a separate room, even though cooking was still often done by the landlady.[88] Middle-class lodgers, of course, could command a higher standard of service and more privacy. One bachelor lodger in the 1880s (with an annual income of £300 a year, paying 30 shillings a week 'all found') complains of the new servant being moody and dour, she 'shuts her eyes' when he gives his orders to 'fetch coals or water or beer, post letters, cook a steak or bring up tea'.[89]

A variety of arrangements was found in holiday accommodation. Wives on holiday in Margate sent letters with minute instructions for bringing groceries by the 'Husbands' Boat' which came down from London on Saturdays: coffee, tea 'and a breast of veal from Fleshby's because Margate butchers are asking preposterous prices'.[90] According to the Tourist Hand Book to the British Isles for 1880, as much as £2 to £6 per week could be paid for staying in the West End of London. However, the writer notes that private lodgings may always be had by the week in nearly every part of the metropolis. Cards for 'furnished apartments' are almost always placed in the windows of houses where there are rooms to let:

> The price of apartments includes attendance in most cases. Extra charges are made for light, use of kitchen fire and washing of bed and toilet linen and usually of boot cleaning.

But the warning is added:

> Strangers should be careful to have a clear understanding as to prices and to fix upon an arrangement which will include all extras. Lodgers may make their own purchases

of provisions or the housekeeper will make them, rendering weekly accounts with the bill.

Supply of Lodgings

If many lodgers were young and single, then it should follow that landlords and landladies would be married or widowed middle-aged people, and table 5.1 suggests that this was often the case.

Attention has been drawn to the taking-in of lodgers as a way of providing a livelihood for widows or other women left without support.[91] In Colchester in 1851, while women made up 19 per cent of household heads in the city as a whole, they constituted 30 per cent of household heads who took in lodgers. For example, in 1861, Emma Bond, a widow aged fifty-seven, lived with her son, a bookbinder aged twenty, and a lodger aged twenty-four. By 1871, the son had moved out and been replaced by two additional young artisan lodgers.

It could be further argued that such a resource was important for married women living with their husbands, particularly those with very young children who did not yet take up much house room or, on the other hand, could not make any financial contribution to the household (figure 5.2).

For couples in late middle age, lodgers would once again fill the beds and supply the income in lieu of grown-up children who had left home. This cyclical pattern is analogous to the domestic economy of peasant households, where the labour

Table 5.1 Lodger households by age of household head: Colchester, 1851

Age of household head	Lodger household	All households
Under 30	16%	16%
31–50	38%	61%
Over 50	46%	23%
Total	100%	100%

Figure 5.2 Household 2: 19 Long Wyre Street, Colchester, 1851

John Bennington	Head	Married	Age 31	Writer and grainer
Elizabeth Bennington	Wife	Married	Age 29	
2 sons aged 3 and 1				
Frederick Morris	Boarder	Single	Age 16	Apprentice writer and grainer

of living-in farm servants was used when the children were very young and again after they had grown up and left home.[92] In both cases, household resources and space were balanced by the presence of non-kin at certain times in the family cycle.

The hatter Fred Willis, who lived in Camberwell in the 1900s, rented a house for 12s 6d per week with six rooms and a scullery. At that time he had four children ranging in age from six to thirteen years old. When he first married, the whole top floor was let unfurnished, but as the family increased, the lodgers decreased. The compositor who inhabited the front room upstairs and who shared supper and all his meals on Sunday with the family, was the last, they hoped, but he was clean, quiet and orderly and they couldn't give up the 10s a week he brought in. Interestingly enough, he also was able to get an apprenticeship in his own trade for the eldest boy, thus demonstrating how lodging could increase the network resources of a nuclear family.[93]

It could be further argued that the taking-in of lodgers would be particularly attractive to ex-domestic servants who had neither the experience nor contacts necessary to find factory work or even, in some cases, outwork.[94] A building worker in London said of his landlady: 'Mrs Jennings had been in service as a cook in a gentleman's family. In order to improve their scanty income, she took in a little washing, and she also washed for myself and fellow lodger.'[95]

Although in one sense taking in of lodgers was seen as being incompatible with middle-class gentility, on the other hand it was a way of supplementing income without the women in the household having to work in public. On these grounds alone, it would appeal to both ex-domestic servants and respectable working men alike. It was also a resource which could be used by middle-class women left without means of support, particularly after the First World War, when gentility was more loosely defined and the euphemism 'P.G.' (paying guest) softened the idea of taking strangers into the house for cash.

An early nineteenth-century American visitor to London gives a vivid picture of a household where he had to supply a character reference to his middle-class landlady:

> I am now comfortably and quietly settled in lodgings with an elderly lady who has good blood in her veins. . . . Comfort, neatness and economy distinguish her household from the cellar to the garret. Nothing is wasted, nothing is wanting. . . . This economy is neither the offspring of meanness nor of avarice, but the rational result of a determination to preserve her independence. Her means are just sufficient with this rigid economy, to enable her to appear with that sober sort of gentility, which is her pride and delight to exhibit. Were she to relax in any one respect, the nice system would lose its balance and fall to the ground.[96]

Taking in lodgers could not only maintain gentility; it could also support dependants at a time when women's wages were often below subsistence level for them-

Figure 5.3 Household 3: 30 Priory Street, Colchester, 1851

Ann Dunningham	Head	Widowed	Age 63	No occupation
Rachel Dunningham	Daughter	Single	Age 29	Machinist
Charles Dunningham	Grandson		Age 10	
Jabez Dunningham	Grandson		Age 6	
Female lodgers ages 19, 19, 19 and 22 – all tailoresses				

selves alone. Elderly parents, younger brothers and sisters, or even illegitimate children could at least be provided with a roof over their heads (figure 5.3).

It is difficult to know when taking in a couple of lodgers became the sole support of a household or individual when in effect it might be considered running a boarding house. In Colchester in 1851, of those households where lodgers were kept, 70 per cent had only one, 17 per cent had two and 13 per cent had three or more. Only one household had five, which was the highest figure in the sample. These proportions are confirmed by Anderson's findings for Preston. From examining the manuscript census, it seems clear that some enumerators used the category 'lodging house keeper' to designate a household head who happened to have one or two lodgers and no other declared occupation; but some enumerators seem to have used this practice much more widely than others. In fact, as Charles Booth knew from his study of London, the line was very difficult to draw. The 1931 Housing Report tried to lay down guidelines for making a distinction between a private household where lodgers were taken in and a lodging house:

In the case of business establishments and boarding houses, where any doubt has arisen in regard to the nature of the occupation, the residents have been included in the private family class when the number of business assistants or boarders was not greater than the number of members of the employer's or householder's family (including domestic servants).[97]

A legal case decided in 1978 put the matter most succinctly. The issue was whether a single woman providing breakfast, tea and Sunday lunch for her five lodgers (as her mother had done in the same house) was, in effect, running a business and thus subject to the Landlord and Tenant Act rather than the Rent Act:

No one factor was decisive; all the factors – the number of lodgers, the money, the size of the house, had to be looked at. She was not reaping any commercial advantage. She was doing it probably because she liked it and no doubt she was good at it.[98]

The proportion of men listed as 'innkeepers' in the census throughout the nineteenth century is 80 per cent, compared to 20 per cent women, while almost exactly the reverse percentages of the sexes are listed as 'lodging house keepers'. While, undoubtedly, men found it much easier to obtain the licence and raise the capital to become an innkeeper, it is possible that the sex of the householder may have influenced the enumerators' description. Certainly this definitional distinction is clear in the separate list of innkeepers' *wives* (61,553 in 1871); of course there is no category of lodging house keepers' husbands.

If the initial capital and/or housing could be found, there were several advantages for women in taking in more lodgers – in effect running a lodging house. Not only could dependants be supported, but enough might be saved for retirement. A somewhat romanticized version of this is the theme of Arnold Bennet's novel *The Old Wives' Tale* (1908), where the heroine, having been abandoned by her philandering husband in Paris, sets up and runs a select boarding house for English visitors and eventually retires in triumph to her native town in the Potteries. In real life, Mrs A.P. Patchett's furniture and fittings for her Nottingham lodging house (three public rooms and nine bedrooms) were valued at £131 1s 6d in 1885.[99]

The 'production' of services to lodgers, however, was by no means the only form of using women's labour at home to augment income or promote the family enterprise. The 1931 Housing Report noted that, as with the definition of a lodging house cited above, a similar rule was applied to 'exceptional families of like character e.g. a doctor with resident patients, a tutor with resident scholars'. But in the nineteenth century, such households were not so exceptional. In Colchester in 1851 there were more households with apprentices than lodgers. Other categories would include tradesmen's wives who serviced residential shop assistants, doctors' wives caring for resident medical students (the standard form of training for general practitioners), and clergymen's wives watching over the young boys boarded and taught by their husbands. While a general servant might have performed the heavier work in such households, the mistress often did light cleaning, the cooking and serving herself, as well as overseeing the provision of clean laundry and other managerial tasks. The necessity for the wife's (or her substitute's) contribution is made clear in the dilemma of Dr Gibson, the widowed country practitioner in Mrs Gaskell's *Wives and Daughters*, who had to cope with two resident students and a lively daughter in her early teens – a situation which propelled him into a second and unhappy marriage. There were also joint enterprises such as the rural pub run by the wife and daughters of the carter who was often away from home in the course of his trade. Not only did the pub increase household resources,

Figure 5.4   Household 4: 'Egerton House', 38/39 Hawley Square, Margate, 1871

Mary Brooks	Head	Single	Age 50	Headmistress
Martha Brooks	Sister	Single	Age 46	Schoolmistress
Jane Brooks	Niece	Single	Age 23	Schoolmistress
Laura Brooks	Niece	Single	Age 15	
Thurza Hill	Governess	Single	Age 22	Schoolmistress

3 female servants, aged 56, 21 and 16
12 female pupils aged 7 to 17 years

Figure 5.5   Household 5: 30 Goodwin Road, Margate, 1871

Clara Searles	Head	Widow	Age 45	Schoolmistress
Helen Searles	Daughter	Single	Age 17	
Annie Culver	Servant to schoolmistress	Single	Age 15	
Catherine Brown	Boarder	Widow	Age 26	
1 boy aged 2				
5 boys aged 7–8				
1 girl aged 10				
Sarah Goodall	Servant to school	Single	Age 19	

but it provided more houseroom for the family and thus directly raised their standard of living.[100]

Similar enterprises are found in those, often all-female, households where middle-class women added their only other meagre asset – education. In Margate in 1871 (see figs. 5.4 and 5.5), in Hawley Square and the two streets running off it, there were nine small private schools, every one of them run by women, who were for the most part unmarried.[101]

Often an elderly relative and/or boarder was added to the household. In fact, many of these establishments were little more than private homes surviving through taking in boarders or fostering children; for example, 'Anglo-Indians' – that is, children sent home without their parents from insalubrious parts of the Empire. An advertisement of the 1880s says: 'Two ladies residing in a pretty cottage would be happy to take charge of a young child. Education, including music etc. if afterwards required.' An advertisement in a newspaper by the wife of a retired naval captain in Southsea resulted in a boy aged six and his three-year-old sister being sent from India to board for three years in what later became known to the world as 'The House of Desolation' in Rudyard Kipling's famous story 'Baa Baa Black Sheep'.[102]

In addition to the convenience and respectability of being able to earn income within the four walls of the house, the provision of domestic services to boarders, lodgers, pupils and others did not require the exercise of any authority except over servants and children, both categories falling within a legitimate feminine domain. However, the correlative assumption that the feminine domain was gentle and uncommercial does not tally with the facts: especially where such activities were the only support of the household, and in particular where lodgings were supplied on a scale large enough to produce a profit, the lot of these servants could be very hard indeed. The lowest form of domestic service was the 'slavey' in a lodging house and was often the fate of young girls from workhouses or orphanages.[103]

In summary, then, rather than investigating the supplying of lodging and boarding in isolation, it should be seen as part of a continuum of positions: wife or female relative helping to service apprentices, pupils, and others, child-minding or fostering children, taking in boarders or lodgers, keeping a small school, running private apartments, a lodging house or hotel.

The Meaning of the Landlady–Lodger Relationship

The fact of having strangers in the house could be seen as – and undoubtedly often was – a heavy burden for the landlady, who had not only to provide the material comforts of home but also to keep the emotional atmosphere on an even keel, to apportion scarce resources of time as well as things, to sooth ruffled feelings and to arbitrate between lodgers, servants and her own family. On the other hand, an enlarged household brought the added interest of contact with the outside world, bringing colour into what might otherwise have been an exceptionally narrow, meagre life. This was particularly true in the case of boarding where meals were served, although one need not go so far as the flippant journalist who said: 'My general experience of boarding houses leads me to think they are kept not so much for profit as for society.'[104]

The importance of these contacts is brought out in an autobiographical novel which gives a detailed account of a middle-class lodging house in the Tavistock Square area of London in the 1890s. The author was a dentist's assistant earning £1 per week. At first she had only room and 'attendance', surviving on boiled eggs and toast at an ABC café, for like many upper-middle-class girls of the period she did not know how to cook. After about a year, the widowed landlady decided to change over to boarders. She is quoted as giving the following reason:

> It will give my chicks a better chance. It isn't fair on them living in the kitchen and seeing nobody. . . . What others have done I can do; something for the children. Mrs Reynolds has married three of her daughters to boarders. I know it's a risk but if you get on it pays better. There's less work in it and you've got a house to live in.[105]

There was always a certain ambiguity involved in extracting payment for the services that would be expected from mothers, wives and other female relatives. Unlike the relationship with a servant, however, the lodger was not on his own home ground; the landlady had considerable control over the conditions of his life. Partially because of this equivocal status, landladies have, on the whole, received a 'bad press'. This may also be due to the fact that the relationship has usually been seen from the point of view of the lodger, the young single hero, while the landlady has shared the generally negative image of the older woman.

On the other hand, the landlady was thought to be too inquisitive and demanding because she was afraid of not being paid enough or because she lived vicariously through her boarders, prying and listening at key holes, examining the sheets of the honeymoon couple. The most devastating portrait we have of that negative, pleasure-denying image is Dylan Thomas's imaginary seaside village, where Mrs Ogmore Pritchard presides over Bay View Cottage, a house for paying guests, 'in her iceberg white holily laundered night-gown under virtuous polar sheets and before she raises the blinds to let the sun in, tells it to mind and wipe its shoes'.[106]

On the other hand, the landlady was seen as the equivalent of the 'tart with the heart of gold', a source of nurturing, always ready to do that little extra without thought of self. This expectation lies behind the patronizing tone of the artisan lodger who said of his landlady: 'I have many times felt sorry to observe that she had gone beyond her means in making a pie or tart, perhaps a custard, merely for the satisfaction of asking me to have a bit.'[107] Thomas Wright, the engineer, remembered the young journeyman from the country, employed in the same place as his father, who lodged with his family: 'As is often the practice of this class with their landladies he calls her "mother" and he strikes her as being like what her first born boy would have been had *he* lived to be three and twenty.'[108] The overtones of the relationship were not only maternal, as Roberts remembers about his local community in the Salford of the 1900s:

> The very word lodger stood, so to speak, pregnant with meaning. In plain fact, of course, many single men spent all their mature lives in other people's homes in a relationship which, despite close quarters, always remained platonic. But circumstances offered scope for scandal and malicious tongues made the most of it. 'Three evils' one learned judge had said, 'most commonly break up marriages: they are selfishness, greed and lodgers'.[109]

There was a feeling that the lodger had access to all sorts of hidden extra privileges through his special relationship to his landlady (and/or her servant and daughter); yet he was never a full masculine adult, a householder.[110] Indeed, an index of this indeterminate status was the *de facto* disenfranchisement of a man who remained in lodgings throughout his adult life. 'In the metropolitan boroughs the number of lodgers [eligible to vote] was estimated at between 200,000 and 300,000 but the number on the electoral register in 1872 was 4,000 in the whole of London.'[111]

The lodger gained these privileges at the expense of the 'legitimate male head of house'.[112] Thus the maternal and sexual came to be fused in a well-recognized if semi-licit relationship between an older woman and younger man, further confused by the handing over of cash for service rendered. The tensions such a relationship produced, including its oedipal implications, may at least partially account for the jokes, songs and stories with a 'Roger the Lodger' motif.[113]

Conclusion

Historians have recently pointed out that the experience of lodging must have been much greater than our 'snapshot' type of statistical data would suggest: as a child growing up in a house with lodgers, occasional or more permanent; as a young person living in lodgings, or a servant waiting on lodgers; as a married householder letting out lodgings. All these positions might have been maintained for relatively short periods, but they gave a variety of household living experience very different from our own nuclear-family dominated lives.[114]

With the decline of house building and massive movements of population during the First World War, the twentieth century saw a temporary increase in lodging and house sharing. By the early 1930s this had been reversed as the demand for lodging slackened. There was less geographical mobility as enterprises became more bureaucratized and occupations more settled. The development of short-distance transport – trams, buses and bicycles – meant that young, single people could live at home and still get to their work. In any case, with a fall in the age of marriage, they were more likely to try to set up independent households at an earlier age.

The growth of the building society meant that owner occupation was increasing. Building societies were attracted to houses designed for nuclear families only. Furthermore, it was much more difficult for a woman to raise a mortgage to buy a house, as opposed to getting control of a tenancy.[115] Municipal housing, too, was more carefully controlled than private lettings had been. On the whole, councils were opposed to the subletting of rooms and, where it was allowed, additional charges were often made. Taken together, these developments meant that the flexibility which had been an especial advantage to women was being removed from the housing market.

The amount of general service expected by the middle class declined after the war, despite the continued high levels of women occupied as domestic servants. Working-class women were being urged rather to take better care of their own families and menfolk, as emphasized by the new moves to scientific motherhood and domestic teaching in schools. The inter-war period was the time when advertising promoted consumption within an 'Ideal Home' where there was no social space for the lodger. The 'final and definite transition' to the small, nuclear-family household (mean 3.04 in 1961) is said to have occurred between the 1920s and 1940s.[116]

Of course lodging for shorter or longer periods has continued, but even among those groups where it was once almost universal, such as students or holiday-makers, it has rapidly declined in the last ten or fifteen years. As a recognized social experience it has, like residential domestic service, almost disappeared. Similarly, family enterprises, from small shops to small schools, have declined numerically, and with them the unpaid labour of wives (and children), while even clergymen's and doctors' wives are increasingly entering the labour market rather than contributing to their husband's work. The one form of family surrogate work which remains in the home and has, if anything, increased is child-minding, in the forms of both fostering and boarding out children who are in the care of the state or private daytime childcare. This is in keeping with the emphasis put on the nuclear family as the natural and best place for children to live.

It has been stated repeatedly that the post-Second World War period has witnessed an 'explosion' in the proportion of married, particularly older, women working: from 8 per cent in 1921 to 60 per cent in 1976. But perhaps what we are seeing is a shift in the location and, to a lesser extent, the kind of work that these women are doing. This shift may ultimately affect the women's view of themselves as it brings them into contact, even if only as 'part-timers', with large-scale private or state enterprises. However, the expectation that this move would, in some way, fundamentally change their consciousness, does not, as yet at least, seem to have materialized, despite a considerable increase in women's trade union membership.[117] This may be partly explained by the fact that in some sense the shift may be seen as a loss of autonomy as the landlady becomes the supermarket employee. The rise of lodging and boarding did not only structure opportunities: women actively helped to shape this alternative or supplementary arena, where they could at least gain a measure of financial and social independence. If it is impossible ever to weigh up the gains and losses, at least this examination of the recent past should be a reminder that there is no natural or fixed separation between a private and a public sphere.

Notes

I should like to thank Anna Davin, Diana Gittins, Diana Leonard, Judy Lown and Sandra Taylor for help and suggestions in the writing of this essay. Support for the research came from the Gulbenkian programme of Lucy Cavendish College, Cambridge.

1   Barbara Taylor, 'The Woman-Power: Religious Heresy and Feminism in Early English Socialism', in Susan Lipshitz, ed., *Tearing the Veil: Essays on Femininity* (Routledge & Kegan Paul, London, 1978).
2   Duncan Crow, *The Victorian Woman* (Allen & Unwin, London, 1971).
3   David M. Schneider, *American Kinship: A Cultural Account* (Prentice-Hall, Englewood Cliffs, NJ, 1968).
4   All examples from Colchester are based on a 1 in 8 sample of the 1851 manuscript census. Colchester was a market town in East Anglia with a population of 20,000.
5   Robert E. Park, Ernest W. Burgess and Roderick D. McKenzie, *The City* (University of Chicago Press, Chicago, 1967); John Rex and Robert Moore, *Race, Community and Conflict: A Study of Sparkbrook* (Oxford University Press for the Institute of Race Relations, London, 1967).
6   John Modell and Tamara K. Hareven, 'Urbanization and the Malleable Household: An Examination of Boarding and Lodging in American Families', in Tamara K. Hareven, ed., *Family and Kin in Urban Communities, 1700–1930* (New Viewpoints, London and New York, 1977), p. 182.
7   J.J. Lee, 'Aspects of Urbanization and Economic Development in Germany 1815–1914', in Philip Abrams and E.A. Wrigley, eds, *Towns in Societies: Essays in Economic History and Historical Sociology* (Cambridge University Press, Cambridge, 1978); Barbara Laslett, 'The Family as a Public and Private Institution: A Historical Perspective', *Journal of Marriage and the Family*, no. 35 (August 1973).
8   Michael B. Katz, *The People of Hamilton, Canada West: Family and Class in a Mid-Nineteenth-Century City* (Harvard University Press, Cambridge, MA, 1975); Michael Anderson, *Family Structure in Nineteenth-Century Lancashire* (Cambridge University Press, Cambridge, 1971).
9   Modell and Hareven, 'Urbanization and the Malleable Household', p. 182.
10 For a critique of this view see W. Breines, W. Cerullo and J. Stacey, 'Social Biology, Family Studies and Anti-Feminist Backlash', *Feminist Studies*, vol. 4, no. 1 (February 1978).
11 Anderson, *Family Structure*; J. Humphries, 'Class Struggle and the Persistence of the

Working-Class Family', *Cambridge Journal of Economics*, vol. 1 (1977).

12 Modell and Hareven, 'Urbanization and the Malleable Household', p. 183; Alan Armstrong, *Stability and Change in an English County Town: A Social Study of York, 1801–51* (Cambridge University Press, Cambridge, 1974).

13 J. Gardiner, S. Himmelweit and M. Mackintosh, 'Women's Domestic Labour', *Bulletin of the Conference of Socialist Economists*, vol. 4, no. 2 (1975).

14 'It is this necessity – to do concrete, historically specific research from a feminist perspective – which could be described as the most important thing that we have learned from our last few years' (Women's Study Group, Centre for Contemporary Cultural Studies, University of Birmingham, 'Women's Studies Groups: Trying to do Feminist Intellectual Work', in *Women Take Issue: Aspects of Women's Subordination* [Hutchinson, London, 1978], p. 11).

15 Martha Blaxall and Barbara Reagan, eds, *Women and the Workplace: The Implications of Occupational Segregation* (University of Chicago Press, Chicago, 1976).

16 R.D. Barron and G.M. Norris, 'Sexual Divisions in the Dual Labour Market', in Diana Leonard Barker and Sheila Allen, eds, *Dependence and Exploitation in Work and Marriage* (Longman, London, 1976), p. 47.

17 A.M. Scott, 'Who are the Self-employed?', in Roy Bromley and Chris Gerry, eds, *Casual Work and Poverty in Third World Cities* (Wiley, London, 1979).

18 *Census*, 1911, General Report, p. 51.

19 *Census*, 1873, General Report, p. xii.

20 In 1871 Order 4 contained 4,014,044 women over the age of twenty or 62 per cent of the total female population (*Census*, 1871).

21 For an examination of the way statistical categories help to shape social reality see Barry Hindess, *The Use of Offical Statistics in Sociology: A Critique of Positivism and Ethnomethodology* (Macmillan, London, 1973).

22 M. Spufford, 'Peasant Inheritance Customs and Land Distribution in Cambridgeshire from the Sixteenth to the Eighteenth Centuries', in Jack Goody, Joan Thirsk and E.P. Thompson, eds, *Family and Inheritance: Rural Society in Western Europe, 1200–1800* (Cambridge University Press, Cambridge, 1976), p. 174.

23 M. Dorothy George, *London Life in the Eighteenth Century* (Penguin, London, 1965), p. 100.

24 Lawrence Stone, *The Family, Sex and Marriage in England, 1500–1800* (Weidenfeld & Nicolson, London, 1977), p. 28.

25 George Gissing, *In the Year of the Jubilee* (Watergate Classics, London, 1947), p. 401.

26 SSRC Oral History Archive, no. 116.

27 H.J. Dyos and D.A. Reeder, 'Slums and Suburbs', in H.J. Dyos and Michael Wolff, eds, *The Victorian City: Images and Realities* (Routledge & Kegan Paul, London, 1973), vol. 1, p. 375.

28 George, *London Life in the Eighteenth Century*, p. 103.

29 Leonore Davidoff, Jean L'Esperance and Howard Newby, 'Landscape with Figures: Home and Community in English Society', this volume, ch. 2.

30 For the origins of these ideas see Catherine Hall, 'The Early Formation of Victorian Domestic Ideology', in Sandra Burman, ed., *Fit Work for Women* (Croom Helm, London, 1979), pp. 15–32.

31 Society for the Promotion of Christian Knowledge, *The Lodgers* (London, 1901), p. 18.

32 Dinah Maria Craik, *Mistress and Maid* (Hurst & Blackett, London, 1863), p. 108.

33 Charles Booth, 'Common Lodging Houses', in *Life and Labour of the People in London*, vol. 1 (Macmillan, London, 1892), p. 206.

34 Raphael Samuel, 'Comers and Goers', in Dyos and Wolff, eds, *The Victorian City*, vol. 1, pp. 123–60.

35 *Parliamentary Papers*, 1852–3, LXXVIII, Common Lodging House Act, Report to the Secretary of State for Home Department, p. 528.
36 *Parliamentary Papers*, 1884–5, XXXI, Housing of the Working Classes, First report of HM Commissioners, Q 12, p. 359.
37 Modell and Hareven, 'Urbanization and the Malleable Household', p. 166.
38 Dyos and Reeder, 'Slums and Suburbs'.
39 *Parliamentary Papers*, 1852.
40 Anthony S. Wohl, 'Sex and the Single Room: Incest among the Victorian Working Class', in Anthony S. Wohl, ed., *The Victorian Family: Structures and Stresses* (Croom Helm, London, 1978).
41 *Parliamentary Papers*, 1859, XXII (Accounts and Papers), W. Harris in 'Report of the Assistant Commissioner of Police on the Conditions of Single Rooms Occupied by Families in the Metropolis'.
42 *Parliamentary Papers*, 1887, LXXI, Housing of the Working Classes, Report of HM Commissioners, Q 4147.
43 *Parliamentary Papers*, 1884–5, LXXI, Rural Report, Housing of the Working Classes.
44 *Census*, 1931, Housing Report.
45 Arthur Sherwell, *Life in West London: A Study and a Contrast* (Methuen, London, 3rd edn, 1901).
46 Fabian Society, *Homes for the People*, Tract no. 26 (London, 1897).
47 Enid Gauldie, 'The Middle Class and Working-Class Housing in the Nineteenth Century', in A. Allan MacLaren, ed., *Social Class in Scotland: Past and Present* (John Donald, Edinburgh, 1976).
48 Leonore Davidoff, 'Mastered for Life: Servant and Wife in Victorian and Edwardian England', this volume, ch. 1.
49 Sandra Taylor, personal communication.
50 National Association for Women's Lodging Homes, *National Conference on Lodging-House Accommodation for Women* (London, 1911).
51 Mrs B. Booth, 'The Need for Real Homes for Women', *National Conference on Lodging-House Accommodation for Women* (London, 1911).
52 Manuscript Census, Public Record Office, RG 10.
53 Count Charles de Rémusat, *La vie de village en Angleterre ou souvenirs d'un exilé* (Didier, Paris, 1862), p. 31.
54 T.S. Simey and M.B. Simey, *Charles Booth, Social Scientist* (Oxford University Press, Oxford, 1960).
55 Eric Partridge, 'Do – Hence to please, to meet the requirements of a person', in *A Dictionary of Slang and Unconventional English*, vol. 1 (Routledge, London, 1937), p. 226.
56 A.J. Munby, Diaries 1861–1875, quoted by permission of the Master and Fellows of Trinity College, Cambridge.
57 This expectation remains as in the Department of Health and Social Security's 'Co-habitation Rule'.
58 M. Finer and O. McGregor, 'The History of the Obligation to Maintain', in *Report of the Committee on One Parent Families*, Cmd. 5629, 1974, Appendix 5, p. 126.
59 Armstrong, *Stability and Change*, p. 180.
60 H.J. Dyos and A.B.M. Baker, 'The Possibilities of Computerising Census Data', in H.J. Dyos, ed., *The Study of Urban History* (Edward Arnold, London, 1971), p. 102.
61 Munby, Diaries.
62 Anderson, *Family Structure*.
63 *Census*, 1863, vol. LIII, p. 33.
64 *Census*, 1851, General Report, p. xxxiv.
65 *Census*, 1851, General Report, p. xxxiv.

66 J. Marle, in *Tom* v. *Luckett* (1847) 5 C.B. 23; 12 J.P. 6; 11 Jur. 993; 136 E.R. 781; J. Willes, in *Smith* v. *Lancaster* (1869) L.R. 5 C.P. 246; 1 Hop. and Colt 287; 39 L.J.C.P. 33; 21 L.T. 492; 18 W.R. 170.

67 Charles Seymour, *Electoral Reform in England and Wales: The Development and Operation of the Parliamentary Franchise, 1832–1885* (Yale University Press, New Haven, 1915).

68 Katz, *The People of Hamilton.*

69 John R. Gillis, *Youth and History: Tradition and Change in European Age Relations, 1770 to the Present* (Academic Press, New York, 1974).

70 *Parliamentary Papers*, 1884–5, Q 15, p. 203.

71 The Colchester sample produced 49 lodgers, 12 female and 37 male. A special sample of 14 subdistricts of the general 1851 census showed that 66 per cent of lodgers were male.

72 Katz, *The People of Hamilton.*

73 Frank McKenna, 'Victorian Railway Workers', *History Workshop Journal*, no. 1 (spring 1976).

74 Raphael Samuel, 'Village Labour', in Raphael Samuel, ed., *Village Life and Labour* (Routledge & Kegan Paul, London, 1975), p. 16.

75 John Burnett, ed., *Useful Toil: Autobiographies of Working People from the 1820s to the 1920s* (Allen Lane, London, 1974), p. 284.

76 Samuel, 'Comers and Goers', p. 152.

77 T. Vigne, P. Thompson and A. Howkins, personal communication.

78 Brian Harrison, *Drink and the Victorians: The Temperance Question in England, 1815–1872* (Faber & Faber, London, 1971), p. 47.

79 Judith R. Walkowitz, *Prostitution and Victorian Society: Women, Class and the State* (Cambridge University Press, Cambridge, 1980).

80 For a critique of the 'snapshot' approach to historical statistics, see L. Berkner, 'The Uses and Abuses of the Census for Family History', *Journal of Interdisciplinary History*, vol. 5, no. 4 (1975).

81 Essex Record Office, D/F 3/3/22 and 56.

82 Michael Holroyd, *Lytton Strachey: A Biography* (Penguin, Harmondsworth, 1971), p. 204.

83 C.W. Chalklin, *The Provincial Towns of Georgian England: A Study of the Building Process, 1740–1820* (Edward Arnold, London, 1974), p. 53.

84 Munby, Diaries.

85 Anderson, *Family Structure*, p. 47.

86 Medical Officer of Health, *Report on Kensington 1899* (London), Appendix 2.

87 Anderson, *Family Structure*, p. 47.

88 Anderson, *Family Structure*; Robert Tressell, *The Ragged Trousered Philanthropists* (Lawrence & Wishart, London, 1955).

89 Anonymous, *Looking for Lodgings and Other Tales* (Brussels, 1885).

90 *All about Margate and Herne Bay* (publicity pamphlet, 1865).

91 Anderson, *Family Structure*; Armstrong, *Stability and Change*; Modell and Hareven, 'Urbanization and the Malleable Household'.

92 L. Berkner, 'The Stem Family and the Development Cycle of the Peasant Household: An Eighteenth-Century Austrian Example', *American Historical Review*, vol. 77 (1972).

93 Frederick Willis, *101 Jubilee Road: A Book of London Yesteryears* (Phoenix House, London, 1948).

94 Davidoff, 'Mastered for Life'.

95 Burnett, ed., *Useful Toil*, p. 285.

96 A New England Man, *A Sketch of Old England* (Wiley, New York, 1822), p. 10.

97 *Census*, 1931, Housing Report.

98 *The Times*, Law Report, 14 April 1978.

99 Nottingham Archives, PL/111/275.

100 M. Winstanley, 'The Rural Publican and his Business in East Kent Before 1914', *Oral History*, vol. 4, no. 2 (autumn 1976).

101 Here was one of the ways in which 'surplus' women were surviving. It is questionable whether the problem of surplus women in the mid-nineteenth century was demographic so much as social, and public concern may have been at least partially due to the publicity given to certain findings of the 1851 census; W.R. Greg, 'Why Are Women Redundant?', *Literary and Social Judgements* (Trubner, London, 2nd edn 1869).

102 Angus Wilson, *The Strange Ride of Rudyard Kipling: His Life and Works* (Secker & Warburg, London, 1977).

103 'Toilers in London', *British Weekly* (London, 1897); Munby, Diaries.

104 'Juloc', *Boarding-House Reminiscences, or, the Pleasure of Living with Others* (T.F. Unwin, London, 1896).

105 Dorothy Richardson, 'Interim', *Pilgrimage*, vol. 2 (Dent, London, 1938), pp. 286–7.

106 Dylan Thomas, *Under Milk Wood: A Play for Voices* (Dent, London, 1966).

107 Burnett, ed., *Useful Toil*, p. 285.

108 [Thomas Wright], The Journeyman Engineer, *Some Habits and Customs of the Working Classes* (London, 1867), p. 210.

109 Robert Roberts, *A Ragged Schooling: Growing Up in the Classic Slum* (Penguin, Harmondsworth, 1978), p. 82.

110 'The Landlady's Daughter' a music hall song of the late nineteenth century:

> Where I'm lodging, oh dear me?
> The daughter of my landlady
> She's a perfect little treet
> Not quite 19, and so neat!
> Talk about a fellow when
> He's made to feel quite easy
> I never knew what comfort was
> Until I met Miss Squeezy. (*Fred Earle Songbook*)

111 Seymour, *Electoral Reform in England and Wales*, p. 364.

112 This was essentially a working-class image. It is striking that the other semi-licit sexual stereotype of Victorian society, the older middle-class man and the young working-class girl (often a servant), gains its piquancy by crossing class lines. It too, of course, involves a cash relationship which masks an oedipal situation. How far either of these reflected reality is very difficult to say.

113 In rhyming slang, a lodger was 'artful dodger': 'The lodger was the butt of many late nineteenth- and early twentieth-century jokes – now almost all obsolescent due to the vast change in post-war social conditions' (Julian Franklyn, *A Dictionary of Rhyming Slang* [Routledge, London, 1960], p. 34).

114 Katz, *The People of Hamilton*; Modell and Hareven, 'Urbanization and the Malleable Household'.

115 Michael Young and Peter Wilmott, *Family and Kinship in East London* (Routledge & Kegan Paul, London, 1957).

116 Peter Laslett, 'The Decline of the Size of the Domestic Group in England. A Comment on J.W. Dixon's Note', *Population Studies*, vol. 24 (November 1970).

117 Friedrich Engels, *The Origin of the Family, Private Property and the State* (Lawrence & Wishart, London, 1972); Wally Seccombe, 'The Housewife and her Labour under Capitalism', *New Left Review*, no. 83 (1974), pp. 3–24.

6

The Role of Gender in the 'First Industrial Nation': Farming and the Countryside in England, 1780–1850

Keep up appearances: there lies the test
The World will give thee credit for the rest
John Trusler, *The Way to be Rich and Respectable*, 1777

By the end of the eighteenth century, a middle class was emerging as a major force in English society.[1] The expansion of capitalist enterprise had transformed forms of property and fostered scientific and practical experimentation, rational acounting and centralized marketing. Commercial, manufacturing, professional and farming families gained in wealth, knowledge and prestige. Their aim was not simply inclusion in the existing system but to challenge the legitimate basis of aristocratic domination. Their wealth flowed mainly from liquid property and skill rather than land, hitherto the major source of political and social honour.[2] As employers of wage labour, manufacturers and farmers faced directly that section of the lower strata being transformed into a propertyless working class. Moreover, the middle class was itself riven by internal divisions: between higher- and lower-ranking families, between provinces and metropolis, Anglican and Nonconformist, Tory and Whig.

Within this context, provincial middle-class consciousness was framed by moral and religious values, embodied in the Evangelical movement, both Anglican and Nonconformist.[3] Concern with individual salvation elevated moral probity above the claims of rank through birth. An intensely moral life was to be supported by the rational principles of property management and work organization, both aspects enhancing commercial trustworthiness at a time when formal business institutions were undeveloped. The emphasis on conversion experience meant that inward grace could be demonstrated by outward individual behaviour; restraint in gait and language, soberness, curbing public display of bodily functions or simply wearing clean linen. Such 'seriousness' challenged aristocratic laxity, exemplified in the countryside by the absentee parson and hard-riding, drinking squire. In London the Prince Regent's circle was notorious for drunkenness, licentiousness and gambling at a time when debt to tradesmen was part of the aristocratic code but anathema to the self-respect of the middle classes whose livelihood and social position depended on commercial trust.[4] The challenge of the middle class was, indeed, seen as a crusade against 'Old Corruption'.[5]

Within the middle class, social honour was claimed through *gentility*, a concept undoubtedly derived partly from gentry culture but reinterpreted in crucial ways.[6] *Gentility* and its lesser derivative, *respectability*, were always heavily gendered categories. A *gentleman's* claim to recognition was his independence signified by his ability to protect and support his dependants (primarily wife and children), a definition with chivalric overtones of reconstructed paternalism going hand in hand with market exploitation.[7] The analogous ideal of *lady* placed women in a protected environment away from independent action in market, street or political forum.

Religious and secular status merged in stressing domestic life, the creation and maintenance of the 'Home' in opposition to the public world. This division evolved into a powerful world-view embodied in the doctrine of 'separate spheres', with its gendered resonance which became a unifying characteristic of middle-class identity. Such concepts are never made from whole cloth but had an inheritance from law, theology, custom and classical learning. Men already claimed natural superiority and a place as representatives of household and family in the body politic. They were seen as potential bearers of rationality and controllers of disruptive forces, particularly female sexuality. Since it was the middle classes who had promoted the potentially disruptive and amoral market forces, they were especially concerned with social order and their apprehensions were fuelled by potential political disorder unleashed by the French Revolution. Relations between the sexes often became a metaphor for such threats to the social fabric.

The central place of home and family also rested on the organization of middle-class property and economic resources. Few institutions had yet emerged for transacting business. Early banks, for example, were liable to sudden collapse and family or local community remained the primary source of capital and credit.[8] The main form of enterprise was the single entrepreneur aided by family and household and expandable into the partnership. Wives, often acting as informal partners, would have been the logical choice, but under the legal convention of 'coverture', at marriage a woman 'died a kind of civil death'; she could not make contracts, sue or be sued or declared bankrupt.[9] Single women and widows, while not legally disabled, were conventually regarded in a similar way. Male relatives were favoured partners: brothers, sons, nephews, brothers-in-law and sons-in-law.

One of the most powerful middle-class forms of property, the trust, also marginalized women. Male relatives acted as trustees investing and managing women's property to produce income for their support while capital was freed for investment in the family enterprise.[10] The liquidity of much middle-class property favoured partible inheritance in contrast to primogeniture practised by the landed gentry, although sons tended to inherit business tools, stock and premises while daughters received household goods, cash and government securities.[11] One result was the intensity of sibling relationships since all life-chances were tied to the family enterprise, a pattern reinforced by the late age at marriage.[12] Women's roles were extended beyond mothers and wives to sisters, aunts, cousins or occasionally non-kin in a pattern of male support exchanged for female service.

Since kin were so important to economic survival, marriage was central. Brothers-in-law were brought in as partners or sisters married existing partners. The priority given to such links is indicated by 'sibling-exchange' marriage frequently found in town and countryside, across all occupations and religious groups. In this practice, two brothers would marry two sisters or a sister and brother from one family would marry a brother and sister from another. Cousin marriages were also frequent, both patterns reinforcing partnership.[13] Women were central in maintaining relationships upon which business and professional operations rested. They contributed further by bearing and rearing suitably large numbers of sons as future personnel,[14] and they cared for apprentices, pupils or shopmen, often kin, who lived in their master's home. In addition, women contributed labour and skills to the enterprise although often behind the scenes, since households were largely still located next to, if not within, the enterprise. Bankers' families lived in the Bank House, schoolmasters' in the School House, millers' in the Mill House, while shops were in the front room from which doctors likewise dispensed drugs. Thus women dealt with customers, helped keep the books and undertook other business tasks while running the house.

Women were also instrumental in exhibiting the family's position through consumption. An effort to keep up appearances and display creditworthiness lay behind much of the expenditure in rising standards of living. Middle-class households bought the furniture, carpets, wallpaper, silver plate, pictures and wheeled vehicles for their renovated or new suburban homes. They read new publications, attended doctors and solicitors, created opportunities for more clergymen, schoolmasters, bankers and architects. This circular process created demand for goods and services which made modest fortunes while fuelling claims to status recognition by the gentry.[15] The necessity to prove probity through life-style increased during the volatile Napoleonic War period. The mingling of family and business finances under unlimited liability made frequent bankruptcies more devastating. High mortality constantly threatened financial support from a husband, father or brother. Thus family and kin, augmented by local and religious community ties, provided a vital source of support. Women, in their active domesticity, were at the heart of these networks.

The contribution of women's property, labour and skill to the enterprise has been outlined. Conversely, men were heavily involved in the household where business and social contacts intermingled, the endless tea-drinking being by no means a purely female affair. Middle-class men, working from the building which housed the home, engaged with their children and the innumerable visiting family and friends. At the same time, these men were active in the expanding public sphere. In addition to their business affairs, men sought political, scientific and cultural recognition through a myriad of voluntary societies, the hallmark of the middle class.[16] Not coincidentally, such organizations were often charitable trusts, their trustees, the same men running the gas companies, insurance societies and renovated grammar schools, further strengthening the masculine image of the public sphere.

Women were peripheral to such organizations. They might give subscriptions or act as spectators at selected events, but were ineligible as effective members. Forms of property, economic institutions and cultural norms framed middle-class masculinity as action and independence while women received support in return for personal services and dependence.[17] At this time, their role promised positive rewards. It was only as the nineteenth century developed, that the price women paid for exclusion from the expanding public world became manifest.

The provincial middle class has usually been taken as an urban phenomenon. It may be argued, however, that similar patterns would emerge wherever conditions for its growth were present. In the last quarter of the eighteenth century farming for profit was well established in the south-eastern and midland areas of England.[18] Here too, Anglicans and Nonconformists were active proponents of domesticity. Therefore, detailed concentration on this local farming community should demonstrate the interaction of class and gender in its historical context. The middle-class challenge might be observed even better in the countryside where gentry and aristocracy were visible than in more middle-class enclaves of provincial manufacturing towns. Farmers were the first to confront wage labourers on a large scale, before the familiar case of manufacture. Thus it is here in the heartland of the upper-class ascendancy, that the men and women of the middle class will be observed as they forged a self-identity in the daily round of business, social and family life.

Despite the growth of manufacturing industry in the late eighteenth century, agriculture remained the basis of English society. Land, in the form of large estates, was owned mainly by the aristocracy. Below them was a larger group of landowning gentry without titles, plus a scattering of owner occupiers. By the mid-eighteenth century, particularly in the grain-growing areas of the midlands and south-east, the uniquely English 'three-tier' system of agriculture was firmly established. Landowners leased out land and farmsteads and were responsible for maintaining buildings, roads, hedges and drainage. The farmers who managed the land were tenants who supplied stock, seed and tools. This division gave a flexibility unlike European peasant farming or even owner occupation of English upland farms of the north and west. Farmers could add or discard acres and move households from farm to farm with changes in labour supply or demand for grain products.

In these areas the system of boarding and lodging farm servants within the farmhouse was giving way to the employment of day-labourers paid in cash. Farm service had been performed primarily by young men and women before marriage whereas day-labour represented a permanently proletarianized workforce.[19] This shift was related to changes in farming practice where arable crops were easing out animal husbandry, an innovation often countered by hostility from the agricultural labouring community.

By the second quarter of the nineteenth century, it was recognized that although landowners provided many of the basic resources, the farmers were 'the active capitalists of English agriculture'.[20] For much of the eastern region, agriculture had become an economic salvation. This area had been the centre of the wool trade through the eighteenth century, its towns and villages prosperous with wool merchants, weavers and spinners. By the 1770s, changes in demand and competition from abroad had eroded trade, the blockade of the Napoleonic War providing the final blow. However, the same factors created a protected market for grain, many woollen mills being converted for grinding corn,[21] while capital salvaged by wool merchants was reinvested in growing grain, malting and milling.[22]

The gulf between prosperous farmers and labourers grew. Farmers became disdainful of manual work alongside their men, spending more time in planning, marketing and managerial functions.[23] The gap widened further when the high cost of corn during the Napoleonic Wars brought wealth to many farmers but lean years to their labourers, whose lives appeared increasingly narrow and vulgar. Rising expectations among farmers were encouraged by newcomers to the countryside. Families with a little capital were drawn by high profits and the prospect of a rural retreat. Many came to grief in the post-war slump, but their influence as carriers of culture was strong. The ex-naval officer John Harriott took over a large farm on marginal lands in coastal Essex, determined to make it pay and enlighten his stolid rural neighbours with innovations such as Sunday schools.[24] At a more opulent level, John Hanson, a wealthy London merchant, bought a small Essex estate as a retreat on which to raise his fourteen children. He was keen to run the home farm on commercial lines while his home became a social centre for the area, displaying genteel domesticity in daily life.[25] The war also brought army officers to market towns, some of whom became part of the Evangelical community while others sponsored balls, assemblies and theatres. Worldly or religious, these families created demands for goods and services, acting as status leaders to the local population.[26] These towns also attracted retired farmers, and farmers' widows and spinster daughters, swelling the ranks of genteel families living on small investment incomes, mingling the cultures of town and countryside.[27]

In any case, farming was not yet a fixed full-time occupation during the period under investigation. For the wealthy banking family of Oakes in Bury St Edmunds (close friends of their neighbour, Arthur Young), the farm was still an important part of their household economy and the banker himself turned out to see the harvest in.[28] Jonas Asplin, an Essex physician, was as concerned about the state of his corn as of his patients.[29] The successful Witham grocer, Thomas Butler, turned the business over to his son and worked the farm whose fields lay behind the shop.[30] Malters and brewers grew their own barley while farming and milling continued in combination.[31] Smaller farms might keep a public house or a shop, work a brickkiln, blacksmithy or small pottery.[32] These enterprises used family labour, custom dictating activities suitable for boys and girls, men and women.

By the 1820s, the standard of living and status aspirations of farming families had been raised. A Suffolk vicar had noted in 1813 how a generation before farmers had 'lived in the midst of their enlightened neighbours like beings of another order; in their personal labour they were indefatigable; in their fare hard, in their dress homely, in their manners rude. We ne'er shall look upon their like again.'[33] There were modest fortunes in farming but it was risky and capital was necessary. Arthur Young, travelling the eastern counties, noted that houses of small farms 'are frequently wretched hovels, not better, if so good, as decent cottages'.[34] At the other end of the scale farmers lived in converted manor houses, for example families like the Hutleys of Power Hall in Witham, Essex, with extended acres, augmented by judicious marriage, who became a force in the local community. Hutley, farming over 1,500 acres, had the option of becoming part of the local gentry but he chose to remain a farmer whose wealth exceeded that of some of his gentry neighbours.[35] Hutley dined regularly with the self-made Witham doctor Henry Dixon, himself the son of a small farmer but who, through marriage, was proprietor of neighbouring Durward Hall, and like many of their mutual friends was active in local politics often opposed to gentry interests.[36]

These substantial farmers, whose wealth and contacts made them powerful beyond the bounds of their villages, were becoming a social anomaly if not an actual threat to the status order of the countryside. By the 1820s, peace had brought a sharp drop in grain prices, combining with bad harvests to turn boom into depression and only larger farms backed by strong credit survived. Yet when the Select Committee on Agriculture sat in 1833 to inquire into the distress, it was maintained that farmers and farmers' wives were loath to give up the tastes they had acquired during the prosperous years of the French wars. 'They may have since been forced to diminish their expenses, but I cannot say that they have returned to their former habits, because they could not have kept their grade in society.'[37]

Local gentry and clergy were threatened by the rising position of farmers while their own fortunes were closely tied to the farming enterprise, a point made painfully clear in the 1820s and 1830s when, as landlords, many were forced to grant rent abatements of farms no longer profitable.[38] Jane Austen encapsulated the social bewilderment expressed by local gentry. In her novel of 1816, *Emma*, the heroine of the title had befriended a young woman of gentry origins who had been at boarding school with the sisters of an up-and-coming young farmer neighbour. This young man read a great deal but not 'what you would think anything of. He reads the Agricultural Reports'. When Emma is asked if she has seen him, she replies that she may have seen him fifty times but has no idea of his name:

The yeomanry are precisely the order of people with whom I feel I can have nothing to do. A degree or two lower, and a creditable appearance might interest me; I might hope to be useful to their families in some way or other. But a farmer can need none of my help, and is therefore in one sense as much above my notice as in every other he is below it.[39]

Austen recognizes here the role of women in giving or witholding social recognition while satirizing the gentry for false pretensions over their farming neighbours. At the same time, radicals such as Cobbett fulminated against upstart farmers who disdained the plain ways and honest oak furniture of his youthful days.[40]

Status problems among farmers were furthered by the wide range of incomes and life-styles. The ambiguous division between managerial and manual tasks for both the farmer and his wife allowed no breaking-point in the scale of status demarcation as between, for example, wholesale and retail trade. Furthermore, in the earlier part of the period under discussion in this essay, young people from small farming families had entered higher echelons of domestic service. Ladies' maids, children's nurses, cooks, grooms and footmen were often recruited from farms and when married settled back in the countryside carrying with them urban standards yet remaining socially tainted in the eyes of the gentry by their service experience.[41]

The ambiguity of farmers' status seemed most disturbing to the clergy, traditional cultural leaders in the countryside, particularly Anglicans with close ties to the gentry but whose incomes might be closer to those of their farming parishioners.[42] Unease about the degree of social intimacy between farmers and clergy surfaces in local sources. An Evangelical curate in rural Suffolk wrote a tale in which the clergyman hero is shocked when his sister is courted by the son of a local farmer, a young man given a gentleman's education which raised him above his station.[43] Clergy–farming relations were exacerbated further by the tithe question particularly where farmers were Nonconformist and clergymen doubled as landowners. But even Anglican farming families might seek to preserve independence by refusing to remove a cap or curtsy to clergy.[44] Nevertheless, Evangelical religion permeated the farming community as much as the urban middle class. Nonconformists and Anglicans recruited farmers as the backbone of revitalized rural congregations.[45] Prosperous farming families drove their gigs to more distant town churches and chapels often staying on for afternoon Sunday services.[46] Here they mixed with trade and professional people, raising aspirations for a more refined life-style.

Religious impetus combined with changing farming practices to emphasize the need for an enlarged education for farmers' children. In 1807, Arthur Young noted that the 'greater opulence of farmers led to improved education of their children and a greater taste for reading'. No longer did incessant drudgery shut him (sic) out from 'intercourse with the world which enlarges the mind and increases knowledge'.[47] More prosperous male farmers mixed socially at markets and other functions, their mobility increasing with ownership of riding-horses and wheeled vehicles. Modern farming also required increased literacy and numeracy for the keeping of accounts and records, writing business letters and keeping up with new literature on farming methods. School curricula were expanded with surveying, geometry and book-keeping alongside Latin and Greek for sons of farmers and tradesmen in the renovated grammar schools and numerous private academies of the market towns.[48] Gentry, clergy and professionals may have felt threatened by the educated, more 'gentlemanly' farmer, but farmers saw education as a means of raising their social status vis-à-vis labourers. In a survey of Suffolk it was stated that the smaller farmers could not afford the annual fees of £40 or £50 for the grammar schools and 'owing to the advantages of the free and parochial schools now spread throughout the county, our labourers' children will be better taught than our own'.[49] Since the clergy were mainly responsible for the drive to educate labourers' children, this further aggravated tensions.

While the sons of farmers were beginning to receive a general education augmented by practical subjects, girls' brief formal schooling and home training alike emphasized the expectation of a domestic future. In Lincolnshire a farmer sent his sons to school but not his daughters as they needed only to milk, sew, cook and bear children.[50] Girls had long been excluded from the grammar schools, many of whose original founding charters had specified that both sexes should attend. The girls' private schools which existed at this time stressed deportment, music, drawing and a smattering of foreign languages in addition to the all-pervasive religious and moral training. Since the content of the education offered to girls from farming families was not directly useful or seen to be relevant to their lives, they were more open to censure for pretentiousness than young men whose schooling might at least turn them into better farmers.

In fact, the standard of living of the family was partially determined by the level of literacy, skill and outlook of its female members. Wives and daughters who had received a better education might manage to keep some literary pursuits and mix more freely with other middle-class women. Jane Saffrey, who had run a boarding school before marrying a Baptist farmer, organized a small magazine and literary society,[51] while Jane Ransome Biddell, daughter of an Ipswich Quaker manufacturer but married to a wealthy Anglican farmer, wrote poetry and mixed with the upper echelons of the town.[52] Yet the literary output of both women is a celebration of domesticity. Commonplace books of young men and women illustrate their differing preoccupations. While all were concerned with moral questions and individual salvation, masculine entries include exercises in measurement, comments on politics, scientific facts, or the weather. The cultural milieu of young women, gleaned from books, newspapers, school stories, local sermons and their diary entries, favoured family relationships, friendship and domestic happenings. Jane Seabrook was a farmer's daughter and future farmer's wife when she kept such a book in her late teens. Her brother-in-law copied for her the well-known homily, 'The One Thing Needful': religious duties, which 'particularly belong to women to gain for her family'. She is daily to read and explain the Scriptures, to lead all family members 'to the alter of God'. If her husband stands aloof from these important duties and 'suffers the cares and troubles of the world more to possess his mind' there is nothing she can do but 'humbly hope and pray'.[53]

Local evidence suggests that farmers' wives, sisters and daughters took seriously their role in creating a domestic atmosphere and training their children. They saw the home as a means of overcoming divisions between master and man, as strong in the countryside as in the town. Earthly homes were a foretaste of the immortality open to all in the heavenly home. In an unpublished poem entitled simply 'Home', Jane Ransome Biddell (farmer's wife) states many of these themes explicitly:

> Alike in day-built shed, or marble hall
> Thy magic name has power o'er every heart
> The quiet nest, through life so dear to all
> The goal from which the spirit may depart.

But home had a different meaning for men and women:

> How sweet the atmosphere around thee thrown
> Where youthful daughters grace thy social hearth
> Nor less, though sadder, is thy influence known
> By son's self-exiled wandering o'er the earth[54]

For both men and women, the material basis of that home was an equally important preoccupation, for both spiritual and worldly reasons. Changes in farming practice and higher levels of income combined at the end of the eighteenth century to institute changes in the layout of farmsteads as well as internal alterations to the farmhouse in keeping with middle-class concerns for privacy, comfort and family life. By the early nineteenth century there had been extensive alterations to existing farms as well as the planning of new farmsteads. New farming methods tidied away many functions into barns and sheds. The use of manure as fertilizer meant providing for its storage which cleared farmyards, while more expensive machinery was kept under cover. The older pattern had been a square of utilitarian buildings with the farmhouse making up the fourth side, no garden to speak of and an entrance through a mucky yard.[55] This was changing as the 'casual chaos' became a 'more planned and purposeful lay-out of the new order'.[56] Many farmhouses were given brick fronts with sash-windows and door lintels covering their old-fashioned muddle of elevations, hiding mud and wattle exteriors. By siting the kitchen and working places firmly at the back and presenting such a front to the road, 'farmhouses could approximate to mere . . . residences that could just as well have appeared in town'.[57] By the 1840s, 'Essex farmhouses and buildings are for the most part substantial and ornamental with neat gardens and choice evergreens.'[58]

The interior layout of the farmhouse also changed. The size of the workforce on larger farms would have prevented traditional boarding of all labourers even without social conventions of family privacy.[59] Initially, labourers were segregated at a separate table in the living kitchen, which later gave way to feeding the men in the 'back-house' (bak'hus) for a midday meal only, while the family ate in a separate kitchen and sat in a parlour. A door to this room avoided entrance through the kitchen, keeping family and hired hands apart. Segregation was not simply a social pretension but part of a desire by farmers' female relatives for freedom from heavy manual tasks. A farmer's daughter who remembered the work involved in the hot dinners and, at harvest, special cakes and home-brewed beer, could understand that farmers' wives welcomed paying men in cash to board themselves although it 'snapped some of the ties which bound the servant and master as fellow creatures'.[60] From the eighteenth to the nineteenth century, the tradition of the harvest supper (in Suffolk, the 'Horkey'), with its special ales, songs and rituals, was transformed from the lavish spread in the common 'house place', with tables laden with roast and boiled meat, plum-pudding and Horkey ale, master and mistress at the head of the table taking part, to a separate meal provided in the kitchen where the farmer and his wife put in an appearance for the final toasts. Later still, the publican was paid to provide the whole affair at the local inn where much heavy drinking took place and women were seldom present.[61]

Furnishings of farmhouses also altered. There were signs of a more rational life-style in wall-clocks and barometers. Stone-flagged floors gave way to carpets, open fireplaces with chimney-breasts hung with cooking and farming implements were replaced by closed grates and overmantels. Curtains and padded chairs or a sofa were introduced. There might be books in cases and possibly a piano.[62] The diary of a farmer's wife covers 1823 when extensive alterations were made to their farmhouse, including new grates and chimney adjustment, a parlour with carpets and curtains, the purchase of pictures and, significantly, bell-pulls to summon the servants from the kitchen. The alterations took over five months and by July, she recorded: 'I feel much pleased that I can prevail on Mr Green (*the new vicar*) to take a glass of wine for the first time at our house.'[63]

Men in farming families also shopped for the new furnishings, helped hang the wallpaper and appreciated the various refinements of their daily lives. However, many, in addition to running the farm, were becoming involved in the voluntary societies which were beginning to redefine the public sphere. For example the Thaxted Book Society, a group of farmers in Essex led by the Nonconformist minister, met monthly to discuss books brought from London. Despite the fact that they met at one another's houses with only the annual dinner held at the Sun Inn, there seems to have been only one woman member.[64] Some organizations built the concept of men's responsibility for dependants into their activities, setting up funds for widows and children while also emphasizing their masculine ambience through ritual dining and drinking. Their meetings were almost always held in public houses and ranged from purely social affairs such as the Chelmsford Beefsteak Club, to more political Whig and Tory strongholds. Freemasonry, too, flourished in the eastern counties and was almost entirely middle class despite its aristocratic patronage at the national level. While innkeepers, tradesmen and professional men tended to dominate in lodges in Colchester and Ipswich, farmers made up 6 per cent of the total.[65]

The contacts gained through an organization like the Freemasons were used by farmers to promote business, but Agricultural Societies and Farmers' Clubs were their special milieu. The latter were less prestigious and had fewer aristocratic titles but they had more working members who exchanged practical information.[66] In Suffolk in 1804 there had been one Agricultural Society, but by 1846 there were five as well as ten Farmers' Clubs.[67] Women might go as spectators to Agricultural Society shows and social affairs but they were totally excluded from the Farmers' Clubs which met in local public houses. Farmers also joined forces to protect their property as rural police were unknown before the 1830s. The Napoleonic Wars and their aftermath of depression meant much unrest among the hard-pressed rural labouring community, with rick-burning and cattle-maiming as well as stealing horses, fodder and food. Attacks were directed at the larger farmers as well as clergy and gentry.[68] Farmers formed the core of rural Protective Associations to track down culprits, raise rewards and follow up prosecutions. These Associations also met in public houses where dining and convivial drinking were combined with business. Only a handful of property-owning widows was scattered among the male membership.[69]

Changes in local administration, transferring church functions to the state, favoured farmers' involvement at village level. The appointment of permanent officials left local people with vestry duties, larger farmers demonstrating their new levels of administrative competence as Poor Law overseers. Traditional offices were attached to the property rather than the person and technically open to widows and single women who worked farms.[70] Up to the 1830s some women exercised this right, helping to take the collection at church services, levying rates and administering relief, for example the notable Mrs Whitehead who dealt with 165 applicants at a single meeting.[71] However, women so acting were potentially anomalous. While the verger, sexton and parish clerk were posts occasionally filled by women, the latter office derived from clerical assistant to the priest, 'a man who is able to make a will or write a letter for anyone in the parish . . . the universal father to give away brides, and the standing god-father to all newborn bantlings'.[72] In parishes with a dearth of literate men, a woman might take on some of these functions. Attitudes of Evangelical clergy to this situation are illustrated by the shocked reaction of the Reverend John Charlesworth, on first taking his appointment in the remote parish of Flowton in Suffolk where he 'found a *woman* acted as the clerk giving out the responses' (his italics). He immediately substituted a male farmer although this man's reading was 'inferior to hers'.[73]

The use of the public house for transacting all types of business was a major obstacle to respectable women's activity in local affairs. The heart of the farmers' world was the market where buying and selling of produce, exchange of information on prices, land availability and farming practice changed hands and bargains were sealed over a drink. On market days the innkeeper and one or two leading farmers organized the weekly 'ordinary' – a meal at a fixed price high enough to exclude labourers.[74] Farmers' wives might accompany their husbands to inns when on a visit to a town, but women seen in public houses were increasingly jeopardizing their reputations. Evangelical opinion equated public houses with sin. While men might have to go to such places in pursuit of legitimate business, women should never be seen crossing their thresholds. In the 1830s, a Suffolk man commented on the notoriety of a female cattle dealer – by that date considered an eccentric – who used to sit with other dealers at the Swan, drinking and smoking a pipe and known locally as 'The Duchess'.[75]

Changes in marketing also hampered women's business activities. The informal open market was superseded by Market Halls and Corn Exchanges. The building of these impressive structures with neo-classical façades was organized by men as committees of trustees or directors. Women might have bought shares as an investment but they never became active committee members.[76] These purpose-built structures were partly promoted to replace fairs. The control of fairs was part of the Evangelical moral crusade against public displays of dancing, singing, drinking and games with an undercurrent of sexuality. The new morality was exemplified by the Essex magistrates' support for Wilberforce's Society Against Vice and Immorality to stop the licensing of local fairs, while an Essex vicar maintained that Chelmsford fair was, indeed, an 'abode of Moral Darkness'.[77] Such strictures were becoming easier to enforce as fairs were being partially replaced by shops or tinkers and packmen travelling to farm doors.

Hunting, too, was becoming a more questionable activity for women. The hunt had traditionally been the place where the three tiers of the English countryside could meet, for even labourers followed the hunt on foot. By the late eighteenth century, more formal subscription packs replaced private arrangements which had allowed women to take part occasionally (Lady Salisbury had once been Master of the Hunt by inheritance). The wildness of the chase, the 'blooding' with the fox's brush – exactly those elements which made it a 'manly exercise' – were inimical to feminine decorum. The costume of pink coat and breeches (evolved from wartime uniforms) was not for ladies whose long skirts when perched on a side-saddle were a further disincentive to hard riding. Emphasis on masculine chivalry, the need to protect women through any supposed difficulty and maintain ceremonious intercourse between the sexes made men feel constrained with women in the chase. 'Surtees', the great hunting journalist, maintained that: 'women are as much in their place at the meet watching and cheering the men on as they are out of it tearing across the country.'[78] Hunting provided an ideal 'male bonding' for all classes, the 'strongest preservation of that natural spirit . . . for a life of active energy, independence and freedom . . . and corrective to effeminacy' in the words of a fox-hunting MP.[79] Meanwhile, the women, whose men had organized the Suffolk Hunt, 'played the harpsichord and the new forte-piano, paid visits to each other, organised balls and made up theatre parties'.[80] Male farmers were thus able to mix with both social inferiors and superiors in market, hunting field, agricultural show, horse-race or club, but such masculine camaraderie had no equivalent for their female relatives. Women's activities were encapsulated by family and friends, the marking of social boundaries through informal shopping and visiting.

Women had traditionally been excluded from the public sphere of politics so that the masculine monopoly of voluntary societies, civic activities and leisure pursuits is not unexpected. The role of women in the economy was more problematic in both farming and the new occupations which were evolving in the countryside. Auctioneers, estate agents and bailiffs were dealing in land and specializing their nascent professions while others became solicitors. The demand for enclosure surveys, the estimation of tithes for commutation into cash, and later the railways, created a lively demand for surveying. Many men practising these skills had risen from the ranks of working farmers while other farmers combined activities.[81] These occupations stressed training on the job and experience. Their professional standards were promoted by newly formed organizations such as the Land Surveyors' Club, forerunner to the Institute of Chartered Surveyors.[82] Women were in no position to grasp such opportunities for they had neither the education, training nor legitimate acceptance in professional circles. A farmer's daughter with a talent for drawing might give a few art lessons to the neighbour's children or use her talents in cookery and needlework for the family.

Even in those areas where farm women had contributed directly to household production, a combination of factors was making them marginal to the economy. Specialization in arable farming and the accompanying use of male waged day-labour affected women's position at all levels of agriculture. The traditional association of men with ploughing and reaping furthered a gradual displacement of female labour from the fields, except for casual seasonal tasks.[83] There is a debate about the origins and timing of the decline in women's field labour, but it is agreed that by the early nineteenth century there was concern about the suitability of fieldwork for women.[84] Whatever the underlying economic reasons, the discussion of women's fieldwork was couched almost entirely in moral terms.[85] Exclusion affected women in farming families, creating difficulties in their enforcement of authority over the now predominantly male labour-force, particularly as they no longer overlooked the men's domestic lives as housemistresses. Supervision of field labour on far-flung acreages meant riding horseback, often alone. While this may have given added status and authority to male farmers, thus 'elevated above their work-force',[86] it ran contrary to notions of feminine decorum. Male farmers could slip into colloquial speech when dealing with labourers but respectable women were in a dilemma since rural lower-class culture was increasingly regarded as crude.

A more serious loss was dairying, traditionally women's work, which was a casualty of the shift to arable agriculture. Cheese and butter rapidly declined from being export products in the eastern counties as 'factors' made the rounds collecting more standardized products,[87] concentrating production in certain areas such as Gloucestershire where men were taking over enlarged operations.[88] Women's dairying which had taken place on almost every farm was slowly phased out, while growing corn and fattening cattle 'give but little trouble to the housewives of the present generation', according to an Essex commentator.[89] By 1843, the Royal Commission on Women and Children in Agriculture announced that the patience, skill and strength needed to produce cheese made this work unsuitable for women.[90] Specialized organization accompanied a move towards more scientific methods of cheese-making. The shift from craft skills to more experimental methods is exemplified in a manual dated 1784 where the male author based his rules on information 'collected from the most experienced Dairywomen of several counties' but then proceeded to upbraid them for their empiricist approach:

> The general way that the art of Dairying has been carried on for Ages has been progressive or traditional, being taught by Mother to Daughter, from common or continual experience, naturally adopting from time to time, the methods that appeared best, from such as have happened to come within their knowledge; without ever calling in the assistance of either materials they use, or knowledge of how to apply them in a Physical or Practical manner.[91]

At this early date the handbook is still designed for women, 'an attempt to instruct or inform Dairy women', despite the 'unthankful office' as the author anticipated the question: 'how should a Man know anything of Cheesemaking?'[92] As long as the process was in transition it was possible for women to contribute. The only entry by a woman in the *Farmer's Magazine* which began in 1800, was an article setting out a gravity test to measure the richness of milk, including the concept of a weighted index.[93] In the 1800s, a Suffolk farmer's wife was commended in the survey undertaken by the newly formed Board of Agriculture for her method of comparing milk from cows of different breeds and feeding habits. William Marshall combined gallantry with approval in his comment: 'This is a charming thought – which conveys to my mind, new and interesting ideas. And I value it the more as it aptly emanates from that of a sensible enlightened mistress of a dairy, whose experiments and observations on the subject in view, are truely scientific.'[94]

By the second quarter of the nineteenth century, only a few avocations were left to farmers' female relatives, activities which hovered between money-making, production for family use and hobbies of interest mainly to the women themselves. Poultry-keeping remained uncommercialized and farms continued to keep a few cows since large-scale sales of liquid milk were not possible until mid-century railroad development. The wife of Robert Bretnall of Witham (prosperous enough to sign himself 'gent' but from his diary more a farmer) kept two cows. In the first week of November, her husband recorded: 'My wife opened her Cow Box found in it saved cash £37 = 9 = 6 allowed for butter and milk for the use of our own house at 1 shilling per week is £2 = 12 shillings or £40 = 1 = 6.' Considering that this would have been a good income for a schoolteacher or curate, Mrs Bretnall had done well with her minuscule herd although how much she benefited personally is doubtful for the next year's entry reads: 'Total amount for the two Alderneys made in the Year £50 = 6 = 6. My wife took for her hard labour in managing the two cows £5 = 0 = 0 and I received £45 = 6 = 6 like all other lazy persons for doing nothing.' Bretnall paid his daughter-in-law small sums for raising puppies for him and his married sister one penny each for ducks she had raised on her farm.[95]

Developments in farming and status considerations had combined to make profitable farming more difficult for women. In the eighteenth century it was still not considered unusual for a farmer's wife, even of fairly high rank, to be seen taking an active role in running the farm. In the 1780s Mary Hardy dealt with her solicitor, directed workmen and recorded in her diary 'the sale of my turnips' and that she 'ground malt for brewing'. She often rode horseback from her home at Letheringsett Hall the twenty-two miles to Norwich to transact business including the purchase of land.[96] On smaller farms where mainly family labour was employed, wives and daughters would contribute directly, particularly at harvest, if not actually raking hay or stacking corn, then brewing and baking to feed casual workers. Even the rather flighty seventeen-year-old Mary Parker, daughter of a farmer, whose mid-nineteenth-century diary is filled with genteel visiting and hints at attachments with young men at chapel, breaks off in June to record that she and her two sisters 'have been working at hay making in the Mill Field' which prevents her visiting but, 'I don't dislike it half as much as I thought.'[97]

Nevertheless, women who wished, or had, to farm on their own were at a disadvantage in the larger scale of operations, in the need for heavier capital investment for tools, fertilizer, seed and better storage facilities, as well as credit to carry over from planting to harvest. Formerly when cash needs had been intermittent and informal borrowing the norm, it had often been the woman's butter, cheese or egg money which provided rent or small sums for stock, a practice recalled disdainfully by the son of a small farmer: 'The farmer's wife was an especial hoarder in making a purse of her own from chickens and poultry of all kinds.' He noted that such a woman had saved £150 in notes over the years, hiding them in the thatch where they were eaten by mice.[98] Under the new conditions, women controlled the necessary large capital sums less often and were not seen as legitimate borrowers for investment. In the burst of prosperity during the Napoleonic War, farmers began to use country banks to raise capital on a larger scale.[99] The ensuing use of cheques created problems for women without credit. Bankers often asked for references and referees were likely to stress 'diligence in business, experience and capital', all elements difficult for a woman to demonstrate.[100]

Farmers' female relatives continued to bring capital and skill to the enterprise but rather in their capacity as family members and kin. At marriage a wife might contribute her savings or inheritance to stock the farm. William Fairhead, whose family had once farmed independently, was reduced to labour as a team man but his fiancée had skills in dressmaking gained when employed by a Norwich family and after marriage 'this remarkable woman' brought the family back into farming.[101] Older women made loans at low interest to family members while women's property in trust or trust-like arrangements could be used as investment on an existing farm or to take on additional land. The trust device seemed to have particular appeal in the farming community, possibly because farmers seldom went into formal partnership to raise capital and were slow to take up other forms of credit. Among the 158 wills examined between 1780–1850 for the Essex town of Witham, virtually all the higher strata of the middle class left their property under some form of trust arrangement, while 43 per cent of the lower strata left theirs directly under the control of their wives. Yet among yeoman and farmers, even among the lesser type, only 19 per cent gave complete control to their wives and 81 per cent left property either in trusts or other regulated forms.[102]

Farm women were pivotal in marriage alliance as a resource. The special relationship between town enterprises such as grocers' shops and farms was often maintained through family ties. For example, three daughters out of the ten children of a Suffolk farming family married Ipswich shopkeepers. In this way farm produce became fresh supplies for town shops travelling along kinship networks.[103] Some farm families had relatives in larger cities, particularly London, so that products would be exchanged for urban contacts and country holidays were traded for placing farm youngsters in town employment. Marriage also linked farming families with nascent manufacture in the countryside or market town. The farmer/surveyor Arthur Biddell enhanced his operations by his marriage into the iron-manufacturing family of Ransome. Biddell's sons' professional careers benefited while the Ransomes were rewarded by close association with their farming customers and by Biddell's knowledge, for they specialized in manufacturing agricultural machinery.[104]

Farm women were instrumental in training young people in farming skills, particularly girls. The Wright family took in the fifteen-year-old daughter of a distant cousin, also a farmer, whose wife had died leaving a houseful of young children. Mrs Wright taught her to bake and the basic skills in running a farmhouse so that she could manage the household for her father.[105] Farmers' wives needed extra hands even if they were not working directly on the land for during the daily round they were kept busy smoking, pickling and preserving food, baking bread, puddings and cakes as well as the daily cooking for large families and, perhaps, the midday meal of labourers. Part of the farming family's claim to local status lay in the ability to 'keep a good table' at a time when three-quarters of the population could drop into destitution if not starvation. Food and farm produce were favourite gifts for maintaining kinship networks and expressing thanks for favours. It was usually the farmer's wife who controlled the distribution of items such as the Christmas goose. The raising of the seven or more children of the average family carried on whether farm work was undertaken or not. Higher standards of childcare had to be fitted into farm life. It was these demands, as much as the often-criticized refinements, which occupied farmers' female relatives by the early nineteenth century.

The efforts of farm women to live a respectable, domesticated life could play a central role in demonstrating the farm as a going concern. Oxley Parker, the Essex agent, noted that the church-going habits of farmers' wives acted in their favour as tenants. The sobriety, sense and experience of a wife could ensure the granting of leases, their terms and possible renewal.[106] Farm women had to balance spiritual and material rewards of domesticity against a direct contribution to productive farm work. The contradiction of these demands was most evident when women attempted to run farms in their own right as widows and spinsters. It was, in fact, usually expected that such women would take on a bailiff or agent to act for them but only those above a certain level of income had this option. In an 1851 sample from Essex and Suffolk, 9.3 per cent of farm households were headed by women, almost all widows.[107] The occasional spinster might farm property she had inherited but single women farming on their own found their scope limited. Louisa Fairhead of Wickham's Bishop in Essex inherited the family farm and ran it 'with equal skill to that of male members of the family' throughout her long life. It is instructive to compare her career with that of her brother who farmed at nearby Birch Holt. Golden Fairhead became a well-known local agriculturalist, a 'familiar figure at different markets', active in the Braxted Agricultural Society and in his local church. His wife, from a successful farming family, played the organ at their parish church and was presumably more refined than her farming sister-in-law.[108]

Age, experience and the mantle of her former husband gave the widow advantages over young and/or unmarried women, but it was still difficult for her to run a farm actively. Records indicate that widows often farmed as a 'holding operation' until a son was old enough to take over.[109] While the combination of widow and young adult son might make it possible to pass the lease from one generation to another, the tenancy system could make a widow's position vulnerable. The landlord or his agent had to be convinced that the widow would be able to carry on a profitable venture. Those landlords who had invested heavily in improvements sought tenants who were 'intelligent and enterprising'.[110] However, the landlords and agents were themselves often imbued with preconceptions about female respectability which was characterized by dependency.

By mid-century, these expectations were less compatible than ever with a woman remaining active in running a farm. George Eliot, a farm steward's daughter, put forward the fictional case of the farmer's widow whose husband's dying wish had been for her to carry on the farm. When she goes to plead her case with the landlord she is dismissed in just these terms, of an appeal to both the supposed capacities and right conduct of femininity. 'You are about as able to carry on a farm as your best milch cow. You'll be obliged to have some managing man, who will either cheat you out of your money, or wheedle you into marrying him.' The landlord goes on to predict that the farm will run down and she will get in arrears with the rent. She argues back that she knows 'a deal o' farming an' was brought up i' the thick on it' and that her husband's great-aunt managed a farm for twenty years and left legacies to her 'nephys an' nieces'. 'Phsa! a woman six feet high with a squint and sharp elbows, I daresay – a man in petticoats; not a rosy cheeked widow like you.' This widow knows that once all the stock has been sold and debts paid she will have hardly anything to live on. Since this is fiction, the secretly benevolent landlord arranges to have a cottage let to her at low rent with a plot for a cow and some pigs where she will be able to live in suitable retirement.[111]

However, landlords in the real world, while subscribing to a similar view of women's place, were not so helpful or often unable to be so liberal. John Oxley Parker, the agent for a large number of landowners in mid-Essex in the 1830s, was called in to negotiate the lease of a widow who had kept on a farm after her husband's death. He, along with her neighbouring farmers and her brother-in-law, urged her to give up the attempt. He noted in his diary in connection with this case how important it was for tenants to have both character and capital. The questions he asked himself about a prospective tenant were: 'Was he an energetic farmer? Did he know his job and use his initiative in doing it?' Oxley Parker finally urged the widow to throw herself on the mercy of the landlord, but to no avail and she had to leave the farm with no compensation.[112]

If maintaining a farm was problematic for women, acting in the market-place, the core function within capitalist farming, was even more of a challenge, for it exposed them to public evaluation. In *Far From the Madding Crowd* Thomas Hardy's heroine, Bathsheba Everdene, tried to farm an inherited property. Hardy uses her situation to portray the deviant nature of such ambition including the sexual provocation of a woman acting independently. In her first appearance at the Corn Market, Bathsheba's co-farmers carried sticks with which they poked at pigs, sheep or 'their neighbours', hardly an option for a respectable young woman. In the Corn Market itself:

> Among these heavy yeomen, a feminine figure glided, the single one of her sex that the room contained. She was prettily and even daintily dressed. She moved between them as a chaise between carts, was heard after them as a romance after sermons, was felt among them like a breeze among furnaces. It had required a little determination – far more than she at first imagined – to take up a position here, for at her first entry, the lumbering dialogues had ceased, nearly every face had been turned towards her and those that were already turned rigidly fixed there.[113]

In this fantasy, Hardy highlights the damaging fact that Bathsheba had to deal with men to whom she had not been introduced by reliable intermediaries.

The model of feminine gentility, unlike its male counterpart, had no place for even managerial involvement in a productive enterprise. Many women went so far as to have nothing to do with the sordid world of business no matter what the cost. Helen Uvedale, a clergyman's widow living in an Essex village on the modest rents from two farms gave the complete management of her property to a local attorney. She had little interest in it except to get maximum rent paid promptly and grumbled at the need for rent abatements in the 1820s. Unlike the model ladies of the religious tracts, she cared little that her tenant had a large family or lacked sufficient capital to farm efficiently. A male farmer/clergyman might have taken charge himself but Helen Uvedale confessed to being too ignorant in such matters for her opinion to count. She had neither education nor experience to expand her operations even had she been taken seriously in the farming fraternity and, most significantly, as a widow she had only a life-interest in the farms. As a result she was unable even to stem the decline of her small property, having placed herself completely in the hands of her powerful if somewhat shady Colchester attorney.[114]

The only completely respectable public presence for women was at church or chapel. They were an important, if usually silent, part of rural congregations where they listened to sermons on, among other subjects, the importance of family life and women's place. However, they could express informal influence in the local congregation as the Independent minister of Kelvedon in Essex found to his cost when he fell out with his deacons and had to solicit farm women's support.[115] In remote villages farming families could be the main representatives of a more refined and religious culture. The farmer's wife who had invited the new vicar to sup wine in her renovated parlour was anxious for his approbation, but she had reserved judgement on his sermons and demeanour when he first came to the parish. Her invitation could be seen as putting the community seal on his tenure of office.[116]

Women took part in the philanthropic activities organized by zealous clerical families, for example the ubiquitous Bible and Missionary Societies. However fancy-work bazaars, garden parties and organized sick-visiting were less well developed in the countryside. Much informal aid to labourers was organized by farm women but Sunday-school teaching remained their staple contribution to the religious effort. In even more remote villages where no clergy resided and no doctor practised, farmers' families might be the only carriers of the more enlightened culture. Some farm women saw themselves playing a leading role against superstition, folk belief and rural ignorance and apathy. Against this they pitted their intense conversionist religious belief and a commitment to rational modes of thought, although many farmers' wives continued to use herbal medicine to perform the role of village midwife, nurse and doctor. But farm women's expertise even in this role was slowly being undermined. In addition to their own commitment to new ideas, enclosure of common lands was cutting supplies of plants for both medicines and cosmetics. The rise of professional medical men, apothecaries and chemists denigrated many of the women's skills and beliefs to the status of 'old wives' tales'.[117]

Yet there is no doubt that educated and religious women were proud of their role. In early nineteenth-century Suffolk, a Quaker farmer's wife, as the sole 'lady' in an isolated village, deliberately exposed her children to smallpox after having them vaccinated to demonstrate to the villagers the efficacy of the new, frightening procedure.[118]

In areas with resident clergy, tension over leadership and status recognition could be played out between women. The Reverend John Charlesworth formed part of a network of Evangelical Anglican clergy in early nineteenth-century Suffolk. His eldest daughter Maria later became author of the best-selling treatises, *Ministering Children* and *The Female Visitor to the Poor*. Her text reveals these anxieties in describing an imaginary school fête, to be the high point of the village year, where farmers' wives and daughters are enlisted to provide food, small farmers' or cottagers' wives to wait at table while the vicar's daughter, presiding from a throne decked with greenery, dispenses prizes as rewards for good and bad behaviour to the village children.[119] In the fantasy, farming families with their new wealth and enhanced education are held firmly in place.

The status ambiguity in the position of farmers which lay behind such fears has been investigated. The symbolic role of farming in English consciousness also played a part. Unlike factory production, farming had a long history, still seen more as a 'way of life' than as a means of earning a living within the cash nexus, a view which lingers to the present.[120] Unlike other sections of the middle class, farmers' families continued to live where they worked. Farmsteads were reorganized instead to separate domestic life spatially and socially from farming operations, but outsiders continued to expect a more unified existence, part of an image of a traditional way of life. As English society became ever more embedded in market relations, as production moved into factories and the population crowded into towns, the yeoman of Olde England with his roast beef and real ale came to embody attributes of independence and patriotism. To this day, John Bull wears the dress of an eighteenth-century farmer.

Within the symbolic imagery of farming, women held a special place and, as so often, they carried the negative qualities of the group as a whole. Claims to spurious gentility and the greed of wives and daughters were seen as prodding the farmers' search for profits, often at the expense of labourers. It was the expensive habits of the women which usurped the 'honest and manly simplicity of manners which has so long dignified the British character . . . the very farmer's daughter has laid aside her stuffs for muslins, her handkerchief for the meretricious display of naked charms, her diffidence for coquetry and the bloom of virtuous industry for the harlotry of paint.'[121] The use of such gendered messages confuses the historian's investigation, already hampered by limited sources from the women themselves. As an eminent historian of rural England has said: 'The farmer's wife and daughters do not emerge very clearly from the contemporary records.'[122]

Neverthless, it is clear from sources we have that the general ideas about gender permeated the countryside as a consequence of increased literacy and general education, through travel, the circulation of newspapers, journals and books, through sermons and lectures and, above all, through lived example. Farmers and farm women alike experienced the contradictions inherent in the middle-class model. Cornelius Stovin, a devout Nonconformist farmer, had a wife manifestly suffering from isolation and chronic ill-health associated with multiple pregnancies. He tried in his bumbling fashion to make up to her for being cut off from genteel refinements in the draughty old-fashioned farmhouse:

> If God permit us to enjoy the great gift of a new or restored, enlarged and more
> commodious dwelling, my Lizzie will find more scope for her tasteful devices. She is

fond of a vase and understands the adornment of a home. . . . I notice a great change
towards a loftier and more refined civilization hallowing our dwellings which had not
taken place during my childhood.[123]

The exclusion of women with ambitions for gentility from active participation in
the running of the farm was complete by the mid-century 'golden age' of high
agriculture. Such ideas were only reaching the Lincolnshire countryside in the
1860s and 1870s when Cornelius and Elizabeth Stovin started their farming life.
Many of the couple's aspirations stemmed from visits to and from their respective
families, particularly Cornelius's first cousin, a doctor in Oxford who was married
to his sister. Cornelius Stovin's bewilderment about his wife's unhappiness is
understandable. The couple were part of a culture which had built an edifice of
gender differentiation whose contradictions bore particularly heavily on women.
As a working farmer pressed with debt, Stovin could scarcely afford to keep a wife
in non-productive refinement (Elizabeth even refused to bake the household bread
although she knew how). To Cornelius, Elizabeth's 'inability for accomplishing
life's duties' was a 'mystery' and, far from being angry, he regarded her weakness
as part of her gentility, her devout, meek, Christian character. The stress on pious
domesticity and the expected pattern of family enterprise meant no reduction in
constant debilitating childbearing which undermined Elizabeth Stovin's health and
strength. Her craving for respite and company was partly the product of beliefs
which made active farming appear vulgar and degrading, especially in comparison
with her town kinsfolk. The wish of such women to move beyond the drudgery of
farm work should not, however, be dismissed as mere snobbery. The grinding
physical labour and social isolation of the farmer's wife must be remembered and
may be a factor in the dearth of their surviving diaries, memoirs and letters.[124]
     By the 1870s English agriculture was once again in a period of depression. It was
the grain-growing midland and eastern regions which were hit hardest. Many
farms were deserted while arable land was converted back to pasture. Towards the
end of the century some farms were taken at extremely low rents by Scots coming
south to seek new opportunities. As farmers willing to take a lower standard of
living while using mainly family labour, they prospered. Their wives willingly
undertook tasks such as mucking out sheds and sties which no English housewife
would contemplate but, as a contemporary observed, 'they came as strangers; they
have no position to lose.'[125] Such a comment demonstrates how deeply the concept
of 'separate spheres' and its association with both gender and class had entered into
the heart of Victorian identity, even to the depths of the English countryside.
     The power of this model has been profound. The impersonal market economy,
constructed as part of the public sphere, became even more identified with men, the
private sphere of individual morality and the home with women. Men began to be
identified by their means of earning a living for themselves and their dependants,
giving the concept of 'occupation' heavy masculine overtones. Women's status
however, remained overwhelmingly familial during this period.[126] The identifi-

cation of manhood with the ability to support a domestic establishment became part of the conditions for the franchise. Women's passive relationship to property was maintained through successive legal reforms and feminine dependence became a serious obstacle to women's wider citizenship claims as well as the narrower issue of suffrage. As the middle class moved into leadership in the late nineteenth century, the model was used to evaluate working-class behaviour and attitudes. It became a standard in administering state policy and dispensing charity, in education and in recognizing working-class claims for social and political incorporation. It was an important part of the culture which the English carried with them to administer the Empire. Contemporary English society continues as the inheritor of this gendered model of the social world.

Notes

1 This chapter is based on a project funded by the Economic and Social Research Council. It concentrates on the counties of Essex and Suffolk and is balanced by a comparative study of Birmingham by Catherine Hall (North East London Polytechnic). The general argument is a joint effort and I am indebted to her throughout. See Leonore Davidoff and Catherine Hall, *Family Fortunes: Men and Women of the English Middle Class, 1780–1850* (Routledge, London, 1992). I also thank Janet Gyford for Essex material and Michael Mann, Sonya Rose and Alison Scott for helpful comments.

2 Harold Perkin, *The Origins of Modern English Society 1780–1880* (Routledge & Kegan Paul, London, 1969).

3 Alan D. Gilbert, *Religion and Society in Industrial England: Church, Chapel and Social Change, 1740–1914* (Longman, London, 1976).

4 R.J. White, *Life in Regency England* (Batsford, London, 1963).

5 E.P. Thompson, 'Patrician Society, Plebian Culture', *Journal of Social History*, vol. 17, no. 4 (summer, 1974), pp. 382–405.

6 D.C. Coleman, 'Gentlemen and Players', *Economic History Review*, vol. 26 (1973), pp. 92–116.

7 Mark Girouard, *The Return to Camelot: Chivalry and the English Gentleman* (Yale University Press, New Haven, 1981).

8 L.S. Pressnell, *Country Banking in the Industrial Revolution* (Clarendon Press, Oxford, 1956).

9 J. Collyer, *A Practical Treatise on the Law of Partnership* (Sweet & Maxwell, London, 1840), p. 72.

10 R.J. Morris, 'The Middle Class and the Property Cycle during the Industrial Revolution', in T.C. Smout, ed., *The Search for Wealth and Stability* (Macmillan, London, 1979).

11 Sample of 623 wills from Birmingham and Witham, Essex.

12 From the present research, the average age at marriage was 29 years for men and 26.5 for women. See also Charles Ansell, *On the Rate of Mortality at Early Periods of Life, the Age of Marriage and other Statistics of Families in the Upper and Professional Classes* (C. and E. Layton, London, 1874).

13 Davidoff and Hall, *Family Fortunes* (Routledge, London, 1992).

14 Davidoff and Hall, *Family Fortunes*. Average family size for couples with children was 7.4.

15 Neil McKendrick, 'Commercialization and the Economy', in Neil McKendrick, John Brewer and J.H. Plumb, eds, *The Birth of a Consumer Society: The Commercialization of Eighteenth-Century England* (Europa Publications, London, 1982).

16 R.J. Morris, 'Voluntary Societies and the British Urban Elites in the Industrial Revolution 1780–1800', unpublished paper.

17 Although women owned property, it was usually in a passive form such as the trust or annuity. Women's position exemplified the 'social closure' resulting from controlling property as possessions rather than as active capital. See the general discussion, although not applied to women, in Frank Parkin, 'Social Closure as Exclusion', in *Marxism and Class Theory: A Bourgeois Critique* (Tavistock, London, 1979), p. 53.

18 For the distribution of arable farming, see P.J. Perry, *A. Geography of Nineteenth-Century Britain* (Batsford, London, 1975), p. 165. The usual divisions within agriculture in this period have been challenged, but the argument in relation to large farmers still stands. Mick Reed, 'The Peasantry of Nineteenth-Century England: A Neglected Class?', *History Workshop Journal*, no. 18 (autumn 1984), pp. 53–76.

19 Ann Kussmaul, *Servants in Husbandry in Early Modern England* (Cambridge University Press, Cambridge, 1981).

20 James Obelkevich, *Religion and Rural Society: South Lindsey, 1825–1875* (Clarendon Press, Oxford, 1976), p. 46.

21 H. Benham, *Some Essex Water Mills* (Essex County Newspapers, Colchester, 1976).

22 John Booker, *Essex and the Industrial Revolution* (Essex County Council, Chelmsford, 1974).

23 By 1859 a local competition in practical skills for farmers' sons attracted only three entrants (Obelkevich, *Religion and Rural Society*, p. 50).

24 John Harriott, *Struggles Through Life Exemplified* (C. & W. Galabin, London, 1807).

25 John Hanson, Journal, 1829, kindness of Jean Harding, Great Bromley, Essex.

26 A.J. Brown, *Colchester in the Eighteenth Century* (privately printed, Colchester, 1969).

27 H. Coleman, *Jeremiah James Coleman: A Memoir* (privately printed, London, 1905). L.C. Sier, *The Blomfields of Dedham and Colchester* (privately printed, Colchester, 1924); Census sample from Davidoff and Hall, *Family Fortunes*.

28 James Oakes, Diary, West Suffolk Record Office, HA 521/1–14.

29 A.J. Brown, *Essex People, 1750–1900* (Essex County Council, Chelmsford, 1972).

30 Witham file from Davidoff and Hall, *Family Fortunes*.

31 R.G. Wilson, *Greene King: A Business and Family History* (Jonathan Cape, London, 1983).

32 George Sturt, *William Smith, Potter and Farmer, 1790–1858* (Caliban Books, Firle, Sussex, 1978).

33 John Cullum, *The History and Antiquities of Hawstead and Hardwick, in the County of Suffolk* (Nicols & Son, London, 1813), p. 252.

34 Arthur Young, *General View of the Agriculture of the County of Essex* (Sherwood, Neely & Jones, London, 1807), vol. 1, p. 45.

35 Witham file.

36 H.N. Dixon, Diary, by kindness of Janet Gyford, Witham, Essex.

37 *Select Committee on Agriculture*, vol. IV (1833), question 10624.

38 C. Shrimpton, 'The Landed Society and the Farming Community of Essex in the late eighteenth and early nineteenth Centuries' (University of Cambridge, Ph.D. thesis, 1966).

39 Jane Austen, *Emma* (Dent Dutton, London, 1976), p. 23.

40 William Cobbett, quoted in Perkin, *The Origins of Modern English Society*, p. 93.

41 J. Jean Hecht, *The Domestic Servant Class in Eighteenth-Century England* (Routledge & Kegan Paul, London, 1956).

42 Obelkevich, *Religion and Rural Society*.

43 Charles Tayler, *May You Like it, by a Country Curate* (Seely, Hatch & Nesbit, London, 1823).
44 Sturt, *William Smith, Potter and Farmer, 1790–1858*.
45 Clyde Binfield, *So Down to Prayers: Studies in English Nonconformity, 1780–1920* (Dent, London, 1977).
46 Catherine M. Marsh, *The Life of the Rev. William Marsh D.D.* (J. Nisbet & Co., London, 1867); Sier, *The Blomfields of Dedham and Colchester*.
47 Young, *General View of the Agriculture of the County of Essex*, p. 66.
48 M. Karr and M. Humphries, *Out on a Limb: An Outline History of a Branch of the Stokes Family, 1645–1976* (privately printed, Essex, 1976).
49 W. and H. Raynbird, *On the Agriculture of Suffolk* (Longman, London, 1849), p. 132.
50 Obelkevich, *Religion and Rural Society*, p. 53.
51 Marjorie Reeves, *Sheep Bell and Plough Share: The Story of Two Village Families* (Granada, London, 1980).
52 Jane Ransome Bidell MSS, Ipswich Record Office, HA2/D/1.
53 Seabrook and Bunting family records, by kindness of M. Mallowartarchi, Colchester, Essex.
54 Biddell, MSS.
55 Martin Shaw Briggs, *The English Farmhouse* (Batsford, London, 1953).
56 Nigel Harvey, *A History of Farm Buildings in England and Wales* (David & Charles, Newton Abbott, 1970).
57 Eric Mercer, *English Vernacular Houses: A Study of Traditional Farmhouses and Cottages* (Royal Commission on Historical Monuments, HMSO, London, 1975), p. 74.
58 Robert Baker, *On the Farming of Essex* (pamphlet printed from *Journal of the Royal Agricultural Society*, London, 1844), p. 31.
59 In a sample from the 1851 manuscript census from Essex and Suffolk, 16 per cent of farms employed four or more men. Of those who employed labour the average number was 8.2 census sample. Essex had one of the highest ratios in the country of employed men per farm – England 1:4.7; Essex 1:8.4; J. Saville, 'Primitive Accumulation and Early Industrialization', *Socialist Register*, vol. 4 (1969), p. 257.
60 Mary Bayly, *The Life and Letters of Mrs Sewell* (J. Nesbit & Co., London, 1889), p. 31.
61 John Glyde, 'The Autobiography of a Suffolk Farm Labourer', in *The Suffolk Mercury* (1894).
62 Royal Institute of British Architecture, *Rooms Concise: Glimpses of the Small Domestic Interior, 1500–1850* (RIBA Exhibit, London, 1981).
63 Anon., 'Diary of a farmer's wife on the Warwick/Leicestershire border', Heslop MSS, University of Birmingham, MS 10/iii/15, 1823.
64 Ethel Simcoe, *A Short History of the Parish and Ancient Borough of Thaxted* (Hart & Son, Saffron Walden, 1934).
65 Ancient Free and Accepted Masons, *Bye-laws of the Angel Lodge, Colchester No. 59* (S. Hoddon, Colchester, 1835); Bro. S.F. Watson, *A History of British Union Lodge No. 114, Ipswich 1762–1962* (W.S. Cowell, Ipswich, 1962).
66 Nicholas Goddard, 'Agricultural Societies', in G.E. Mingay, ed., *The Victorian Countryside*, vol. 1 (Routledge & Kegan Paul, London, 1981).
67 Raynbird, *On the Agriculture of Suffolk*.
68 Janet Gyford, 'Men of Bad Character: Property Crime in Essex in the 1820s' (University of Essex, MA dissertation, 1982).
69 Peter King, 'Prosecution Associations in Essex, 1740–1800', quoted by kind permission of the author.
70 A.J. Brown, Department of History, University of Essex, personal communication.
71 Eliza Vaughan, *The Essex Village in Days Gone By* (Benham & Co., Colchester, 1930), p. 29.

72 J.E. Oxley, *Barking Vestry Minutes and other Parish Documents* (Benham & Co., Colchester, 1955), p. 28.

73 J.P. Fitzgerald, *The Quiet Worker for Good: A Familiar Sketch of the late John Charlesworth* (Darlton & Lucy, Ipswich, 1985), p. 15.

74 B.A. Holderness, 'The Victorian Farmer', in G.E. Mingay, ed., *The Victorian Countryside*, vol. 1 (Routledge & Kegan Paul, London, 1981).

75 Glyde, 'The Autobiography of a Suffolk Farm Labourer'.

76 Joan Thirsk and Jean Imray, 'An Improved Corn and Cattle Market at Saxmundham', in Joan Thirsk and Jean Imray, eds, *Suffolk Farming in the Nineteenth Century* (Suffolk Records Society, Ipswich, 1958).

77 S. Golding, 'The Importance of Fairs in Essex, 1750–1850', *Essex Journal*, vol. 10, no. 3 (1975), pp. 50–66, esp. p. 62.

78 R.S. Surtees, 'Analysis of the Hunting Field', in E.W. Bovill, *The England of Nimrod and Surtees, 1815–1854* (Oxford University Press, London, 1959), p. 91.

79 White, *Life in Regency England*.

80 Derek Wilson, *A Short History of Suffolk* (Batsford, London, 1977), p. 126.

81 J. Oxley Parker, *The Oxley Parker Papers: From the Letters and Diaries of an Essex Family of Land Agents in the Nineteenth Century* (Benham & Co., Colchester, 1964).

82 John Oxley Parker from Essex was one of the founder members. See F.M.L. Thompson, *Chartered Surveyors: The Growth of a Profession* (Routledge & Kegan Paul, London, 1968).

83 Michael Roberts, 'Sickles and Scythes: Women's Work and Men's Work at Harvest Time', *History Workshop Journal*, no. 7 (spring 1979), pp. 3–27.

84 K.D. Snell, 'Agricultural Seasonal Unemployment, the Standard of Living and Women's Work in the South and East, 1690–1860', *Economic History Review*, no. 34 (1981), pp. 407–37.

85 John Glyde, *Suffolk in the Nineteenth Century: Physical, Social, Moral, Religious, and Industrial* (Simpkin, Marshall & Co., London, n.d.), p. 367.

86 Obelkevich, *Religion and Rural Society*, p. 50.

87 G.E. Fussell, *The English Dairy Farmer, 1500–1900* (Frank Cass, London, 1966).

88 Ivy Pinchbeck, *Women Workers and the Industrial Revolution, 1750–1850* (Frank Cass, London, 1969).

89 John Player, *Sketches of Saffron Walden, and its Vicinity* (G. Youngman, Saffron Walden, 1845), p. 57.

90 E.W. Martin, *The Secret People: English Village Life after 1750* (Phoenix House, London, 1954). For a different outcome, see Joan M. Jensen, 'Women and Industrialisation: The Case of Buttermaking in Nineteenth-century Mid-Atlantic America', in *Promise to the Land: Essays on Rural Women* (University of New Mexico Press, Albuquerque, 1991).

91 Josiah Twamley, *Dairying Exemplified, or the Business of Cheese Making* (J. Sharp, Warwick, 1784), p. 13.

92 Twamley, *Dairying Exemplified*, p. 10.

93 Mrs Lovi, 'Method of Ascertaining the Richness of Milk', *Farmers Magazine*, vol. 21 (August 1820), p. 63.

94 William Marshall, *The Review and Abstract of the County Reports of the Board of Agriculture* (Board of Agriculture, London), vol. III, *Eastern Department 1818*, p. 463.

95 R. Bretnall, Diary of a Witham Farmer, Essex Record Office, D/DBS, F.38.

96 Mary Hardy, *Diary* (Norfolk Record Society, Norwich, 1968). It is interesting to note that 'farmer' connotes a man. There is no feminine equivalent except 'lady farmer'. The women living on farms have to be called farmer's wife, daughter, sister, niece as the Registrar's Office noted when giving directions for collecting the census.

97 Mary Alice Parker, Diary, 1867, by kindness of William Lister, Leicester.

98   H.N. Dixon, 'Reminiscences of an Essex County Practitioner a Century Ago', *Essex Review*, vol. 25 (1916), p. 71.

99   Christy Miller, 'The History of Banks and Banking in Essex', *The Journal of the Institute of Bankers* (October 1906), pp. 319–30.

100 Shrimpton, 'The Landed Society', p. 221.

101 A.F. Fairhead, *The Fairhead Series* (privately printed, Essex, n.d.), pp. 1–10.

102 One hundred and fifty-eight wills from Witham in Essex, 1780–1855.

103 Thirsk and Imray, 'Suffolk Farmers at Home and Abroad'.

104 Biddell, MSS. See also Reeves, *Sheep Bell and Plough Share*.

105 Bayly, *The Life and Letters of Mrs Sewell*. This pattern is confirmed in George Eliot's *Adam Bede* where Mrs Poyser, farmer's wife, has taken in Hetty Sorrel, her husband's niece, to train in dairying and also gave a home to her own orphaned niece, Dinah, in return for childcare and general household duties.

106 Oxley Parker, *The Oxley Parker Papers*.

107 Sample of 1851 manuscript census for Essex and Suffolk, see Davidoff and Hall, *Family Fortunes*.

108 Fairhead, *The Fairhead Series*.

109 Sample of wills and census. Mrs Clements, 'Essex Farmers' Accounts, 1783–1795', *Essex Review*, XLVII (1938/39), p. 87.

110 E.L. Jones, ed., *Agricultural and Economic Growth in England, 1650–1815* (Methuen, London, 1967).

111 George Eliot, 'Mr Gilfil's Love-Story', in *Scenes of Clerical Life*, vol. 1 (William Blackwood, Edinburgh, 1856), p. 158.

112 Oxley Parker, *The Oxley Parker Papers*, p. 107.

113 Thomas Hardy, *Far from the Madding Crowd* (Macmillan, London, 1969), p. 102

114 Shrimpton, 'The Landed Society', p. 170.

115 Revd. J. Fielding, *A Series of Letters Addressed to the Church and Congregation Assembling at the Great Meeting, Coggeshall* (privately printed, Coggeshall, 1815).

116 Anon., 'Diary of a farmer's wife'.

117 Charles Phythian-Adams, 'Rural Culture', in G.E. Mingay ed., *The Victorian Countryside*, vol. 2 (Routledge & Kegan Paul, London, 1981).

118 Bayly, *Life and Letters of Mrs Sewell*.

119 Maria Charlesworth, *The Female Visitor to the Poor* (Seeley, Burnside & Seeley, London, 1846).

120 Howard Newby, *Green and Pleasant Land? Social Change in Rural England* (Hutchinson, London, 1979).

121 William Green, *Plans of Economy; or, the Road to Ease and Independence* (J. Hatchard, London, 1804), p. 10.

122 G.E.Mingay, *English Landed Society in the Eighteenth Century* (Routledge & Kegan Paul, London, 1963), p. 246.

123 Jean Stovin, ed., *Journals of a Methodist Farmer, 1871–1875* (Croom Helm, London 1982), p. 182.

124 Sue Ann Armitage, 'Wash on Monday: The Housework of Farm Women in Transition', unpublished paper, 1982, by kindness of the author.

125 Thirsk and Imray, 'Suffolk Farmers at Home and Abroad'.

126 Which may help to explain why domestic service, a 'quasi-familial' role, became heavily feminized in the late nineteenth century. See Davidoff, 'Mastered for Life: Servant and Wife in Late Victorian and Edwardian England', this volume, ch. 1.

7

Where the Stranger Begins: The Question of Siblings in Historical Analysis

The sibling is the beginning of the stranger.
Japanese Proverb

That tender union, all combin'd
Of Nature's holiest sympathies
'Tis Friendship in its loveliest dress
'Tis Love's most perfect tenderness.
Mary Ann Hedge, 'Brother and Sister', 1832

From the thundering majesty of Greek tragedy to the brutal Icelandic sagas, down to the sentimentality of such Victorian verses as the above, the relationship of brother and sister has haunted our cultural heritage. And in everyday late twentieth-century lives some of the most powerful emotional bonds as well as practical human interactions remain between brothers and sisters.[1] In the rare cases where historians have noticed sibling relationships, their importance has been evident. Obvious examples would be found in inheritance patterns, for land and other property as well as in the hidden transfers of labour and income, sometimes reciprocal but very often from sisters to brothers.[2] Both in youth and as adults, siblings have been key links in patterns of migration, for gaining access to housing, waged work and support of all kinds. Sisters and brothers have acted as surrogate parents (and children), informal teachers, adult co-residents, friends and even, on occasion, lovers.

Despite the centrality of this relationship, both historically and in contemporary life, it remains strangely neglected, relegated to a fragmentary footnote of the historical record. To understand why, it must first be understood as embedded within the seemingly ubiquitous phenomena of kinship and family.

The concepts of kinship and family are themselves products of Western cultural thought, culled from ideas about religion, nationality, ethnicity, social class, welfare and health provisions, division of property, notions of social honour, of 'the person' and all of these framed by perceptions of gender.[3] Since the early 1960s, their problematic status has been reinforced by a series of major debates among anthropologists as to just what kind of phenomenon kinship, in particular, actually refers to. Is it an empirical set of overlapping relations that are genetic, genealogical and social? Or is it the *meanings* of relationships which must have kin-specific content? 'It [kinship] is a social tie or it is nothing.'[4] Is it a set of symbolizing actions whose emotional charge encourages enduring and practical ends? Or is it simply a set of questions posed by Western social scientists using their own unrecognized cultural presuppositions as a basis for their models?[5]

All we can claim at the moment is that for modern (and even postmodern) Western societies, family and kinship still provide systematic patterns based on symbols as well as structures which try to make sense of the basic problems of order and individual identity connected with birth, socialization and succession. They have been seen, therefore, as the 'building-blocks' of society as well as a symbolic idiom of political and economic relationships, and, as such, they have to respond to (and make meaningful) *change* as well as that which is stable.

Furthermore, it is now evident that while ultimately rooted in physical reproduction both kinship and family are centrally organized around an assumed gender order; indeed it has been argued that the gender and kinship systems are mutually constructed since kinship is based on the division between politico-jural and domestic domains.[6] In Western societies, this has meant that historically what may appear to be a natural order has been heavily moulded by those power centres of culture and material resources, the church and the state.[7]

Legal definitions have both reflected and helped to shape kinship systems. For example in Britain, according to law, family arrangements are seen as governed by principles not applicable to dealing with strangers, and consideration for family is 'partly value but partly love and affection'.[8] The Christian church, too, in its efforts during the early Middle Ages to break the power of kin-based groups by the abandoning of Germanic notions of fraternal kinship in favour of Roman principles, has played a part in emphasizing the married couple and direct descent over the role of collaterals.[9]

The power of definition is especially significant in the case of siblings whose social relations are organized along horizontal lines (at least theoretically), as collaterals, rather than through vertical lines of filiation. Unlike spouses, however, siblings have no direct effect on reproduction – in a word, the sibling relationship is the structural basis for neither the formation of families nor their continuation. On the contrary, their presence can be potentially divisive, fragmenting material, cultural and emotional resources. In this sense, siblings occupy the boundaries between familial and the non-familial, possible strangers. And this 'boundary issue' seems to be inherent whether the family is primarily focused on direct-line inheritance (a stem form) or the independent conjugal family of our own time.[10]

The analysis of historical change is further complicated by the issue of from whose viewpoint these structures, symbolic orders and organizing principles have been created. In the nineteenth century, when the concept of kinship systems was being formed, it was the central adult 'ego', usually male, who was the focus of the the grid of kinship. Recently, however, there has been a shift in perspective: family and kinship systems are increasingly regarded as *process*. Taking a life-cycle as well as family-cycle view should make it possible to appreciate more marginal positions such as siblings as well as some household members who are usually defined as non-kin – for example lodgers or servants. In practice, however, this change has made little impact on either contemporary or historical studies. One reason for this may lie in the problem of definition.

At first sight, defining *brother* and *sister* might seem deceptively simple. Since human beings are capable of reproducing more than one offspring over a lifetime, the sharing of at least one common parent would be enough to ensure the categories. But immediately there are gradations implied by the expectation of a two-parent norm, so that we have *half-siblings* who share one physical parent but not the other, and *step-siblings* who share a parent through remarriage but not through physical reproduction.[11] The latter category raises issues about whether it is the 'blood' relationship (consanguinity) or social kinship through marriage (affinality) – or both – which should be the defining characteristic of kin relations, including siblingship.

Although affines are not 'real blood', they are often treated as such, as are affines' relatives, as in the case of husband's brother, wife's sister and so forth. In sorting out these complexities, it is well to note that the notion of a distinct 'blood relative' used in this way seems to have been fully developed only at about the turn of the twentieth century,[12] and may thus be anachronistic when unproblematically projected on to the historical record.

Finally, there are numerous categories of 'fictive siblings', that is, unrelated individuals linked through either a common place within the family/household or the creation of forms of 'blood brotherhood', often through the ritual mingling of blood, combined with oaths of loyalty.[13] Varying forms of fictive kin merge with notions of *friendship* which concentrate on peer bonds. But it is important to remember that friendship has also often implied patronage and clientage, reciprocal but highly inegalitarian forms of social linkage. Historians have paid little attention to the concept of friendship but it is evident that its meaning has varied widely. Even as late as eighteenth-century England, just as the word *family* encompassed non-relatives, *friend* also referred to kin.[14]

The instability and variability of these definitions is to be found both historically and in a wide variety of cross-cultural contemporary studies. For example, in societies with a matrilineal focus, a brother has special interest in his sister's children who, in turn, recognize him, rather than their physical father, as the central masculine figure.[15] These questions of definition are only the beginning and do not take into account the multiple levels and multiple meanings – structural, symbolic and psychic – which cluster around the sibling relationship.

Yet despite such variance, a common theme seems to run through the notion of brotherhood and sisterhood, one which is related to basic issues of personal identity and the formation of *self*. The myth of Narcissus, searching for himself in his own reflection, is echoed in many beliefs about siblings. But, as with parts of the self, brothers and sisters can represent rejected traits, values and behaviours;

they can repel as well as attract. Because of their shared parentage, all siblings, whether of the same or different sex, seem to possess a special quality of 'unity in difference', a mirroring of the self, two parts of one whole 'split along the faultlines of ambivalence'.[16]

There are several reasons for the inherent tension between identification and repulsion among siblings, a quality captured in George Eliot's phrase 'a like, unlike', in her poem 'Brother and Sister'. One reason for this is the probable sharing of childhood experiences within the household, Eliot's 'two flowers growing on one stem'.[17] The effects of a mutual infancy and childhood are expressed in a passage written in the 1830s by Arthur Tennyson, whose hero speaks, significantly, about a foster-sister with whom he later fell in love:[18]

> She was my foster-sister: on one arm
> The flaxen ringlets of our infancies
> Wandered, the while we rested: one soft lap
> Pillowed us both: a common light of eyes
> Was on us as we lay: our baby lips
> Kissing one bosom, ever drew from thence
> The stream of life, one stream, one life, one blood.

The shared childhood, the shared name and the sharing of family resources as well as traditions could also bring out the opposite emotions of envy or disengagement. Precisely because the bonds could be threateningly and smotheringly close, there was often rivalry and the enhancement of difference. From Cain and Abel onwards, in Western culture, the struggle over parental love, resources and rewards has often meant that brothers and sisters spell trouble. Clinical practitioners today have recognized what may be obvious in everyday life, that emotional ambivalence, while part of all intimate relationships, seems to be particularly acute between brothers and sisters. 'A rapid shift of "hot and cold" acceptance and rejection, closeness and distance seems more characteristic of these ties than any other', and – media attention notwithstanding – conflict and violence within families is most common between siblings although contained within a relatively safe environment and often condoned by adults.[19]

In structural terms, siblings are not always the equals portrayed in the model or the ideal. Given the long period in which a parent is capable of generating children (even for women well over twenty years), some siblings will be of an age that is more like a parent than peer generation to those born later in the family. And in cultures which emphasize masculine primacy, all brothers, including the younger, start with power and privilege over all sisters, no matter what the age differences.[20]

This potential age gap between siblings large enough to create pseudo-generational differences muddies the categories of 'parents' and 'children' and confuses clear authority lines. Although families with large numbers of offspring would obviously be more likely to exhibit such a pattern, two or three siblings could still be widely spaced, a likelihood much increased in step- and half-sibling relationships.[21] A striking example of what such a gradation of ages might entail was the arrangement, common until at least the mid-twentieth century, whereby the illegitimate baby of an elder daughter would be brought up as the offspring of her parents. Often the child would never know that those he or she considered mother and father were in fact grandparents and that the 'elder sister' was his or her birth mother. The discovery of this relationship in later life could be traumatic, but its meaning would depend on actual relations within the family and on the wider community context.

Since a common childhood milieu is usually a large constituent in creating a sibling relationship, one of the most significant qualities of the role is its impact on the moulding of gender identity, in emotional terms as well as behaviour. Particularly in cultures which differentiate sharply between the genders, inculcating appropriate forms of femininity and masculinity into young children is a high priority. The sexual division of labour, from tasks to emotions, can be rehearsed by brothers and sisters in a way not possible in single-sex and only-child families or households. The tension between prescribed gender ideals and the realities of physique, personality, birth order and relationship to parents and other adults in the household has produced some of the most salient 'family dramas'.[22]

In modern Western society some of the most vivid memories of what femininity meant to young girls are in relation to their brothers. In some cases this could mean pride in carrying out a womanly role, being 'little mother' to others in the family. In others it could be bitterness about curtailment of free time and allocation of fewer family resources.[23] In particular, girls' personal loyalty towards and involvement with their brothers' concerns may have been stressed, while the boys in the family took for granted both their right and their duty to turn to external pursuits. A brother acting as instructor, guide or 'window on the world' for sisters, was also being initiated into the wider sphere outside the family, an opportunity often denied many girls.[24] This pattern has been widespread but may have differed significantly depending on class, family and community culture. For example in many sections of the British working class girls took an active role in gaining employment and might well have acted for their brothers.

For the nineteenth-century bourgeoisie, from which so much of our literary heritage derives, there was an almost compulsive focus on contrasting masculine and feminine categories, at a time when these attributes were integral to bourgeois identity.[25] The way this could be played out through sibling relationships echoes in Victorian texts. Harriet Martineau had helped bring up her younger brother James as well as a sister. But in early adulthood she and James had a violent disagreement over religious beliefs which was never reconciled. The attachment Harriet felt for James was the strongest passion of her life; obsessive love tinged with envy is evident in her statement that 'brothers are to sisters what sisters can never be to brothers as objects of engrossing and devoted affection', a sentiment also expressed in numerous diaries, memoirs and letters of the period.[26] Such attachments could be to a brother's advantage, as in families where the sister contributed to his education and occupational mobility, or where she forwent part of her own patrimony or worked to provide income for his further training and/or capital for his 'setting up' in a trade, profession or an enterprise.[27]

Between brothers and *between* sisters, too, siblings can provide models to be emulated or rejected. Since there is always a range of masculine and feminine behaviours and meanings available, children and young people are acutely aware of same-sex siblings as models, sometimes identifying with one another but sometimes rejecting such identification. In some cases, these patterns take the form of rebellion against parents and authority figures; in others, a sister or brother can become conformist as a kind of rejection of a rebellious sib. This truism of everyday life, has a long history as in the biblical story of Jacob, the wicked, and Esau, the righteous; brothers completely different in character and destiny. 'How could it be that these two, who were for one another day and night, could have come from the same womb?'[28]

Thus although both same- and opposite-sex siblings provide models, the *content* and the *form* of sister–sister and brother–brother interaction may differ according to the general expectations of gender roles. Brothers and sisters represent the comparative reference group *par excellence*, effective kin from birth and, unlike friends, social givens.[29] In their shadow, decisions – subconscious as well as conscious – are made about life-choices, even in situations where those choices are severely limited by material and financial deprivation. While the significance of siblings has varied over time and place, the relationship remains one of the most significant of reference points of those restricted social comparisons which contribute to social order, even though it has been widely ignored by academic disciplines concerned with human motivation and action.

The historical picture of siblings is also blurred because kinship relations have so often been used as metaphor. The idea of 'a double singleness' has made both same- and cross-sex siblings a favourite device for exploring some of the social, moral and spiritual questions in many cultures. When potential identification is greater, as in the case of twins, the fascination about individual identity and consciousness is even more marked. Many cultures assign special and magical qualities to twinship, either good or evil, sometimes to the point where one twin may deliberately be killed at birth.[30] In literature, cross-sex twins have often been used to explore the limits of gender boundaries by switching identities, usually with the girl twin in disguise as her brother, thus providing a variant of cross-dressing transgression.[31]

Creation myths, too, have often used the theme of brother–sister marriage, alliances which were supposed to produce offspring with superhuman powers. Brother–sister incest as an explanation of human origins is found in almost every culture including the Judaic-Christian tradition. (Adam and Eve were, in a sense, 'siblings' and their children, Cain and Abel, each married their sisters.)[32] The understanding of such myths and beliefs has to be refracted through the beliefs and values of Western cultures, an inheritance shot through with deeply disturbing emotions surrounding the erotic content of sibling interaction. While incestuous brother–sister relationships evoke horror with their implication of familial and social chaos, they also hold strong fascination, being seen as 'an attempt by fragmented man to achieve wholeness and immortality', perfect oneness in a somehow purer and spirtual union.[33] In modern dream analysis, particularly Jungian, brother–sister erotic attraction is interpreted as the masculine and feminine parts of the self seeking each other, and in the archetypical images of the collective conscience, 'brother–sister marriage is a spiritual and mystical union as much as a sensual and sexual union'.[34]

Since the nineteenth century, this attraction, this yearning for wholeness, has usually been debated within a context of concern about the biological consequences of inbreeding. At the present time, however, a great deal of confusion exists over the issue of incest in general. In the first place, there is no longer a consensus that inbreeding between even close relatives, let alone degrees of affinity as distant as cousins, does have negative consequences such as higher infertility, mortality and morbidity rates in the offspring of such unions; it is possible that co-adapted gene complexes are to some extent actually preserved by inbreeding.[35]

Furthermore, while it does seem to be the case that almost all known societies have some kind of prohibition on sexual intercourse between brothers and sisters as well as parents and children, the causes and mechanisms of this pattern are widely disputed, from Freudians who claim the natural eroticism of all family relationships to upholders of the 'Westermark effect' which posits an inbuilt aversion to such mating as protection against debasing the gene pool (or those who uphold both positions and distinguish between ultimate and proximate causes).[36] Nor does this type of sociobiological discussion throw much light on prohibitions against sexual relationships between kinship through marriage rather than 'blood'.

The 'incest taboo' is not a simple concept, and cultural rules prohibiting sexual relations between relatives is not the same thing as 'inbreeding avoidance'. In part this is because the term *relatives* is ambiguous since it can refer to cultural rather than genetic categories.[37] The situation, too, has changed during the nineteenth and twentieth centuries as erotic desire and 'sexuality' have become more firmly disassociated from procreation through a variety of contraceptive means. What is more, these discussions, centred on the negative genetic effects on human populations, are seldom linked to the legal, religious and moral revisions which have greatly reduced the degrees of kinship forbidden in marriage.[38]

The more the topic of brother–sister incest in particular is investigated in different contexts, the less sure are our conclusions. Even one of the best-known exceptions to sibling incest, brother–sister intermarriage among the Hawaiian and Egyptian Ancient Kingdom royal houses, is under dispute. In relation to the latter, modern Egyptologists have found little hard evidence for the commonly held belief in widespread sibling marriage in the Ancient Kingdom, even among ruling families. Of those few cases actually documented, almost all alliances were between 'half' sisters and brothers and much confusion has been caused by the use of the word *sister* as a term for wife.[39] Sociobiologists admit, too, that even if such marriages did exist as a means of maximizing the transmission of genetic relatedness to one's offspring, instances of full sibling marriages among royalty need to be treated with caution.[40]

But if such liaisons existed (in these or in other cultures), their rationale is far more likely to have been complicated by cultural and social factors including a definition of sexuality which has changed historically. The whole issue of erotic attachment between siblings has been summed up by admitting that 'relatives in many cases do not avoid (all) sexual or incestuous contact, nor do they avoid the same kind of sexual contact from one culture to the next, nor is all sexual activity between relatives necessarily considered incestuous'.[41]

These debates and uncertainties are a warning that the interpretation of a seemingly 'natural' relationship such as that between brothers and sisters is heavily influenced by contemporary views. It was, perhaps, in the Romantic movement of the late eighteenth and early nineteenth century, with its rejection of Enlightenment individualism, that brother–sister attachments have received most attention.

Again and again, European writers around this period, turned to the story of Sophocles' *Antigone*, a play which has usually been interpreted as exemplifying the state in opposition to private conscience, but which can also be seen as being centrally about kinship, the bonds of 'common blood' and in particular the ties between brother and sister. In *Antigone* the insistence that the sister be allowed to bury her brother in direct contradiction to the laws of the city is part of the assumption that, in death, males pass from the domain of the polis back to that of the family, for it is there that ritual burial, the ultimate holy duty surpassing man-made law, will be performed.[42] Implicitly, these 'revisionist' interpretations equate the family with women, the polis with men and use the brother–sister bond as their symbolic expression. In this they follow Hegel who also was inspired by the 'Antigone' theme, but explicitly rejected any hint of incestuous attachment and claimed that it was precisely the asexuality of brothers and sisters which allowed them to encapture most perfectly the elements of essential masculinity and femininity.[43]

Both erotic and pure versions call attention to the expectations surrounding the significance of sisters to brothers in our nineteenth-century inheritance. As the Enlightenment individual, freed from the trammels of community and family, became the hero of modernism, men – and it was mainly men in this role – felt a hunger for human bonds. Women, as mothers, sisters and wives, might provide one such refuge, male friends another. Sisters, less psychically dangerous than mothers, and without the sexuality (with its potential for childbearing) of wives, seem to have embodied the perfect ideal. Nineteenth-century life and literature overflow with accounts of the centrality of sisters to spiritual values, as in the case of William Gladstone whose 'sainted sister', Anne, seven years his senior, in her fervent religious belief and faith that he was God's instrument in the world, underpinned both his own Christian beliefs and his remarkable self-confidence.[44] Among numerous other nineteenth-century writers, Charles Dickens often used brother–sister relations to illustrate the moral (feminine, natural affection) values as opposed to the inhumanity of utilitarian political economy.[45]

While the saliency of brother and sister ties, like those of friendship, may have intensified in response to the isolation of individualism and an increasingly urban environment, economic and demographic changes should not be overlooked. In Britain, from the early modern period onwards, the practice of primogeniture among the upper classes put a strain not only on the eldest son's position *vis-à-vis* younger brothers but also on all sisters. On the other hand, sister–sister and brother–sister ties may have been 'the closest in the family', given the type of marriage and parent–child interaction at the time.[46]

In more middling strata, where partible inheritance of property was the norm, siblings were part of the complicated network of kin shading into 'friends' and neighbours, which was vital in supporting the family enterprise. Among the poorer levels of society children might leave the parental home early in the hope of becoming self-supporting and there was a widespread pattern of youthful living-in farm service, domestic service and apprenticeship, which meant that large numbers of young people lived apart from siblings during their formative years.[47] We still know relatively little about peer-group relations during these periods of service: did they imitate and substitute for those of siblings or were they friendships and relationships of a different order?[48]

But in late eighteenth-century England, with the growth of outwork and by-industries, more of these young people were living at home and thus in closer contact with brothers and sisters who would now be part of youth groups, working, playing and courting together.[49] As the middling groups grew in size and importance, the pattern of family enterprise in farming, manufacturing, commercial ventures, trading and the professions gave primacy to family labour and kin recruitment.

Sons and nephews as well as younger brothers provided by far the largest pool of personnel for these enterprises; brothers often went into partnership with the husbands of their sisters or the sister would subsequently marry a brother's partners. As with peasant landholders, in a significant number of cases two brothers from one family would marry two sisters from another, or a brother and sister from one would marry a sister and brother from another, a pattern common among populations where resources – land, tools, stock, education or whatever – were divided under partible inheritance.

Unmarried sisters expected to contribute labour and often capital as well to their family's enterprise, whether run by a father or brother; they also expected to act as housekeeper to adult single brothers, carers of their married siblings' children, and, in turn, to be supported by the family enterprise. Their emotional as well as economic and cultural assets were heavily invested in the family. Thus brothers and sisters, brought up together, often educated at home together, with a common culture and common inheritance, had good reason to elevate the sibling relationship. In such circumstances, deep affection, even passionate attatchment, meant that when conflicts arose, which they almost inevitably did, especially over deployment of resources and inheritance, bitterness and hatred could result.[50]

Large numbers of children in a family meant that the older siblings acted as an 'intermediate' generation between the parents, now in late middle age, and their youngest offspring. In this capacity they could exercise considerable authority, setting up apprenticeships, arranging marriage partners and generally controlling behaviour. Elder siblings provided leadership using a range of behaviours from autocratic bullying to responsible guidance. In adulthood, as youngish uncles and aunts, they could also become a vital substitute for elderly or ailing parents and grandparents.

A similar pattern has been noted in rural areas where families depended on small plots or land tenancies. Here, too, 'parents could not be chosen, but it was possible to express preference for such and such a brother or sister'.[51] Such coalitions and jockeying for place were rather different from the Romantic stereotype which concentrated on one dyad, often an elder brother and younger sister, in keeping with a dominant gender stereotype.

In the mid-nineteenth century, with a high birth rate and gradually falling child mortality, these groupings gave some choice among sibling loyalties which was particularly important for sisters, who would be expected to serve and keep house for brothers but might well also depend on them for maintenance.[52] For example, among Lancashire textile manufacturers, 'kinship was dominated by that persistent feature of the 19th century bourgeois household, unmarried siblings, not only . . . "redundant" sisters but brothers postponing marriage'.[53] At all levels of the society, brothers and sisters, sometimes orphaned, could close ranks against outsiders. Certainly the callousness with which nineteenth-century charities, as well as local and state authorities split up orphaned sibling groups was deeply resented.[54]

The depths of emotional attatchment among nineteenth-century siblings – including erotic overtones – is brought out in that feature of English Victorian culture so puzzling to twentieth-century commentators, the intense debates over legislation that had outlawed marriage with a deceased wife's sister early in the nineteenth-century. State intervention in such a moral and personal issue was unusual (incest was not made a criminal act in England until 1908) since the church was regarded as the authority in these matters. For over seventy-five years, debates in and out of Parliament, in novels and a stream of articles (even mentioned in a celebrated Gilbert and Sullivan song), centred on the dangers of sister-in-law liaisons.[55]

Much of the tension arose because of the practical exigencies caused by a wife's death in childbirth and the attraction of remarriage to the most likely caretaker of the bereft young children. Nevertheless, the preoccupation with the 'Deceased Wife's Sister' may indicate some 'displacement' of anxieties about relationships not with the wife's sister but with the husband's *own* sister(s). In this context it should be noted that the remarriage of a widow to her brother-in-law is remarkably absent from the discussion.

By the mid-twentieth century, with the growth of larger economic organizations in manufacturing, commerce and retailing and more formal educational requirements for the professions, the necessity to recruit family labour directly into management had declined markedly. Individual mobility, new sources of finances and the growing importance of professional managers meant that non-kin were often actively sought; and by the late twentieth century what had been regarded as the desirable pooling of kinship skills and resources in the nineteenth century is now branded as pyschologically and socially suspect 'nepotism'. Even small 'family enterprises' now try to separate business and family affairs, as in the case of the engineering firm where a father and his two sons worked together but deliberately eschewed close personal links, claiming that 'business keeps us apart'.[56]

This may be an extreme case, and help in gaining jobs or opening up career opportunities for nieces and nephews as well as among siblings should not be minimized. Through to our own day, *informal* contacts and resources between siblings and among nieces, nephews, aunts, uncles and cousins can be vital, especially in times of crisis. Even among the poorest, for example, an oldest daughter might often be instrumental in holding together a family and providing opportunities for younger members after the overburdened, worn-out mother had either died or faded into chronic invalidity.[57]

The accelerating decline in the birth rate in all classes has meant that for generations born after the First World War, the number of siblings has declined sharply. In the last thirty years with the two-child family as the norm, there is no longer an intermediate generation of elder siblings. With the possible exception of upper-class families, an extensive network of uncles, aunts and cousins has melted away. To a certain extent these familial categories have been replaced by the 'composite' families of step- and half-kin created by divorce and remarriage, but the meanings attached to these relationships are not yet clear.

Although family and kin networks are still important in occupational choice and recruitment, and despite the survival of small family businesses and farms in most Western countries (in varying proportions), it is evident that by the last quarter of the twentieth century sibling relationships are no longer central to the organization of economic life. Economic organization has, in turn, been shaped by the falling birth rate which has drastically stripped the numbers of siblings in each family. These changes have undoubtedly narrowed the experience of living with kin, but they are not enough to explain the curious absence of interest in and recognition of sibling ties manifest in late twentieth-century culture.

The reasons for this neglect in academic and intellectual circles are complicated. In addition to the structural and demographic changes already cited, the dominance of psychological, particularly psychoanalytic, interpretations of the family have tended consistently to draw attention to the vertical ties of parent and child. Yet despite the overwhelming amount of material on this issue, a *sociologically* and *culturally* informed theory of childhood remains sketchy.[58] And despite the efforts of historians of childhood, it is still even unclear what relations were held to constitute 'the child' or when childhood in its contemporary sense was first instituted.

The dominance of psychic models in this field has meant that when sibling interaction is actually noted, it often figures as displacement for a deeper oedipal pattern; brothers and sisters are regarded as pale reflections of the central parental drama. One unfortunate result of this view has been to downplay the importance of brother–sister incest and violence.[59] The authors of one of the few full-scale American studies of siblings remark that none of the classical theories of personality and psychological development portrayed brothers and sisters, aunts and uncles, as important in socialization.[60]

Within family studies and family history, too, overwhelming attention has been paid to marriage and parent–child interaction, the nucleated triad. The post-Second World War orthodoxy, exemplified by Talcott Parsons's functionalist explication of American kinship as necessarily nuclear, was challenged by Peter Laslett and the British Cambridge Group for the Study of the History of Population. However, their rebuttal consisted of finding a nucleated family already in place several centuries earlier. Both statement and critique centre on parent–child, vertical relationships.[61]

It is true that recent interest in inequalities within the family has drawn attention to birth order among siblings, especially over the issue of primogeniture and the allocation of resources. Nevertheless, what emerged from a large conference and subsequent publications on this topic, was that what the contributions 'collectively demonstrate is the complexity of inter-sib relations'.[62]

Nor did the move from using snapshot images of the family to a 'life-course' approach necessarily alter the focus. Generational studies have concentrated on vertical transmission and again neglected horizontal ties.[63] Even where the numbers of children in the family are recognized as important, the comparison has been *between* families of different sizes rather than an examination of relationships *within* the family.

Only a handful of 'urban anthropologists', with their sensitivity to kinship systems, have recognized the continued saliency of brothers and sisters in mid- and late twentieth-century life.[64] In particular, the disruption brought about by emmigration and geographical mobility away from parents, other kin and local community led to special dependence and cooperation among siblings lasting into adulthood; for example shared housing and other resources. As in one American study, the brothers and brothers-in-law joined one another in small shops or worked in the same factory, the sisters shared housework and motherly duties so that, if there was more than one baby crying, whichever mother happened to be around would pick up and breast-feed the child. But when the immigrants had settled into the new culture and the generation born in the new country grew to adulthood, sibling relationships, like those between neighbours, lost their primary place.[65]

It should not be surprising then, that within the other social sciences there persists a similar lack of attention to peer-generation relationships. Economic thought focuses either on the single individual *or* takes the household (family) as the unit. When household constitutes the main economic 'actor', its internal relationships are ignored, not only those of husband and wives (as feminists have pointed out), but also those of siblings, other kin, lodgers, and servants.[66]

Political theory, too, comes from a tradition which names the senior male as representing the household, a construction ultimately derived from Western and Middle Eastern traditional religious thought. It is this model of the family which has been used as the basis for the state, with wives, children, younger siblings and servants representing categories of 'non-person'. In the nineteenth century, as a concept of *contract* replaced particularistic notions of kin within political thought, the underlying ideas about kinship and gender remained integral to that construction.[67] Unfortunately, the centrality of kinship in the formation of political theories has not often been recognized. Thus, despite massive attention to history of the family by historians such as Peter Laslett and Lawrence Stone, there has been little effort to link specific family relationships to the formation of the state.[68] David Schneider, again an anthropologist, does suggest that societies built around democratic values would tend to stress egalitarian ties and here siblings would provide a prototype. Referring to American society, he claims that 'horizontal solidarity with collateral kin can be thought of as an integral part of a social system which requires a high level of coordination and mutual dependency but which at the same time, values a high level of autonomy, freedom of choice and egalitarianism'.[69]

But the connections between such democratic expectations and actual kinship remain obscure. It is true that notions of brotherhood and sisterhood have been used to invoke ideas of inclusion and identity in national or racial terms. A well-known example is found in the early nineteenth-century anti-slavery campaign which coined the slogan: 'Am I not a man and a brother? Am I not a woman and a sister?'[70] The idea of brother and sister as used here, however, implies a childish immaturity and expectations of subordination to the 'parent' culture.

There is also evidence that siblings have provided the model for utopian communities in many times and places, which is not surprising since, despite the growth of both contract theory and bureaucratic organization, kinship remains even now in many ways a primary model of all social relations.[71] Enclosed monastic communities (of either sex), confraternities, fraternal organizations such as the Freemasons, millenarian sects, as well as trade unions and socialist parties, have all used fictive sibling and friendship structures with their naming practices (Brother, Sister, Comrade) to signify a levelling of social position. For example, in a study of a mixed-sex utopian community, Lyndal Roper calls attention to the title 'marital sister' (*eeswester*) used for wife, and she believes that the model of brother–sister relations was meant to emphasize equality, kinship and similarity, rather than difference, and thus spiritualize the marriage relationship.[72]

However, if fraternal organizations are examined carefully, there is almost always a tension towards reverting to parental models, or at least leadership with a 'Big Brother', and mixed-sex communities invariably stress masculine authority. Brotherhood rests ultimately on fatherhood; the existence of all-male groups which aimed at internal equality were part of a wider culture based senior on masculine privilege.[73] Although in studies of these various organizations and communities, the sibling metaphor is noted, it has tended to be taken for granted; siblings are part of the air we breathe while it is parental, particularly patriarchal, hierarchy which gets explanatory attention.

Nevertheless, less formal evidence, that based on childhood memories, written autobiography and oral histories, shows that the lives of ordinary people as much as those of the famous resonate with vivid portraits of actual brothers and sisters – cherished, detested, admired, reviled. The nineteenth-century pantheon of creative artists and writers seems particularly sibling-rich: Wolfgang Amadeus and Maria Anna Mozart; Friedrich and Christophine Schiller; Johann Wolfgang and Cornelia von Goethe; François and Lucile Chateaubriand; William and Dorothy Wordsworth; George Byron and Augusta Leigh; Charlotte, Emily, Ann and Branwell Brontë; Friedrich and Elisabeth Nietzsche; Felix and Fanny Mendelssohn; William, Henry and Alice James; Thomas and Carla Mann; Virginia Woolf and Vanessa Bell (Stephens), to name but a few. Much of our literary and cultural heritage harks back to such individuals who had strong, complicated and sometimes difficult relationships with siblings. Our own childhood imagination continues to be filled with many brother–sister scripts in the staple of fairy tales which have such an abiding hold on Western imagination, even in a 'Disneyfied' form.[74]

How long will this continue? In the last analysis it is the experience of sharing a life with other people within an identity labelled 'family' which turns an abstract kinship model into a concrete relationship. For young children in our own time, it seems to be the *person* who is more important than the category, and even with older children it is the relevance of the relationship which influences children's knowledge of kinship terms.[75] Hence, the common practice of children calling close adult friends of parents 'Uncle' and 'Auntie'. The unusually low mortality rates in contemporary societies have inevitably changed the meaning of sibling relationships. The experience of being 'chosen' to replace a dead sibling by his or her parent, parents or even the whole family is now very rare but was once widespread (hence the custom of sometimes giving the new same-sex sibling an identical name to the dead child). The powerful psychic and emotional effects of being a 'replacement' or surviving child are now much less often an enduring childhood experience.[76]

Because parents now have a greater possibility of surviving until their children are self-sufficient, there is little necessity felt to use siblings as guardians of their nieces and nephews – in fact many modern parents prefer to name friends – although *informal* contacts and mutual exchange between adult siblings are clearly present in many cases. Especially in old age many sibling pairs appear to re-establish closer relationships.[77] A large grey area between personal preference and duty colours relations between the middle-aged dyads and triads of the small-family era. However, there usually remain two issues where these ties are forced to come to the fore: the care of elderly parents and the division of property and resources, particularly after the death of parents, and even sometimes before. Little attention has been paid to either of these issues in professional social work or family counselling literature although modern novels often take the death of the parents and the gathering of the grown-up brothers and sisters as a focus for dramatic construction.[78]

The reasons for 'not seeing' the importance of sibling relationships are manifold – economic and demographic change, legal constructions, political and psychological theories, social practices, psychic processes of denial and projection. Historically, there has undoubtedly been a reduction in the saliency of this relationship along with changes in its form, shifts which may be further complicated by the growing numbers of single-parent, one-child families. Yet both the idea and reality of brothers and sisters (uncles and aunts, nieces, nephews and cousins), still have remarkable purchase in making sense of contemporary life. In a recent American report on sibling rivalry, few adult siblings had severed their ties completely and one-third of those interviewed used words like 'competitive' and 'hurtful' to describe their relationship – negative but still emotionally charged evaluations.[79]

We continue to take for granted siblings as a constant and universal presence dictated by our common humanity. At the same time, as Martine Segalen has asked, 'If relationships with the kinship group are such an abiding phenomenon, why has their existence been so often hidden and, indeed, denied over the last 20 years or so?'[80]

Such a paradox may tell us something about the gap between everyday existence and the categories used by academics and intellectuals. In stretching horizontal bonds away from the nuclear triad, siblings are capable of building a web of intimate and trusting relationships and could be a model for nascent civil society. Their dearth, for example in those areas of China where the one-child family policy has been successful, has made for highly competitive and self-centred individualism. Where there are very few or no siblings, the symbolism of siblingship may loom larger, part of our yearning for a historical Golden Age. Perhaps it is only when siblings are no longer part of everyday experience that we can begin to talk and write about them.[81]

And in an such an era of much reduced, one-child, lone-parent families, what might take the place of siblings, aunts, uncles, nephews, nieces and cousins? In psychic terms, egalitarian friendship can also evoke the search for intimacy. One of the few serious studies of friendship concludes that friends can overcome the isolation of individuals, 'by subtraction, as it were when two become one, or by doubling, when each of the friends acquires a second self'. As siblings once did, friends promise wholeness but wholeness is also friendship's problem; the delicate balance in wanting to be ourselves and wanting to be close to other people as well.[82] But the striking difference is that while friends – to an extent – are chosen, siblings remain a 'given'. It is just possible that trust among friends may hold one key to genuinely democratic structures and values, embedded in a kind of intimacy unknown to our historical past.[83]

Notes

A brief version of this chapter has appeared in *Quaderni Storici*, n.s., vol. 83, August 1993. I should like to thank Alan Campbell, Delfina Dolza, John Gillis, Diana Gittins, Norma Grieve, Esther Goody, Helen Hirsch, Elaine Jordan, David Lockwood, Judith Okely, Ruth Perry, Rayna Rapp, Sonya Rose, Elaine Showalter, Maila Stivens, Marilyn Strathern, Paul Thompson and Patrick Wolfe for suggestions and help in preparing this essay. In particular I am grateful to David Heath (University of Essex, Department of Biology) and Ross Crozier (Institute of Human Genetics, LaTrobe University) who provided guidance on the literature about human inbreeding.

1 In particular the importance of the sister relationship has been recognized in feminist literature: Adrienne Rich, 'Sibling Mysteries', *The Dream of a Common Language* (W.W. Norton, New York, 1978); see also Brigid McConville, *Sisters: Love and Conflict within the Lifelong Bond* (Pan, London, 1985); Toni McNaron, *The Sister Bond: A Feminist View of a Timeless Connection* (Pergamon Press, London, 1985); Drusilla Modjeska, ed, *Sisters* (HarperCollins, London, 1993).

2 In the nineteenth-century British textile industry, for example, where young women's wages from the mills or outwork enabled brothers to move into other occupations and sometimes freed younger sisters for more independent careers. Diana Gittins, 'Marital Status, Work and Kinship: 1850–1930', in Jane Lewis, ed., *Labour and Love: Women's Experience of Home and Family 1850–1940* (Blackwell, Oxford, 1986); Clare Evans, 'The Separation of Work and Home? The Case of the Lancashire Textiles 1825–1865', University of Manchester Ph.D. thesis, 1991.

3 Rayna Rapp, 'Toward a Nuclear Freeze? The Gender Politics of Euro-American Kinship Analysis', in Jane Collier and Sylvia Yanagisako, *Gender and Kinship: Essays Toward a Unified Analysis* (Stanford University Press, Stanford, 1987); Marilyn Strathern, *After Nature: English Kinship in the Late Twentieth Century* (Cambridge University Press, Cambridge, 1992).

4 David Schneider, *A Critique of the Study of Kinship* (University of Michigan Press, Ann Arbor, 1984), p. 101.

5 A useful summary of the debates over these issues is provided in Chris Harris, *Kinship* (Open University Press, Milton Keynes, 1990), pp. 27ff.

6 Collier and Yanagisako, *Gender and Kinship*, p. 7.

7 Susan Staves, *Married Women's Separate Spheres: Property in England, 1660–1833* (Harvard University Press, Cambridge, MA, 1990).

8 *Halsbury's Laws of England* (Butterworth, London, 4th edn, 1977), vol. 18, p. 137.

9 Jack Goody, *The Development of the Family and Marriage in Europe* (Cambridge University Press, Cambridge, 1983), p. 142.

10 Sylvia Yanagisako, *Transforming the Past: Tradition and Kinship among Japanese Americans* (Stanford University Press, Stanford, 1985), p. 193.

11 The ambiguity this creates is well brought out in legal wrangles over the ruling that if
    a tenant died without issue having a half-brother, the latter could not inherit as he was
    only related by half-blood, a rule finally abolished in 1833 (J.H. Baker, *An Introduction
    to English Legal History* [Butterworth, London, 1979], p. 228).
12 Sybil Wolfram, *In-Laws and Outlaws: Kinship and Marriage in England* (Croom Helm,
    London, 1987).
13 See Robert Brain, *Friends and Lovers*, ch. 3, 'Friends in Blood' (Paladin, London, 1977).
14 Naomi Tadmore, ' "Family" and "Friend" in *Pamela*: A Case-Study in the History of
    the Family in Eighteenth-Century England', *Social History*, vol. 14, no. 3 (October
    1989); see also the discussion of friendship in Leonore Davidoff and Catherine Hall,
    Family Fortunes: Men and Women of the English Middle Class (Routledge, London,
    1994); Graham Little, *Friendship: Being Ourselves with Others* (Text Publishing,
    Melbourne, 1993).
15 Esther Goody, 'Separation and Divorce among the Gonja', in M. Fortes, ed., *Marriage
    in Tribal Societies* (Cambridge University Press, Cambridge, 1972); Thomas
    Beidelman, 'The Filth of Incest: A Text and Comments on Kaguru Notions of Sex-
    uality, Alimentation and Aggression', *Cahiers D'Etudes Africaines*, vol. 12, no. 1 (1972);
    see also Martine Segalen, *Historical Anthropology of the Family* (Cambridge University
    Press, Cambridge, 1988).
16 Ruth Perry, 'Brotherly Love and Brotherly Hatred in the Fiction of Frances Burney',
    unpublished paper delivered to the Modern Languages Association, December 1990;
    Elaine Jordan 'Literary Doubles: Brothers and Sisters', unpublished notes – by kind
    permission of the authors.
17 George Eliot, 'Brother and Sister', in 'The Spanish Gypsy', *Collected Works* (London,
    1901), p. 587.
18 Arthur Tennyson, *The Lover's Tale* (C. Kegan, Paul & Co., London, 1879), p. 20.
19 G. Einstein and M. Moss, 'Some Thoughts on Sibling Relationships', *Social Casework*,
    November 1967, p. 553; M. Straus, R. Gelles and S. Steinmetz, *Behind Closed Doors:
    Violence in the American Family* (Anchor Books, New York, 1980).
20 Gerald S. Levanthal, 'Influence of Brother and Sister on Sex-Role Behaviour', *Journal
    of Personality and Social Psychology*, vol. 16, no. 3 (1970). This point has emerged in
    present thinking which focuses on the dyad rather than a 'universal' nuclear family:
    Ruth Busch, 'If the Hsu fits . . . An Extension of the Hypothesis Relating Kinship and
    Culture Developed by Francis L.K. Hsu', *Journal of Comparative Family Studies*, vol.
    8, no. 3 (autumn 1977). For a striking example of a powerful eldest sister whose formal
    role was continually subordinated to her younger brothers see E.M. Forster, *Marianne
    Thorton: A Domestic Biography 1797–1887* (Harcourt Brace, New York, 1956).
21 William R. Beer, *Strangers in the House: The World of Stepsiblings and Half-Siblings*
    (Transaction Publishers, New Brunswick, NJ, 1989).
22 Extreme identification seems to occur when other support systems for children break
    down. Even opposite-sex siblings sometimes identify strongly, as, for example in the
    case of Charles Lamb who became the carer of his sister Mary after she had murdered
    their mother. In his caring role, Charles felt as if he had thus avoided the 'impertinence'
    of manhood. Jane Aaron, ' "Double Singleness": Gender Role Mergence in the Auto-
    biographical Writings of Charles and Mary Lamb', in Susan Gloag Bell and Marilyn
    Yalom, eds, *Revealing Lives: Autobiography, Biography and Gender* (SUNY Press,
    Albany, 1990).
23 Envy of brothers' opportunities is found in memoirs spanning centuries and class
    groups. For example: *Memoirs of the Life of the Late Mrs. Catherine Capp*, edited by her
    daughter, Mary (Longman, London, 1822); Hannah Mitchell, *The Hard Way Up: The
    Autobiography of a Suffragtte and Rebel* (Virago, London, 1977). In religious households
    the realization that they, unlike their brothers, could never become preachers seems to

have been particularly painful. *Autobiography of Elizabeth M. Sewell*, edited by Eleanor Sewell (Longman's, Green & Co., 1908); Katherine Sklar, *Catherine Beecher: A Study in Domesticity* (Yale University Press, New Haven, 1973).

24 'Wordsworth's "beauty" and "fear" are nature's ministries devoted gratuitously and unconditionally to the growing boy, while for George Eliot, "the fear and the love" are purely human.' The implication is that the girl will give up everything for love of an elder brother (Margaret Homans, 'Eliot, Wordsworth and the Scenes of the Sister's Instruction', *Critical Inquiry*, vol. 8 no. 2 (winter 1981), pp. 39, 26.

25 See Davidoff and Hall, *Family Fortunes*; E.J. Hobsbawm, *The Age of Capital 1848–75* (London, 1977).

26 Harriet Martineau, *Autobiography* (London, 1877), 3 vols, vol. 1, p. 99.

27 See, for example, Mary Ryan, *Cradle of the Middle Class: The Family in Oneida County New York, 1790–1865* (Cambridge University Press, Cambridge, 1981).

28 Lawrence Kushner, *Honey from the Rock: Visions of Jewish Mystical Renewal* (Jewish Lights Publishing, Woodstock, VT, 1977), p. 38.

29 Bert N. Adams *Kinship in an Urban Setting* (Markham, Chicago, 1968), p. 117; for the concept of 'reference group', see Robert K. Merton, 'Continuities in the Theory of Reference Groups and Social Structure', in *Social Theory and Social Stucture* (Free Press, Glencoe, IL, 1975).

30 Robert Brain, *Friends and Lovers*, 'Friends as Twins'.

31 See, for example, Viola and Sebastian in Shakespeare's *Twelfth Night*, but there are many other examples, e.g. Sarah Grand's *The Heavenly Twins* (1894) was used to explore controversial themes at the height of first-wave feminism in Britain.

32 In particular the widely used Germanic/Scandinavian legend of Sieglund and Sieglunde, the brother–sister pair who were parents of the hero, Siegfried (basis for the Wagnerian Ring Cycle) which also became the basis for the powerful short story, 'Blood of the Walsungs' by Thomas Mann. Luciano Santiago, *The Children of Oedipus: Brother–Sister Incest in Psychiatry, Literature, History and Methodology* (Libra Publishers, Roslyn Heights, NY, 1973).

33 Kaythern B. Maguire, 'The Incest Taboo in *Wuthering Heights*: A Modern Appraisal', *American Imago: A Psychoanalytic Journal for Culture, Science and the Arts*, vol. 45, no. 2 (summer 1988), p. 218.

34 Roderick Peters, *Living With Dreams* (André Deutsch, London, 1990), p. 139.

35 See W.M. Shields, *Philopathy, Inbreeding and the Evolution of Sex* (State University of New York Press, Albany, 1983).

36 See the extensive debates including evolutionary and sociobiological positions in Nancy W. Thornhill, 'An Evolutionary Analysis of Rules Regulating Human Inbreeding and Marriage' (with commentaries), *Behavioural and Brain Sciences*, vol. 14 (1991).

37 Gregory C. Leavitt, 'Sociobiological Explanations of Incest Avoidance: A Critical Review of Evidential Claims', *American Anthropologist*, vol. 92, no. 4 (December 1990).

38 For a thought-provoking although somewhat mechanistic view on this topic, see J.R. Fox, 'Sibling Incest', *British Journal of Sociology*, vol. 13, no. 2 (1962); see also Robin Fox, *The Red Lamp of Incest* (E.P. Dutton, New York, 1980).

39 Jaroslav Cerny, 'Consanguineous Marriages in Pharonic Egypt', *Journal of Egyptian Archaeology*, no. 40 (1954); Shafik Allam, 'Geschwisterehe', in W. Helck and W. Westendorf, eds, *Lexikon der Ägyptologie*, no. 11, Wiesbaden, 1977; I am indebted to Stephen Quirke, Department of Egpytology, British Museum, for the above information.

40 R. Bixler, reply to Nancy Thornhill, 'An Evolutionary Analysis of Rules Regulating Human Inbreeding', p. 266.

41 Leavitt, 'Sociobiological Explanations of Incest Avoidance', p. 984, n. 1.

42 Robin Fox, 'The Virgin and the Godfather: Kinship Law versus State Law in Greek

Tragedy and After', in *Reproduction and Succession: Studies in Anthropology, Law and Society* (Transaction, New Brunswick, NJ, 1983).

43   See Fox, ibid, on George Steiner's discussion of *Antigone*; and A. and H. Paolucci, eds, *Hegel on Tragedy* (Harper Torchbooks, New York, 1975), p. 268.

44   Peter Jagger, *Gladstone: The Making of a Christian Politician: The Personal, Religious Life and Development of William Ewart Gladstone* (Pickwick Publications, Harwarden, Clwyd, 1991).

45   Daniel Daneau, 'The Brother–Sister Relationship in *Hard Times*', *The Dickensian*, vol. 40 (1964); see also Michael Slater, *Dickens and Women* (Stanford University Press, Stanford, 1983).

46   Lawrence Stone, *The Family, Sex and Marriage in England, 1500–1800* (Weidenfeld & Nicolson, London, 1977), p. 115.

47   Leonore Davidoff, 'The Family in Britain 1750–1950', *Cambridge Social History of Britain* (Cambridge, 1990), vol. 2.

48   For some discussion of these issues see John Gillis, *Youth and History: Tradition and Change in European Age Relations 1770 to the Present* (Rutgers University Press, New Brunswick, NJ, 1974).

49   John Gillis, *For Better for Worse: British Marriages 1600 to the Present* (Oxford University Press, Oxford, 1985).

50   A family of two parents and eight children living in the household represents 45 sets of personal relationships and a potential of 28,500 combinations. See James Bossard, *The Large Family System* (University of Pennsylvania Press, Philadelphia, 1956).

51   Called 'elective affectivity' by anthropologist Martine Segalen, in '"Avoir sa part": Sibling Relations in Partible Inheritance Brittany', in Hans Medick and David Warren Sabean, eds, *Interest and Emotion: Essays on the Study of Family and Kinship* (Cambridge University Press, Cambridge, 1977), p. 133.

52   For the British population as a whole, in the mid-nineteenth century 12 per cent of ten to fourteen year olds were living in households with sibling groups of more than six but this would not take into account elder brothers and sisters who had left home and might well be higher for middling and upper-class families. Michael Anderson, 'Households, Families and Individuals: Some Preliminary Results from the National Sample from the 1851 Census of Great Britain', *Continuity and Change*, vol. 3, no. 3 (1988).

53   A.C. Howe, 'The Lancashire Textile Masters, 1820–60: A Social and Political Study', University of Oxford, D. Phil. thesis (1980), p. 94. A quarter of the relatives living with heads of households were their siblings or siblings-in-law. Anderson, 'Households, Families and Individuals'.

54   Eileen Simpson, *Orphans: Real and Imaginary* (Weidenfeld & Nicolson, New York, 1987); Joy Parr, *Labouring Children: British Immigrant Apprentices to Canada, 1869–1924* (Croom Helm, London, 1980).

55   Nancy Anderson 'The "Marriage With a Deceased Wife's Sister Bill" Controversy: Incest Anxiety and the Defence of Family Purity in Victorian England', *Journal of British Studies*, vol. 21, no. 2 (1982); Harriet Martineau's one novel, *Deerbrook* (1839), centres on a doctor who realizes he is in love with his resident sister-in-law; Charles Dickens had a close attachment to his wife's younger sister, which he, after her death, transferred to a yet younger sister; both sisters lived for long periods in his household (Slater, *Dickens and Women*).

56   Adams, *Kinship in an Urban Setting*, p. 132.

57   For example, 'Mighty', sister of the hero in Raphael Samuel, *East End Underworld: Chapters in the Life of Arthur Harding* (Routledge & Kegan Paul, London, 1981).

58   Mailia Stivens, 'Theorizing Childhood', unpublished paper, University of Melbourne, October 1993.

59   For example Elizabeth Fishel, *Sisters: Love and Rivalry inside the Family and Beyond*

(Morrow, New York, 1979); Harry Musinger and Adele Rabin, 'A Family Study of Gender Identification', *Child Development*, vol. 49, no. 2 (June 1978); for this view of sibling incest, see G.W. Berry, 'Incest: Some Clinical Variations on a Classical Theme', *Journal of the American Academy of Psychoanalysis*, vol. 3, no. 20 (April 1975); Vera and Allen Frances 'The Incest Taboo and Family Structure', *Family Process*, vol. 15, no. 2 (June 1976), and a feminist challenge in Ellen Cole, 'Sibling Incest: The Myth of Benign Sibling Incest', *Women and Therapy*, vol. 1, no. 3 (fall 1982).

60 Michael Lamb and Brian Sutton-Smith, *Sibling Relationships: Their Nature and Significance across the Lifespan* (Lawrence Erlbaum, London, 1982), p. 4.

61 Talcott Parsons, 'The Social Structure of the Family' in Ruth Aushen, ed., *The Family: Its Function and Destiny* (Harper, New York, 1949); Peter Laslett, 'Introduction: The History of the Family', in Peter Laslett with Richard Wall, eds, *Household and Family in Past Time* (Cambridge University Press, Cambridge, 1972).

62 Richard Wall and Lloyd Bonfield, 'Dimensions of Inequalities among Siblings', introductory essay to a special issue of that title, *Continuity and Change*, vol. 7, no. 3 (December 1992), p. 269.

63 Glenn Elder, 'Family History and the Life Course', *Journal of Family History*, vol. 2, no. 4 (winter 1977).

64 Bert Adams, *Kinship in an Urban Setting*; Raymond Firth, Jane Hubert and Anthony Forge, *Families and their Relatives: Kinship in a Middle-Class Sector of London* (Routledge & Kegan Paul, London, 1969); Yanagisako, *Transforming the Past*.

65 Judith E. Smith, *Family Connections: A History of Italian and Jewish Immigrant Lives in Providence, Rhode Island 1900–1940* (State University of New York Press, Albany, 198?), p. 102; Yanaisako, *Transforming the Past*.

66 Michèle A. Pujol, *Feminism and Anti-Feminism in Early Economic Thought* (Edward Elgar, Cheltenham, 1992).

67 See this volume, ch. 8.

68 Robert Wheaton, 'Observations on the Development of Kinship History 1942–1985', *Journal of Family History*, vol. 12 (1987).

69 Elaine Cumming and David Schneider, 'Sibling Solidarity: A Property of American Kinship', *American Anthropologist*, vol. 63 (1961), p. 505.

70 Catherine Hall, 'Competing Masculinities: Thomas Carlyle, John Stuart Mill and the Case of Governor Eyre', in *White, Male and Middle Class: Explorations in Feminism and History* (Polity Press, Cambridge, 1992), p. 270.

71 Michael Roper, *Masculinity and the British Organization Man since 1945* (Oxford University Press, Oxford, 1993).

72 Lyndal Roper, 'Sexual Utopianism in the German Reformation', *Journal of Ecclesiastical History*, vol. 42, no. 3 (July 1991), p. 404.

73 Mary Ann Clawson, 'Fraternalism and the Patriarchal Family', *Feminist Studies*, summer 1980, and her *Constructing Brotherhood: Class, Gender and Fraternalism* (Princeton University Press, Princeton NJ, 1989); McGuire, *Friendship and Community*.

74 Lily E. Clerkx, 'Family Relationship in Fairy Tales: A Historical Sociological Approach', *The Netherlands Journal of Sociology*, vol. 23, no. 2 (October 1987). It might be argued that children identify with the brothers and sisters as segmented parts of themselves *vis-à-vis* an orphaned state, wicked stepmothers, etc. Nevertheless, the sibling *category* still seems to have great emotional purchase.

75 Nancy Benson and Jeremy Anglin, 'The Child's Knowledge of English Kin Terms', *First Language*, vol. 7, pt I, no. 19 (1987).

76 For a striking account of this phenomenon see Andrew Birkin, *J.M. Barrie and the Lost Boys* (Constable, London, 1979).

77 Janet Finch, 'Family Obligation, Kinship and Social Change', paper delivered to University of Essex, Department of Sociology, March 1990.

78   While mother–daughter relationships are a strong theme in literature on caretaking of
     the elderly, chronically ill and disabled, almost no attention has been paid to siblings
     (in-law), nieces and nephews (personal communication, Jane Lewis, Department of
     Social Administration, London School of Economics).

79   Janet Mersky Leder 'Adult Sibling Rivalry', *Psychology Today*, January/February,
     1993.

80   Segalen, *Historical Anthropology of the Family*, p. 103.

81   John Gillis, personal communication.

82   Little, *Friendship*, pp. 15, 250, 255.

83   When totalitarian regimes begin to invade personal relations, a retreat inwards to the
     closest bonds may, at least for a short time, hold at bay the political invasion of trust
     between people. Thomas Mann's story of a post-First World War brother and sister
     whose semi-incestuous games cut them off from the destruction of their bourgeois
     security by the effects of massive inflation ('The Blood of the Walsings') was eerily
     played out in real life by his son, Klaus, and daughter, Erika, during the rise of Nazism.
     See Klaus Mann's novella and play *Siblings and the Children's Story*, translated with an
     introduction by T. Alexander and P. Eyre (Marion Boyars, London and New York,
     1992).

8

Regarding Some 'Old Husbands' Tales': Public and Private in Feminist History

There is no easy passage from 'women' to 'humanity'
Denise Riley, 1988

Prologue

A central platform of feminist critique and attempted revision of mainstream thought has focused on the construction and boundaries of classifications: of femininity and masculinity, women and men, woman and man. These classifications have been, in turn, linked to the construction of other highly significant categories, the complicated – and slippery – notions of *public* and *private*.

The everyday usage of a public and private distinction has led to much confusion. When feminists, mainly anthropologists, first focused on the distinction, there was an apparent universal sexual asymmetry that fitted neatly into a public/private dimension. This was then used, often implicitly, to *explain* women's powerlessness.[1] However, the obvious objection to the automatic connection of women with the private (or the 'natural') is the nonsensical logic which would then make men 'naturally' cultural or 'naturally' rational.[2]

This convention, indeed, has continued to be part of the problem, for the public/private divide has played a dual role as both an *explanation* of women's subordinate position and as an *ideology* that constructed that position. As Ludmilla Jordanova has argued, 'The distinction itself has to be treated as an artefact whose long life history requires careful examination.'[3] Furthermore, like gender itself, public and private have been used as a rich source of metaphor.

For feminist historians, the *public/private* distinction has been linked to the notion of *separate spheres*, one of the most powerful concepts within women's history since its recrudescence in the 1960s. Such binary distinctions have come under attack from a range of theoretical positions, including powerful feminist solvents which stress multiplicity, plurality and the blurring of boundaries. Yet there continues to be fascination with the seeming separation of private and public life in our own late twentieth-century situation as we juggle the multilayered psychic structures of femininity as well as confronting feminine roles of daughter, wife and mother with professional identity and/or political activism. In Ann Snitow's memorable phrase: 'Modern women experience moments of free fall. How is it for you, there, out in space near me? Different I know. Yet we share – some with more pleasure, some with more pain – this uncertainty.'[4]

Nevertheless, out of the confusion a consensus is emerging that public and private are not (and never have been) 'conceptual absolutes', but a minefield of 'huge rhetorical potential'.[5] Despite their instability and mutability, public and private are concepts which also have had powerful material and experiential consequences in terms of formal institutions, organizational forms, financial systems, familial and kinship patterns, as well as in language. In short, they have become a basic part of the way our whole social and psychic worlds are ordered, but an order that is constantly shifting, being made and remade.

Historians grappling with this complicated web of structures, meanings and behaviours have had to work on a number of different levels. Should these dichotomous categories be treated only in terms of languages, or of attitudes and values? Or should they be described in terms of the organization of space, time, the location of people? Are, and were, they ideologies imposed, cultures created, or simply a set of given boundaries to be observed? If the 'separate spheres' of home and work, to take one derivation, was 'a trope which hid its intrumentality even from those who employed it'[6] then how can we retrieve more than the most partial picture 100 or 200 years later?

Part of the problem is the form in which historians of women have entered the debate. For example, in a discussion of the eighteenth century, the claim has been made that:

> At bottom, the separation of the home and workplace, the rise of the new domestic woman, the separation of the spheres, and the construction of the public and private all describe the same phenomenon in different words.[7]

This may, indeed, be the way these ideas have come to be used, but it is a profound misunderstanding to think that they are either analytically or descriptively the same thing. For example, while conceptual dichotomies such as public and private are constructed with a drive to fix boundaries between at least two *different* constructs which can be separated and contrasted, the concept of *domesticity* and its concomitant, *domestic ideology*, seems historically to have no other 'half'. (The literal opposite of domesticity would be the wild or untamed or, alternatively, foreign or strange, as in domestic goods versus foreign imports.)

Until recently, debates about the public and private have taken the domestic for granted as well as being unaware of a gender dimension. The most common distinction has focused on the state as representative of the public in contrast with private organizations such as the church, voluntary societies and, particularly, privately owned business or professional enterprises. At times this private sector has been conflated into 'civil society', regarded as 'above all else, the sphere of private interest, private enterprise and private individuals.'[8] In this formulation, civil society would include a notion of 'private life' the family and sexuality,[9] especially in discussions of totalitarian as opposed to democratic regimes.

There has been unease, however, about the place of morality within these distinctions, for neither the modern state nor the private enterprise was conceived in moral terms.[10] In England, this was re-echoed in late nineteenth-century legal debates about the relationship of the individual to the state at the time of increased separation of law and legal forms from ethical concerns.[11] The distinction between justice and morality (the good life) subsumes a gendered notion of public versus private spheres which runs like a thread through social-contract tradition from John Locke to John Rawls, and which contains 'a fundamental ambiguity governing the term *privacy*'.[12]

This uncertainty has continuously resurfaced. Its latest manifestation is explicitly linked to gender issues as seen in debates over the work of writers such as Carol Gilligan and Catherine Mackinnon.[13] But, these discussions make little reference to the terms 'public' and 'private'. On the other hand, in the nineteenth century, debates about these terms could be at a level which had no feminine component at all. Given that men were the 'unmarked' and therefore invisible category, the gendered nature of these assumptions has not until very recently been part of the debate. At the same time the whole edifice was predicated on an unspoken assumption about a shadow world of reproduction, sexuality and at least parts of the morality which had come to be jettisoned from the public realm as the constructs developed through the nineteenth century. Domestic, personal life, regarded as embedded in the biological, universal and pre-social, remained outside the terms of debate, an exclusion which has been used to restrict the universe of *legitimate* public, and hence political, contestation.

Thus the institutions of family, kinship, marriage and parenthood, which should have been central to debates on the public and private, have been either neglected or taken for granted.[14] And within feminist history, while aspects of these institutions and their cultures have been extensively researched, the categories have rarely been interrogated. Meanwhile, family history and demographic history have proceeded, for the most part, as quite distinct from women's history, much less a feminist approach. But the family and household remain the primary 'mediating institutions' in gender systems. They are the crucible within which individuals, both psychologically and symbolically, learn to speak a gendered language as well as the languages of their many other identities, ethnic, racial, national, sexual.

It is within the family – however that has been constituted – that formation of both body and psyche, literally and symbolically, first takes place. By laying most emphasis on understanding gender distinctions at the social level, particularly within the sexual division of labour, feminist research has at times, paradoxically, fallen back on some biological constants, especially those related to birth and breast-feeding. The body thus becomes too much the bearer of the timeless and static. Only by refocusing on the body can feminist research apply the logic of change and, therefore, redeem a site of some of our deepest conceptual sources of gender construction,[15] including the imbrication of masculinity and femininity with the public and private.

In applying conceptual understandings to such a range of levels, in floundering through such a conceptual and linguistic minefield, feminist historians have to be clear about what they are trying to do. As with most human institutions and cultural forms, *public* and *private* have a long history; they represent both continuity and change. Among many groups and in many cultures they do not even appear as relevant concepts.[16]

In the sections that follow, my focus will be on the public and private as they were understood through the 'long nineteenth century' (*c*.1780–1914) in England, the period and place in which the other essays in this collection have been set. For the practising historian, in particular, it is vital to locate concepts in use at the time as well as those we have inherited.

In Part I the discussion concentrates on the conceptual level, including the inherited ambiguity, complexity and changing nature of some key ideas and their derivations: *rationality*, *the individual*, *property*, *the market*. The point has been emphasized that it is this history which lies behind our received and seemingly unproblematic current assumption of a distinction between the public and private.

For the working historian, the *consequences* of such constructs (often quite unintended by their proponents), the power and resources deployed in attempts to make – or keep – a particular view of the world dominant, are of equal signficance. The development of financial, industrial and even technological organization, the layout of buildings and towns, manners and dress, the formation of group boundaries and identities – all can ultimately be traced back to beliefs and ideas held by various peoples.

But this approach makes no claim for the primacy of ideas. On the contrary, organizations with their hierarchies of relationships, the web of laws and customs, the transformation of ideas into stone, brick and mortar which far outlast their origins, all may have an independent impact on the conceptual systems as well as behaviours of many generations beyond the original formulations. For example, the most important post-1850 industry in England, the building trade, flourished with the construction of the great municipal, civic and voluntary society public buildings, on the one hand, and private homes, many of them in new suburbs, on the other.

Part II examines the consequences of the gendered nature of the root concepts considered in Part I. In particular, it examines the way these ideas and the relationships, organization and distribution of power associated with them have structured the particular English public and private domains. Specific areas covered include: the gendered nature of class relations; the relation of men to the putative private sphere; and, especially, the relation of women to the public sphere.

PART I   ADAM SPOKE FIRST AND NAMED THE ORDERS OF
THE WORLD

Forging Concepts

Many eighteenth-century beliefs were built on binary conceptions existent in early modern Europe, including the already accepted inwardness of mental life and a division between people and objects. This was a conception of a different order to most other cultures.[17] The sixteenth and seventeenth centuries had witnessed a gradual shift from the idea that witches could cause good or bad fortune, or that evil agencies resided in people, to a realization that what befell individuals and groups might be due to environmental effects. Here is found the 'nascent statistical sense' which saw proto-scientific patterns in seemingly random behaviours.[18] A type of rational thought and its technological application was emerging from which symbolic and expressive dimensions had been to a great extent purged.[19]

Particularly under the influence of Descartes and the impact of the French Enlightenment, a modern discourse arose which made reason the source of knowledge of the world and separated the knower from the known. When combined with the existing Judaic-Christian division between spirit and flesh, these ideas have been seen as an attempt to create a rational order from chaos and 'to escape from history, culture and human finitude' but to which the body (and its material mortality) was the chief impediment to human objectivity'.[20]

Within such a Cartesian scheme of mind and body, the 'mind had no sex', and thus held out the potential for freedom from sex prejudice. Yet the effacement of value behind objective fact, in conception as well as practice, meant that woman, so closely defined by her bodily materiality, was a particular case of the universal, while man was both the universal human and the particular male – an asymmetry underlying all claims to rational universalism.[21]

Emerging objectivity in scientific, commercial and other bodies of knowledge claimed universality but, by the eighteenth century in actual historical configurations, the idea of rationality was masculine throughout.[22] By the mid-nineteenth century, rational expertise as found in science, medicine and the legal system gradually became the major source of intellectual authority. This often took the form of universal laws which drew ever further from what came to be regarded as the ignorance of 'old wives, tales' (sic). Even the notion of an unconscious (or subconscious) mind, taken up in the later nineteenth century, developed as part of a philosophical as well as medical discourse which had begun to examine the phenomenon of consciousness.[23]

In the economic sphere, the rational calculation of income was torn away from the moral community. Accounting, surveying, practices of estimating everything from crop yields to the calculation of time units were coming to be set in universalized standards.[24] The practical rationalization of space as well as time marked, for example, by the invention of the Ordnance Survey, formed the context in which Enlightenment thinkers formulated their projects.[25]

The mind set at the heart of rationality was not only the basis of a variety of developing thought systems and practices but also had a deep effect on everyday interactions between men and women. An abstract mode of thought focused only on certain types of information, but denied that these values, desires and commitments were to (or from) a given position. The effect was to deny the non-unitary, non-rational, relational character of subjectivity.[26]

Desire and fantasy were segregated as an intensified religious realm, or funnelled into the category women (and children) as wife, mother or prostitute (and, incidentally, leaving no recognized space for male homoeroticism). The impartial voice of reason universalized the masculine out of personal existence so that the 'ontological centre has vanished in its own neutrality', always leaving women as the shadow on the margins, visible, ironically, only in an 'emphasized' form.[27]

In this way, nineteenth-century rational masculinity withdrew from the body. And with its disembodiment went a casting-off of sexuality so that only women could be consituted as sexual beings – in Victorian parlance, women were THE SEX while men's sexuality was reincarnated in a naturalized biology. Max Weber, the greatest student of rationality, a man more insightful, if more troubled, about such matters than most, stated the opposition with its implied gender connotations:

> Rational ascetic alertness, self-control and methodical planning of life are threatened most by the peculiar irrationality of the sexual act which is ultimately and uniquely unsusceptible to rational organization.[28]

The difficulty of coming to grips with the issue of sexuality from these various, probably incommensurable, positions has been exemplified in Judith Walkowitz's investigation of the earnest discussions among a small group of London's late nineteenth-century intelligentsia within a 'Men and Women's Club'. This group gathered with the specific aim of a scientific discussion of relations between the sexes. But the limitations of rationalist discourse for expressing desire for both men and women were soon revealed. Women especially felt the silencing and denial of a sense of sexual danger as well as the misogynist origins of such a procedure. It is not surprising that the Club survived for only a few years.[29] It may be significant that some of these women, like their counterparts who later became active in the movement for scientific state socialism, the Fabians, turned to writing fiction as a way of expressing themes and feelings denied by the available languages of rational science and rational politics.[30] Women's writing has probably attracted most attention as a form of their resistance to this formulation, a resistance which in fact set up a dialogue of challenge to the dominant models, but a challenge which, significantly, had to take a different *form*.[31]

The core idea associated with the drive to rationality was *the individual*, the self conceived as the source of knowledge and meaning. This concept, too, was fashioned on a long-standing foundation of Judaic-Christian, Hellenic and Roman culture and was consolidated in the seventeenth and eighteenth centuries by many of the developments already described. While recognized as a keystone in Western modernism, in many ways the term 'individual' has been largely taken for granted, used as a common sense.[32] In England in particular, individualism has mainly been explored in relation to political and economic liberalism; the discussion has centred on the nature of the individual in relation to public collectivities.

It was only individuals who could enter into civil and commercial contracts; it was the individual – rational and free – who represented both political and, ultimately, moral authority. The individual, however, had by definition to focus on *difference*. Individualism was predicated on the idea of a 'dichotomous other' which carried a covert dimension of power.[33] Down through the nineteenth century the 'otherness' of designated non-individuals can be traced in the construction of age groups, class, ethnic, racial and national categories as well as gender.

The basic elements of individualism cluster around an idea of socially recognized and legitimate autonomy. The individual is sovereign in matters concerning himself: individuals have capacity for action in transformation of their environment; furthermore, a form of action that is planned, calculating and rational is implied.[34] Above all, as an individual, 'everyman is naturally the sole proprietor of his own person and capacities'.[35]

Such meaning has deeply gendered implications, for it rests on a double understanding of the individual *subject*. The subject can be an initiator, the subject who acts, but that actor needs a subject upon which to act, who was subjected to his authority. It is as if masculine self-fabricated subjecthood could only be attained at the cost of another – so often a feminine, or at least feminized, other's subjection. Thus the two meanings of subject were fractured along gender lines from the start, a position with obvious political implications for the category *woman*.

Eighteenth- and nineteenth-century discussions about the meaning of childhood and adult status, for example, reveal a deep unease about dealing with embodied, live human beings, yet beings who were not seen to possess such 'proprietorship'.[36] Nevertheless, whatever defined the individuality of the child, if that child was a boy, time would bring full adulthood. The obverse of manliness was often not so much femininity as childishness. It may be significant that boys who spent their first five or six years wearing little skirts with leading strings tied to their shoulders were ceremonially 'breeched' into adult masculine garb when they passed out of the hands of mothers and nurses to masculine pursuits. Girls remained in petticoats all their lives.

The nineteenth-century male domestic servant, too, was a role where dependence and masculinity were increasingly at odds. The servant displayed his master's authority in the ribbons on his shoulders and the colours of his livery. He had an image of being both sexually disruptive and effeminate; a 'kept' person, the bird in a cage (a sexualized image also applied to wives), he was derogated as 'a flunky', the opposite of the manly independent worker. The stereotypical name for a male domestic servant often used by employers instead of his given name was *John Thomas*. To this day, John Thomas is an English euphemism for penis. The servant is here identified as the ultimate 'tool' of his master. Significantly, there is no such connotation for the female analogue, *Mary Ann*.

In addition to servants and children, the status of individuals who were defined as paupers and those dependent on charity, formally through the state or on voluntary donations, was also dubious. But it was above all within marriage, the institution founded upon a core of reproductive sexuality, that women's subjecthood was evident, both symbolically and practically. As expressed by the law, an individual was, 'when defined fully, a legal personality',[37] but upon marriage, women died a kind of civil death, losing legal personality along with potential capacity for active agency in either civil or commercial life.

Individual, then, implied mastery over others who were conceived as dependants and objects. And as the nineteenth century progressed, the enlarged concept of citizenship was framed around the idea of the individual.

It has been pointed out, however, that this conception of the rational individual contains an inherent contradiction. For the norms of rationality and standardization, the impersonal and abstract mode, if carried to their logical conclusion would tend to overwhelm the autonomous free individual, forcing him (sic) into a standardized statistical category. Recognition of this contradictory outcome coincided with the economic and political turmoil of the late eighteenth and early nineteenth centuries when these concepts were being forged in their modern form; men continued to search for alternative worlds where the self and personal morality might be protected, if not flourish.

One reaction to this dilemma was to create a form of idealized individual subject who made his own world: the artist, the genius and the extramundane Romantic hero, much influenced by continental culture. The Romantic archetype was conceived as transcendent to a particular milieu or even physical space; 'the autonomous individual became the literary counterpart of laissez-faire economics, free trade and the minimalist state'.[38] Although the original German conception had contained a space for women, particularly within the complementarity and potential equality of Romantic love, even there a sediment of essentialist masculinity's relation to the 'external world' persisted.[39] Once transferred to the British context, however, it was evident that the archetypical Romantic could only be masculine wherever he appeared: in 'ethical responsibility, civic identity, artistic representation or economic behaviour'.[40]

The late eighteenth-century, Evangelical religious revival – the rise of Methodism and other enthusiastic forms of Anglicanism as well as Evangelical movements within Nonconformist sects – also cleared a space for a more moral or ethical individualism. Intense examination of the soul in the interests of submission to Christ drew constant attention to the notion of self. The religious construction of the self embraced more feminine characteristics of service and, paradoxically, self-denial.[41] Yet the very intensity of this spiritual search put men under severe tension between the demands of masculine self-assertion and agency on the one hand, and the obliteration of self which marked Christian salvation on the other.[42]

For men, it was the family, where the adult male represented and supported all others defined as within his orbit, which was the ordained space where individuality – as differentiated from abstract individualism – could be maintained. By building on former notions about the master/father, the nineteenth-century concept of 'head of household', as defined in the newly created *Census of Population*, could be combined with individualism. Nevertheless, alongside the rational abstract and masculine individual, there followed a shadowy figure based on a different order of morality, an apolitical, less bounded self, associated with personal emotion, parenthood and, increasingly, notions of good taste. Although this conception could be taken up by men, its highest expression came to be the bodily incarnation of delicate Victorian middle-class womanhood. Exponents of classical liberalism and utilitarian thinkers alike were content to leave the sphere of 'moral and domestic economy' to what was conceived as the natural order of the family.

The importance of this usually unspoken dimension of nineteenth-century individualism has been highlighted for the 1830s and 1840s when artisans and labourers queried its basic tenets. Working-class communities were hammering out their own version of morality and gender. Eventually a conception of the adult male as value-creator as well as supporter of dependants also became incorporated into a version of working-class culture producing one version of late nineteenth-century masculinity.[43]

Thus individualism did not just inhabit political liberalism or doctrines of political economy. If we accept the premise that the individual was based on difference – and, in particular, sexual difference – then it follows that views of what constituted the sexual and its relationship to gender must also have been affected during this period. Though only limited attention has been paid to this question so far, it would seem that in the seventeenth century it had been recognized that both women and men had carnal appetites, but sexuality was not yet an entity divorced from other aspects of life. Within this view, women were held to be especially sexually voracious, their appetites especially threatening.[44] By the end of the eighteenth century, an idea of *sexuality* as a separate entity began to appear. Yet that sexuality did not take the same form for men and for women, and it differed again for ladies and women, gentlemen and others. Class, nationality and gender – all were related to this novel phenomenon.

By the beginning of the nineteenth century, lines of sexual identity were hardening. A definition of femininity – at least for the literate classes – was evolving into a passionless maternity or weak sensuality, only roused by men's action. Such a view may seem to sit strangely with the Victorian positioning of women as 'the sex'. The key to such an involuted construction lies in the disembodied masculinity previously discussed. Rational individual man had become a 'Cartesian mind that happened to be located in biological matter in motion'.[45] Male sexuality was banished to a naturalized realm and often visualized as an hydraulic model, or in keeping with the dominant market metaphor, a spermatic economy of saving and spending.[46]

Distancing from the body was inherent in rational individualism. This perception, for example, underlay Hegel's conception that man's real and substantial life was the state, science, combat, work – activities which brought him into opposition with the outside world *and* himself.[47] Man as knower, man as doer, man as the latter phrase implies, was potentially capable of self-control (including sexual 'continence') denied to dependent and demeaned others.

During the nineteenth century, for men, the location and timing of both work-processes and sexuality became more compartmentalized. Play and leisure now became defined as the opposite of occupation or work; *ergo*, sexuality was equated with the frivolous, the childish, the feminine. Beauty and desire were confined to women's bodies. If promoted by men's bodies, such desire was transmuted to a fascination with muscularity or romanticized physical strength, or typecast as deviant effeminacy with homoerotic overtones. The leeching away of colour, varied and sensuous texture and detail from middle- and upper-class men's clothing in exchange for sombre, dark and shapeless suits by the mid-nineteenth century is emblematic of this transformation. Thus the interplay of views about rationality, individuality and sexuality can be followed in the complicated web of gendered meanings mapped out on the grid of the human body.[48] By mid-century a cartography had been created which distinguished lady from woman, respectability from pauperism and, increasingly, the English from the foreign, particularly colonial, dark-skinned (and ex-slave) others.[49]

The importance of these constructions partially rested on the central place of *property* in English culture and law. The qualifications for English political leadership had long rested on the basis of property. In the seventeenth century, the conception of property had begun to shift from a set of *rights* to a *thing*. Rights to property were now seen as 'unlimited in amount, unconditional in the performance of social functions and freely transferable'.[50] By the eighteenth century, absolute property, originally conceived as land, extended to the growing forms of liquid capital in real estate, stock and plant, bonds and shares. But this type of property, especially now that land was increasingly available for mortgage, was identified as a personal and *individual* possession.

The ultimate posession of property was possession of the individual self – the men able to dispose of property in themselves as well as in objects, to control (if necessary to sell) their bodies, their skills and their labour. Not surprisingly, many of these constructions emerged during the eighteenth- and nineteenth-century debates over slavery in the colonies as well as relations between employer and workman as opposed to master and servant.

Property relations were now based on the idea of a rational, free individual acting through contract. The individual man (with the possible exception of aristocratic heirs constrained by entail) moved beyond the family as the basic property-owning unit. Women, children, servants and other dependants were defined as belonging *through* the family, *through* the relationship of master and servant. They lacked, precisely, that freedom to dispose of themselves. As Henrietta Moore has said, 'concepts of property are ultimately bound up with concepts of the person' and woman's capacity to own in an active sense depends on her legal and actual separation from other people.[51]

By the nineteenth century, there are numerous examples of such a conception in action, one of the most powerful being the expectations written into the New Poor Law of 1834, which abolished an allowance system based on needs of the known local population and used instead a rationalized division into categories of destitution. The attempt to single out able-bodied individuals (almost always adult men) using incarceration in a gaol-like workhouse for the first time assumed complete dependency of wife and children – at least in theory. The Bastardy Amendment to the Poor Law which put all responsibility for illegitimate children on to the woman, reinforced both Evangelical as well as individualist assumptions.[52]

The importance of this position was highlighted from the third quarter of the nineteenth century in a series of legal debates and cases centred on the issue of whether or not women could be considered *persons*. One of the most famous 'persons' case centred on the attempt of sufficiently qualified women to enter the University of Edinburgh medical faculty. British judges, working without a written constitution and in a system which rested heavily on the precedent of common law, formed the argument that women were not persons. They based this argument on the so-called protected position of women within the family.[53] A *person* had to be free to 'own' himself.

It is true that some women, within the family and particularly as producers of male children, were considered to play a vital role as *conduits* of property. They had certain, highly circumscribed, rights as property owners. However, these provisions were mainly meant to ensure that the family property would pass safely from their own fathers to their sons.[54] In the lower and middle classes widows also had some control over property, including the goodwill of small businesses and rights to continue their dead husband's trade.[55] Such variations bring out strikingly the crucial role of marital status in the construction of the nineteenth-century category 'woman' as opposed to the rational individualism which constructed 'man'.

These basic ideas about *rationality*, *individualism* and *property*, and their gendered nature, ran deep into the consciousness, the mental maps of the articulate and powerful. They were the groundwork upon which conceptions of public and private were built. And it was the collection of masculine personae, the individuals inhabiting a range of public domains, that made up the potential public of the community and the nation. Women, children, servants, the poor, the foreign were seen as having no community, no inherent right to a national identity on their own behalf; they were mobile as they followed their natural masters.

Constructing a Political Public Sphere

Early modern historians have emphasized that households at every social level were both 'public' and 'private' in the modern sense of the dichotomy. Productive work, political decision-making, festival and ritual all took place where people lived and ate; the division between house space and street or village green was not rigidly drawn. The notion of a separate and 'private' life was less evident than in the modern period.[56] Slowly, from the sixteenth century onwards, this pattern began to change, although in uneven, halting fashion. For example, the houses of the well-to-do began to separate sleeping quarters from more public rooms by the use of staircases and corridors.[57] The picture is confusing, however, and the intricate relationship of these developments to gender has yet to be explored in detail.

From at least the time of the early Greeks, there has been some notion of a public sphere, if not a public place. The English language, indeed, leaves evidence of some underlying continuities. Could it be significant that, as Nancy Fraser tells us, there is an etymological connection between 'public' and 'pubic', 'a graphic trace of the fact that the possession of a penis was a requirement for speaking in public' and mirrored in a similar linguistic connection between 'testimony' and 'testicle'?[58]

From long before the modern period, then, the conceptual relationship between *public* and *masculinity* has been marked, the male adult head was the representative of his family and household to the larger world, whatever the actual arrangements on the ground. The ability to exercise licit authority within a public arena, however the latter was defined, was based on the possession of independence and agency. These were qualities equated with virility and a fundamental constituent of a privileged masculine status – a status, however, by no means available to all males.[59] As in the case of the rational individual, those in a servile condition to the will of another, for example serfs or slaves, were not rightfully capable of taking part in political discourse or political action. Since women were only to be regarded through their subordinate relationship to master, father, brother or husband, there was no way they could be conceived of as members of the polis. Once again, the equivocal position of widows in some situations is instructive here.

Neither the Protestant Reformation nor the leaders of the sixteenth- and seventeenth-century scientific revolution challenged these inherited notions. They continued to influence the substantial changes in legal systems as these shifted from a basis in feudal military service. Throughout all these developments, it was women's dependence through marriage which remained the key to the construct of that category; the older notion of male guardianship shifted ground but was not abandoned.[60]

Eighteenth-century Enlightenment culture built on these traditions of classical republicanism and civic humanism, particularly in the concept of 'civic virtue', of which 'republican virtue' was a variant.[61] As a challenge to the absolutism of monarchy and aristocracy, those men (sic) who could gather in rational discourse –

in other words literate men of some property – would promote an ideal of the common good.[62]

The most powerful case for the idea of a 'bourgeois public' as a high moment in social development has been made by Jürgen Habermas.[63] The nub of his argument derives from a critique of classical (pre-Gramscian) Marxist analysis which makes a fatal elision between the state and the public, neglecting the area of 'civil society', a space where consideration of the common good can be *rationally* discussed and promoted, a *reasoned* discourse in which arguments, not status or traditions, were to be decisive.[64] Habermas's 'privatized individual' in these constructions is consistently, if unconsciously, masculine.

The Habermas formulation, 'civic society', also bears a striking resemblance to the implicit bourgeois and male image of the eighteenth century. Civic virtue itself rested on a notion of abstracted and rational individualism which encoded a potent form of masculinity. As Joan Landes writes in connection with the French Revolution, 'the exclusion of women from the bourgeois public was not incidental but central to its incarnation . . . the bourgeois public is essentially, not just contingently, masculinist'.[65] The ignoring of gender as a formative element in civic society is enhanced by Habermas's placing of the formation of subjectivity, the precondition for creating the public, within (and moving outwards from) the patriarchal conjugal family. In this he is not far removed from those Enlightenment thinkers who saw virtue as being naturally formed within the conjugal family.[66] Women's demarcation within the bourgeois family would have made the move outwards extremely problematic.

For even while paying homage to putative feminine superior morality, women's supposed erotic appeal to male passions was seen as a corrupter of civic virtue, a point Mary Ryan's citation of this American Freemason's Toast to Women from 1828 illustrates well:

> The Fair Sex-Excluded by necessity from participation in our labors; we profess equality, the presence of woman (sic) would make us slaves, and convert the temple of wisdom into that of love.[67]

Dismay at the supposed fall of this public man into the welter of mass democracy[68] has been challenged by the idea of alternative, if subaltern and contesting, 'publics' on the part of sections within the working class, ethnic minorities and even of women. In other words, the simple assumption of *the* public has to be fractured into a *variety* of publics, all of them making claims to legitimacy and some of them found in unlikely places such as city streets, village greens or the public house (sic). Ceremonies such as parades, the ritual celebration of holidays as well as the more familiar all-male territories of certain voluntary societies or Working Men's Clubs could become contested areas where 'outsiders' might make their mark.

But these, too, have to be seen as areas where statements about gender relations were being made. It has been argued that the organization of coffee houses and debating societies – the archetypical site of the new democratic civic space –

consciously excluded women in contrast to salon culture and the political intrigue of aristocratic/gentry households.[69] Yet there appears to have been a paradox in this ambitious project of reform: 'a new-modelling of the code for the public conduct of men in accordance with the norms of private mixed company'.[70] This code included control of alcohol and was one of the aims of contemporaneous Freemasonry. Such elements of restraint were part of wider notions of domesticity clustering around the private sphere which were being applied to men's public behaviour. But these same novel standards of propriety also assumed that ladies would remain at home and would not take part in public discourse, as witnessed by the lively exchanges over women's role in the London debating societies of the 1780s.[71]

Yet women were actors as well as spectators in those places defined as 'public'. Women could, and did, openly or covertly challenge the equation of the public arena as a purely masculine preserve. In a range of strategies from leading food riots to raiding brothels, from acting as an audience to or participants in 'street theatre', to boycotting the shops of political opponents, to writing and publishing across a range of genres and – especially towards the end of the nineteenth century – even within local politics women were present, although often overlooked by contemporary observers as well as historians.

Women also resisted exclusion and enlarged their role in institutions where the gender boundaries were not so firmly drawn. The feminine ideal had a recognized place in the church, together with that other site of moral authority, philanthropic activities, even if real women still found themselves marginalized and constrained in many ways. For some sections of society the church did not fit neatly into a public/private dichotomy at all, precisely because of the recognized presence of women (and children).[72] It should be noted in this connection that Habermas completely neglects any discussion of religion as part of the public.

The nineteenth century represents the apogee of bourgeois culture, most particularly the myriad voluntary societies and pressure groups which have been taken as the key to Britain's middle-class identity.[73] The same period that witnessed the development of the modern state also spawned the growth of 'quasi-public' arenas associated with claims for middle-class incorporation into leadership. Many of these organizations were for men only; others followed a pattern of the more prestigious men in leadership positions with women and lower-middle-class subalterns doing much of the local and routine work.

Meanwhile, in the social realm, nineteenth-century upper- and upper-middle-class 'Society', with its female power-brokers in the form of political hostesses, blurred distinct lines between political institutions and the household.[74] The confusion and debate over the status category *gentility*, differentiated as it was for *gentlemen* and *ladies*, indicates that in practice, at this level, the public/private divide was not easily sustained. What were the correct worldly duties for upper-class women as opposed to the private concerns of nursery, kitchen and parlour? How far did duty reach beyond the family, beyond 'people like us', our class? These issues affected both men and women, although in different ways.

Even beyond these tensions, however, the construction of a private sphere within the home as a peculiarly feminine domain, undoubtedly did give some nineteenth-century women a power base from which to make counter-claims on civil society, creating the possibility for the basis of a 'women's culture'. This concept, which has been heavily criticized by recent feminist historians, still deserves some attention. Mary Ryan, for example, has shown how the decline of 'public' holiday ritual and its replacement by home-centred festivities such as the modern Christmas, began well before being co-opted by commercial interests. Women, as by far the majority of 'shoppers', took over the public spaces of cities and towns in carrying out preparations for such putatively private rituals.[75]

Yet for all these novel and ingenious ways in which feminist thinkers have remodelled the idea of the public as a contested concept as well as contested space, the fact remains that, in both civic society and the state, public is usually understood in its original, highly rational, individualist and masculinist sense. Among other consequences, this has meant that in both iconography and fact women who enter, and are seen to be, in those places, spaces and times defined as public are open to suspicion. The terms *public women* and *women of the streets* immediately conjure up the prostitute – a primary marker of 'woman' as solely a sexual being. By the late nineteenth century, the 'fallen woman', by her independent and public behaviour now cast out beyond the pale of respectable society, was an image resonating across all classes.[76]

The exceptional difficulty women faced on entering the *formally defined* political domain and their continued lack of an authoritative political style reflects the way public life has been constructed as a key element in masculinity, of the category *man*. This point is driven home by implicit imagery, as in the incongruity of feminine clothing in political, professional and business settings, so obvious to nineteenth-century feminist activists, holding on to their hairpins, great flapping hats and floor-length skirts in the rough and tumble of political meetings. But the practical as well as image problems of women dressing for going into the public domain is not overcome to this day – whether to flaunt femininity in ruffles and short skirts or go for 'power dressing' in tailored suits? Not to speak of the lack of pockets for pens, keys, etc., a lack hardly compensated for by the ubiquitous, if not ridiculous, handbag.

The masculine nature of formal public institutions has been especially evident in certain branches of the state, for example in foreign affairs. A close examination has shown how the state itself is 'constituted by gender relations and shaped by the vicissitudes of sexual politics'.[77]

Finally, it should never be forgotten that throughout the modern period the public realm, and increasingly the state, had become the single legitimate arena for the use of force. Up to the end of the eighteenth century, the fighting of duels to settle disputes marked a certain type of class-specific masculinity.[78] By the mid-nineteenth century, procedures such as duelling and the reign of the justices of the peace with their amateur constables (roles filled by men) were phased out and the organs of the state took over the regulation of disputes through police forces. It was taken for granted that women would be excluded from these new offices. Early twentieth-century attempts to introduce women into the police force and armed services have raised some of the most fiercely debated, and ridiculed, passages in modern sexual politics.[79]

Most women, by definition, have been denied direct access to that ultimate form of agency: the openly observed and sanctioned power over their own body and possession of others' bodies in the name of the whole community. Belief in the inherent masculinity of war – the ultimate legitimate violence – was created precisely by leaving that which was seen as feminine behind, by the supposed capacity to rise above what femininity symbolically represented. In this conception, men in war moved into the universal and truly ethical because they transcended 'womanhood'. Women were regarded as the embodiment (sic) of the individual material body, of natural feelings and private interests. They were able to serve their nation only by negation, by giving up what was most precious in the private sphere, that is their fiancés, husbands, brothers and sons. As the famous First World War poster proclaimed, 'Women of England say "GO" '.[80]

The almost universal embargo on women bearing arms, the supreme case of the use of legitimate violence, became a keystone in the arch of gender dimorphism.[81] This has a particular resonance in England's long, feudal-based link between arms-bearing and landownership, the almost mystical basis of landed property as the sole basis for leadership. In the imagination of English nineteenth-century nationalism this continued, even if much of the rhetoric for such a 'tradition' came to be sifted through the mock-chivalry of middle-class culture as in the novels of a Sir Walter Scott.

Constructing an Economic Public Sphere

There is no question that the reconsideration of 'the public' has been tremendously liberating to feminist thought, not least in opening debates about the relationship of a gendered state to a gendered civil society. Encouragingly, some of this work uses an empirical as well as a theoretical approach.[82] But confusion remains where 'public' also may refer to the official economy of paid employment within the market, as opposed to the multiple tasks and activities carried on outside the cash nexus (mainly, although not only) within the family and household.[83]

In the model used by many feminist political theorists, while recognizing that economic inequality has crucial effects for the exercise of power within the political sphere, there is a tendency to set aside the market as an external factor.[84] But historians should be aware that the eighteenth-century project of creating the post-Enlightenment public included the *division* of 'an economy' from 'the polity'. Indeed, carving up the world into these separate arenas of specialized knowledge became one of the great transformations of the nineteenth century. The claims for demarcation and specialized expertise were themselves linked with a form of mas-culine prowess. 'Woman' tended to be held in a category which was both more general, i.e. unspecialized, *and* more particular, i.e. less implicated in universal and rational discourse.[85] Indeed, the effort to separate 'an economy' as a special domain with its own iron laws from politics and the state was part of the clamouring masculinity of the eighteenth- and nineteenth-century bourgeois challenge.[86]

Unfortunately, feminist historians, who have done so much excellent empirical research have, on the whole, tended to take for granted the construction of a separate market based in the monetary economy, on the one hand, and the family/household on the other. The emphasis has been on demonstrating the productive and demanding nature of unpaid work, with waged work (or, for the better off, the organization of kinship and the ownership of property) treated as separate from familial life. The effort has been to find women *in* the waged economy. Marxist analysis, which does understand the market as a social construction and thus offers a key to the problem, has not prevented even Marxist-feminist analysis from regarding the economy as a separate entity with its own laws of operation.[87] This myopia may be partly due to the way contemporary organizations and discourses have been built up and have firmly institutionalized a market economy. However, it is up to historians to show how this was created, on what terms and with what assumptions.

Before the mid-seventeenth century, the periodic chaos and uncontrollability, the 'fickleness' of commercial transactions had, at times, been associated with the feminine. 'Lady Credit' was equated with 'fantasy, passion and dynamic change . . . sought passionately and inconstantly and with . . . hysterical fluc-tuations of the urges towards it'.[88] The market, which was to become the central concept for rational political economy, was still a place where the trader expected to make personal ventures within it, not against it. Market-places and fairs with their rituals of exchange were not free but hedged round with protective measures reinforced by guilds, city authorities and merchants themselves.[89]

By the eighteenth century, the personal contact in a bargain over the exchange of material goods or services began to be replaced by more abstract pricing and accounting systems. Credit began to take on a new dimension of financial worth, increasingly divorced from its other meaning, 'reputation'.[90] Women's 'credit', however, continued to be largely defined by sexual availability, through ties to her male relatives, thus emphasizing the gendered colouring which flooded the gradual development of a market concept.[91]

Well into the eighteenth century, there was still much suspicion of the growing 'paper screen' of credit mechanisms and fierce antagonism to the new breed of agents, factors and money-men who operated the system. Nevertheless, a concep-tion of inexorable laws, cast more like the mechanical laws of gravity – rational and immutable, open to interpretation and manipulation only by the knowing (mascu-line) subject – developed alongside institutions such as banks, stock exchanges, corn and other commodity markets. Such laws were predicated on quantitative properties in people as well as land and moveable goods; all included the common denominator of price.

The assignment of a calculable value to more and more areas of lived experience grew with the increase in circulation of money. Money was becoming a currency to measure all value but what could not (or what was ruled as should not) be so measured; what did not have a price, now was defined as of no value. One definition of a private sphere was precisely all which lay outside the pricing mentality. As for the woman embedded in the domesticity coming to epitomize that type of private domain, as innumerable funeral orations declared, 'her price was above rubies'.

If we look closely at the eighteenth-century construction of *political economy*, these developments are reflected in the shift from Adam Smith's wider concerns, his consideration of moral sentiments, to the later work where he develops the tradition of making women and their work – both productive and reproductive – invisible, ignoring the sexual division of labour and its fundamental contribution to the capitalist system.[92]

Women and the domestic sphere are nowhere mentioned in the major works of Ricardo or Malthus on political economy – despite the latter's interest in population analysis.[93] The new science (sic) of economics took as its starting-point the rational, individual 'economic *man*', operating in a supposedly gender-neutral market; economics itself was defined in terms of the work of men.[94]

Nevertheless, as with the underlying concepts of rationality and the individual, the market and its relationship to morality became – as it has remained to this day – a matter of continuing contention.[95] Amoral liberal economics remained tied to a moral social organism, caught in the struggle to divide production and consumption, commerce and philanthropy, economy and family. One consequence of this tension was that, as Maxine Berg has pointed out, by defining women and children's work within the labour market, 'as a problem of social morality rather than economics, Whig reformers could protect political economy from the criticisms of its methodology and its doctrines on industrialization'.[96]

There is further evidence of the clouded relationship between the economy and private morality in the way timekeeping, accounting procedures and writing were used to control religious and household as well as business affairs.[97] While 'political economists were moving away from their earlier concern with general social issues toward purely economic considerations'[98] the basic unit of business still remained the family enterprise, and was not fully defined until after the introduction of limited liability in the 1850s.

Long into the nineteenth century, in English law, the firm or enterprise was treated as a 'person', a legal individual. One reason that it was possible to operate with such a fiction was because, as we have already seen, that 'individual', that 'economic actor', was a masculine fiction. So, too, were partners in a partnership, the other main form of business organization, assumed to be male.[99] It was not until the third quarter of the century that a concept of the business corporation emerged, not coincidentally at the same period as the neo-classical school of economics signified a transformation from a labour-based to a utility-based theory of value.[100] Under the influence of Alfred Marshall, one of the leading figures in this shift, the concept of the labour market as completely distinct from the household had a direct effect on the English *Census of Occupations* which, in turn, gave total primacy to the model of narrow economic rationality which has become the template for modelling economies worldwide.[101]

Knowledge of this past history establishes that the concept of *an economy* is built on an already-taken-for-granted private sphere of physical, emotional and social reproduction usually organized through the family, the daily and life-cycle re-creation of human beings as well as institutions without which the free-floating and abstract market could not exist.[102] It is a conception which applies to all aspects of the market – for property and money as well as for labour.

This market model was the cornerstone of the new 'science' of economics. Creating, using and surviving the laws of the market bolstered middle-class masculinity. While aristocratic manhood might have once given unquestioned prestige and power, the market came to be defined as a new battleground where men could test their virility and celebrate previously despised notions of *work* (while at the same time amassing fortunes to challenge the immense resources of landowner-ship). Adam Smith himself argued that the market was a place where the individual could make himself visible through his *independence*, proved by his ability to support his own domestic dependants: 'to balance the dependants of the great, and he has no other fund to pay for them from but the labour of his body and the activity of his mind'.[103] As the eighteenth century advanced, honour was increas-ingly understood to be a particularly stable and solid form of credit but the content of honour had to be transformed to include 'work' as part of *manhood*.[104]

Manhood, independence (and its concomitant ability to support dependants) and work were becoming an indivisible entity for the early nineteenth-century middle class summed up in Carlyle's 'Gospel of Work' where life was seen as a battle and 'God-like Labour' became man's supreme and essential activity. By knowing his work and doing it, a man perfected himself. The man who delighted in his business, 'He shall stand before Kings'; the chivalry of work was far nobler than the chivalry of fighting wars.[105]

By mid-century, the belief in an individual as captain of his fate bit deeper into the social fabric. Some working-class men had begun to repudiate notions of manhood based on physical prowess and to focus on control of passion, sobriety and a form of domesticity which, even among radicals, cast women as sisters and wives to the artisan community rather than actors in their own right.[106] The short-lived Owenite feminist effort was superseded by men eager to defend their honourable status as craftsmen from cheap female and juvenile labour.[107]

For the notion of the male breadwinner which lay at the heart of nineteenth-century masculinity was not only imposed from above. A negotiated version of middle-class domesticity was partially adopted within large sections of the working class, despite the fact that only a narrow stratum could afford to put its precepts into practice.[108] At the same time, long experience of work-processes shaped working-class men's 'property in skill' which underlay claims to masculine exclusivity; domestic respectability and property in labour laid the foundations for working-class men's claim to the franchise of 1867 and 1884.[109]

As feminists have been pointing out for some time, such a basically masculine conception automatically and irrevocably excludes much of the work that women do and have done.[110] This can be traced in the way the word *work* itself has narrowed over the nineteenth century. For upper- and middle-class women, their 'work' came to mean amateur sewing, embroidery and fancy needlework. For working-class women it could refer to both waged labour and all their multiple household duties. But by the late twentieth century, across the class spectrum, work has come to be almost solely limited to waged labour outside the home.

It is not surprising, then, that waged labour for women has historically been problematic; nor is it surprising that the ideal that women should never have to 'work' became a fundamental part of the dominant Victorian ethic. The phrase 'working woman' had an uneasy and derogatory overtone compared to the dignity of 'the working man'. These are not just semantic niceties but rather reflect the fact that, as Joan Acker points out, 'the labour of men is . . . privileged because only that labour, conceptualized as gender-neutral, is theorized in the concepts that allow us to understand the system as a whole'.[111]

The implications of these assumptions have been profound, but so pervasive as to be often overlooked. The most obvious is the continued effort to keep the category 'woman' as attached to society via the family and thus part of the moral domain, untainted by the market.[112] Conversely, there has been a constant effort not to muddy the waters in creating a model of the market. For example unpaid work has been deliberately excluded in the concept of the Gross National Product.

One result of these procedures has been that women's skills and experience have been consistently conceived as generalized, almost natural, attributes of femininity. Thus every woman was expected to be able to cook, clean the house, sew, take care of invalids and young children. A girl's childhood was defined by absorbing expertise in these tasks as part of core feminine identity; if she did not do so it was considered a personal and moral failure. Ever since the introduction of formal schooling in the second half of the nineteenth century, there have been debates about whether and how these feminine skills should be taught. Attempts to turn them into 'Domestic Science' have not usually succeeded and their status has remained uncertain if not despised.

One reason for such low regard is the widespread availability of often semi-trained women able to carry out these tasks anywhere, anytime. Such extensive 'dilution of skill' has meant that it has been almost impossible for women to close ranks and create scarcity. It was recognized by contemporaries that governesses were a depressed and despised group for the same reason that needlewomen were a distressed class; as every woman could read, write and sew a little, every uneducated woman who was destitute became a seamstress and every educated (or half-educated) woman became a governess. But frequently it was the women themselves who were blamed for the work being 'ill done'.[113]

The ability to perform these tasks, in some cases to an exceedingly high standard, when undertaken by women for the households as sisters, wives, mothers, aunts or servants was hardly defined as expertise at all in comparison to, say, artisanal skills carefully cherished and protected by male practitioners. Thus the benefits of trade union or professional association formal training and occupational closure have seldom been available to women. The existence of armies of amateurs hovering in the wings would undermine such attempts. Quite aside from the pressures of childcare, housekeeping and 'people work' on women's time and energy, this fundamental *dis*attachment from the labour market put women, as a category, at a permanent disadvantage, as innumerable studies have shown. Sidney Webb puzzled over fitting women into the wage labour system in the first issue of *The Economic Journal* in 1891. In trying to make sense of the differentials paid to women and men for similar work (which he failed to do) he noted that '. . . it is impossible to overlook the fact that woman has something else to sell besides her labour' and but he went on to condemn the prevailing assumption that women needed less, in terms of both physical and mental demands.[114]

What is not nearly so often recognized is that this disadvantage for women has structured an *advantaged* labour market for the category 'men'. The existence of large amounts of low-paid, casual work, often done by women, allows for the organization of smaller numbers of highly paid, more expert positions almost always filled by men.[115] During industrialization, cheap female labour performed manual operations at home as well as in factories and workshops, giving skilled male labour incentives for formal training and disciplined work patterns. Employers, too, had the benefit of being able to unload finishing processes on outworkers, mainly women.[116] Thus the concept of the 'unproductive housewife' which emerged in the latter part of the nineteenth century was not just a by-product of a new definition of productive labour that valorized participation in the market (as even some feminist analysis has suggested);[117] it lay at the foundations of the original, masculine conception. The sexual division of labour has deeply affected the way work itself is structured. The nineteenth-century development of medicine into low-status, lower-paid care (female nurses) and high-status, more highly rewarded diagnosis and treatment (male doctors) is only one of the most striking examples.

Similar assumptions constrained those women who did operate in the economic sphere from gaining recognition and capitalizing on their success. For example, in a small town where a local tanner was fêted with a dinner at the inn in celebration of his many minor public posts as well as his business achievements, the equally prosperous female owner of the biggest millinery establishment in town could not possibly have received such formal recognition.[118]

Gender, then, affects the way the labour market and work were *defined* as well as how they operated. From Poor Law institutions to charitable bodies, women's *un*employment (particularly married women's) was consistently overlooked as non-problematic if not non-existent, for if employment is essentially male, women's unemployment becomes difficult to confront.[119]

Similarly, women's access to property had been partially defined through the doctrine of 'coveture' where, under common law, her legal and economic personality was incorporated into that of her husband. Even single women, although technically able to operate in the property market as 'feme sole', tended to be considered as dependent, as beneficiaries rather than generators of property. Through the long process of reform of married women's property from the mid-nineteenth century, attempts were made to give wives' property protection from the total control of their husbands in imitation of the system enjoyed by wealthier women under laws of equity. Nevertheless, these piecemeal measures, along with divorce and marriage-reform legislation, never addressed the basic construction of gender relations as constituted through marriage and kinship. And this formulation continued to survive permeation by the idea of contract which transformed most other social relationships at the time.[120]

These constructions of labour and property concealed the fact that women's capital, their labour and their reproductive powers were often appropriated by male relatives through institutional forms such as the trust. Individually, women's resources were put towards furthering a family estate, farm or enterprise in return for support. In the aggregate, women's resources provided a crucial source for development of capital as well as labour, a fact often overlooked in traditional economic history.

Because of the way the category 'woman' had been reconstructed in relation to the concept of the labour and property markets, real women's mediated position was always riddled with tension, evident in the difficulties which have plagued the analysis of a range of institutions. Prostitution – that is, putting under the rubric of the market that which was supposed to be most distinct from its abstracted impersonal form – has continued to evoke particular revulsion. Part of the fascination with prostitutes, their identification with pornography and perverse practices, rests on this transgression of such deeply held notions of distinctions between these realms. This was exemplified in the 1860s and 70s debates over state regulation of prostitution through the Contagious Diseases Acts as well as the late nineteenth-century moral panic over social purity and 'white slavery'.[121] In Laura Englestein's words prostitution was 'the Enlightenment in nightmare form – a caricature of universalism, a network of global intercourse, of interchangeable private female parts loosed from the domestic into the public sphere, transforming the particular (my wife, your daughter) into a public woman accessible to all men.'[122]

Similar processes can be seen at work in the development of welfare systems around the same period. Once the immutable assumption of female dependency is understood, it could be argued that the emerging welfare state helped to create the very gender relations it took as normative by basing benefits on an insurance system structured around the male wage.[123]

We also know that living, breathing women continued their productive activities and engaged in the world of the market economy in many guises, from paid employment to investment; the exceptional wealthy woman could and did wield considerable power, especially in her local community.[124] Yet women's contribution was, and to an extent still is, defined as external to the model of an economy. Economic institutions, from banks and commodity markets to stock exchanges, were founded as male territories. Their architecture, organization and legal regulations discouraged, if they did not preclude, women's participation. The London Stock Exchange, for instance, finally allowed women to operate on the floor only in 1973.

These organizational constraints were serious obstacles for both individual women and women as collective actors. Even after later nineteenth-century reforms, although women could possess income and property, they found it difficult to amass or readily control *active* capital.[125] Laws of inheritance which denied married women capacity to direct the use of their property after death (and could curtail even that of widows by the terms of their husbands' testaments) compounded this basic economic weakness.[126] The ultimate logic of this situation was that women as individuals and more especially *as a group* were virtually incapable of generating lasting wealth. As Martha Vicinus has vividly illustrated, in the late nineteenth century communities made up of single women free from family ties, which began to spring up around such organizations as schools, settlement houses and nursing orders, had great difficulty surviving as economically viable, public organizations.[127]

PART II AS YE SOW, SO SHALL YE REAP:
CONCEPTS AND THEIR CONSEQUENCES

Gender, Class and Status

The gendered substructure under discussion has had massive impact on Western political and social institutions and systems of thought, as well as on people's lives. The concept of the rational individual and his domain, the category of public sociality became not only an idealization of nineteenth-century society in general but also the primary orientation of social scientific inquiry. Indeed, the extension of the idea of science to social science has been seen as a key moment in the creation of a liberal public sphere.[128]

The fledgling discipline of sociology was moulded during the volatile decades of the early nineteenth century, coterminous with, and contributing to, the struggles for dominance of these basic concepts. The keystone of the sociological edifice, the concept of *class*, was based on the premise of a totally separate productive order. In this formulation, family and kinship were taken as necessary but natural corollaries and were constructed around a similar concept of the individual self.[129]

The category 'woman' was explicitly located within the construct of family and kinship, just as 'man' was assumed within the economy, polity and the realms of knowledge. Sociologists (and historians influenced by them) have assumed the family as secondary and peripheral, always responsive to changes in the public sphere, although some latter-day social historians have begun to argue that, in special cases, lines of influence might have run the other way.

But both assumptions rest on the original gendered dualisms already explored. The proliferation of 'hyphen solutions', such as Marxist-feminism, to bind together the separate spheres has not proved adequate. It is increasingly evident that the most valiant attempts to extend concepts of rationality or universalism to women, and thus to embrace them within the class system, are bound to founder on the fact that, as Joan Scott reminds us, these 'languages' are already dualistic and already gendered.[130]

For in classical Marxist and Weberian as well as more modern, formulations class is based on assumptions about an economic sphere derived from neo-classical economic theory.[131] The implied abstract notion of a *mode of production*, as separated from consumption and other social tasks, assumes a separate productive order which embraces the fiction of disembodied actors with capacity to sell labour away from the person (the body) of the labourer. But since women were defined by their familial relationships, they potentially lacked both the ability and the legitimacy to sell their labour *freely*. Implicit in this disability was the idea that women were inevitably embodied beings, trailing their sexuality always with them, while men were somehow abstracted from their own material substance.

The 'domino effect' of such a model can be readily appreciated. The basis of class analysis rests on the relationship of individuals and groups to the economic structure of society. It follows, then, that if women as a category (and married women in particular) were outside the basic capitalist system centred on production, they could never become – at least directly – part of the class structure and, *pari passu*, take part in class action. Indeed, within the middle class, women were often viewed as trivial, non-political creatures, while within the working class, women, with their constant carping about domestic concerns, might be regarded as a dead weight pulling down the political aspirations of the the rational working man.

While sociologists have wrestled with these issues particularly in relation to class identity and voting behaviour, most historians have been rather more unsophisticated, often using a rule-of-thumb descriptive notion of class. In so doing they unconsciously betray their lack of understanding of the way gender has structured that concept. Witness, for example, such phrases as 'the working classes with their wives and families'.[132] In her critique of E.P. Thompson, Joan Scott notes that 'the organization of the story and the master codes that structure the narrative are gendered in such a way as to confirm rather than challenge the masculine representations of class'.[133]

Feminist historians should keep in mind that such conceptual limitations go back to the underlying concept of a market economy, which informally also excludes paupers, servants, children (and in the USA, blacks or in the UK, the Irish) from class analysis. These groups are thus precluded a place within class action, an exclusion which would be extended in colonial situations, carried as part of the cultural baggage of an expanding Empire. Ultimately, male, adult, ethnic superiority has had the power to impose the original definitions from which our models are derived.

Class, which plays such a powerful role in modern British culture, is, however, more complicated than such models, both in the experience of everyday life and in the hands of social investigators. A working definition of class usually employs some non-economic, even symbolic, indicators of boundaries beyond the question of ownership of the means of production. As the sociologist, Rosemary Crompton has recently admitted, in practice it is exceptionally difficult to separate *theoretically* as well as empirically the 'economic' from the social or 'cultural'.[134]

The traditionally invoked sociological division between *manual* and *non-manual* occupations emphasizes other, more relational, aspects of class. These 'status considerations' or claims to social honour, must ultimately depend on having the wealth and resources to maintain them. It is generally recognized, however, that social honour is never exactly synonymous with material and financial power, as, for example, in the case of the *nouveau riche* entrepreneur on the one hand, or the impecunious gentry on the other. Wealth or force do not translate easily into high status for usually life-style intervenes, and that life-style may take more than one generation to inculcate. The escalating difficulties of class analysis raised by the expansion of the salariat, developments of later twentieth-century technologies and a large, mainly feminized service sector indicate that the standard (and ungendered) version of class analysis may need to become more complicated and nuanced.[135]

As illustration, let us consider the early nineteenth century, the period when classical social scientific thought was being formed. At that time the growth of more specialized functions, larger-scale operations and market contacts beyond the local area meant that men with resources in property or skill became more responsible for the external affairs of buying and selling. The small manufacturer no longer donned an apron to handle his goods physically, but remained closeted in his counting house or dealt with customers, while the farmer of larger acreage spent much of his time at market, only riding out to the fields to give orders from on high to labourers on foot.

The deep-seated derogation of *manual* work, the preoccupation with clean, unblemished 'non-working' hands, was built into class relations at a deep, even subconscious level; early factory workers were, for instance, referred to simply as (genderless) 'hands'. For men, however, while markers such as clean, soft hands might establish a higher position in the class hierarchy, too great a preoccupation with dress, with cleanliness and finicky attention to personal appearance, might border on the effeminate.

Commercial and professional occupations which exhibited such features, particularly those under the authority of an employer or master such as clerical and salaried workers, as well as the despised male domestic servant, had an even less positive masculine image. By contrast, the rugged independent craftsman, despite his dirty apron and calloused, blackened hands, was clearly a *man*. Both class and gender components were thus part of identity but in complicated and sometimes contradictory ways.

Middle-class women, or at least those whose menfolk were owners of some wealth-producing enterprises or had sufficient income from fees or salaries, also took part in this delicate restructuring of the meaning of work during the nineteenth century. They had no more taste for grinding toil than their men who preferred the ledger and pen to the plough, anvil or loom.

Younger and lower-status women (and sometimes men) had, for centuries, carried out the most toilsome, noisome tasks such as heavy lifting, fetching water, dealing with garbage and the contents of slop-pails and chamber-pots. But in the nineteenth-century middle-class home, the wife, daughters and sisters were doing less manual work and were hiring, increasingly, lower-class recruits to take over the drudgery of the 'housework' and childcare. The women of the household were still busy with the myriad tasks to be done, but the amount of housework had escalated with divided living and working space as well as a novel, complicated, variety of furnishings, carpets, curtains, crockery, clothing – a much higher material and social standard of living.

Yet middle-class women's relationship to manual work was, and still is, not as clear-cut as men's. How much of childcare, for example, should be turned over to others when the physical care of children was so intermingled with their intellectual, moral and spiritual development? What of food provision, cooking and meal preparation when women's role as nurturer and caretaker was central to feminine identity? Through the nineteenth and well into the twentieth century, the mark of genteel womanhood was white, unblemished hands. Women's dress, with tight waist, billowing crinoline or great bunched bustle and trailing skirts, was designed to make strenuous physical work difficult, if not impossible. Women carried middle-class status on their bodies, yet their tasks were never as clearly differentiated as for men.

As subordinates themselves, women did not so clearly exercise the power of authority. But in addition, they were more intimately bound up with the *relational* aspects of class. In their social rounds, in philanthropic activities and dispensing charity, they were cultivating, smoothing and negotiating the relationships created and sustained by the productive sphere. In a word, they were deeply implicated in the marking of class boundaries. In particular, they were concerned with the other side of the circle, that is, *consumption*. Since men were so closely associated with generating income through 'work', women came to be increasingly associated with correctly consuming the products of that work, an activity increasingly located in the differentiated private sphere of the 'Home'.[136]

Despite recent attempts at delineating class groups as based on life-style where taste comes to be a resource deployed by groups in the social hierarchy,[137] consumption cannot be understood outside relations of production, but needs to be seen as part of it. The desire for goods and services created the demand for goods and services, but was also implicated in the workings of productive activity. For example, in the early nineteenth century, when banks and other financial institutions were rudimentary, a middle-class man's 'worth' was judged not only by his own appearance and behaviour, his contributions to charity, membership of voluntary societies, his house(s), and his carriage, but also by the standard of demeanour and life-style of his whole household, particularly the sexual honour of his womenfolk.

Partly because of prescriptive statements of the time, partly because of our own perceived separation of production/public from consumption/private, interaction between these spheres has been constantly overlooked. Yet recent feminist historical studies of institutions such as the department store show the intimate connection between 'shopping' as a mainly feminine activity and the commercialization of consumption which drew women into the wage-labour market.[138] The recent work of such feminist historians as Alice Kessler-Harris and Joy Parr demonstrates how widening the boundaries of the economic to include household affairs has decentred workplace history and reforged the analysis of politics as well as class: the household is no longer construed as a private domain, rather it is the source of conciousness that generates public activity.[139]

It is also too often forgotten that cross-class interaction took place not only between employer and workman, but also between mistress and servant, who between them were responsible for organizing and displaying the family life-style in the home. In fact, the line between those servants working for the productive enterprise and for the home was not rigidly made until well into the nineteenth century. When more service activities were later drawn into the cash nexus, many of the features of personal service were carried over in the form of secretaries, shop assistants and nurses – not, coincidentally, posts largely staffed by women.

These myriad connections point to the need for a reconceptualization of societal hierarchies to incorporate more than the narrowly based class model. The nuances of relational status have to be recognized as a crucial site of group interaction which, in some cases, can cross traditional 'class' lines. Within the nineteenth-century working class, for example, the division between *rough* and *respectable* was not unlike the *genteel/ungenteel* divisions within the middle class; both rested on judgements of worth, partly material and partly moral.[140]

The core of nineteenth-century femininity had been constructed as outside the amoral market. Thus the feminine, always regarded within a familial context, became an idealized carrier of morality. With the late nineteenth-century decline of both formal religious belief and commonly held 'people's wisdom', the 'Home' and

'Motherhood' became even more powerful spiritual and emotional icons.[141] Women, putatively placed in the private sphere and commanding a central role in representing the family in face-to-face relationships, were often the controlling force in local status systems which relied on moral regulation, from the 'old wives' of villages and small towns, to the 'Queen Bees' of the urban slum court to the dowager matrons of London's West End.

Middle-class women were harnessed to the 'moral enterprise' of building status reputation for the family, which had been especially important in creating commercial and professional probity in an era before limited liability freed family assets from the devastation of business failure. It is striking how the nineteenth-century uplift literature for such women likens their duties to the *business* of creating and maintaining the ethical fabric of society. Yet when women attempted to enforce a set of moral values upon men of their own status group, as in late nineteenth-century moral reform or social purity campaigns, these men became uncomfortable and restive, accusing women of being prudes or killjoys, in other words defending their claims to men's privileges as males.

This contradictory situation draws attention to the importance of rethinking the categories *men* and *women* as part of what might be called in Weberian terms a status system. For it is status – attributions which give people certain group identities and preclude them from others – which, in the last analysis, determines the life-chances of individuals and groups. One of the main purposes of a status order is to protect the privileged by providing them with a resource not easily acquired by others[142] – in this case masculinity. The way status operates is most clearly seen in the way certain groups such as 'women' or 'blacks' have been denied inclusion into civil society as well as full citizenship rights. And it is status allocation which gives – or withholds – opportunities to manipulate marketable skills since these skills depend on estimations of social worth.

But as we have seen, 'woman' was defined by being outside the realm of legitimate marketable skill; and in terms of her own status *qua* woman she was systematically disadvantaged, although these disadvantages took different forms at different class levels. Instead, most women used their role as status markers and enhancers in the interests of wider class, religious and kinship groups, families and the individual men to whom their own fortunes were attached. When women did operate on their own account it was through the alternative realm of possible opportunities given by their embodied definition – the marriage market or its equivalent, a commercialized sexuality through a range of relationships from prostitution to co-habitation. The only women exempt from selling or bartering their sexuality for support were aristocratic or other wealthy heiresses.

In this context, it may be significant that sexuality was a commodity seldom 'sold' by adult, white, English men – precisely those groups whose identity has been most clearly included in analysis of the *class* system. Class, like 'the economy' or rational discourse to which it is so closely related, is thus a conceptual system which through its inherent nineteenth-century masculinity is cleansed of identification with human reproduction or desire.

What, then, of considering women and men as *separate* status groups in terms of their interests, access to monopolies of power, knowledge and material resources? Certainly if status is determined by the proximity to the creative and charismatic centres of society,[143] then women *as a group* – not in their capacity as kin to men – were, and still are, on the periphery. The higher reaches and inner circles of such centres – the churches, political parties, armed services, universities, law courts, business corporations, trade unions – remain adamantly masculine if not wholly male.

Unlike any other status groups, however, for example those based on ethnicity, racial category, nationality, religion or language, men's and women's ability to close ranks *against each other* is complicated. Men could, and did, use their privileged position to create all-male organizations and spaces. Yet, obviously, the usual strategies of endogamy, accompanied by exclusive commensality, which, along with linguistic barriers, are such potent creators of group identification, would be extremely difficult to maintain completely between men and women (after all, 49 per cent of children are boys and in their early years at least, usually cared for by women). As banal a truism as it may be and, science fiction notwithstanding, even if somehow total permanent segregation of the sexes were possible, the most likely result would be the dying-out of populations.

In pressing for an inclusive analysis of difference, it may be overlooked that class position and identity, like those of race, ethnicity and religious affiliation, are always built on the assumption of physical and cultural reproduction. When all is said and done, that reproduction *must* include diverse, but always present, gender orders.

Multiple Publics, the 'Social' Semi-Public and the Private Sphere

So far the discussion has focused on the creation of political and economic 'public' domains and indicated how gender was basic to their formation. The way these constructions constrained beliefs and behaviours in nineteenth- and early twentieth-century English society has been further explored. From the seventeenth century onwards, however, there had emerged a range of other public spheres. Indeed, as we have seen, the creation of different and specialized public arenas was in itself part of masculine identification in contrast to the resolutely generalized, private and domesticated world of women.

Among the most influential of differentiated publics, the area of science and medicine has begun to attract attention from feminist historians. As long as scientific practice was linked to household production, female relatives of scientific practitioners could take part and were sometimes the unacknowledged driving force in the enterprise. Female aristocratic patrons, in both fact and imagery, mediated for bourgeois scientific men.[144] But when scientific knowledge began to be conceptualized as rational and abstract, women were cooled out. By the later nineteenth century, practising scientists came to be equated with the detached, distinguished male expert focusing his gaze on, revealing and conquering, the feminized subject: 'Nature'.[145] 'Woman' (and thus sexuality) represented the irrationality of superstitious 'old wives' tales' in opposition to progressive rational scientific procedure.

The worlds of art and cultural production have a similar history although complicated by the early nineteenth-century Romantic movement which, as we have seen, took the male protagonist outside society altogether into a No Man's (sic) Land of individuality and genius. The extra-mundane performance of such men, however, took place in a remarkably public arena and, like all the other publics, remained dependent on the unacknowledged contributions of excluded, mainly female supporters.[146] To take part in this public, in the world of the studio culture as protagonist rather than muse or model, in Griselda Pollock's words, women had to choose between being human and being a woman.[147]

A variety of public organizations developed as part of a growing working-class culture, the trade unions being the most obvious. As oppositional to the dominant culture some, such as the Cooperative Movement, had more space to incorporate feminine interests, if not women themselves. The most incisive analyses of gender relations as well as a few attempts at practical rearrangements had been put forward by Owenite socialists early in the century.[148] Working-class movements themselves faced exclusion from participation in civil society and the state. Anna Clark has argued that during the period of Chartist debate, middle-class commentators had used gendered notions of virtue, expressed in the discourses of civic humanism, separate spheres, Malthusianism and political economy to create and maintain this general exclusion. It was contested that working-class men qualified for the masculinity of traditional citizenship.

Therefore, in addition to claiming property in skill and labour, working men turned to arguing that reason, rather than property itself, should be the basis for political participation. In so doing, they created a possible space for women who, it could be maintained, had reason too. It was also argued that the 'People' should have rights beyond property – the right of humanity for survival. The problem came in defining who were the People and, if they included women, did these women exhibit reason? The inclusion of women in the rubric of radical politics varied, with textile communities where many women were employed in mills and were members of trade unions, not surprisingly, being more receptive to their contribution.[149] Nevertheless, by the 1850s, it was clear that it had fallen to the men to speak to the outside world.[150]

By the late nineteenth century, the growth of state organization, voluntary society concern with working-class life and shifts in patterns of employment within an expanding urban culture emphasized a version of working-class respectability more squarely based on marriage and a species of domesticity.[151] The 'residuum' was at least partially defined by deviance from expected gender behaviour.[152]

The twentieth-century Labour Movement retained an underlying conception based on the gendered worlds derived from the triumph of political economy's fundamental categories, despite these variations and the inherent difficulty in maintaining expected gender distinctions based on a male breadwinner and dependent wife and children.

Each one of these segmented public worlds had rational man at its centre, embodied woman at the periphery. Nevertheless, such masculine domination of publics was by no means unproblematic. From around the third quarter of the nineteenth century, the emergence of a separate semi-public realm of 'the social', as distinct from the economic and political, began to take shape. This was, in part, a result of negotiation and protest from politically active women seeking to gain entry into the public arena through engagement with local issues and philanthropy, seen as extension of familial concerns.[153] But the conception of a separate social sphere also remained a source of constraint, limiting what became known as 'women's issues' – the family, children, health and welfare – thus minimizing feminine influence in the 'real' business of politics and the economy.

At the same time as an acknowledged realm of social life was claiming the attention of charity workers and nascent civil servants, there also existed an informal world of high politics linked to 'Society', the intermingling of political influence with entertainment based on kinship and a common upper-class culture. But by the 1880s this was gradually giving way to more professional party politics, a shift signalled by measures such as the secret ballot, the creation of party agents and the reform of local govenment.[154] Nevertheless, middle-class domesticity had never been unconditionally adopted by the gentry and aristocracy where men ran their estates or entered politics using the manor house as a base while women attended to the public functions of entertaining and social functions which were the hallmark of their station. The wife and daughters of the church dignitary, the diplomat, the headmaster, the admiral had as clear a position as the woman who had 'married a country house'; ideally, none of them would have spent much time in the nursery or any at all in the kitchen except, possibly, to give orders.

Many upper-class women were already active in a semi-public social sphere. Their middle-class counterparts, however, tended to be the backbone of those organizations and movements making up the feminized and depoliticized domain of welfare action aimed at those lower down the social scale. Together with an emerging feminist movement, several aspects of family and sexual relations began to enter into public discourse, the best known being the Anti-Contagious Diseases Campaign aleady referred to.

But in the 1860s and 1870s, there were other, less obvious issues which raised passionate public reactions, suggesting that the tensions generated by gender relations could surface under the increasing pressure of proto-feminist reactions. One such was the furore over the practice of leaving infants with paid caretakers (wet-nursing and 'baby-farming'); another was the bitter controversy over definitions of permitted power over – and violence towards – wives. A sense of unease colours discussions of such practices which, in many cases, had gone unnoticed for decades.[155]

Such debates indicate that the definition of what was public did not remain static, but shifted over time. One might ask, for example, whether the political and salon hostesses who continued to operate as important but informal power-brokers were in a public or private sphere? Because of the particular structure of gender relations, the vaunted Victorian 'women's influence' was not without a tinge of reality; the power of 'pillow talk' should not be underestimated. And towards the end of the nineteenth century, women were finding a more genuinely public voice in writing, editing and publishing as well as providing an influential readership.

Of course women had been engaging in all these activities as soon as literacy touched lower than a narrow elite band. The difference in the late nineteenth century was that they were able to do so more frequently in their own voice and through a wider range of more sympathetic outlets.[156] Yet it must be kept in mind that all these activities were still conducted in the semi-privacy of bedroom, parlour or study. Genteel women, at any rate, were seldom to be found roaming freely around the environs of Grub Street, not at least without a male sponsor or protector.

Variation, change, blurred boundaries – all left spaces for regrouping the gender components of these cornerstones of modern English society. Even in those public preserves most intensely masculine in character, the category 'woman' was always part of the definition, if in no other way as the shadow without which there can be no image projected. Fantasized 'others' never can be totally evaded, either conceived in the form of those who are *not* like the group with power to define or as those in whose supposed interests the powerful legitimate the actions that they take. Emphasis on *difference* could be conveyed as misogyny or chivalry, two sides of the same coin.

There can be no doubt, then, that an understanding of 'the public sphere(s)' is central to feminist history. Once this is accepted, it follows that key questions about the creation of *identity* have to be extended beyond family, home and childhood. The ragged frontiers between public and private must be recognized as a site where identity – of race, ethnicity and class and sexual orientation as well as gender – is formed.

In this respect, it may be unfortunate that feminists' rightful preoccupation with questions of identity has often privileged, rather than simply recognized, the psychic level. Psychoanalytic perspectives, in particular, may be used in a manner which inevitably draws attention away from the public or deals with it crudely as a *deus ex machina*. But there is no inherent opposition between recognizing the power of the public and giving equal weight to the dynamic place of psychic structures in gender identities, behaviour and symbolism. Happily there have been some recent encouraging signs that feminist historians are using psychological concepts, but carefully placed within specific historical situations.[157]

With these developments, in a sense, feminist history has come full circle. Recognition that identity for women as well as men is forged by both individual life situations and by the construction of the idea of the public confirms the original point that the private has to be taken not only as problematic, but also as a social construction. In revising these conceptions of the public, we can appreciate that a simple equation of the private with home and family has obfuscated important assumptions about gender. For example, historians of the family have taken for granted that men, who were seen to be prime actors in the public, were somehow not constituted in the family at least not beyond childhood. In this they followed the nineteenth-century convention that the attainment of manhood was achieved by leaving childish – that is, familial – identity behind. To quote John Demos's classic study of family life in colonial America:

> The family, in particular, stands quite apart from most other aspects of life. We have come to assume that whenever a man leaves his home 'to go out into the world' he crosses a very critical boundary.[158]

Furthermore, many men, who spent so much of their time in the public world of waged work and a selection of formal organizations, also had access to a 'private' life spent in non-domesticated (public?) spaces such as theatres, racecourses, boxing rings, clubs, the market-square. Even their most private, 'sexual', activities came to be shared between the home and the public arenas of café, pub, saloon, inn and brothel.[159] It could be argued that these strongly masculine spaces, quite as much as the domestic hearth, were seen to provide a haven against the harsh world of the market but within a culture of masculinity where paternalistic and fraternal relationships flourished unimpeded by claims from dependent and/or demanding womenfolk.[160]

The category 'women', on the other hand, (and married women in particular), even those who may have spent much time in public places, was defined by a limited kind of all-embracing privacy: 'the easy divorce of public and private had no real meaning for them'.[161]

Women in Public and Feminism

Understanding the complicated and shifting relations between public and private – politics, work (science, art, religion, philanthropy, warfare) and home, men and women – could help to unravel the tangles which have plagued recent efforts to study the history of women in public as well as the history of feminism, overlapping *but by no means synonymous* topics. It could also aid efforts to grapple with the notoriously tricky issues of *equality* and *difference*, for both classifications are predicated on a gender-neutral public realm into which women can/should, or cannot/ should not be fitted.[162]

Analyses of nineteenth-century British politics have concentrated on class and class action; given the previous explication, this means that women may have conceived, and responded to, such action differently from men. For example, a recent Australian study shows how the struggle between a nascent urban 'gentry' and the existing commercial leadership in a provincial city was experienced as political conflict of interests by men, but as a struggle for social (status) relations among women from the same strata and even the same families.[163] Or take the story of women's place in the history of British Chartist politics: not only the issues raised but the *form* of organizations adopted had an unacknowledged but heavily gendered dimension.[164]

What is defined as 'political action' may have been, at least in part, what was defined as masculine, but recent feminist questions have pushed out the boundaries of 'political' to encompass other arenas of conflict. Such redefinition shifts the boundaries of the private as well as the public. It has, for example, come to light that throughout the modern period some women apparently chose not to marry (although they often remained part of kinship and family groups). Could this and the 'silent strike' involved in the deliberate limitation on births from the third quarter of the nineteenth century represent a type of women's politics within the private realm?[165]

Women were also entering the public arena more openly; some from middle-class backgrounds literally transferred their private life into public institutions – settlement houses, schools, hospitals, colleges. In such cases living away from a familial home itself was a public action where women expected to be involved in business, labour, welfare and charity as workers (whether or not they were actually financially self-supporting). In this they followed a tradition of working-class women who had acted as Poor Law workhouse matrons and similar less glorified positions.[166]

Such women, however, tended to be exceptional. More often, those who did become politically active usually had to do so through an already male-defined domain with male-structured institutions and rituals, for example pressure groups, political parties or trade unions. This was largely a result of women's location in the family, which gave a particular cast to the relational aspects of class, sections of classes, interest groups, religious affiliations and ethnic groups.[167]

Those women who began to identify their interests as coinciding with other women rather than, or as well as, with men of their own strata, were in a particularly stressful position. Their loyalties stretched between family and class on the one hand, and a status identity as *women* on the other. During the period of the suffrage campaign, specific issues such as complete sexual equality in voting rights, as opposed to working-class representation in Parliament through a male-only working-class franchise, affected women from all strata of society, since most suffragists brought to their campaigning pre-existing class and party loyalties.[168] Women within traditional party auxiliaries such as the Women's Liberal Party Federation experienced a classic conflict between feminism and party loyalty raised in various disputes – over the employment of barmaids, for example, when their interests as women lay with supporting temperance. This stance opposed official Liberal Party policy, backed by the liquor trade, which cynically used feminist arguments to support 'equal employment opportunities'.[169] Simultaneous affirmation and denial of 'women' as a particular grouping was endemic among Labour Party members through to the inter-war period.[170]

Too often historians have seen such conflicts either as instances of the equality/difference divide or as personal conflicts between the demands of a woman's immediate family on the one hand, and devotion to the 'first Women's Movement' on the other. But because women were so deeply implicated in relational aspects of the social hierarchy, their disloyalties were often interpreted as much wider than the simple disregard of familial duty – although that was serious enough. Such women were also 'letting the side down', disengaging from their special role in moral – and thus social – boundary maintenance of their particular group, whether that be of a social stratum or even of the English 'race'.[171]

What few could face up to was that campaigns which used liberal principles of individual autonomy and equality, or even those claims which were made on the basis of women's place within the family, would ultimately unleash the radical contradictions of the public/private divide, including the rational individual man and the feminized, dependent woman.[172] In some ways anti-feminist rhetoric was more aware of this potential than others were, or have been since.

Family loyalties mediated women's public commitment in complicated ways. Working-class women in areas where waged work was customary and available, such as in textiles or shoemaking, were often torn between a virtuous independence which renegotiated their womanliness in terms of supporting their families by their waged work, and the more remote bonds which brought together all women: married and unmarried, housewives, outworkers, workshop and factory women. Such cases highlight the tension between consciousness of identity as workers and as women.[173]

But even when 'going public', many women did so (and do so now), to protect and further their position within the bounds of the category 'women' as it has been constructed within the home and family. From the early nineteenth-century involvement in the Anti-Slavery Movement, many women entered political campaigns around issues generally designated as domestic and private.[174] Claims of equality within the male-defined public sphere, on the other hand, could be seen as a double threat, first to the 'foundation of personal identity, social stability and the moral order' but also contributing to the destruction of feminine culture. That culture crucially included claims on men for support and protection, so that the exposure of women as autonomous individuals 'devoid of nurturing, affiliative virtues' seemed to weaken that position.[175] In the face of such powerful 'secondary gains', equal-rights feminist issues have often been difficult to keep on the agenda. In summing up the complexities of these positions, the concept of 'cooperative or pacific conflict' has sometimes been employed, although such notions tend to glide over the power differentials embedded in many nineteenth-century gender relationships.[176]

Women acting *as a group in their own interests* have been met with particular virulence. The reaction points to the outrage felt at the putative disloyalty

perceived in those women who sought individual autonomy, as if there was something almost obscene in the feminine guardians of morality and status boundaries
presuming to take part in the political domain as individuals. The nineteenth-
century epithets 'strong-minded', 'unsexed', 'spayed women' applied to such
women entering the public arena in their own right betray a fear of embodied
sexuality bursting asunder the abstraction of that sphere.

The nineteenth-century embargo on women speaking and writing in public,
from the pulpit as well as the political platform, was an integral part of this process
(although, as we now know, ironically, thousands of women did write, if not speak
'in public' places). How could it be otherwise if the category of 'women' came to be
understood as conditional, dependent on a relationship to 'their' men? And masculinity, full manhood, was at least partly defined as the ability 'to speak' for others.
All types of masculine interests, parties and groups as well as individual men, have
consistently used female symbolism, the protection of 'their' women, as central to
masculine dignity and power, including power over other men[177] – the all-male
dining or drinking ritual gathering rounding off the evening with the toast: 'To the
Ladies, God Bless Them'.

It is thus understandable that the call to women to move beyond family, class or
other group and identify with their fellow (sic) sisters as women, which was sent out
by the nineteenth-century Women's Movement, invoked similarly passionate devotion from its followers. Martha Vicinus's original and illuminating discussion of
the spiritual as well as embodied character of the British militant suffrage campaign
emphasizes how the peculiar construction of 'women' both as a category and as a
group, energized and moulded that movement,[178] for feminism, like women, grew
from an idea of self which was embodied.

The same forces which constructed women as the key figures of the moral order,
however, as we have seen, deprived them of access to major institutions and the
means of generating group resources in time, energy, money, organization, buildings and training. Their efforts at group action were often ridiculed, their attempts
to create rituals or traditions of their own were written off as trivial and tawdry.
Women's public appearances were always open to sexual innuendo because the
category 'woman' had been defined as embracing the sexual from which the
category 'man' had been exempt.

For many women, the courage necessary to act in formal public arenas was
formidable and it is encouraging that such efforts are being sought out and recorded. Yet feminist historians in their enthusiasm for finding 'women in public'
have tended to overlook the distinctions between women acting as familial, class or
other group members rather than as (or in addition to) 'women'. As Joan Landes
has written, the Women's Movement could not take possession of a public sphere
that had been enduringly constituted along masculinist lines.[179] In practice, the way
nineteenth- and early twentieth-century individual women experienced these divisions in their excursions into the public domain may not have been so clear-cut,

but in terms of the effectiveness of women's group action, they were vital. Recent historical inquiry into such varied groups as the Women's Cooperative Guild, the Mothers' Union, the Women's Institutes and the Townswomen's Guilds as well as the women's auxiliaries of the major political parties shows the extent of activity compared to purely feminist organizations.[180]

The varied, detailed historical studies of women in public, as well as of feminist organization and action, carried out over the last decade have demonstrated beyond doubt the variety of versions of public life. Somehow, we have to give full play to that lively and fluid vision while recognizing problems created by the categories with which we do our historical work. How far did the masculinity of public institutions, language and imagery affect women's view of themselves, including the transgressive behaviour and, later into the twentieth century, definitions of lesbianism? Were there ways in which women used the male language of the public to their own advantage and as disruptive of public discourse? What were the long-term effects of such disruption?

To answer such questions we have to listen carefully to the use of 'public' and 'private' in the language of historical actors themselves.[181] How to acknowledge that exclusion from political thought, economic and social theory and tradition might have, under certain circumstances, actually left women free to grasp the initiative? Where and under what circumstances were some women in some places able to shift the terms of debate, including the definition of what was political, what was economic, what was social – indeed, what was public and what was private?

Epilogue

Given the structure of gender categories and their centrality to the nineteenth-century concept of the family with its attendant male breadwinner, female house-wife, non-working child roles, as well as the language of femininity and masculinity, it is not difficult to understand why women in public life posed such a threat to identity – for both men and women. In a period of such rapid technologi-cal change, geographical and social mobility, together with the later nineteenth-century loss of religious faith among the middle and upper classes, a sense of self, of identity, was crucial to psychic as well as material survival. And in the twentieth century, that sense of self turned increasingly inward towards a private and ulti-mately sexual self.

As the whole edifice of rational individualism and the public/private division has come to be taken for granted, and is solidly established within state, educational and economic bureaucracies, it is the concept of 'sexuality' which has come to 'hold the key to the hermeneutics of the self'.[182] The same dichotomies that produced languages of equal rights and, by implication posited sexual difference, also shaped the erotic realm, 'exaggerating divisions between carnality and love, desire and reason, excitement and companionship which profoundly scarred men as well as women'.[183]

The novelty of such a world-view is evinced in the case studies, mainly of lesbian and gay identity, which have begun to investigate how sexuality and sexual orientation as a core part of Western identity grew as part of the differentiation of the public and private. Homosexual identity as we know it could not exist unless sexuality as part of a private realm had not already been carved away from a putatively public sphere.[184]

'Sexuality', the desires and fantasies it accompanies, as well as the physical reproduction it implies, cannot be cut away from the rest of human life with impunity. The Cartesian schema, in its defiant gesture of masculine independence from physicality and thus from what was defined as the feminine, was a claim which was also a compensation for a profound loss.[185]

We are beginning to recognize through a variety of empirical studies that often independence was elevated and loss denied by categorizing women (and with them 'effeminate' Jews, blacks or native inferior others) as mired in their biology. These groups represented potentially disruptive procreative forces which male individuality had to subdue – the particularistic, familial ties that civic man must rise above and that some men would attempt to educate/rescue women from.[186]

While women had the potential to give birth to babies and thus renew populations, inevitably, these frail and mortal human lives must, in their turn, end. It was within the abstract masculine realm that the power of infinite and indestructible generativity would lie. In the seventeenth and eighteenth centuries, it was men, through the social contract, who give birth to civil society.[187] It was early nineteenth-century engineers and entrepreneurs through their 'all but miraculous creations', the machines, who appeared to give birth by immaculate conception, and in the process endow machine-based industrial production with women's life-creating function.[188] In the later nineteenth century, it was only men, it seemed who, 'could give birth to the political entity, the imperishable community of the nation'.[189] Such appropriations of reproduction and gestures towards immortality were built upon, as they served to maintain, the division between the public and the private.

We, in the late twentieth century, are the inheritors of a world structured by these categories and these conceptions. They continue to operate subtextually and informally to the disadvantage of women (and other subordinate groups) long after explicit formal restrictions on women's entry into the public realm have been lifted.[190] As in every human society, constructing such categories represents our culture's way of coming to terms with the mysteries of creation and of mortality. The difference from all previous cultures is that nineteenth-century England, through its Empire and the diffusion of its economic and military dominance, through its values, technologies and language, had the power – certainly never uncontested but nevertheless always present – to shape not only our destiny but potentially that of a goodly portion of our total planet.

Notes

The main arguments in this essay were first presented to the interdisciplinary symposium, 'The Construction of Sex/Gender – What is a Feminist Perspective?', Swedish Council for Research in the Humanities and Social Sciences, Stockholm, 1990. The thoughtful discussions around subsequent presentations in Britain, Norway, the USA and Australia have offered many useful new insights. A brief version has been published in *Passato e Presente*, no. 27, September–December 1991, and *L'Homme: Zeitschrift für feministische Geschichtswissenschaft*, 1993. The present version incorporates many of the ideas published in my article, 'Adam Spoke First and Named the Orders of the World: Masculine and Feminine Domains in History and Sociology', in Helen Corr and Lynn Jamieson, eds, *The Politics of Everyday Life: Continuity and Change in Work and Family* (Macmillan, London, 1990).

I am grateful for advice and suggestions about these ideas from discussion with Carole Adams, Monika Bernold, Barbara Caine, Delfina Dolza, Christe Hammerle, Alice Kessler-Harris, Catherine Hall, David Lee, Jane Lewis, Susan Margarey, Jill Matthews, Jane Rendall, Sonya Rose, Alison Scott, Eleni Varikas, Ulla Wikander and especially to my colleague Ludmilla Jordanova for her critical but always supportive suggestions. Diana Gittins provided invaluable editorial critique as well as encouragement in revising this version. Finally, my thanks to Citlali Rouirusa who provided the title.

1   Olivia Harris, 'Households as Natural Units', in Kate Young, Carol Wolkowitz and Roslyn McCullagh, eds, *Of Marriage and the Market: Women's Subordination in International Perspective* (CSE Books, London, 1981).
2   There was an extended debate on this topic in the 1970s, starting with Michelle Rosaldo, joined by Edward Ardener and Sherry Ortner. See in particular Sherry Ortner, 'Is Female to Male as Nature is to Culture', in M. Zimbalist Rosaldo and L. Lamphere, eds, *Woman, Culture, and Society* (Stanford University Press, Stanford, 1974). This was answered by Nicole-Claude Mathieu, 'Man–Culture and Woman–Nature?', *Women's Studies International Quarterly*, vol. 1, no. 1 (1978).
3   Ludmilla Jordanova, 'Women's Testimonies on "Public" and "Private" in Eighteenth-Century England', paper delivered at the conference on the public and private spheres in early modern Europe, University of Exeter, March 1993, by permission of the author.
4   Ann Snitow, 'A Gender Diary', in Marianne Hirsch and Evelyn Fox-Keller, eds, *Conflicts in Feminism* (Routledge, London, 1990), p. 137; see also Nancy Hewitt's elegant plea for a concept of 'compound identities', studying elements both in isolation and as a whole. Nancy Hewitt, 'Compounding Differences', *Feminist Studies*, vol. 18, no. 2 (1992), p. 318.
5   Jordanova, 'Women's Testimonies', p. 6.
6   Linda Kerber, 'Separate Spheres, Female Worlds, Women's Place: The Rhetoric of Women's History', *Journal of American History*, vol. 75, issue 1 (1988), p. 30.
7   Amanda Vickery, 'Golden Age to Separate Spheres? A Review of the Categories and Chronology of English Women's History', *Historical Journal*, vol. 36, no. 2 (1993), p. 412.
8   Carole Pateman, 'Feminist Critiques of the Public/Private Dichotomy', in *The Disorder of Women: Democracy, Feminism and Political Theory* (Polity Press, Cambridge, 1989), p. 122.
9   Nancy Fraser, 'Rethinking the Public Sphere: A Contribution to the Critique of Actually-Existing Democracy' in Craig Calhoun, ed., *Habermas and the Public Sphere* (MIT Press, Cambridge, MA, 1992).

10   Geoff Eley, 'Nations, Publics and Political Cultures: Placing Habermas in the Nine-teenth Century', in Calhoun, ed., *Habermas and the Public Sphere*.

11   G.R. Rubin and David Sugarman, 'Changing Views of Credit, Economy and the Law', in *Law, Economy and Society 1750–1914: Essays in the History of English Law* (Professional Books, Abingdon, Oxfordfordshire, 1984).

12   Seyla Benhabib, 'Models of Public Space: Hannah Arendt, the Liberal Tradition and Jürgen Habermas', in Calhoun, ed., *Habermas and the Public Sphere*, p. 90.

13   See Drucilla Cornell, *Beyond Accommodation: Ethical Feminism, Deconstruction and the Law* (Routledge, London, 1991).

14   Pateman, *The Disorder of Women*. Feminist sociologists seem to have been more aware of the centrality of family and kinship than some historians. See, for example, Carol Smart, *The Ties That Bind: Law, Maniage and the Reproduction of Patriarchal Relations* (Routledge & Kegan Paul, London, 1984).

15   Eva Lundgren, 'The Hand That Strikes and Comforts: Gender Construction in the Field of Tension Encompassing Body and Symbol, Stability and Change', in Maud Edwards et al., eds, *Rethinking Change: Current Swedish Feminist Research* (Swedish Science Press, Uppsala, 1992); see also the discussion of motherhood, the embodied connection and their relationship to the category of 'person', in Susan Bordo *Unbear-able Weight: Feminism, Western Culture and the Body* (University of California Press, Berkeley, 1993).

16   Chandra Mohanty, Ann Russo and Lourdes Torres, eds, *Third World Women and the Politics of Feminism* (Indiana University Press, Bloomington, In, 1991).

17   See the discussion in, for example, Mercia Eliade, *The Myth of the Eternal Return* (Princeton University Press, Princeton, 1954).

18   Keith Thomas, *Religion and the Decline of Magic* (Weidenfeld & Nicolson, London, 1971), p. 656.

19   Charles Taylor, 'Rationality', in Steven Lukes and Martin Hollis, eds, *Rationality and Relativism* (MIT Press, Cambridge, MA, 1992), p. 94.

20   Susan Bordo, 'The Cartesian Masculinization of Thought', *Signs: Journal of Women in Culture and Society*, vol. 11, no. 3 (spring 1986), pp. 440, 450.

21   Erica Harth, *Cartesian Women: Versions and Subversion of Rational Discourse in the Old Regime* (Cornell University Press, Ithaca, 1992), pp. 1, 12. A particularly powerful case for the consequences of this mode of 'faulty generalization', or 'false universality', is made in Elizabeth K. Minnich, *Transforming Knowledge* (Temple University Press, Philadelphia, 1990), especially ch. 5.

22   G. Oaks, *Georg Simmel: On Women, Sexuality and Love* (Yale University Press, New Haven, 1984).

23   H. Ellenberger, *The Discovery of the Unconscious* (New York, 1970). Thanks to Sandra Ellesley for this reference. See also 'Unconscious', in Raymond Williams, *Keywords: A Vocabulary of Culture and Society* (Fontana, London, 1983).

24   For the importance of this development to the early nineteenth-century provincial middle class in England and its relationship to gender, see Leonore Davidoff and Catherine Hall, *Family Fortunes: Men and Women of the English Middle Class* (Routledge, London, 1992).

25   David Harvey, *The Condition of Postmodernity* (Blackwell, Oxford, 1990), p. 258.

26   Wendy Holloway, 'Gender Difference and the Production of Subjectivity', in Julian Henriques et al., eds, *Changing the Subject* (Methuen, London, 1984), pp. 252–8. It may be of interest that dedicated proponents of 'rational choice' models for all areas of social action have begun to doubt the usefulness of their chosen approach. For example see the review of Jon Elster's work by Martin Hollis, 'Why Elster Is Stuck and Needs to Recover his Faith', *London Review of Books*, 24 January 1991.

27   Jock Norton, 'Intimacy, Independence and Masculinity: Keeping a Distance at Close

Quarters', in Patricia Grimshaw et al., eds, *Studies in Gender: Essays in Honour of Norma Grieve* (Committee for Gender Studies, University of Melbourne, 1992), p. 74.

28 Max Weber, 'Religious Ethics and the World: Sexuality and Art', in G. Roth and C. Wittich, eds, *Economy and Society* (Bedminster Press, New York, 1968), vol. 2, p. 603.

29 Judith Walkowitz, 'Science, Feminism and Romance: The Men and Women's Club, 1885–1889', *History Workshop Journal*, no. 21 (spring 1986).

30 Polly Beales, 'Fabian Feminism: Gender, Politics and Culture in London, 1880–1930', Rutgers University, Ph.D. thesis, 1989.

31 For a splendid example of writing (and reading) as resistance for women, see Elaine Showalter, 'Family Secrets and Domestic Subversion: Rebellion in the Novels of the 1860s', in Anthony Wohl, ed., *The Victorian Family* (Croom Helm, London, 1978).

32 Nicholas Abercrombie, Steven Hill and Bryan Turner, *Sovereign Individuals of Capitalism* (Allen & Unwin, London, 1986), p. 1.

33 N. Luhman, 'The Individuality of the Individual: Historical Meanings and Contemporary Problems' in T. Heller and D. Wellberry, eds, *Reconstructing Individualism: Autonomy, Individuality and Self in Western Thought* (Stanford University Press, Stanford, 1986).

34 Abercrombie et al., *Sovereign Individuals*, p. 81.

35 C.B. Macpherson, *The Political Theory of Possessive Individualism* (Oxford University Press, Oxford, 1962), p. 270.

36 Ludmilla Jordanova, 'Conceptualizing Childhood in the Eighteenth Century: The Problem of Child Labour', *British Journal for Eighteenth-Century Studies*, vol. 10 (autumn 1987).

37 Abercrombie et. al., *Sovereign Individualism*, p. 34.

38 Lucien Goldman, quoted in Abercrombie et al., *Sovereign Individualism*, p. 26.

39 Ursula Vogel, 'Humboldt and the Romantics: Neither *Hausfrau* nor *Citoyenne* – the Idea of "Self-Reliant Femininity' in German Romanticism" in E. Kennedy and S. Mundus, eds, *Women in Western Political Philosophy* (Wheatsheaf Books, Brighton, 1987).

40 Heller and Wellberry, eds, *Restructuring Individualism*, p. 1; some psychologists too, have noted the consequences of such a narrow definition of the individual, resulting in a psychic fragmentation, 'each individual struggling with his daimones. If there is only one model of individuation can there be true individuality?' (Thomas More, ed., *The Essential James Hillman: A Blue Five* [Routledge, London, 1994], p. 40).

41 Nancy Armstrong, as a literary historian, has argued that women were in fact the first group to have a strong sense of self: *Desire and Domestic Fiction: A Political History of the Novel* (Oxford University Press, New York, 1988); see also Polly Young-Eisendrath, 'The Female Person and How We Talk about Her', in Mary M. Gergen, ed., *Feminist Thought and the Structure of Knowledge* (New York University Press, New York, 1988).

42 For a detailed discussion see Davidoff and Hall, *Family Fortunes*, pt I.

43 Barbara Taylor, *Eve and the New Jerusalem: Socialism and Feminism in the Nineteenth Century* (Virago, London, 1983); Anna Clark, *The Struggle of the Breeches: Gender and the Making of the British Working Class* (University of California Press, Berkeley, CA, 1995); R.L. Smith and Deborah Valenze, 'Mutuality and Marginality: Liberal Moral Theory and Working-Class Women in Nineteenth-Century England', *Signs: Journal of Women in Culture and Society*, vol. 13, no. 2 (winter 1988); Iain McCalman, *Radical Underworld: Prophets, Revolutionaries and Pornographers in London, 1795–1840* (Clarendon Press, Oxford, 1993).

44 Roy Porter, 'Mixed Feelings: The Enlightenment and Sexuality in Eighteenth-Century Britain', in P.-G. Boucé, ed., *Sexuality in Eighteenth-Century Britain* (Manchester University Press, Manchester, 1982).
45 Sandra Harding, 'The Instability of the Analytical Categories of Feminist Theory', *Signs: Journal of Women in Culture and Society*, vol. 11, no. 4 (summer 1986), p. 661.
46 B. Barker-Benfield, 'The Spermatic Economy: A Nineteenth-Century View of Sexuality', in M. Gordon, ed., *The American Family in Socio-Historical Perspective* (St Martin's Press, New York, 1973).
47 Joanna Hodge, 'Women and the Hegelian State', in Kennedy and Mendus, eds, *Women in Western Political Philosophy*.
48 Robert W. Connell, *Gender and Power* (Polity Press, Cambridge, 1987).
49 See Catherine Hall, *Male, White and Middle Class: Explorations in Feminism and History* (Polity Press, Cambridge, 1992), pt III.
50 Sugerman and Rubin, eds, *Law, Economy and Society: Essays in the History of English Law*, introduction, p. 27; for background to debates about property see Alan Ryan, *Property* (Open University Press, Milton Keynes, 1987), especially the chapter on property and personality.
51 Henrietta Moore, *Feminism and Anthropology* (Polity Press, Cambridge, 1988), p. 71.
52 Pat Thane, 'Women and the Poor Law in Victorian and Edwardian England', *History Workshop Journal*, no. 6 (1978); see also Ursula Henriques, 'Bastardy and the New Poor Law', *Past and Present*, no. 37 (1967).
53 The arguments used by these judges included what a modern lawyer has described as the myth of sexual complementarity which shrouded the enforced subordination and exclusion of women; the myth of judicial neutrality which masked judicial support for male domination; and the myth of professional integrity which veiled economic and domestic self-interest. See Albie Sachs, 'Britain: Are Women "Persons?"', in Albie Sachs and Joan Hoff Wilson, eds, *Sexism and the Law: A Study of Male Beliefs and Judicial Bias* (Martin Robertson, Oxford, 1978), p. 57; see also Henrietta Moore, 'Women as Persons', in her *Feminism and Anthropology*.
54 Susan Staves, *Married Women's Separate Property in England, 1660–1833* (Harvard University Press, Cambridge, MA, 1990), especially the conclusion.
55 Maxine Berg, 'Women's Property and the Industrial Revolution', *Warwick Economic Research Papers*, no. 382, Department of Economics, University of Warwick (1992).
56 Barbara Harris, 'Women and Politics in Early Tudor England', *Historical Journal*, no. 33 (1990).
57 Mark Girouard, *Life in the English Country House: A Social and Architectural History* (Yale University Press, New Haven, 1980).
58 Fraser, 'Rethinking the Public Sphere', p. 114.
59 See, for example, B.C. Verstraete, 'Slavery and the Dynamics of Male Homosexual Relationships in Ancient Rome', *Journal of Homosexuality*, vol. 5, no. 3 (1980).
60 Merry E. Wiesner, *Women and Gender in Early Modern Europe* (Cambridge University Press, Cambridge, 1993).
61 The relationship of both femininity and women to the political sphere and the construction of the domestic was somewhat different in the United States, as is to be expected. See Linda Kerber, *Women of the Republic: Intellect and Ideology in Revolutionary America* (University of North Carolina Press, Chapel Hill, 1980).
62 Pateman, *The Sexual Contract*; for a detailed discussion of these issues in the Scottish Enlightenment and its influence on British culture, see Jane Rendall, 'Virtue and Commerce: Women in the Making of Adam Smith's Political Economy', in Kennedy and Mendus, eds, *Women in Western Political Philosophy*.
63 J. Habermas, *The Structural Transformations of the Public Sphere: An Inquiry into a Category of Bourgeois Society* (MIT Press, Cambridge, MA, 1989).

64 Calhoun, ed., *Habermas and the Public Sphere*, pp. 2, 10.
65 J. Landes, *Women and the Public Sphere in the Age of the French Revolution* (Cornell University Press, Ithaca, 1988), p. 7.
66 Habermas, *The Structural Transformation of the Public Sphere*, p. 43; Rendall, 'Virtue and Commerce'.
67 Ryan, *Women in Public*, p. 27; see also her 'Gender and Public Access: Women's Politics in Nineteenth-Century America', in Calhoun, ed., *Habermas and the Public Sphere*.
68 R. Sennett, *The Fall of Public Man* (Knopf, New York, 1977).
69 Linda Colley, 'Womanpower', in *Britons: Forging the Nation* (Yale University Press, New Haven, 1992).
70 E.J. Clery, 'On the Coffee House Myth: Women and the Public Sphere, England 1652–1712, unpublished paper, 1991, by permission of the author.
71 Mary Thale, 'Women in London Eighteenth-Century Debating Societies', *Gender and History*, vol. 7, no. 1 (1995).
72 Davidoff and Hall, *Family Fortunes*; see also Frank Prochaska, *Women and Philanthropy in Nineteenth-Century England* (Oxford University Press, Oxford, 1980).
73 Robert J. Morris, 'Voluntary Societies and British Urban Elites, 1780–1850', *Historical Journal*, no. 26 (1983).
74 L. Davidoff, *The Best Circles: 'Society', Etiquette and the Season* (Century Hutchinson, London, 1986); Patricia Jalland, *Women, Marriage and Politics 1860–1914* (Clarendon Press, Oxford, 1986).
75 Ryan, *Women in Public*; even working-class women did manage to use institutions like courts of law under some circumstances. See Ginger Frost 'I shall Not Sit Down and Crie: Women, Class and Breach of Promise of Marriage Plantifts in England, 1850–1900', *Gender and History*, vol. 6, no. 2 (1994). Carolyn Steedman argues that the obscurity resulting from women's absence in social and political conceptions of the public allowed them actually to operate across a wide political spectrum. See *Childhood, Culture and Class in Britain: Margaret Macmillan, 1860–1931* (Virago, London, 1990).
76 For a stimulating and nuanced discussion of this historical milieu, see Judith Walkowitz, *City of Dreadful Delight: Narratives of Sexual Danger in Late-Victorian London* (Virago, London, 1992).
77 S. Franzway, D. Court and R.W. Connell, *Staking a Claim: Feminism, Bureaucracy and the State* (Allen & Unwin, Sydney, 1989), p. x.
78 Donna Andrew, 'The Code of Honour and its Critics: The Opposition to Duelling in England 1700–1850', *Social History* vol. 5, no. 3 (October 1980).
79 Lynn Amidon, ' "Ladies in Blue": Feminism and Policing in late Nineteenth- and Early Twentieth-Century Britain', University of Essex, MA thesis, 1986.
80 Genevieve Lloyd, 'Selfhood, War and Masculinity', in Carol Pateman and Elizabeth Gross, eds, *Feminist Challenges* (Allen & Unwin, Sydney, 1986).
81 For a useful overview of this work see Martha Ackelsberg and Irene Diamond 'Gender and Political Life: New Directions in Political Science', in Beth Hess and Myra Marx Ferree, eds, *Analysing Gender: A Handbook of Social Research* (Sage Publications, London, 1987).
82 Ruth Pierson, ' "Did Your Mother Wear Army Boots?": Feminist Theory and Women's Relation to War, Peace and Revolution', in S. MacDonald, P. Holden and S. Ardener, eds, *Images of Women in Peace and War: Cross-Cultural and Historical Perspectives* (Macmillan, London, 1987); Eleanor Hancock, 'Women, Combat and the Military', in Renate Howe, ed., *Women and the State: Australian Perspectives* (La Trobe University Press, Melbourne, 1993).
83 There is some recognition of the blurred lines between these publics but with little

understanding of how they are linked to gender constructions. See, for example, E. Meiksins Wood, 'The Separation of the Economic and the Political in Capitalism', *New Left Review*, no. 127 (1981).

84   For example, Carole Pateman and Nancy Fraser both give considerable recognition to the economic sphere but do not incorporate it directly in their analysis, a position analagous to J.S. Mill's in the nineteenth century. However first-wave feminists did often take the economic into their account, possibly because at that time both institutionally and intellectually the domains were not so clearly divided. See Jane Rendall, 'Nineteenth-Century Feminism and the Separation of Spheres: Reflections on the Public/Private Dichotomy', T. Andreasen et al. in *Moving on, New Perspectives on the Women's Movement* (Aarhus University Press, Aarhus, 1990).

85   The identification of masculinity with the specialized or differentiated and femininity (and thus women) with the undifferentiated or 'essence' has been a strand in much nineteenth-century European thought including some psychoanalytic formulations which equate undifferentiation with women's supposed lack of an integrated ego or celebrate the more particular/emotionally enhanced feminine which is easily elided to refer to actual women. See D.S. Wehr, *Jung and Feminism: Liberating Archetypes* (Routledge, London, 1988).

86   For an elaboration of this argument, see Davidoff and Hall, *Family Fortunes*, especially pt II.

87   For an extreme early (non-Marxist) example, see Lee Holcombe, *Victorian Ladies at Work: Middle-Class Working Women in England and Wales, 1850–1914* (David & Charles, Newton Abbott, 1973). These questions have been acutely addressed in M. Molyneux, 'Beyond the Domestic Labour Debate', *New Left Review*, no. 116 (1979). There have also been some imaginative exceptions, see particularly Miriam Glucksman's concept of 'total social labour' in *Women Assemble: Women Workers and the New Industries in Inter-War Britain* (Routledge, London, 1990) and A. Kessler-Harris, *A Woman's Wage: Historical Meanings and Social Consequences* (University of Kentucky Press, Lexington, 1990), introduction.

88   J.G.A. Pocock, *Virtue, Commerce and History: Essays on Political Thought and History, Chiefly in the Eighteenth Century* (Cambridge University Press, Cambridge, 1985), p. 99.

89   Jean-Christopher Agnew, *Worlds Apart: The Market and the Theater in Anglo-American Thought 1550–1750* (Cambridge University Press, Cambridge, 1986), p. 38.

90   Joyce Appleby, *Economic Thought and Ideology in Seventeenth-Century England* (Princeton University Press, Princeton, NJ, 1978).

91   Susan Amussen, *An Ordered Society: Gender and Class in Early Modern England* (Blackwell, Oxford, 1988).

92   Rendall, 'Virtue and Commerce'.

93   Michèle Pujol, *Feminism and Anti-Feminism in Early Economic Thought* (Edward Elgar, Aldershot, 1992), pp. 42ff.

94   A tradition culminating in the statistically orientated professional economics championed by Alfred Marshall at the end of the nineteenth century. However, this view also heavily influenced government officials and others involved with social policy decisions including the Registrar General's office. See E. Higgs, 'Women's Occupations and Work in the 19th-Century Census', *History Workshop Journal*, no. 23 (spring 1987).

95   Robert Gray, 'The Languages of Factory Reform in Britain, *c*.1830–1860', in Patrick Joyce, ed., *The Historical Meaning of Work* (Cambridge University Press, Cambridge, 1987).

96   Maxine Berg, *The Machinery Question and the Making of Political Economy* (Cambridge University Press, Cambridge, 1980), p. 296.

97 Margaret Hunt, 'Time Management, Writing and Accounting in the Eighteenth-Century Trading Family: A Bourgeois Enlightenment', *Business and Economic History*, 2nd series, vol. 18 (1989).

98 Gregory Claeys, *Machinery, Money and the Millennium: From Moral Economy to Socialism: 1815–1860* (University of Princeton Press, Princeton, NJ, 1987), p. 40.

99 G.R. Rubin and David Sugarman, 'Changing Views of Credit, Economy and the Law', in *Law, Economy and Society*; see also Davidoff and Hall, *Family Fortunes*, pt II.

100 Pujol, *Feminism and Anti-Feminism in Early Economic Thought*.

101 For the British census see Higgs, 'Women, Occupations and Work in the 19th-Century Census'; for the influence of this model throughout the contemporary world and on major international agencies, see Marilyn Waring, *If Women Counted: A New Feminist Economics* (Macmillan, London, 1989).

102 For an explication of these insights, see Christine Delphy and Diana Leonard, *Familiar Exploitation: A New Analysis of Marriage in Contemporary Western Society* (Polity Press, Cambridge, 1992).

103 Maria L. Pesante, 'A Calm, Composed, Unpassionate Serenity: Public and Private in Adam Smith's *Theory of Moral Sentiments*', paper presented to 'The Public Sphere in Eighteenth-Century Europe', Eighteenth-Century Studies Group Symposium, University of Exeter (May 1992), by permission of the author.

104 Agnew, *Worlds Apart*, p. 175.

105 Thomas Carlyle, 'The Modern Worker', Book III, *Past and Present* (London, 1899), p. 273.

106 Clark, *The Struggle of the Breeches*; McCalman, *Radical Underworld*.

107 Taylor, *Eve and the New Jerusalem*.

108 Keith McClelland, 'Some Thoughts on Masculinity and the "Representative Artisan" in Britain 1850–1880', *Gender and History*, vol. 1, no. 2 (summer 1989); R. Danon, *Work and the English Novel: The Myth of Vocation* (Croom Helm, London, 1985).

109 John Rule, 'The Property of Skill', in Joyce, ed., *The Historical Meaning of Work*; T.R. Tholfsen, *Working-Class Radicalism in Mid-Victorian England* (Croom Helm, London, 1976). While neither of these studies is aware of the implications, the notion of *manhood* is obviously imbued with gender characteristics.

110 For a particularly good English example, see Deborah Valenze, 'The Art of Women and the Business of Men: Women's Work and the Dairy Industry *c*.1740–1840', *Past and Present*, no. 130 (February, 1991).

111 J. Acker, 'Making Gender Visible', in R. Wallace, ed., *Feminism and Sociological Theory* (Sage, Newbury Park, CAl, 1989), p. 75. Acker here points out that at the most abstract level of Marxist theory, women's labour is as 'gender-neutral' as men's but she acknowledges that an analysis of concrete situations must always be made within specific social formations where women's labour is definitely gendered.

112 Davidoff, 'The Rationalization of Housework', this volume, ch. 3.

113 W.R. Greg, 'Why are Women Redundant?', *National Review*, vol. 15 (1862).

114 Sidney Webb 'The Alleged Differences in the Wages Paid to Women and Men for Similar Work', *The Economic Journal*, vol. 1 (1891), pp. 660 and 661.

115 A sociological study of the banking industry makes this point and shows how men's mobility is also fostered at the expense of women. Rosemary Crompton and Gareth Jones, *White-Collar Proletariat: Deskilling and Gender in Clerical Work* (Macmillan, London, 1984). For a broader application of these ideas within the literature on developing societies and the way men operating in the informal sector gain by the existence of low-paid casual women's work see A. Scott, 'Informal Sector or Female Sector?: Gender Bias in Urban Labour Market Models', in Diane Elson, ed., *Male Bias in the Development Process* (Manchester University Press, Manchester, 1991).

116   Judith McGaw, 'No Passive Victims, No Separate Spheres: A Feminist Perspective on Technology', in Stephen H. Cutcliffe and Robert C. Post, eds, *In Context: History and the History of Technology* (Lehigh University Press, Bethlehem, PA, 1989), p. 183; Sonya Rose ' "Gender at Work": Sex, Class and Industrial Capitalism', *History Workshop Journal*, no. 21 (1986).

117   Nancy Folbre, 'The Unproductive Housewife: Her Evolution in Nineteenth-Century Economic Thought', *Signs: Journal of Women in Culture and Society*, vol. 16, no. 3 (spring 1991).

118   Davidoff and Hall, *Family Fortunes*, pt II.

119   G. Marshall, 'On the Sociology of Women's Unemployment, its Neglect and Significance', *Sociological Review*, vol. 32 (1982); Clare Evans, 'Unemployment and the Making of the Feminine during the Lancashire Cotton Famine', in Pat Hudson and W.R. Lee, eds, *Women's Work and the Family Economy in Historical Perspective* (Manchester University Press, Manchester, 1990).

120   Staves, *Married Women's Separate Property in England*, p. 229.

121   Judith Walkowitz, *Prostitution and Victorian Society: Women, Class and the State* (Cambridge University Press, New York, 1980).

122   Laura Englestein, *The Keys to Happiness: Sex and the Search for Modernity in Fin-de-Siècle Russia* (Cornell University Press, Ithaca, NY, 1992), p. 300.

123   Susan Pedersen, 'Gender, Welfare and Citizenship in Britain during the Great War', *American Historical Review*, vol. 95, no. 4 (October 1990), p. 1006; Jane Lewis, 'Gender and the Development of Welfare Regimes', *Journal of European Social Policy*, no. 3 (1992).

124   For a striking and carefully documented example see Jill Liddington, 'Ann Lister of Sibden Hall, Halifax (1791–1840): Her Diaries and the Historian', *History Workshop Journal*, no. 35 (1993).

125   For the distinction between property as possession and as active capital, see: F. Parkin, 'Social Closure as Exclusion', in *Marxism and Class Theory: A Bourgeois Critique* (Tavistock, London, 1979), p. 53.

126   C. Delphy and D. Leonard, 'Class Analysis, Gender Analysis and the Family', in R. Crompton and M. Mann, eds, *Gender and Stratification* (Polity Press, Cambridge, 1986).

127   See the illuminating discussion in Martha Vicinus, *Independent Women: Work and Community for Single Women 1850–1880* (University of Chicago Press, Chicago, 1985).

128   Calhoun, *Habermas and the Public Sphere*, p. 37; see also Anna Yeatman, 'Gender Differentiation of Social Life in Public and Domestic Domains', *Social Analysis: Journal of Cultural and Social Practice*, no. 15 (August 1984).

129   Jane Collier and S. Yanagisakdo, eds, *Gender and Kinship: Essays Toward Unified Analysis* (Stanford University Press, Stanford, California, 1987), introduction.

130   Joan Scott, 'A Reply to Criticism', *International Labour and Working-Class History*, no. 32 (fall 1987).

131   Acker, 'Making Gender Visible'; R.E. Bologh, *Love or Greatness: Max Weber and Masculine Thinking – A Feminist Enquiry* (Unwin Hyman, London, 1990).

132   Quoted in R.J. Morris, *Class, Sect and Party: The Making of the British Middle Class; Leeds 1820–1850* (Manchester University Press, Manchester, 1990), p. 196; E.P. Thompson has a similar formulation for the 'common people'. He denies that they 'married wives and begat children in order to exploit them' – presumably women are not part of the common people. See 'Happy Families', *Radical History Review*, no. 20 (1979), p. 48.

133   Joan Scott, 'Women in *The Making of the English Middle Class*', *Gender and the Politics of Class* (Columbia University Press, New York, 1988), p. 72.

134   Rosemary Crompton, *Class and Stratification: An Introduction to Current Debates* (Polity Press, Cambridge, 1993), p. 207.

135   D. Lockwood, *The Blackcoated Worker: A Study in Class Consciousness* (Clarendon Press, Oxford, 1989), postscript.

136   This does not mean that men took no part in consumption. On the contrary they spent a great deal of time and thought on buying and fitting goods for the home although there tended to be some differentiation between masculine goods – wine, carpets, carriages, horses, large items of furniture – and feminine – smaller items, curtains, kitchenware, tableware, decorative materials. For a general discussion see Neil McKendrick, John Brewer and J.H. Plumb, eds, *The Birth of a Consumer Society: The Commercialization of Eighteenth-Century England* (Europa Publications, London, 1982).

137   The issue of consumption, taste and taken-for-granted behaviours in the construction of classification has been explored in detail in Pierre Bourdieu, *Distinction: A Social Critique of the Judgement of Taste* (Routledge, London, 1986).

138   Susan Benson, *Counter Cultures: Saleswomen, Managers and Customers in American Department Stores 1890–1940* (University of Illinois Press, Urbana, 1988); Gail Reekie, *Temptations: Sex, Selling and the Department Store* (Allen & Unwin, St Leonards, NSW, 1993); fears about the role of female shopping activities as blurring the distinction between market and home are explored in Erika Rappaport 'A Husband and his Wife's Dresses: Consumer Credit and the Debtor Family in England 1864–1914', in Victoria de Grazia and Ellen Furlogh, eds, *Conspicuous Constructions: Essays on Gender and Consumption* (forthcoming).

139   Alice Kessler-Harris, 'Treating the Male as "Other": Redefining Parameters of Labor History', *Labor History*, vol. 34 (spring/summer 1993); Joy Parr, 'Keynsianism, Consumerism and Gender Politics in Canada and Sweden 1943–56', paper delivered to 'New Directions in Women's History', Schlesinger Library, Radcliffe College, March 1994.

140   On the relation between status honour, official power and wealth see Max Weber, 'Class, Status and Party', in H. Gerth and C.W. Mills, eds, *From Max Weber: Essays in Sociology* (Oxford University Press, New York, 1948).

141   This has been particularly ignored for the working class. But for an analysis of the idealization of 'Our Mam' as the centre of family life, see Ellen Ross, *Love and Toil: Motherhood in Outcast London 1870–1918* (Oxford University Press, New York, 1994).

142   Murray J. Milner, *Status and Sacredness: A General Theory of Status Relations and an Analysis of Indian Culture* (Oxford University Press, New York, 1994), p. 32.

143   Edward Shils, *Centre and Periphery: Essays in Macrosociology* (University of Chicago Press, Chicago, 1982).

144   Londa Schiebinger, *The Mind Has No Sex? Women in the Origins of Modern Science* (Harvard University Press, Cambridge, MA, 1989).

145   L. Jordanova, *Sexual Visions: Images of Gender in Science and Medicine Between the Eighteenth and Twentieth Centuries* (Harvester Wheatsheaf, Hemel Hempstead, 1989).

146   C. Battersby, *Gender and Genius: Towards a Feminist Aesthetics* (Women's Press, London, 1989).

147   Griselda Pollock, 'Painting, Feminism and History', in Michèle Barrett and Ann Phillips, eds, *Destabilizing Theory: Contemporary Feminist Debates* (Polity Press, Cambridge, 1992), p. 56.

148   Taylor, *Eve and the New Jerusalem*.

149   This section owes much to the analysis in Anna Clark, *The Struggle of the Breeches*; see also Jutta Schwarzkopf, *Women in the Chartist Movement* (Macmillan, London, 1991).

150   Sally Alexander, 'Women, Class and Sexual Differences in the 1830s and 1840s: some

Reflections on the Writing of Feminist History', *History Workshop Journal*, no. 17 (1984).

151   See John Gillis, *For Better, For Worse: British Marriages from 1600 to the Present* (Oxford University Press, Oxford, 1986).

152   Jane Lewis on Helen Bosanquet and Fabian Women's understanding of the difficulties in her *Women and Social Action in Victorian and Edwardian England* (Edward Elgar, Aldershot, 1991); Ross, *Love and Toil*.

153   Denise Riley, '*Am I That Name*'; Lewis, *Women and Social Action*.

154   Davidoff, *The Best Circles*.

155   Margaret Arnot, 'Infant Death, Child Care and the Law: "Baby-Farming" and the First Infant Life Protective Legislation of 1872', *Continuity and Change*, vol. 9, no. 4 (August 1994); James Hammerton, *Cruelty and Companionship: Conflict in Nineteenth-Century Married Life* (Routledge, London, 1992).

156   There is a vast literature on women as writers and readers. The standard work tracing some of these changes over the nineteenth century, however, remains Elaine Showalter, *A Literature of their Own* (Princeton University Press, Princeton, NJ, 1977).

157   Alex Owen, *The Darkened Room: Women, Power, and Spiritualism in Late Victorian England* (Virago, London, 1989); for a more problematic example see Lyndal Roper, 'Witchcraft and Fantasy', *History Workshop Journal*, no. 32 (autumn 1991).

158   John Demos, *A Little Commonwealth: Family Life in a Plymouth Colony* (Oxford University Press, New York, 1974), p. 186; but see also a more recent example: 'The individual – his wife and family' (James Casey, *The History of the Family* [Blackwell, Oxford, 1989], p. 15).

159   Peter Bailey analyses the shifts in place and form of some of these activities at the end of the nineteenth century in 'Parasexuality and Glamour: The Victorian Barmaid as Cultural Prototype', *Gender and History*, vol. 2, no. 2 (1990).

160   Mary Ann Clawson, *Constructing Brotherhood: Class Gender and Fraternalism* (Princeton University Press, Princeton, NJ, 1989); Marilyn Lake, 'The Politics of Respectability: Identifying the Masculinist Context', *Historical Studies*, no. 22 (April 1986).

161   Phillipa Levine, ' "So Few Prizes and So Many Blanks": Marriage and Feminism in Later Nineteenth-Century England', *Journal of British Studies*, vol. 28, no. 2 (April 1989), p. 151.

162   Jane Rendall, ed., *Equal or Different: Women's Politics 1800–1914* (Blackwell, Oxford, 1987), introduction; Joan Scott, 'Deconstructing Equality-versus-Difference; or the Uses of Post-Structuralist Theory for Feminism', *Feminist Studies*, vol. 14, no. 4 (spring 1988).

163   Penelope Russell, *A Wish of Distinction: Colonial Gentility and Femininity* (Melbourne University Press, Melbourne, 1994).

164   Clark, *The Struggle of the Breeches*; see also Dorothy Thompson, 'Women, Work and Politics in Nineteenth-Century England: The Problem of Authority', in Rendall, ed., *Equal or Different*.

165   The notion of 'domestic feminism' in connection with the fall in the middle-class birth rate was first put forward in the 1970s, by Daniel Scott Smith among others, but these ideas have resurfaced in more sophisticated form. See, for example, the concept of the 'silent strike' in Lucy Bland 'Marriage Laid Bare: Middle-Class Women and Marital Sex 1880–1914', in Jane Lewis, ed., *Labour of Love: Women's Experience of Home and Family 1850–1940* (Blackwell, Oxford, 1986), p. 138; Kerreen Reiger, *The Disenchantment of the Home: Modernizing the Australian Family 1880–1940* (Oxford University Press, Oxford, 1985).

166   Vicinus, *Independent Women*; Sarah Deutsch, 'Reconceiving the City: Women, Space and Power in Boston 1870–1910, *Gender and History*, vol. 6, no. 2 (1994).
167   Recent interest in the relationship of gender to national identity has raised similar issues in a variety of contexts. See Catherine Hall, Jane Lewis, Keith McClelland and Jane Rednall, eds, 'Gender and National Identity', Special Issue, *Gender and History*, vol. 5, no. 2 (1993).
168   Sandra Stanley Holton, *Feminism and Democracy: Women's Suffrage and Reform Politics in Britain 1900–1918* (Cambridge University Press, 1986), p. 5.
169   Claire Hirschfield, 'A Fractured Faith: Liberal Party Women and the Suffrage Issue in Britain 1892–1914', *Gender and History*, vol. 2, no. 2 (1990), p. 190.
170   Claire Collins 'Women and Labour Politics in Britain 1893–1932', University of London, Ph.D. thesis, 1990; Pat Thane, 'Visions of Gender in the Making of the British Welfare State: The Case of Women in the British Labour Party and Social Policy, 1906–1945', in Gisela Bock and Pat Thane, eds, *Maternity and Gender Policies: Women and the Rise of the European Welfare State* (Routledge, London, 1991).
171   Lockwood, 'Class, Status and Gender', p. 233.
172   Mary Lyndon Shanley, *Feminism, Marriage and the Law in Victorian England 1850–1895* (Princeton University Press, Princeton, NJ, 1989), p. 20.
173   Clare Evans, 'The Separation of Work and Home? The Case of the Lancashire Textiles 1825–1865', University of Manchester, Ph.D. thesis, 1991; Mary Blewett, *Men, Women and Work: Class, Gender, Protest in the New England Shoe Industry 1780–1910* (University of Illinois Press, Urbana, 1988); Alice Kessler-Harris, 'Gender Ideology in Historical Reconstructions: A Case Study from the 1930s', *Gender and History*, vol. 1, no. 1 (1989).
174   Claire Midgeley, 'Anti-Slavery and Feminism in Nineteenth-Century Britain', *Gender and History*, vol. 5, no. 3 (1993).
175   Jane Sherron DeHart, 'Gender on the Right: Meanings Behind the Existential Scream', in Special Issue, 'Gender and the Right', Nancy Hewitt, ed., *Gender and History*, vol. 3, no. 3 (1991), p. 248. See also Susan Kingsley Kent, 'The Politics of Sexual Difference: World War I and the Demise of British Feminism', *Journal of British Studies*, no. 27 (1988). Such a position takes seriously the 'secondary gains' which some women could hold through marriage (or as dutiful sisters or daughters) in terms of men's attention and support. For the power, as well as the costs, of this position, particularly in its psychic dimension, see Jean Baker Miller, *Toward a New Psychology of Women* (Beacon Press, Boston, MA, 1976).
176   Amartya Sen, 'Gender and Cooperative Conflicts', in Irene Tinker, ed., *Persistent Inequalities: Women and Third World Development* (Oxford University Press, Oxford, 1990); see also Emily Grosholz, 'Women, History and Practical Deliberation', in Mary Gergen, ed., *Feminist Thought and the Structure of Knowledge* (New York University Press, New York, 1988).
177   Mary Ryan, 'Gender and Public Access: Women's Politics in Nineteenth-Century America', in Calhoun, ed., *Habermas and the Public Sphere*.
178   Martha Vicinus, 'Male Space and Women's Bodies: The Suffragette Movement', in her *Independent Women*.
179   Landes, *Women and the Public Sphere*, p. 202.
180   Kate Beaumont 'Women and Citizenship in England 1928–1950', unpublished paper by permission of the author; Jean Gaffin and Jarid Thomas, *Caring and Sharing: The Centenary History of The Cooperative Women's Guild* (Holyoake Books, Manchester, 1983).
181   Jane Rendall, 'Nineteenth-Century Feminism and the Separation of Spheres: Reflections on the Public/Private Dichotomy'.
182   Robert A. Padgug, 'Sexual Matters: On Conceptualizing Sexuality in History', in K.

Peiss and C. Simmons, eds, *Passion and Power: Sexuality in History* (Temple University Press, Philadelphia, 1989); David M. Halperin, 'Is There a History of Sexuality?', *History and Theory*, vol. 28 (1989), p. 271.

183 Dina Copelman, 'Liberal Ideology, Sexual Difference and the Lives of Women': Recent Works in British History', *Journal of Modern History*, vol. 62, no. 2 (June 1990), p. 325.

184 Jeffrey Weeks, *Sex, Politics and Society: The Regulation of Sexuality since 1800* (Longmans, London, 1981).

185 Bordo, 'Cartesian Masculization of Thought', p. 451.

186 Englestein, *The Keys to Happiness*, p. 302. Public discussions of sexual behaviour and the nature of sexuality reached a crescendo in England in the early decades of the twentieth century. For a particularly illuminating case study of attempts to link public and private life through sexuality, see Jane Lewis, 'Intimate Relations between Men and Women: The Case of H.G. Wells and Amber Pember Reeves', *History Workshop Journal*, no. 37 (1994).

187 Pateman, *The Disorder of Women*, p. 45.

188 Judith Newton, 'Sex and Political Economy in *The Edinburgh Review*', in *Starting Over: Feminism and the Politics of Cultural Critique* (University of Michigan Press, Ann Arbor, 1994).

189 Marilyn Lake, 'Mission Impossible: How Men Gave Birth to the Australian Nation: Nationalism, Gender and Other Seminal Acts', *Gender and History*, vol. 4, no. 3 (1992), p. 307.

190 Fraser, 'Rethinking the Public Sphere', p. 32. For an original view of many of these issues in the Norwegian context see Tordis Borchgrevink and Øystein Gullvåg Hotter, eds, *Labour of Love: Exploring Gender, Work and Family Interaction* (Avebury Publishing Ltd., Aldershot, forthcoming).